Terrorism, Politics, and Human Rights Advocacy

OXFORD STUDIES IN AFRICAN POLITICS & INTERNATIONAL RELATIONS

General Editors
Nic Cheeseman, Peace Medie, and Ricardo Soares de Oliveira

Oxford Studies in African Politics and International Relations is a series for scholars and students working on African politics and International Relations and related disciplines. Volumes concentrate on contemporary developments in African political science, political economy, and International Relations, such as electoral politics, democratization, decentralization, gender and political representation, the political impact of natural resources, the dynamics and consequences of conflict, comparative political thought, and the nature of the continent's engagement with the East and West. Comparative and mixed methods work is particularly encouraged. Case studies are welcomed but should demonstrate the broader theoretical and empirical implications of the study and its wider relevance to contemporary debates. The focus of the series is on sub-Saharan Africa, although proposals that explain how the region engages with North Africa and other parts of the world are of interest.

Terrorism, Politics, and Human Rights Advocacy

The #BringBackOurGirls Movement

TEMITOPE B. ORIOLA

Great Clarendon Street, Oxford, OX2 6DP,
United Kingdom

Oxford University Press is a department of the University of Oxford.
It furthers the University's objective of excellence in research, scholarship,
and education by publishing worldwide. Oxford is a registered trade mark of
Oxford University Press in the UK and in certain other countries

© Temitope B. Oriola 2024

The moral rights of the author have been asserted

All rights reserved. No part of this publication may be reproduced, stored in
a retrieval system, or transmitted, in any form or by any means, without the
prior permission in writing of Oxford University Press, or as expressly permitted
by law, by licence or under terms agreed with the appropriate reprographics
rights organization. Enquiries concerning reproduction outside the scope of the
above should be sent to the Rights Department, Oxford University Press, at the
address above

You must not circulate this work in any other form
and you must impose this same condition on any acquirer

Published in the United States of America by Oxford University Press
198 Madison Avenue, New York, NY 10016, United States of America

British Library Cataloguing in Publication Data

Data available

Library of Congress Control Number: 2024902412

ISBN 9780198886976

DOI: 10.1093/oso/9780198886976.001.0001

Printed and bound by
CPI Group (UK) Ltd, Croydon, CR0 4YY

Links to third party websites are provided by Oxford in good faith and
for information only. Oxford disclaims any responsibility for the materials
contained in any third party website referenced in this work.

For Mami, Ms Felicia Oriola. Ó dàbò o (goodbye).

Acknowledgements

This book would not be possible without the support of several individuals and organizations. I appreciate the time of members of the #BringBackOurGirls movement in Abuja. They provided incredibly helpful insight into the micro-mechanics of the movement. I am grateful for the opportunity to interact with Dr Obiageli Ezekwesili, Aisha Yesufu, Bukola Sonibare, Dr Manasseh Allen, Florence Ozor, and many others to whom anonymity was promised. Thank you for the opportunity to interview several of you and be a participant observer at the sit-out. I appreciate family members of the kidnapped girls who summoned the courage to participate in interviews. I interviewed Elvis Iyorngurum, an incredibly brilliant #BBOG member, in summer 2015. Elvis passed away later that year. I had no idea that the young man I interviewed only had a couple of months to live. Elvis seemed conscious of time as he battled a fatal illness. He was involved in the #BBOG movement until his dying days. Good night, my friend!

I deeply appreciate the officers and rank-and-file members of the Nigerian Armed Forces who participated in the study. Thanks to Major General Chris Olukolade, former Director of Defence Information, and Major General Mobolaji Koleosho for interactions on the positionality and challenges of the armed forces. I am grateful to several others who must remain anonymous.

Funding from the Department of Sociology, Faculty of Arts and Office of the Vice President (Research) at the University of Alberta, Canada is gratefully acknowledged. Steve Patten, former Associate Dean Research, Faculty of Arts, supported this endeavour. I appreciate the Institute of International Education (IIE) for two tenures as a fellow of the prestigious Carnegie African Diaspora Fellowship Program (CADFP). My Carnegie Fellowship at the University of Port Harcourt (2015) and University of Ibadan (2017) were instrumental in completing this project. Professor Abi Derefaka, Director of the Institute of Niger Delta Studies, University of Port Harcourt, was an outstanding host. The former Dean of the Faculty of Social Sciences, University of Ibadan; Professor Ayodele Jegede; Professor Oluwatoyin Odeku, Director of the Office of International Programs; Dr Funke Fayehun; and Professor Rashidi Okunola (former Head, Department of Sociology), among others, played a huge role in making my three-month visit to the University of Ibadan a fruitful and memorable exercise.

The editors and staff at Oxford University Press have been amazing partners throughout the process. Thank you for what you do.

My colleagues and friends, Rita Abrahamsen, Pius Adesanmi (rest in peace), Charles T. Adeyanju, Omolade Adunbi, Bonny Ibhawoh, W. Andy Knight, Cyril Obi, and Paul Ugor, have consistently epitomized true friendship. Thank you Adekunle Adeyanju, Donald Fajemisin, Sunkanmi Famobio, Idowu Ohioze, and Dean Robert Wood for your friendship. My siblings (Abosede, Yemisi, Oluwafemi, and Ayorinde) have been supportive over the years. Thank you for everything. Special thanks to Oksana Kyrylovych for being incredibly supportive. Responsibility for any errors or omissions is solely mine.

Temitope B. Oriola
Edmonton, Canada

28 February 2023

Contents

Introduction	1
1. Boko Haram and the Chibok kidnapping	22
2. 'The fight for the soul of Nigeria and the world': The #BringBackOurGirls movement	63
3. Framing of the #BringBackOurGirls movement: Lessons for grassroots advocacy	117
4. #BBOG, members' social positionality, and politics	152
5. Outcomes of the #BringBackOurGirls movement	199
6. Conclusion	234
Bibliography	243
Index	270

Introduction

This book provides an insider–outsider analysis of the #BringBackOurGirls (#BBOG) movement. The movement was formed by a group of influential women through an elite middle-class coalition to advocate for the rescue of 219[1] girls kidnapped by the Islamist fundamentalist group, *Jama'at ahlis Sunnah lid Da'wat wal Jihad* (People Committed to the Propagation of the Prophet's Teachings and Jihad) or Boko Haram. The kidnapping occurred on 14 April 2014 at Government Secondary School, Chibok, Borno state in Northeast Nigeria. Although the #BBOG movement has become synonymous with the growing utility of social media, this book demonstrates that there is a lot more to the #BBOG movement than just hashtags and internet activism.

The #BBOG movement is a fascinating sociological phenomenon. It is arguably the first 'lives matter' or human rights *global* campaign whose authorship and provenance emanated directly from Africa. This is a fundamental shift from the 'white-savior' model demonstrated in #stopkony, for example.[2] #BBOG also demonstrates how a women-led non-violent social movement came to be perceived as a major threat to regime stability. This is interesting given the treatment of #BBOG by successive governments formed by two political parties engaged in major contestations for political power. The experience of #BBOG also depicts a learning curve for women-led autonomous social movements, which came of age with the #ENDSARS protests against police brutality.[3] The ascendance, trajectory, global spread, and outcomes of #BBOG are of interest beyond Africa. The #BBOG phenomenon is of worldwide interest vis-à-vis protest in authoritarian democracies and transnationalization of the framing of social movements from the Global South.

The #BBOG movement is a ruthlessly efficient ideational machine for political and social change. It embodies the engagement of contemporary, women-led social movements in Africa in systematic (re)structuring of institutional and non-institutional actions, beliefs, and practices. A hybridized communication process, which seamlessly combines the time–space compression of social

---

[1] Two-hundred-and-seventy-six girls were kidnapped. Fifty-seven of the girls escaped on the night of their abduction.

[2] The 'Kony 2012' documentary on Joseph Kony, the leader of the Ugandan Lord's Resistance Army, demonstrates the schism between the priorities of Africans and citizens and governments of Western countries. See Cole's (2012) 'The White-savior industrial complex' in *The Atlantic*.

[3] For more on #ENDSARS, see Ojedokun et al. (2021).

media with the relative fidelity and territoriality of traditional media, is at the heart of this complex, multifaceted exercise. The result is a potent entity that transcends its offline membership, possesses significant symbolic power, and generates results.

The advocacy of #BBOG transformed the Chibok kidnapping into a *social problem* in a sociological sense. This is remarkable, given that kidnapping had become relatively unspectacular in Nigeria and that there were other major crises around the world. #BBOG engaged in an ideational process of contestation over meanings, legitimacy, and authenticity vis-à-vis the Chibok kidnapping. The interplay of actors, such as the Nigerian state and its allies, international non-governmental organizations (NGOs), and other institutional and non-institutional entities led to the rise of a social problem industry with the Chibok girls at the epicentre.

The #BBOG experience speaks to the texture of the African state and its military architecture, opposition politics, and challenges to human rights advocacy. The findings also concern peace and security in Africa, the war against terrorism in the Lake Chad Basin, perpetuation of social problems in developing societies, and outcomes of social movements in the postcolony.

Human rights activists in Africa confront a trifecta of social conditions: (a) a neocolonial state fractured by socio-political and economic problems, (b) a region conflicted by national interests and colonial history, and (c) an international community with geopolitical priorities. The arguments of the book include the following:

The #BBOG movement is a global leader in 'lives matter' politics and a new episode in women-led social movements in Africa

#BBOG is an important dimension of global 'lives matter' politics and advocacy. It has played a catalytic role in subsequent human rights movements, such as the #ENDSARS. #BBOG championed kidnapped girls in the poorest Northeast corridor of Nigeria in sub-Saharan Africa as rights-bearing persons despite their socio-economic background. This is an important accomplishment in a context where the lives of the poor do not generally garner any robust state or global concern. Therefore, #BBOG advances the long lineage of African women's movements devoted to fighting for the rights of women and young girls. #BBOG represents a relatively new episode of women's rights movements in Africa: its repertoire of protest and overall strategic approach demonstrate the depth and richness of the social, symbolic, cultural, and political capital of its conveners and their middle-class allies. The movement epitomizes the increasing embeddedness and significant positionality of highly educated and socially conscious women in the body politick and their capacity to problematize state legitimacy and effectiveness.

The double bind of the involvement of elite women/mothers in grassroots advocacy

The involvement of elites in grassroots advocacy in developing societies is a double-edged sword. Elites bring significant advantages as well as baggage to social movements in Africa due to the nature of politics and weak institutional structures. This imperils a movement's objective. The engagement of elite women in #BBOG had a profound impact on the rise, international spread, acceptance, and reputation of the movement. Elite women's engagement as 'social mothers' advocating for the rescue of the Chibok girls provided opportunities and public interest that could not be accomplished by the biological mothers of the kidnapped girls. This speaks to a social class dimension to the functionality of motherhood as a socio-political and cultural resource. However, the involvement of elite women in the advocacy for the kidnapped girls enmeshed the movement in the intricate labyrinth of partisan loyalties and individual ambitions. Many of the contradictory ideological leanings, intra-elite squabbles, and political ambitions of the co-conveners pre-date the movement but have had significant impact on #BBOG and influenced its outcomes—for better *and* worse.

Nonetheless, the kidnapping of the Chibok girls might have generated no state action without the involvement of elite women/mothers in the grassroots advocacy for the rescue of the victims. A protest by the mothers of the victims held in Chibok before the formation of #BBOG did not yield any significant media or public attention. The mobilization by the coalition of elite mothers and their middle-class allies, starting in Abuja—the federal capital, made the issue a national and international matter in a context where kidnapping had become common. The involvement of elite women therefore challenged reticence to use the powers of the state to rescue the poor in an extremely socially marginal part of Nigeria. This gave many of the victims a chance to survive.

Refraction of the #BBOG movement's framing

Movement activists in authoritarian or quasi-democratic contexts, particularly in Africa and Latin America, should think local and act local. This means they need to be cognizant of their environment, avoid framing and tactics that may be deemed antagonistic to the government, and ensure social and discursive distance between their advocacy and opposition parties, who may wish to identify with the cause for political purposes. Activists in the Global South need to work conscientiously with key local institutional actors that are relevant to their cause. The framing adopted by #BBOG enmeshed the movement in partisan politics that pre-dated the movement. This complicated the dynamics of the movement's socio-political environment. The international attention generated by the framing of #BBOG had historically specific resonance with local contestations for political power. The political allegiances and activities of some prominent leaders of the movement before and during #BBOG activities influenced local reactions to the movement's framing. These factors led to the alienation of key political actors in Nigeria who could have helped achieve the movement's objective.

Four master frames of the #BBOG movement are identified and explicated. These are the *motherist or maternalist, human rights, girl-child's right to education*, and *state failure framing*. The framing of #BBOG is bifocal in orientation. On one hand, the motherist or maternalist framing was developed as a motivational and mobilizational tool for Nigerian women at the start of the movement in April 2014. The girl-child's right to education framing also resonated in Nigeria. The state failure framing superseded other framing approaches as the President Goodluck Jonathan government (2010–2015) was lethargic in its efforts to rescue the girls. #BBOG began to shift its focus to external actors to help rescue the girls, particularly after the first six months of the abduction. Discursive emphasis was placed on the ineptitude, decadence, and corruption of the Nigerian state and internal decay of the military. This book problematizes the framing of #BBOG. The framing of #BBOG impacted its political context, and the international attention generated by the framing reverberated in the contestation for presidential power. This has influenced the outcome of the movement in both intended and unintended ways.

The study contributes to framing theory in relation to authoritarian or quasi-democratic societies. The effects of internationalized framing are refracted through four major variables in the national political context. These are (a) closeness of movement mobilization to a major event in the political process, particularly elections; (b) the nature of the cause; (c) primary beneficiaries of movement activities; and (d) the social positionality of key movement leaders—political affiliation and ambitions—before and during movement activities. These variables influence the efficacy and outcomes of framing within the context of human rights advocacy in Africa, where elections are matters of life and death.

The internationalization of the #BBOG framing: Tactically useful but also a strategic error

The national opportunity structure influences the outcomes of local struggles in developing societies more than opportunities in the international arena. The framing of #BBOG was internationalized on the distinctive belief of the movement's leadership that the government would act to rescue the girls when confronted with 'international embarrassment'. However, despite #BBOG spin-offs around the world, the movement was not transnationalized in a conventional sense. #BBOG resisted offers of monetary and logistical support from international organizations around the world. The movement was also careful to not become formally affiliated with, or tied to, organizations that might institutionalize any form of cooperation on the struggle. Refusing to formally transnationalize the movement was appropriate for the movement's political context, but internationalizing the framing was inappropriate for the national political opportunity structure. The internationalized framing privileged developments and opportunities in the global arena over the national context. This epitomizes a strategic error by #BBOG despite the global popularity of the movement and the symbolism of highly influential global elite (e.g. world leaders and their spouses, actors, and miscellaneous celebrities) identifying with the cause. Internationalizing the framing of #BBOG demonstrates three interrelated political miscalculations: first, the failure to think through the step between mobilizing opinion and practical efforts to achieve the main objective of the movement, second, the assumption that the Nigerian government could be compelled or shamed into taking action on an issue it had little interest, third, the presupposition that Western powers would help to rescue the girls if the Nigerian government was unwilling, or unable, to act.

The book argues that while #BBOG confronted a lethargic state regarding the rights of citizens, the social positionality of the movement's elite members could have been deployed to engage with key state institutions and local actors to rescue the girls. Such an approach required an emphasis on in-person, face-to-face direct discussions with the military elite and major figures in the ruling party. This would have meant relying on 'back channels' and informal relationships as well as eschewing or minimizing the use of the state failure master frame. Overall, the analysis in the book demonstrates that the #BBOG movement chose ideological puritanism over pragmatism vis-à-vis the rescue of the girls.

Nevertheless, #BBOG's choice in this regard was not necessarily whimsical: the back-channel approach carried a significant risk—co-optation by the government and probable damage to the credibility and reputation of the leaders of the movement.

#BBOG's governance and repertoire of protest: Major internal divisions in the movement

Contemporary social movements in Africa confront internal challenges in relation to decision-making, bureaucratization, governance structure, ethno-religious allegiances, and oligarchization. #BBOG began to haemorrhage elite members shortly after its formation in April 2014. Differences over how to engage the government and the overall tone, diction, framework, and protest tactics generated irreconcilable differences a few weeks into movement activities. As the leadership of the movement began to coalesce around two-time federal minister and former vice-president of the World Bank Africa, Dr Obiageli Ezekwesili, a direct, arguably non-diplomatic no-nonsense approach was firmly established. Some #BBOG members, particularly from Northern Nigeria, wanted a more conciliatory approach once Muhammadu Buhari became president of Nigeria on 29 May 2015. Such members became increasingly alienated and began to avoid movement activities. Attendance at the daily protest began to dwindle as some members questioned the utility of the movement's approach and wanted a seat at the table with the Buhari government. The leadership, led by Ezekwesili, believed that #BBOG was a pure advocacy movement and needed to avoid co-optation by the government.

Divisions within #BBOG have also been shaped by the problems of 'superstar' activists and fundamental disagreements over decision-making and strategic direction of the movement. The book argues that there are five categories of #BBOG members: *regime-neutral die-hards, regime-change emergency activists, committed pragmatists, non-committal advocates,* and *totemic elite members*. These divisions shape, and are influenced by, oligarchization within #BBOG, despite efforts to ensure an atmosphere of democratic decision-making. The four sources of oligarchization within #BBOG are analysed. These are *level of commitment, resources, regime neutrality,* and *interpersonal relations with top leaders of the movement*. The internal divisions within #BBOG have serious implications for social movements in the Global South. These include clearly stipulating criteria for membership, decision-making procedures, defining and refining a movement's strategic direction in consonance with empirical realities, dealing with ethno-religious and political differences among members, preventing oligarchization, and ensuring engaged membership over the long haul.

#BBOG advocacy: Creation of a social problem industry, which contributed to a multidimensional exploitation of the Chibok girls and their community

The #BBOG experience and exploitation of the Chibok girls have broad implications for the intractability of social problems in developing countries and the engagement of international governmental and non-governmental actors in local struggles. #BBOG inadvertently heralded a social problem industry centred on the exploitation of the Chibok girls. This industry has become an international business. A constellation of actors—human rights advocates, school administrators, politicians, seemingly unsuspecting humanitarians, and an assortment of local and international NGOs within and outside Nigeria—has engaged actively in exploiting the Chibok girls. Forms of exploitation include the use of some Chibok girls to raise funds at public events and public relations campaigns. These activities have proven psychologically costly to the Chibok girls. The findings have implications for how social movements in developing countries may avoid turning their cause into an opportunity for material gain by self-interested national or international governmental and non-governmental actors.

The contextual seven-stage model: Engaging with how a social problem industry develops

The book proposes a contextual seven-stage model regarding how a social condition becomes transformed to a social problem and the development of a social problem industry. First is the *overpass stage* wherein a harmful social condition exists, and affects a number of people, but is ignored by those with political and economic power despite its effect on a section of the population. Second is the *elite mobilization stage*, which involves intervention by a range of well-situated individuals. Third is the *validation stage*, in which a social condition becomes recognized as a social problem in a sociological sense, with one or more organizations devoted to the 'cause'. Fourth is the *governing authority response stage*. This tends to be unpredictable in developing countries. There are three probable response trajectories at this stage. Fifth is the *bifurcated trajectory stage*, in which the social problem may (a) be resolved or (b) fester. Sixth is the *internationalization stage*, in which the engagement of actors at the local and national levels may interpellate international actors, and seventh is the *dénouement stage*. The social problem may become exacerbated as various actors become self-perpetuating in the teething social problem industry. This model contributes to social problem theory through its dynamism and non-linearism—a major weakness of existing scholarship. The chances of an industry developing around a social problem increase from the fifth stage, while some social problems may terminate at the third or fourth stages. In other words, the probable outcome in the odyssey of a social condition is fluid and context-dependent. This model presents an orientation that is better suited to understanding the careers of social problems and the underlying industry in developing countries with limited state capacity and relatively weak institutions.

The nebulous nature of international 'support' for grassroots movements in developing countries

The #BBOG experience signposts the need for activists, particularly in the Global South, to be clear about what 'support' means for their cause. There is also a need to be cognizant that generating awareness about a social problem is not necessarily the same as specific, tangible, and empirically verifiable action to solve a problem. There was little practical and visible assistance by international actors to rescue the Chibok girls, despite the internationalized framing and globalized televisual display of support by heads of states and celebrities. Approximately six months into the advocacy, #BBOG activists became increasingly disappointed that the lives of scores of kidnapped young women did not garner tangible rescue efforts beyond media commentaries about 'standing with' the Chibok girls, their families, and the #BBOG activists. #BBOG's faith in the international community was misplaced and, ultimately, unrealistic. In the end, the lives of young women from the Northeast corridor of the poorest part of Nigeria did not matter to key international players. Movements, particularly in developing countries, must be wary of media-saturated, highly popularized, and performative online support for their cause. Such support is merely symbolic and transient. It is an indicator of the fad of the moment. Grassroots movements in the developing world should focus on local support for their objectives.

Problems in the Nigerian political process and the military inhibited efforts to rescue the Chibok girls

The military bureaucracy is often the nucleus of contestations for political power, particularly in African countries, with a history of coups and military dictatorships. The impact of the percolation of Nigeria's ethno-religious divisions into the fabric of the military provides a lens through which to examine how the political process and pre-existing divisions affect the African military. The political, religious, and ethnic identities of many senior officers in the Nigerian military were mobilized prior to the 2015 presidential elections. Their ethnic and religious subjectivities were exploited in the contestation for presidential power by the two major political parties. Several senior officers began to openly identify as 'PDP officers' or 'APC officers'. These were the acronyms of the two parties—the People's Democratic Party and All Progressives Congress—at the centre of contestation for presidential power. APC officers worked to ensure the failure of efforts to defeat Boko Haram during the Jonathan administration. A triumphant Boko Haram was considered favourable to the electoral chances of the APC candidate, former military head of state, General Muhammadu Buhari. Officers' political identities were symbolically delineated on the basis of ethnic and religious affiliations. These issues poisoned social relations among military personnel at the Army and Defence Headquarters in Abuja and barracks across Nigeria. The military was highly polarized and therefore ineffective several years into the war against Boko Haram.

This book argues that 10 major factors within the Nigerian political process and the military made rescuing the Chibok girls and defeating Boko Haram difficult. These were (a) corruption, (b) intelligence leaks/sabotage, (c) alienation of the public, (d) shortage of arms and ammunition, (e) inadequate coordination of security operations, (f) 'strategic blunders' of political leaders, (g) the rise of actors benefiting from the problem, (h) nepotism, (i) toxic politics in the military, and (j) troops' perception of the war against Boko Haram as a 'rubbish mission'. #BBOG responded to its external environment and the movement's relationship with the military fragmented. This contributed to poor civil–military relations in the war against Boko Haram.

Five dimensions of state repression against #BBOG

#BBOG demonstrates significant strengths from within and outside the movement. These are largely due to the social positionality of its conveners. The strengths have been useful to prevent more direct and egregious forms of state action against the movement. Nonetheless, #BBOG has faced major challenges in efforts of two successive Nigerian governments to repress the movement using state law enforcement officers as well as highly placed elected leaders and financially induced regular citizens. State repression against #BBOG, the evidence demonstrates, has five major dimensions. These are (a) a coordinated physical attack by state-sponsored thugs, (b) bomb threats, (c) smear campaigns, (d) attempts to sponsor chaos and leadership change in the movement, and (e) intimidation through false arrests. The book demonstrates how the #BBOG brain trust strategized to avoid the outcome sought by state agents through each of the episodes of repression. #BBOG's strategies in countering state repression are instructive for other movements, particularly in the developing world.

The risks of acceptance of a social movement as a legitimate actor in a cause

There are risks to a movement's acceptance as a legitimate actor in a cause despite the potential to create political opportunities. In particular, social movement collaboration with the state may lead to erosion of legitimacy. The Nigerian government's overture to #BBOG in 2017 to participate in a tour of Sambisa forest, where the Chibok girls were believed to be kept by Boko Haram, and assess military infrastructure in the area created an existential crisis for #BBOG. The government's perspective was to demonstrate to the activists the efforts of the government to rescue the Chibok girls. This was an unsolicited political opportunity. Activists must be cautious about political opportunity delivered to them seemingly on a platter. The Sambisa episode fragmented #BBOG internally and also created a public relations problem. The government put #BBOG in a bind: there were risks with accepting or declining the offer. Members were divided over whether or not #BBOG should honour the government's invitation. The steps taken by the government indicated political manoeuvring aimed at the movement's credibility. For example, the invitation was leaked to the press before #BBOG could respond, and the timeline (five days) was unreasonable for meaningful preparation by the movement. The findings demonstrate that while accepting such an opportunity may sometimes be reasonable, movements should prepare for the consequences of collaborating with the government, particularly in the Global South. The evidence indicates that the intrigues encompassing such collaboration may entangle a social movement in toxic national politics, generate mistrust among members, and tarnish its reputation.

The #BBOG movement: Contradictory outcomes

Contradictory outcomes often plague social movements. The #BBOG movement has spurred many national and international institutional and non-institutional actors to provide social benefits to many of those affected by Boko Haram. However, the popularity of the advocacy has had an unintended consequence—the prolonged captivity of the girls. This contradictory perspective on the impact of #BBOG on the struggle for the release of the Chibok girls is widespread among a broad range of participants in the study. The consensus in the military is that #BBOG made it more difficult to find the girls because the movement increased the Chibok girls' ransom value. Boko Haram recognized their social value, put them under a higher security regimen than other captives, and used them as bargaining chips. Other victims of Boko Haram are also being neglected relative to the Chibok girls.

#BBOG's significant impacts on its cause and the broader political process

#BBOG has had major impacts. Its impacts transcend its original cause (the rescue of the Chibok girls), despite the contradiction noted above. The impacts of #BBOG include the release of 106 girls through negotiations. The evidence demonstrates that the relentless efforts of the movement compelled the government to act: the activities of #BBOG had become so compelling that, in order to save face, the government had to negotiate with Boko Haram. #BBOG's visionary approach and impact are evident in the fact that the movement designed the blueprint for psychotherapy and other (educational) activities for rehabilitation of victims before any of the girls were released, despite the refusal of the government to acknowledge the contributions of #BBOG. The channelling of resources to rebuild schools in Northeast Nigeria since 2014 is due largely to the #BBOG advocacy. The #BBOG advocacy has also had an impact in greater attention to the education of the girl-child in Northern Nigeria. #BBOG has also produced indirect impacts such as support for internally displaced persons in the Northeast region.

There are wider and structural impacts of # BBOG. For example, #BBOG has advanced the frontiers of non-violent protest in Nigeria. #BBOG also contributed to a seismic political change in Nigeria—the first electoral defeat of an incumbent president. The evidence demonstrates that the advocacy of #BBOG invigorated international support for political change in Nigeria. The movement's framing regarding governmental incompetence and inability to rescue the kidnapped Chibok girls severely affected the credibility and legitimacy of the Jonathan government (2010–2015). This was instrumentalized by then opposition party, the APC, which adopted a 'change' mantra, publicly ingratiated itself with #BBOG, and committed to rescuing the Chibok girls and defeating Boko Haram.

#BBOG's innovativeness: Combining the strengths of social and traditional media alongside offline, on-the-ground mobilization

#BBOG has been globally celebrated for its use of social media technology. This is a significant aspect of the movement's mobilization. However, this book argues that #BBOG's popularity was partly in its hybridized communication process—a coalescence of the instantaneity of social media with the reach of traditional media. The study articulates #BBOG's *media sense*: engagement of traditional media through an email list of journalists, media organizations, and an assortment of bloggers, who regularly received the movement's statements in addition to deploying the personal social media handles of members and those of the movement. The Chibok kidnapping did not automatically generate worldwide interest. The core members of #BBOG's strategic media engagement team interviewed in this study are bewildered by the assumption that the kidnapping of the Chibok girls somehow generated global attention once the #BBOG conveners began to tweet and post messages on Facebook.

In addition, #BBOG mobilization combined social media with assiduous offline work. Focusing almost exclusively on #BBOG's social media rigour and reach ignores the movement's meticulous and challenging offline efforts. Therefore, this book argues that #BBOG is more than a social media phenomenon and could not have made any gains, particularly within Nigeria, where internet access was relatively limited during its mobilization, without its offline mobilization and engagements.

Nigeria's complexity and politics

Thurston (2018) emphasizes the role of Nigeria's contentious politics in the rise and spread of Boko Haram. He underscores the relevance of the conduct of elections, endemic corruption, chronic inequality, and a twin issue—violence and the approach to conflict management. Elections in Nigeria are keenly contested but also produce impossible results because of massive rigging (Thurston 2018). This has contributed to the use of political thugs armed by politicians for the purposes of intimidating opponents and other electoral malpractices. This practice is one of the notable sources of arms and ammunitions, which contributed to the insurgency in Nigeria's oil-rich Niger Delta region from the late 1990s (Oyefusi 2008). This is evident in other African countries such as Kenya, Cote d'Ivoire, Democratic Republic of Congo, Rwanda, Liberia, and Sierra Leone, among others. It has often led to breakdown of order (Allen 1999; Dunn 2009; DeJesus 2011).

There is fatalistic acceptance of the widespread nature of corruption within government and across society. Estimates of outright loss of state revenue due to official corruption provide a glimpse of the scale of the problem. For example, Nigeria lost $380 billion to corruption between 1960 and 1999, according to the Economic and Financial Crimes Commission (Human Rights Watch 2007) and another $32 billion during the administration of President Goodluck Jonathan between 2010 and 2015 (Awojulugbe 2017). Government ministers, former heads of state, other top politicians, and military generals, among others, are indicted routinely but rarely jailed for corruption. Such was the level of bureaucratic corruption in Zaire (now Democratic Republic of Congo) that an official newspaper noted that the medical services sector's mottos were *Pave ou tu creves* ('Unless you pay, you die') and *Un medecin qui ne percoit pas d'honorares est un imbecile* ('A physician who does not collect illicit fees is foolish') (Gould and Mukendi 1989: 430).

Nonetheless, bureaucratic corruption is only one manifestation of corruption. Citizens are also involved in corrupt practices as a routine part of daily life. For instance, a clerk at an office of the organization responsible for a university entrance examination, the Joint Admissions and Matriculations Board office, Makurdi, Nigeria claimed that a snake swallowed approximately $100,000 that she ought to have remitted to the examination body (BBC 2018).

In *The State in Africa: The Politics of the Belly* (2009), Jean Francois Bayart develops a theoretical framework for understanding the routine functioning, morphology, rationality, or 'governmentality' of the African state. Bayart argues that the African state operates within the labyrinth of *politique du ventre* or the 'politics of the belly'. Bayart takes the term 'politics of the belly' from a common Cameroonian expression, which he acknowledges is analogous to the familiar macrosociology of the popular term 'national cake' (p. 90) in Nigeria. The stomach, or the belly, is a 'metaphorical insignia and signification of the problematic socio-historical contours and dynamics of such states. The belly is also an organizing apparatus for the conduct of politics' (Oriola [2013] 2016: 177). For Bayart, the African state 'functions as a rhizome of personal networks, and assures the centralisation of power through the agencies of family, alliance and friendship, in the manner of ancient kingdoms, which possessed the principle attributes of a State within a lineage matrix, thereby reconciling two types of political organisation' (pp. 261–262). In other words, the African state is neither fully traditional nor bureaucratic in the Weberian sense.

Nigeria exemplifies the politics of the belly—what a former governor in Ekiti state, Nigeria, Ayo Fayose, calls 'stomach infrastructure'. Stomach infrastructure, as Governor Fayose puts it, is 'a way of life' (Premium Times 2016b).[4] There is existential struggle to control the machinery of the state as an avenue of enhancing the quality and quantity of one's consumption. To eat, as Bayart argues, entails nourishing oneself as well as to 'accumulate, exploit, defeat, attack or kill' (p. 269). The machinations of the politics of the belly is reminiscent of Mbembe's (2003) 'necropolitics'. Bayart (2009) describes it as 'a matter of life and death' (p. 238). The presidency is the ultimate prize—the papacy of graft—in the attempt to eat within a politically toxic atmosphere. This speaks to how political actors in 'counterfeit democracies' use various means (such as bribery, ballot box stuffing, and violence) to win elections (Cheeseman and Klaas 2018: 34). State officials and those seeking political power, as demonstrated in this book, play deathly politics with the lives of citizens as a routine part of attempts to eat. The ostensible use of Boko Haram as a tool to win elections in the Northeast (c. 2003) is a basic fact about the organization. Intelligence reports from 2014 showed that a former governor of Borno state, Ali Modu Sheriff, was a 'major financier of the terrorist sect' (Premium Times 2014b). Kaka Shehu Lawan, attorney general and commissioner of justice in Borno state, released a statement in 2016 arguing that

---

[4] Governor Fayose appointed a 'personal assistant on special duties and stomach infrastructure' in 2014 (Badejo 2014). The term in fact appears to have originated from Fayose's opponent in a governorship election. Fayose defeated incumbent governor Kayode Fayemi, who was criticized by the people for refusing to provide 'what he cynically referred to as "stomach infrastructure"—food and other consumables—to the residents' (The Scoop 2017). Fayemi learned his lesson. He began providing stomach infrastructure in late 2017 as he prepared to run for his old office. Fayemi won the election in a massive money-for-vote scheme in July 2018 (Atoyebi 2018). This example demonstrates the complicity of the masses. The masses are not innocent in the corruption within the state (Bayart 2009).

former Governor Ali Modu Sheriff's likely desperation for power in 2003 and his arrogance is what led us to the violence of the Boko Haram insurgents that has led to the deaths of over 20,000 persons, displacement of over 2.5 million citizens and destruction of property worth three trillion naira.

Lawan's statement supports the findings of a 2014 panel (the Galtimari panel) set up by the Goodluck Jonathan administration to examine the rise of Boko Haram (Premium Times 2014c). Ali Modu Sheriff was elected chair of the former ruling party, the PDP, despite allegations of terrorist financing. Ali Modu Sheriff's case is one example of the complexity of the Nigerian state and the entanglement of key actors within the toxic politics and problematique of Boko Haram.[5]

Nigeria's population is estimated at 225,082, 083 people.[6] The complexity of the country is accentuated by over 252 identifiable ethnic groups speaking over 400 languages (Mensah 2005: 73). Muslims make up 50%, Christians 40%, and indigenous believers 10% of the population. The founding fathers were, from the onset, sceptical about the prospects of the country prior to British handover of governance in 1960. The leader of the Action Group party, Chief Obafemi Awolowo, who was a leading nationalist and later premier of the Western region, made a famous statement in 1947 that has become an insignia of Nigeria's political intricacies:

> Nigeria is not a nation. It is a mere geographical expression. There are no 'Nigerians' in the sense as there are 'English', 'Welsh', or 'French'. The word 'Nigerian' is merely a distinctive appellation to distinguish those who live within the boundaries of Nigeria from those who do not.
> (cited in Ogundiya 2009: 285)

A leader of the Northern People's Congress (NPC), Sir Abubakar Tafawa Balewa, who would become Nigeria's first and only prime minister, offered similar assessment in 1948. Balewa noted:

---

[5] However, House of Representatives member Dr Asabe Vilita Bashir, who served in the cabinet of Ali Modu Sheriff, notes that Ali Modu Sheriff worked alongside security agencies to 'reduce the effect' of Boko Haram. She argues, 'As a Muslim, if he went outright to fight them, it will be a problem because they will say that he is fighting his own religion so he had to do it intelligently along with the security agents.' She considers the idea that Sheriff sponsored Boko Haram a 'joke' (personal interview, Abuja 2015).

[6] Based on a 2022 estimate. See 'CIA World Factbook', https://www.cia.gov/the-world-factbook/countries/nigeria/summaries/#people-and-society. Accessed 24 February 2023.

> Since 1914 the British Government has been trying to make Nigeria into one country, but the Nigerian people themselves are historically different in their backgrounds, in their religious beliefs and customs and do not show themselves any sign of willingness to unite ... Nigerian unity is only a British intention for the country.
>
> (cited in Ogundiya 2009: 285)

The NPC was reluctant to support agitations for Nigeria's independence due to the level of development of the North relative to the South. Ahmadu Bello, the Sardauna of Sokoto and leader of the NPC, was unambiguous in his assertion that the 'Northern Region does not intend to accept the invitation to commit suicide.' The NPC formed the national government in partnership with the National Council of Nigeria and the Cameroons (NCNC) and received Nigeria's independence from the British on 1 October 1960. Nnamdi Azikiwe, the leader of the NCNC became governor general (and later president, following Nigeria's decision to become a republic in 1963). The Sardauna chose to serve as premier of the Northern region, and one of his lieutenants, Tafawa Balewa, was sworn in as prime minister.[7] A succession of military coups followed less than six years after independence. The structures laid down before independence became major sources of division between the North and the South. These included census figures, results of the 1959 elections, and the number of seats allocated to each region (Miners 1971).

Consequently, political troubles began early. Opposition politicians from the South attempted to change imbalances in the political system. Miners (1971: 9, 11) notes that

> Radicals in the South became convinced that the rule of the NPC could only be ended if the constitution were radically revised. The NPC were equally certain that the constitution as it stood guaranteed the dominance of the North over the rest of the Federation for ever, and refused to contemplate any but the most minor alterations.

There were attempts to take over power by army officers prior to the first coup of 15 January 1966 (Miners 1971). Major Kaduna Nzeogwu and several other officers, mainly from the Eastern region, led the first successful coup. This cast the coup as ethnicized military action.

---

[7] Odumegwu Ojukwu, leader of the ill-fated Biafra Republic describes Ahmadu Bello as someone whose 'perception of Nigeria was perhaps different from mine. He was more of a continuation of the Sheikh Uthman Dan Fodio's grand design than the creation of a modern Nigeria' (Ojukwu 1989: 160).

A counter-coup by Northern officers occurred in July 1966. The coup brought General Yakubu Gowon to power. The Eastern region, led by Colonel Odumegwu Ojukwu, decided to secede to form Biafra Republic. The secessionist attempt led to a civil war from 1967 to 1970. Gowon was toppled by General Murtala Muhammed in July 1975. General Muhammed was killed in a coup in February 1976. His deputy, General Olusegun Obasanjo, became head of state and organized elections. General Obasanjo voluntarily relinquished power to a democratically elected president, Alhaji Shehu Shagari, on 1 October 1979. Shagari was toppled in a military coup led by General Muhammadu Buhari in December 1983.

Officers, led by General Ibrahim Babangida, removed General Buhari from office in August 1985. Babangida superintended multiple failed elections and a structural adjustment programme, which worsened economic conditions. Babangida relinquished power on 26 August 1993 and installed an interim national government (ING), headed by Chief Ernest Shonekan, following his decision to annul the 12 June 1993 elections. The elections were believed to have been won by Chief MKO Abiola, a billionaire philanthropist. General Sani Abacha deposed the ING on 17 November 1993. General Abacha died in power on 8 June 1998 under mysterious circumstances. General Abdulsalam Abubakar took over power and organized elections. Former military Head of State General Olusegun Obasanjo was sworn in as civilian president on 29 May 1999. President Obasanjo served two terms, made an unsuccessful bid for an unconstitutional third, and handed over power to Alhaji Umaru Yar'Adua on 29 May 2007. President Yar'Adua had major health issues and died in May 2010, less than three years into his tenure, and his deputy, Goodluck Jonathan, was sworn in as president. President Jonathan won a substantive term in 2011. His opponent was a retired general and former military dictator, Muhammadu Buhari.

General Buhari was, again, the main opposition contestant in 2015 when President Jonathan ran for a second term. A coalition of political parties, the APC, was formed. The APC fielded General Buhari as candidate for president. The ruling party, the PDP, which had been in power since the return to civilian rule in 1999, fielded the incumbent president, Goodluck Jonathan. President Jonathan lost his bid for re-election.[8] This marked the first time an incumbent

---

[8] President Jonathan telephoned the challenger and offered his congratulations. This singular gesture is believed to have prevented bloodshed in Nigeria. Multiple sources from the military confirmed that intelligence reports indicated that several countries with interests in Nigeria had made evacuation plans for their citizens. A journalist for a major world news organization confirmed that several of his colleagues had received instruction to cover the 'breakdown' and 'remains' of Nigeria.

president would lose an election in Nigeria. As demonstrated throughout this book, the quest to win the 2015 presidential elections significantly polarized Nigeria along ethnic and religious lines and exacerbated toxic politics. Toxic politics has had major effects on the routine functioning of major institutions, particularly the military. This would have repercussions for perceptions of human rights activists and the demands made on the state before and after the elections.

There are 36 states and 6 geopolitical zones in Nigeria. The geopolitical zones are Northcentral, Northeast, Northwest, Southeast, South-South, and Southwest. The Northeast geopolitical zone comprises six states: Adamawa, Bauchi, Borno, Gombe, Taraba, and Yobe. The Northeast is a microcosm of the ethnic and linguistic diversity of Nigeria. It has various ethnic groups such as Hausa, Kanuri, Shuwa, Marghi, Higi, Marghi, Shuwa, Bachama (Bwatiye), Mbula, Wurkun, Jukun, Kanakuru, Tera, Gudduri, Tula, Waja, Tangale, Jara, Babur/Bura, Chibok, Kilba, Bolewa, Karaikarai, Ngamo, Ngizim, Vere, Gude, and Yungur (Institute for Peace and Conflict Resolution [IPCR] Abuja 2017: 155). Borno state, the most expansive of all the six Northeast states, has an estimated 70,000 sq. km (IPCR Abuja 2017).

The Northeast is the most fundamentally challenged in a country generally undergoing major social economic and developmental problems (Office of the Senior Special Assistant to the President on SDGs 2016; UNDP (United Nations Development Programme 2016a). The IPCR (2017: 152, 155) notes, in its '2016 Strategic Conflict Assessment of Nigeria', that the Northeast is

> *unarguably the worst-hit part of the country in Nigeria's war against terrorism* ... Socio-economically, the geo-political zone comprises states that are leading amongst the dismally performing socio-economically. The region records the highest level of mortality rate, has the highest number of males with no formal education and the second with the highest number of females with no educational attainment ... As at 2010, the National Poverty Profile produced by the National Bureau of Statistics (NBS) reported that 69 percent of the entire population of the zone can be categorised as 'Absolute Poor'.
>
> (NBS 2012: 16; italics added)

The socio-economic and political situation in Nigeria, and the conditions in the Northeast in particular, provide an important background to what follows in this book.

Organization of the book

The remainder of the book is divided into six chapters. The contents of Chapters 1–6 are summarized below.

Chapter 1 'Boko Haram and the Chibok Kidnapping' provides an historical context and overview of the Boko Haram phenomenon: its ascendance, ideology, grievances, objectives, recruitment, and fragmentation. Data from the Global Terrorism Database (GTD) is analysed to demonstrate the trends, targets, and tactics of Boko Haram's operations. The chapter also explores the kidnapping of the Chibok girls and provides insight into the research process of this book, its scope, and limitations. This chapter contributes to understanding the evolving tactics of Boko Haram and its social position within a broader movement for Islamization across West Africa. The chapter also increases understanding of the kidnapping of the Chibok girls.

Chapter 2 '"The fight for the soul of Nigeria and the world": The #BringBackOurGirls Movement' analyses the rise of the #BringBackOurGirls movement. It investigates the formation, organizational structure, core values, and tactics of the #BBOG movement. It also focuses on the communication process, mobilization, and funding of #BBOG. Internal challenges such as the question of defining who a #BBOG member is, decision-making, and debates over strategic direction are analysed. The findings show that the #BBOG movement is an effective, delicately managed, yet internally complicated ideational machinery. It is anchored on the deployment of the broad range of talents of its highly educated leaders and members and a hybridized communication strategy. This chapter demonstrates that despite widespread perceptions about #BBOG's social media sophistication and efficacy, its communication process in reality combines the rhizomatic instantaneity and intercontinental reach of social media platforms such as Twitter ('X') and Facebook with the multiple publics offered by traditional print and electronic media. The analysis shows why members who form the nuclei of the strategic team (ST) and strategic communication team (SCT) of #BBOG are surprised at the presumption that the movement walked into a worldwide media spotlight.

The findings of this chapter provide the first systematic attempt at unpacking the internal organizational dynamics of the #BBOG movement. The chapter contributes to the literature through an analysis of how internal variables may enhance the status of a social movement and globalize its struggle. This is relevant to social movements in developing societies that aim to popularize their struggle beyond national borders and garner international attention.

Chapter 3 focuses on 'Framing of the #BringBackOurGirls Movement: Lessons for Grassroots Advocacy'. This chapter analyses the ideational infrastructure of the #BBOG movement. It interrogates the #BBOG movement's diagnosis of the kidnapping of the Chibok girls as well as its prognostic and motivational framing. The chapter articulates four main master frames in #BBOG. The #BBOG framing is bifocal. On one hand, the maternalist framing and the girl-child's right to education framing were predominantly internally orientated to the Nigerian audience. On the other hand, the human rights and state failure framing were mainly externally orientated and garnered significant support in the international community. However, the state failure framing, while accurately articulating prevailing realities in Nigeria, alienated key actors in the political and military elite. The framing also unintentionally enmeshed the movement in toxic presidential politics.

This chapter engages with the framing of #BBOG—beyond the movement's widely acknowledged deployment of maternalist or motherist framing. It cross-articulates #BBOG publicity material and interviews with key leaders and members of the movement to present a clear picture of how the cause was discursively represented by #BBOG. This chapter contributes to the literature by identifying the framing of #BBOG and the consequences of the movement's framing. Beyond framing identification and analysis, the chapter enhances theory-building on factors that influence how a movement's framing is perceived by opponents and bystanders. The analysis contains major lessons for grassroots movements and human rights activists in Africa and the developing world in general.

Chapter 4 'The #BBOG, Members' Social Positionality, and Politics' explores the embeddedness of #BBOG within Nigeria's toxic political environment. It problematizes the social position and politics of key leaders of the movement such as Oby Ezekwesili, Hadiza Bala Usman, and Aisha Yesufu. The chapter explores the implications of the engagement of several members in partisan politics before and during #BBOG activities vis-à-vis the entrenchment of the movement in toxic presidential politics. It also problematizes the broader consequences of appointment into key positions in the APC-led government of several leaders of #BBOG. This chapter also articulates a typology of #BBOG members. Five categories of members are explored.

The chapter contributes to the literature on elite women's involvement in social movement advocacy in Africa. Elite women bring significant expertise, network, and know-how to grassroots advocacy, as is widely recognized in the literature on women's rights in the Middle East and North Africa. However, the chapter challenges and contributes to the literature by investigating the quality and consequences of the baggage elite women inadvertently bring into grassroots social movements. This emphasizes the salience of gender and class in movement outcomes. The chapter also contributes to the literature on the politics and consequences of acceptance of a social movement as a legitimate actor in a defined cause or field. It argues that such acceptance exacerbates internal challenges, such as decision-making and the strategic direction of the movement, and makes the movement susceptible to external interference, particularly by state agents. It also demonstrates that such acceptance may attenuate but does not make a movement immune to state repression. The findings challenge existing literature on acceptance and legitimization of social movements and the particularities of authoritarian or quasi-democratic contexts. These have major implications for social movement organizations in developing societies.

Chapter 5 'Outcomes of the #BringBackOurGirls Movement' investigates the social consequences of #BBOG. The outcomes of #BBOG are juxtaposed with a major internal document of the movement 'The Strategic Angle to #BringBackOurGirls', which attempts 'scenario building' for the movement.[9] A composite of two out of three scenarios hypothesized by #BBOG applies to the current situation—110 girls are back while 112 are still missing.[10] This chapter demonstrates that movement outcomes are far more dynamic, unpredictable, and complicated than envisioned by the #BBOG movement. The outcomes of the #BBOG movement are multifaceted, significant, and transcend the rescue of the Chibok girls. This chapter contributes to the literature on social movement outcomes and the sociology of social problems. It enhances our understanding of how certain national and international actors seek to benefit from local struggles. The chapter also demonstrates the implications of the findings for the perpetuation of social problems in poor countries and the efficacy of grassroots activism.

The final chapter, Chapter 6 'Conclusion', presents a review of the findings and contributions of the book. The chapter also offers suggestions for future research.

---

[9] #BBOG internal document no. 2.
[10] See http://www.bringbackourgirls.ng. Accessed 19 October 2023.

1
Boko Haram and the Chibok kidnapping

Introduction: Islamic movements in Northern Nigeria

There is a robust marketplace of ideas about Islam in Northern Nigeria. Muslims in Northern Nigeria have always had vigorous debates about the place of Islam in society and its multifarious forms and texture. Evidence suggests that militant interpretations of Islam constitute just one crucial dimension of a highly complex conversation spanning the past two centuries (Meagher and Mustapha 2020). This chapter does not purport to analyse the entire debate or its many trajectories. Rather, it aims to engender understanding of the context and ascendance of Boko Haram. The works of Abdul Raufu Mustapha (2014, 2018), a Northern Nigerian scholar and Mustapha and Meagher (2020), provide nuance and contextually rich analyses. In particular, Mustapha's edited book *Sects & Social Disorder: Muslim Identities and Conflict in Northern Nigeria* (2014) is a compendium for a non-sensationalized and grounded understanding. Mustapha argues that 'Religion simultaneously constrains and enables action by its adherents, but does so in a way heavy with social memory and the institutional residue of the past' (p. 1). He notes that religion is used as 'the idiom' for mobilizing communities at war and 'also [an] important lens through which wider social and political processes, not directly related to the divine, play themselves out in societies like Nigeria'. Besides, Islam is both an 'identity and political expression' in Northern Nigeria (Meagher and Mustapha 2020: 9; see also Mohammed 2015). This approach recognizes the salience of religion in and of itself and its co-mingling with socio-political, cultural, and economic issues as well as its instrumentalization for non-religious ends. Consequently, this chapter adopts Mustapha's 'sociology of Muslim societies, rooted in their agency, ideals, history, challenges and material conditions' (2014: 2) to understand Boko Haram.

As Last (2014: 18) argues, 'the Muslim *umma* in northern Nigeria has never been without religious dissidence'. The history of Islamic movements in Nigeria dates back to the Fulani jihad of 1804 led by Usman Dan Fodio. Dan Fodio was a Sunni Muslim reputed for theological expertise and social justice advocacy on behalf of poor Muslims. His exploits attracted the attention of traditional authorities. Dan Fodio and his followers were targets of attacks by the traditional ruler of Gobir, Yunfa, who began his reign in 1801. Yunfa sought to assassinate Dan Fodio and his followers. Dan Fodio mobilized his followers, mainly warriors from the Fulani ethnic group and Hausa *talakawa* (the poor) to depose Yunfa and take over governance of Gobir. The jihad was successful and marked the beginning of a long military and religious expedition all over what would become Northern Nigeria.

The Fulani jihadists deposed rulers who were accused of 'un-Islamic observances'—adulterating Islam with traditional religious practices (Keddie 1994: 479). Acts such as sale and consumption of alcohol and presence of women in public spaces without hijab or burqa were construed as immoral. The jihad was extremely popular among the predominantly Hausa peasants because of widespread corruption, the imposition of a cattle tax, and failure to observe Islamic laws on inheritance. By 1809, the jihadists had deposed most of the Hausa kings. The jihadists had two main objectives: introduction of a puritanical version of Sharia law and conversion of the locals to Islam (Loimeier 2012; Comoli 2015). The Sokoto Caliphate was established with Dan Fodio as the inaugural sultan. Dan Fodio's son, Muhammed Bello, and his brother, Abdullahi, helped to nurture the Caliphate to maturity. The Sokoto Caliphate was the largest state in Africa at the height of its military prowess (Keddi 1994). The Sokoto Caliphate embodied a powerful trifecta—religious authority, military power, and political authority. The politico-religious dynasty marked the institutionalization of extremely conservative Islam in Northern Nigeria (Hickey 1984). It redefined the role of religion in public life by creating a hybrid political machinery where the Church and state were indistinguishable. It also established conventions of gender relations and limited severely women's role in society.

On 27 July 1903, the British defeated the troops of the Caliph, Attahiru Ahmad at Burmi. This signalled the defeat of the Sokoto Caliphate. The entire region became the Northern protectorate. The defeat occurred 42 years after the annexation of Lagos. This meant that, for nearly half a century, Christian missionary activities, colonial administration, and trade promoted by the British had taken off in the colony of Lagos and Southern Nigeria. This contributed to a gap in education and social development between the North and the South. The British introduced a system of 'indirect rule', which retained the traditional structures largely intact. However, the traditional rulers, emirs, and the sultan, were under the authority of colonial officials. The British established Nigeria in 1914 by amalgamating the Northern and Southern protectorates.

The intermingling of the colonialists with the *Umma* in the Caliphate led to issues relating to secularization and moral decadence in Northern Nigeria—the ostensible focus of the Caliphate on this-worldly rather than otherworldly affairs. The British colonialists were considered 'White infidels' (Adeleye 1972: 194). Some Muslims also believed that being subjected to the rule of Christian officials was a fate more deplorable than death (Clarke 1987). There was a sense of betrayal, given that, in the face of superior military might, the Caliphate had entered into a pact with the British colonialists to guarantee its relevance. The clamour for 'reform and revivalism' emerged and 'dissent became a defining feature of emirate society' (Mustapha 2014: 2). The ensuing struggles have contributed to internal strife within the Muslim community (Mustapha 2014: 2).

Rapid changes (Hashim and Walker 2014), a rise in individualization and religious fragmentation (Mustapha and Bunza 2014), disagreements over the meaning of sacred texts and *takfir* (or excommunication), and changing attitudes towards the state (Mustapha 2014) are some of the factors underlying religious dissidence in Northern Nigeria. Several Mahdist (millenarian) movements had begun to rise up in the early days of the Caliphate but assumed a different dimension as colonial occupation took off. Some local mallams, operating via underground networks, declared themselves the 'Expected Mahdi' with the mission to deliver the *Umma* from its colonizers (Adeleye 1972). These movements were, however, largely uncoordinated and relatively innocuous (Miller 1936). For instance, one mallam proclaimed himself the forerunner of the Mahdi and called for the 'extermination of all unbelievers, including Europeans' (Adeleye 1972: 196). This was in February 1906. He was immediately imprisoned, but another mallam soon breached British troops and was sentenced to death by the native court.

The exception to the generally manageable series of religiously inspired uprisings was the Satiru rebellion, which occurred from February to March 1906. The village of Satiru near Sokoto was the epicentre of Mahdist movements. The chief of Satiru declared himself Mahdi in 1904 and had a son he named Prophet Isah or Jesus Christ (Adeleye 1972). The eschatological implication was that the appearance of the Mahdi indicated the end of time and would herald the materialization of Prophet Isah, who would, single-handedly or in collaboration with the Mahdi, defeat the anti-Christ (Adeleye 1972). The Sultan ordered the arrest of the Mahdi but he died while awaiting trial. His son, Prophet Isah, took over the reins of leadership of Satiru. He attacked the village of Tsomo, purportedly because Mallam Yahaya, the chief of Tsomo, questioned the status of Isah as a prophet and refused to support the movement in Satiru

(Adeleye 1972). The British viewed the attack on Tsomo as an affront on 'all authority' and sought to destroy the Mahdist movement in Satiru (1972: 198).

After the defeat of two forces sent to crush the rebellion, the British mobilized a larger contingent of troops on 10 March 1906 under the leadership of Major R. H. Goodwin—21 officers, 9 European non-commissioned officers, and 517 Africans as well as several local horsemen. The explicit aim was to ensure that 'so dangerous a body of fanatics should be not merely defeated but annihilated' (R.H. Goodwin, cited in Adeleye 1972: 205). The number of Satiru fighters had been overrated—estimates had been as high as 5,000, although Major Goodwin claimed that they were met by no more than 1,500 persons. What followed has been described as a 'holocaust' (Adeleye 1972: 205) perpetrated by British forces with the aid of the Caliphate. An estimated 500–1,000 persons were killed in Satiru to crush the rebellion. The Sokoto native court convicted the leaders of the rebellion and the Sultan approved their public execution at the Sokoto market place.

The Satiru rebellion had major consequences for Islamic movements and religious populism in Northern Nigeria. First, the Caliphate aligned itself with powerful actors who were perceived as foreign, infidel, and exploitative. The 'Sultan and the aristocracy of Sokoto overreached themselves to a point of barbarity in their anxiety to prove their loyalty to the British overlords' (Adeleye 1972: 207). This was viewed as a betrayal of Islam and the people. Second, the entire Satiru affair had social and psychological consequences for colonial rule as well as public perceptions of the Muslim Fulani rulers, who had by then grown in wealth despite the poverty of their people. Third, Satiru also eroded the religious or spiritual authenticity and legitimacy of the Caliphate. The traditional rulers were reduced to political stooges in service of Christian colonialists on Muslim land. A gradual dismantling of the political authority and legal strength of the Caliphate emerged thereafter, although it retained its symbolism and traditional significance among the people. Sharia law was rolled back and, like customary law in Southern Nigeria, had to be compatible with the English common law.

The Northern People's Congress (NPC) was established in 1949 and quickly became a platform for conservative politics in the North. The NPC's objective was to 'unite the peoples of northern Nigeria, retain northern regional autonomy within Nigeria, and enhance the power of traditional Muslim rulers' (Oxford Dictionary of Islam 2018). The Northern Elements Progressive Union (NEPU) was formed in 1950 to challenge the growing influence of the NPC and its alignment with the elites. Mallam Aminu Kano, a Fulani aristocrat, led NEPU. Aminu Kano believed that the 'Anglo-Fulani aristocracy' had failed the masses (Ngwodo 2015). NEPU's slogan was 'Sawaba' or 'freedom'. This was intended as a critique of British domination and the feudal structures entrenched by the Fulani aristocrats. NEPU campaigned for mass education and the rights of women. Ngwodo (2015) notes that

> NEPU's revolutionary agenda zeroed in on the fundamental problem of the North by lamenting that in 1950 its fifteen million people who had been under British rule for nearly a century had only one doctor, and not a single engineer, economist, lawyer . . . The progressives astutely understood that the education gap between North and South fuelled Northern paranoia about its potential post-colonial domination by the better resourced Eastern and Western regions and also fortified the status of the conservative elite.

There was a British policy to curtail the spread of Western-style education in the North (Ngwodo 2015). The situation was exacerbated by the reluctance of the Caliphate and a cultural environment that was suspicious of the proselytizing potential of Western education.

In 1954, the Muslim Students' Society of Nigeria (MSSN) was established to meet the demands of Muslim students who wanted an organization to serve as a forum for engagement on issues relating to Islam and the challenges they faced, 'especially in the face of hostile colonial and evangelical environment then prevalent in the country' (MSSN, University of Ibadan 2018). By the 1970s, some branches of MSSN in the North had begun to demonstrate increased radicalization. For instance, members of the Ahmadu Bello University (ABU), Zaria branch invaded the Faculty Club and destroyed alcoholic products in 1979. They were influenced by the Iranian revolution and the rise of an Islamic theocracy (Thurston 2018). The MSSN ABU chapter secretary general, Ibrahim al-Zakzaky, became vice-president of the national MSSN in 1979. Al-Zakzaky established an organization called the Muslim Brotherhood and renamed it the Islamic Movement in Nigeria (IMN) in the early 1980s (Zenn 2013; Thurston, 2018). Al-Zakzaky's movement centred on Shia Islam, although most Nigerian Muslims were (and remain) predominantly Sunni. This would have ramifications within and outside Nigeria. The new movement was instantly moored into pre-existing struggles in the house of Islam—the battle for supremacy and transnational influence between Sunni Saudi Arabia and Shia Iran. Such has been the impact of Iran that '(d)espite Nigeria's geographic and cultural distance from Iran, there is no region outside of the Middle East where Iran's ideology has a greater impact than in northern Nigeria' (Zenn 2013). A Shia Muslim community, which was previously absent in

Nigeria, grew within a period of 30 years to about 5% of Nigerian Muslims as of 2013 (Zenn 2013) or 10–15 million persons (Shadjareh and Choudhury 2014).

Al-Zakzaky is at the centre of the spread of the Iranian brand of Shia Islamic ideology in Nigeria. Al-Zakzaky has had relative success in transforming 'the IMN from student activism to a mass movement that called for "a second jihad" to implement Shari'a in Nigeria' (Loimeier 1997; Zenn 2013). The first jihad implied in the statement refers to the Fulani jihad of 1804. This suggests an orientation that the IMN was a revival of what had begun in the days of Dan Fodio. The IMN criticized the Northern aristocracy, Nigeria's secular government, and its moderate Muslim office holders and their supporters. Besides Sharia law, the IMN's central objective is to establish an Islamic state in Nigeria. Iran supports its activities despite repeated denials by al-Zakzaky (Zenn 2013; Comoli 2015).

The IMN and Sunni Muslims have been embroiled in several violent clashes. For example, the desire of IMN imams to seek leadership positions in mosques in Sokoto state in 2005 led to sectarian violence between IMN and Sunnis (Onapajo 2017). Security forces were deployed against the IMN following the conflict. They destroyed the IMN headquarters in Sokoto as a response to the assassination of a Sunni preacher in 2007 (Onapajo 2017). The preacher had apparently supported the 2005 state action on IMN and his death was construed as retaliation by IMN. However, al-Zakzaky maintained that state forces were deliberately targeting the IMN by assassinating Sunni Imams while blaming the IMN in order to weaken the movement (Zenn 2013).

The IMN has been at the receiving end of egregious shows of force by the state. For instance, Nigerian soldiers killed 34 persons and injured over 100 in Zaria, Kaduna state within a 2-day period during the annual al-Quds Day procession, which the IMN held to support the Palestinian cause (Shadjareh and Choudhury 2014). This was one in a series of brutal crackdowns on protests by the IMN (Amnesty International 2018). There have been multiple extrajudicial killings and state-sponsored brutality against the IMN.

Another Islamic movement, Maitatsine, led by Muhammed Marwa, gained prominence in the late 1970s and early 1980s. Marwa migrated to Kano from Cameroon in 1945. His followers grew to an estimated 8,000–12,000 followers in 1980 (Aghedo 2014). Marwa was a Qua'anic preacher who 'rebelled against many popular opinions . . . denouncing certain parts of the Holy Qur'an and even criticizing Prophet Mohammed' and condemned Western influence (Falola 1998: 146). Maitatsine means 'one who curses', a name which referred to Marwa and his group because of his strong critique of orders such as the Tijaniyya and Qadiriyya (Aghedo 2014: 234). Marwa was imprisoned and deported on several occasions between 1961 and 1975. The shock value of Maitatsine to the Umma in Nigeria included his condemnation of widely accepted Islamic observances and equating 'himself to the position of the Holy Prophet, saying that Mohammed was not the last prophet' (Aghedo 2014: 234).

Marwa and his followers were given an eviction notice by Abubakar Rimi, the governor of Kano state, in November 1980. On 8 December 1980, Maitatsine members destroyed police vehicles, killed four police personnel, and took over their weapons. The Maitatsine showdown with state security forces in 1980 resulted in the death of 4,177 people. Several hundreds more died in conflicts related to Maitatsine between 1980 and 1985 (Agbiboa 2013).

There have been several other sporadic and seemingly uncoordinated or leaderless episodes of religious violence in Northern Nigeria. Kaduna state has been a hotbed of such episodes. One such occurred at Advanced Teachers College, Kafanchan, on 6 March 1987. Reverend Bako, a preacher who had converted from Islam to Christianity, delivered a message common to all monotheistic religions—'Ours is the one true route to God.' Muslim students were enraged and a fight ensued along religious lines. About 152 churches were destroyed, and properties of Christians were torched. Isa Mohammed, the emir of Kafanchan, claimed that the violence was an act of terrorism by social misfits.

Islamic movements in Nigeria took on a different texture following the end of military rule in May 1999. An establishment-driven form of religious fundamentalism developed among newly elected officials in Northern Nigeria. Ahmed Sani Yerima, the governor of Zamfara state, led the efforts with the introduction of Sharia law in 1999. Eleven other governors in Muslim-dominated Northern states swiftly introduced Shariah law as it proved extremely popular. In Zamfara state, Sharia law was implemented with a heightened sense of seriousness. The right hand of Buba Jangebe was amputated in March 2000 following his conviction in a Sharia court for stealing a cow. This was the first in a series of highly publicized cases in which the punishment did not seem to fit the crime. Nonetheless, despite global outcry, the punishments enjoyed broad (but not universal) appeal in the North. Some of the recipients of the punishments supported the measures. Jangebe, for instance, was quoted by the BBC as stating that 'I thank God for the amputation' (Olukoya 2002). The punishments were largely accepted as the will of God.

Other leaderless cycles of violence also demonstrated the dynamics of social problems and the collision of world views and values in Nigeria. The crisis over plans to host the Miss World pageant in 2002 is one prominent example. The deadly riots over cartoons published in Denmark on 30 September 2005 presented another episode of widespread, and seemingly leaderless, cycles of violence. Violence over protests against the Danish cartoons reached Nigeria on 18 February 2006 in Maiduguri, Borno state, and Katsina state. Most of the 16 persons who died were Christians who were killed in Maiduguri by protesters (BBC 2006; Hill and Asthana 2006). More people died in Nigeria over the Danish cartoons than any other country. The closest country to Nigeria's casualty figures was Afghanistan, where 12 persons were killed prior to the outbreak of Danish cartoon-related violence in Nigeria.

The clamour for Sharia law in 1999 was catalysed by the reintroduction of democratic governance, which allowed the federating units a level of autonomy over their affairs, including authority over Sharia law in their jurisdictions (Agbiboa 2013). This was, however, circumscribed by the federal constitution, which laid down guidelines within a tripartite system of laws. Non-Muslims were excluded from governance by Sharia law. There were differences in how Sharia law was practised in the 12 Northern states in which it was introduced. Consequently, in states such as Borno (where the governor, Ali Modu Sheriff, had a working relationship with Boko Haram, with the latter helping with implementation), the Nigerian constitution set a limit on the use of Sharia law. This was a major source of grievance for those supporting puritanical Sharia law. Public support is generally high for organizations advocating Islamization and state governments that attempt to implement Sharia law in Northern Nigeria, despite the setback to full implementation of Sharia law and Islamization (Adesoji 2011). What these cases suggest is that 'Far from representing an embedded tradition of jihadism, Islamic violence in Northern Nigeria is simply political violence in a largely Muslim society, expressing a range of different political meanings from revolution to elite struggles over power to inarticulate social protest' (Meagher and Mustaphas 2020: 9).

Boko Haram

The Salafi Islamic fundamentalist group, *Jama'at ahlis Sunnah lid Da'wat wal Jihad* (People Committed to the Propagation of the Prophet's Teachings and Jihad) or Boko Haram arguably constitutes one of the greatest existential threats to the survival of the Federal Republic of Nigeria since the 1967–1970

Civil War. Boko Haram was formed in 2002 (Osumah 2013; Agbiboa 2014).[1] Local people in Maiduguri called the growing sect the 'Nigerian Taliban' and 'Yusufiyyah sect' in its early days (Onuoha 2010: 55). The name Boko Haram has, however, stuck. The meaning of the term 'Boko Haram' has been the subject of speculation. A widespread interpretation is that Boko Haram means 'Western education is forbidden and deceitful' (Matfess 2017: 10) or 'Western education is sin', an erroneous translation despite its broad use (Loimeier 2012).[2] Thurston (2018: 16) offers a nuanced interpretation. He argues that Boko Haram roughly translates to '"Western culture is forbidden by Islam" or "the Westernized elites and their way of doing things contradict Islam"—not just in schools but also in politics and society.' This interpretation is supported by evidence from Boko Haram. In a statement released on 9 August 2009, 'We speak as Boko Haram', published by Nigeria's *Vanguard* newspaper, Boko Haram argued,

> First of all ... Boko Haram does not in any way mean Western education is forbidden as the infidel media continues to portray us. Boko Haram actually means 'Western civilization' is forbidden. The difference is that while the first gives the impression that we are opposed to formal education coming from the West, that is Europe, which is not true, the second affirms our believe [*sic*] in the supremacy of Islamic culture (not Education), for culture is broader, it includes education but not determined by Western Education. In this case we are talking about Western ways of life which include: A constitutional provision as it relates to, for instance the rights and privileges of Women, the idea of homosexualism, lesbianism, sanctions in cases of terrible crimes like drug trafficking, rape of infants, multi-party democracy in an overwhelmingly Islamic country like Nigeria, blue films, prostitution, drinking beer and alcohol and many others that are opposed to Islamic civilization.
> (cited in Vanguard 2009)

The explanation provided in the official statement indicates that Boko Haram represents a repudiation of secularism (Kassim and Nwankpa 2018: 87). Therefore, it has not only an otherworldly focus but also a 'thisworldly' concern with political life, the boundaries of morality, gender roles, and the quest

---

[1] There are indications that it was founded in 1995 under the name *Ahlulsunna wal'jama'ah hijra* and led by one Abubakah Lawan, who left Nigeria to study at the University of Medina, Saudi Arabia (Onuoha 2010; see also Aghedo and Osumah 2012). Onuoha (2014: 3) does admit that the origin of Boko Haram is 'not clear' (see also Weeraratne 2015).

[2] Loimeier (2012) analyses why the Arabic or Islamic term *haram* cannot be equated with the Christian term 'sin'.

for the pre-eminence of Islamic civilization. The statement demonstrates that while a lot of attention is focused on its opposition to Western-style education, Boko Haram's objectives are much broader and more comprehensive.

The role of state repression is crucial to any nuanced understanding of Boko Haram. The massive overreaction of the British colonialists and their aristocratic allies at every phase of the Satiru movement marked the start of a trend that has become familiar in post-independence Nigeria—excessive use of force by state agents against protest movements. This has often exacerbated relations between the state and religious, as well as secular, challengers of authority.[3] Mohammed (2015: 19–20) argues that the transformation of Boko Haram to

> an arms-bearing sect was in part the making of security agencies, which approached the situation as one of 'law and order' and responded as such, with disastrous consequences. There was no attempt to perceive the issues raised by the movement in its broader multifaceted prism as political, social and economic... The security agencies serially mismanaged the crisis from the onset and in the process pushed the movement to the extreme end of the spectrum.

Mustapha's (2014: 147) analysis provides a similar conclusion: 'It is testament to the poor management of the situation by political and military authorities at all levels of the Nigerian federation that this transformation from a rag-tag mob in 2003 to a so-called caliphate in 2014 was able to take place unchecked.' In other words, state repression altered the trajectory of Boko Haram in fundamental ways. The extrajudicial killing of Muhammad Yusuf and hundreds of his followers by state forces in July 2009 was a watershed moment in the trajectory of Boko Haram.

Overall, the dynamics of the conflicts in relation to Islamic fundamentalist movements in Northern Nigeria include (a) conflict or schism *within* specific Islamic groups, (b) conflict *between* Islamic groups, and (c) conflict between Islamic fundamentalist groups and Nigerian security agencies (Oriola and Akinola 2017). Other discernible dimensions include (a) diffusion of issues from other parts of the world, which are weaponized for violent acts in Nigeria; (b) violence between Christians and Muslims, who may not necessarily belong to radical Islamic groups; and (c) deployment of indiscriminate violence on whole communities by Islamic groups as well as (d) reprisal attacks

---

[3] For instance, the extrajudicial execution of the Ogoni Nine in 1995 served as watershed in the transformation of a largely non-violent environmental justice movement in the Niger Delta to a violent insurgency by the late 1990s (see Ikelegbe 2005; Oriola [2013] 2016).

by Christians for losses incurred during any of the above. Issues relating to Islamic movements speak to fundamental differences over the meaning and boundaries of freedom of speech, religion in the face of secularism, morality, and Western education. These issues also encompass gender relations and debates over the 'place' of women and the popular appeal of entities promising a return to true Islam.

The foregoing is not intended to provide a comprehensive exposition of the history and dimensions of Islamic movements in Nigeria or the rise of Boko Haram. Loimeier (2012: 138) problematizes Boko Haram as a 'result of social, political and generational dynamics within the larger field of northern Nigerian radical Islam'. Agbiboa (2013: 3–4) buttresses this perspective:

> extremist Islamic movements in northern Nigeria should be considered a movement of restoration since their overriding goal continues to be the enforcement of Sharia in the spirit of earlier times as inspired by Usman dan Fodio and the sharia-governed Sokoto Caliphate. Boko Haram ... is the latest and most violent manifestation of this restoration movement.

The messages of Muhammed Yusuf, the founder of Boko Haram, demonstrate the link between his missionary activities, including deployment of violence and miscellaneous issues highlighted above—the Miss World controversy, the Sharia law debacle, and the battle between Christians and Muslims in Kafanchan. Muhammed Yusuf delivered a lecture, 'Tarihin Musulmai' (History of Muslims), in 2008, which demonstrates the significance of the context. Yusuf argues,

> They insulted the Prophets, Jesus and Muhammad. They believed that since they combined the two Prophets, the people would feel indifferent. They are Christians, but they said the Prophet Jesus had a prostitute (*karuwa*), and the Prophet Muhammad, too, had a prostitute. At the time, the only reaction to this statement was the burning of the newspapers, but they were neither arrested nor charged in court. This event came to pass. Then one rash lady at the time of beauty pageant, Daniel, also perpetrated the same injustice. And before that period, in Kafanchan one Reverend Bako also insulted the Prophet as well ... So they will just insult the Prophet, then kill the Muslims and live in peace. [...] Now that all these events are happening, all the time I am always thinking: Why is it that whenever these events happen, they will just say: 'Sorry, you should exercise patience, wait for what the government will do or let us plead to the government to take measures'. Always that is

what they say. Then Allah made me understand that it is not like that. What will stop them from insulting the Prophet or killing the Muslims is jihād. But how are we going to carry out the jihād? With whom are we going to carry out the jihād? *Allah made me understand that first and foremost, we must embark upon the preaching towards Islamic reform. Then, we will have to be patient until we acquire power. This is the foundation of this preaching towards Islamic reform. It was founded for the sake of jihād and we did not hide this objective from anyone.*

(cited in Kassim 2017; italics added)

There are four phases in the evolution of Boko Haram. These are 'substate missionary activism', 'substate jihadist and an al-qaeda connection', 'national jihadist and al-qaeda affiliation', and 'transnational jihadist and the integration into AQIM and ISIS' (Gray and Adeakin 2015: 189–194). The first two phases denote the transformation of Boko Haram from a localized collection of religious zealots in Maiduguri, Borno state, Nigeria to one that actively sought ties with al-Qaeda within a global jihadi fervour, respectively. The third phase underscores the transformation of Boko Haram to an organization with an al-Qaedaesque nationalism. The fourth phase emphasizes Boko Haram's growing embeddedness within transnational jihadi networks, particularly ISIS (Islamic State of Iraq and Syria). Boko Haram pledged allegiance to ISIS on 7 March 2015. The death of Yusuf led to leadership tussles which created multiple centres of power. Given state counterterrorism operations, a highly decentralized structure emerged with multiple commands, subcommands, and operational cells, particularly between 2011 and early 2014 (Onuoha 2012; Zenn 2020). Each stage above represents growing territorial expansion, broader political objectives, and a significant rise in the use of violence.[4] The next section draws on the Global Terrorism Database to articulate the trends, patterns, and trajectories of acts of terrorism perpetrated by Boko Haram.

Trends and patterns of Boko Haram's activities

Analyses of the Global Terrorism Database (GTD) demonstrate the patterns of violence of Boko Haram. The annual number of terrorist activities in Nigeria was relatively low prior to 2009, when intense activities of Boko Haram commenced (Mantzikos 2014). Boko Haram has changed the scale of political violence in Nigeria.

---

[4] For more on Boko Haram, see Mustapha (2014, 2018, 2020) and Thurston (2018).

Fig. 1.1 indicates that 19,125 deaths and 9,062 injured persons were recorded from 2,289 attacks by Boko Haram between the years 2010 and 2020.[5] Fatalities from Boko Haram's attacks peaked in 2014 (5,621 from 381 attacks), although the highest number of attacks was carried out in 2015 (439) and resulted in 5,309 fatalities.

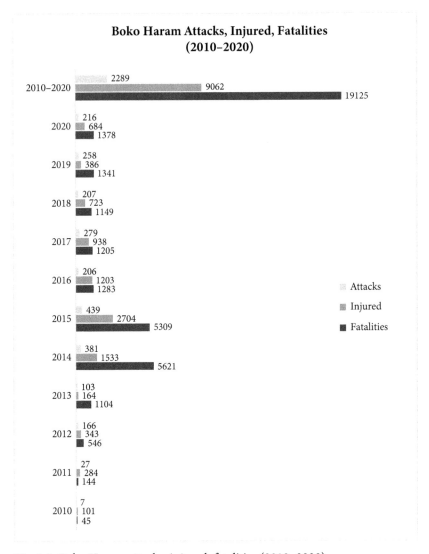

Fig. 1.1 Boko Haram attacks, injured, fatalities (2010–2020)

Source: Based on data from the Global Terrorism Database.

[5] The most recent year for which data was available in the GTD at the time of production process.

Fig. 1.2 shows the distribution of Boko Haram's attacks, persons injured, and fatalities by country. Nigeria is the epicentre of Boko Haram's operations, as is widely acknowledged. There were 1,841 attacks by Boko Haram, which produced 7,015 injured persons and 15,394 fatalities in Nigeria between 2010 and 2020. Cameroon is second with 285 attacks, 1,021 injured persons, and 1,968 fatalities within the same period.

Fig. 1.3 demonstrates the number of Boko Haram's attacks by target and provides a clear picture of their focus of operations. Boko Haram carried out a greater number of attacks (1,299) on private citizens and property than other targets between 2010 and 2020. Military targets were second with 421 attacks within the same period. The police (103 attacks) were third and religious figures/institutions (94 attacks) were fourth, while businesses (78 attacks), 'unknown' (75 attacks), and educational institutions (54 attacks) were fifth, sixth, and seventh, respectively. Attacks on the military and the police have produced major cycles of violence due, in part, to retaliation by affected troops.

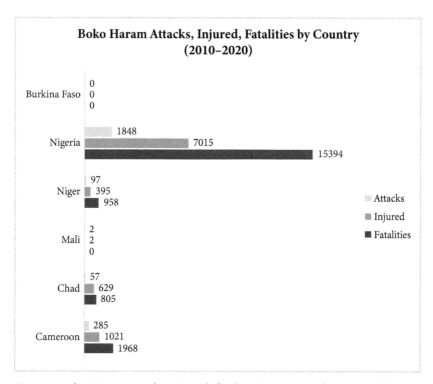

Fig. 1.2 Boko Haram attacks, injured, fatalities by country (2010–2020)
Source: Based on data from the Global Terrorism Database.

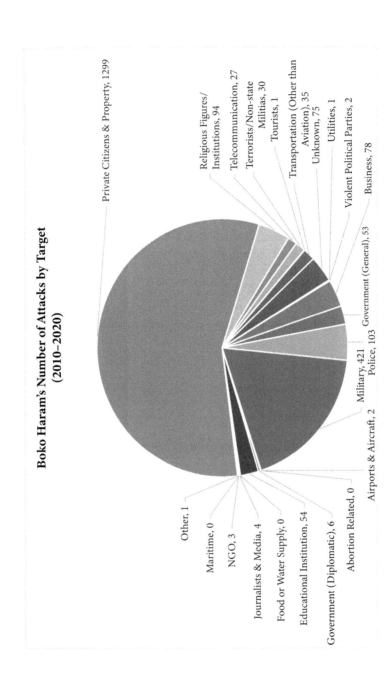

Fig. 1.3 Boko Haram, number of attacks by target (2010–2020)

Source: Based on data from the Global Terrorism Database.

Civilians are often caught in the crossfire. Though ranked third, educational institutions have been used by Boko Haram to kill or kidnap large numbers of students. For example, Boko Haram attacked Federal Government College, Buni Yadi, Yobe state on 25 February 2014. Fifty-nine boys were massacred: some were slaughtered with knives and many were shot, while others died when all 24 buildings in the school were set ablaze (Hemba 2014; Matazu 2014). One of the key moments of the gruesome killing was widely reported in the media: 'Teachers at the school in Buni Yadi said the gunmen gathered the female students together before telling them to go away and get married and to abandon their education' (BBC 2014a). There is no record of sexual molestation of the girls in that particular encounter. This incident revealed Boko Haram's approach to gender: males had to be killed while females existed purely for the purposes of marriage[6] and childbearing. In the organization's mind, attempts to educate females constituted a waste of time; it was irreligious and a forbidden deployment of women's reproductive energies (Oriola 2017).

Fig. 1.4 shows Boko Haram's attacks by number of injured persons and fatalities by attack type. The chart demonstrates that armed assault is Boko Haram's preferred attack type (911 attacks, which led to 1,767 injured and 10,369 fatalities). Bombing/explosion is second with 689 attacks, which produced 6,353 injured and 5,127 fatalities. Hostage-taking/kidnapping is third with 267 incidents, which produced 574 injured and 1,643 fatalities.

Boko Haram is a prolific user of suicide bombers in the global terrorism landscape. Fig. 1.5 shows that Boko Haram executed 365 suicide bombings between 2010 and 2020. These led to 4,470 injured persons and 2,748 fatalities. Most of Boko Haram's suicide bombings occurred in Nigeria (269 attacks, 3,251 injured, and 2,155 fatalities).

Fig. 1.6 distils Boko Haram's suicide bombings in Nigeria to the subnational level. Borno state in the Northeast has been the focus of Boko Haram's suicide-bombing operations (207 attacks, which led to 1,790 injured and 1,342 fatalities). Adamawa (15 attacks, 508 injured, and 317 fatalities) and Kano (10 attacks, 378 injured, and 212 fatalities) are second and third, respectively.

The increase and changes in Boko Haram's tactics and attacks are fundamentally linked to Nigeria's political process. As demonstrated throughout

---

[6] The marriages are often forced on young teenage and prepubescent girls and arguably provide a cover for sexual abuse.

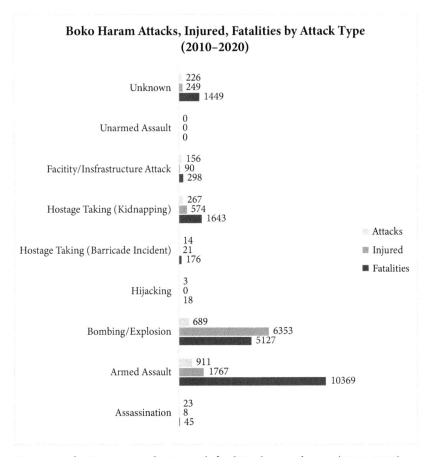

Fig. 1.4 Boko Haram attacks, injured, fatalities by attack type (2010–2020)
Note: For attacks with more than one attack type, the primary (i.e. first) attack type was used.
Source: Based on data from the Global Terrorism Database.

this book, Boko Haram festered largely because of multiple interconnected variables intrinsic to contestation for power and politics. Concerning Boko Haram's overall territorial scope of action, evidence from the GTD demonstrates that the organization had attacked (as of 2013) 20 of the 36 states in Nigeria and the Federal Capital Territory, Abuja. Its activities are particularly focused on Northeastern Nigeria. Overall, analysis of the GTD indicates that Boko Haram spread from one state (Borno) in 2009 to 17 states in 2014. However, its activities occurred in six states in 2016. The decline in its territorial reach coincides with renewed military efforts to decapitate the organization.

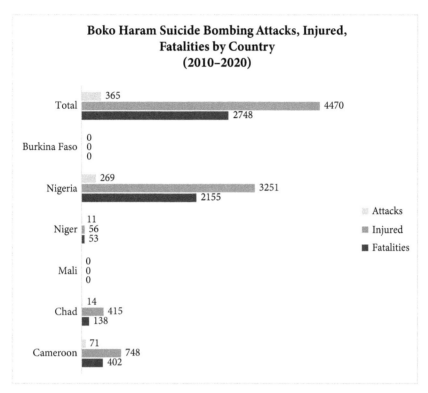

Fig. 1.5 Boko Haram suicide bombing attacks, injured, fatalities by country (2010–2020)
Note: Suicide bombings are attacks where there is evidence that the perpetrator did not intend to escape from the attack alive.
Source: Based on data from the Global Terrorism Database.

Boko Haram's ideology

There are three crucial terms to engage with in an attempt to understand Boko Haram's ideology: *Salafism, jihadism* and *Salafi-jihadism* (Thurston 2018: 18). Salafism means 'predecessors' and has 'special resonance' within Sunni Islam (p. 19). Salafism can be traced to twentieth-century Saudi Arabia. Salafis adhere to a 'literalist understanding' of both the Quran and Sunna (Thurston 2018). Doctrines of Salafism were widely propagated and spread to countries like Nigeria (Thurston 2018). While the term 'jihadism' means 'struggle', 'effort', or 'strive', its interpretation has since acquired a new texture. It refers to an ideology that was influenced by the Muslim Brotherhood from the 1960s to the 1990s and has developed into a focus on militant action

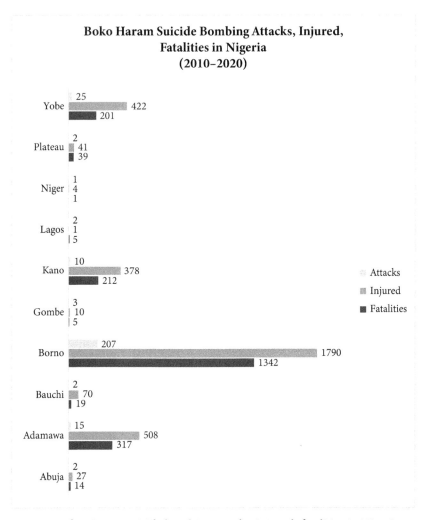

Fig. 1.6 Boko Haram suicide bombing attacks, injured, fatalities in Nigeria (2010–2020)

Note: Suicide bombings are attacks where there is evidence that the perpetrator did not intend to escape from the attack alive.
Source: Based on data from the Global Terrorism Database.

(Thurston 2018: 20). Oriola and Akinola (2017) argue that the complexion of Boko Haram's jihad uniquely combines classical or territorial jihad with a narrative alignment with global jihad. Classical or territorial jihad (*fard al ayn*) requires individual duty in place of collective responsibility to join efforts to depose an alien or unbeliever regime, while traditional jihad (*fard al kifaya*) stipulates that the defence of Muslim territories is a joint responsibility of all Muslims, and consequently, such a struggle is not required of everyone

(Nilsson 2015). Boko Haram's struggle draws inspiration from Salafi-jihadism (Thurston 2018).

Boko Haram considers itself a part of a broader global jihadi movement. Boko Haram pledged allegiance to ISIS in 2015 and changed its name to *Wilayat Ghart Ifriqiya* or Islamic State West Africa Province.[7] However, prior to 2015, Abubakar Shekau aimed to be under the auspices of al-Qaeda. His views were expressed in an undated letter found at Bin Laden's compound in Abbottabad, Pakistan in May 2011. Shekau noted in the letter that

> we have listened to your tapes and have heard your news, such as the tapes of al-Qa'ida and its shaykhs, like Usama Bin Laden ... and Dr. Ayman al-Zawahiri, Abu Musab al-Zarqawi ... But now what we have left is to learn about the system of the organization and how it is organized.

Shekau showed interest in engaging with Bin Laden's deputy and underscored the imperative of 'unification' and 'speaking with one voice'. Shekau never publicly pledged allegiance to Bin Laden or al-Qaeda (Joscelyn 2016), but his letter is unequivocal about Boko Haram's desire to be part of a global jihadi movement, which was a critical objective of Bin Laden (Nilsson 2015; Schmid 2015).

There are six major reasons to support the idea that Boko Haram is internationalist in scope and thus embedded within the global rise of jihadi terrorism (Solomon 2012). First, Boko Haram named itself as the 'Nigerian Taliban' and 'Black Taliban'. This suggests a mimetic and mutually contagious process. Second, there were allegations that Mohammed Yusuf, the founder of Boko Haram, had received money from al-Qaeda; third, Boko Haram claimed that its members received training in countries such as Afghanistan, Iraq, Algeria, Lebanon, and Mauritania, and some of Boko Haram's top leaders were widely believed to have met with al-Qaeda in the Islamic Maghreb; fourth, Boko Haram seemed to also have ties with al-Shabaab. Fifth, Boko Haram is believed to be part of the Movement for Unity and Jihad in West Africa, a coalition of terrorist groups dedicated to jihadi activities in the West African region and, sixth, the geographic spread of Boko Haram across the Lake Chad region suggests that it is a transnational organization (Solomon 2012: 7–8).

A tripartite analytical framework embedded within the notion of Islamism, which entails the adherence of actors to, and propagation of, a 'particular strand of Salafist political Islamic ideology' to understand Boko Haram has

---

[7] Divisions within Boko Haram are explained later in the chapter.

been proposed (Gray and Adeakin 2015: 186). The components of Gray and Adeakin's (2015) framework are missionary Islamism, activist Islamism, and jihadist Islamism (p. 186). Missionary Islamism focuses on provision of social services as a way of propagating Islam in society and is systematically orientated towards the poor through health care, aid, and education, while activist Islamism (*al-harakat al-islamiyya al-siyassiyya*) operates in the form of collective action such as mass protests, demonstrations, and riots (Gray and Adeakin 2015: 187). Gray and Adeakin (2015) argue that Boko Haram deployed a combination of missionary Islamism and activist Islamism until late 2003, when it began to adopt more extremist tactics. Jihadist Islamism implies the use of indiscriminate violence through invocation of 'al-jihad', or holy war to achieve political objectives (p. 188). Attacks on the government of Yobe state in late 2003 marked this trajectory in Boko Haram's operations.

Three fundamental elements—ideology, tactics, and objectives—'divide and define Islamists' (Gray and Adeakin 2015: 186). The focus on Boko Haram's ideology in particular provides a critical corrective to the largely structuralist orientation of the literature on Boko Haram (but see Roeflofs 2014; Sändig 2015). Nonetheless, focusing on ideology is only a start in terms of understanding meaning construction and propagation by terrorist groups (Snow and Byrd 2007). Indeed, ideology is often 'reified and treated as a given rather than as a topic for analysis, and thus glosses over the discursive ideological work required to articulate and elaborate the array of possible links between ideas, events, and action' (Snow and Byrd 2007: 133).

Boko Haram uses three major master frames: the *return to true Islam master frame*, the *injustice master frame*, and the *war against the infidel master frame* (Oriola and Akinola 2017). Oriola and Akinola note that 'the master frames draw on an assortment of Boko Haram's doctrinal beliefs and serve as signifying vehicles through which Boko Haram presents itself and interpellates the audience' (p. 11). For instance, the meta-narrative of the Boko Haram phenomenon is the return to true Islam master frame (Oriola and Akinola 2017). Oriola and Akinola note the five interconnected aspects of the return to true Islam master frame. These are negation of democracy, opposition to Western education, ultra-conservative beliefs about gender relations (specifically the status of women), the construction of Christianity as 'paganism', and the establishment of an Islamic Caliphate (p. 11).

Boko Haram's use of the injustice master frame encompasses grievances over inequality and killing of its leader, Mohammed Yusuf, and several of its members by state forces (Oriola and Akinola 2017). The role of repression in the indiscriminate use of violence by Boko Haram is widely acknowledged (Sändig 2015). Mass arrests and deaths of suspects in state custody have further radicalized the organization (Amnesty International 2015b). The approach of the Nigerian state has attracted local and international criticism. For example, 21 US academics who worked primarily on issues relating to Africa wrote to then Secretary of State Hillary Clinton on 21 May 2012. They implored Secretary Clinton and the US government to suspend plans to designate Boko Haram as a 'foreign terrorist organization' (FTO). The scholars argued,

> An FTO designation would... increase the risk that the US becomes linked—whether in reality or perception—to abuses by the security services.... [It] would effectively endorse excessive use of force at a time when the rule of law in Nigeria hangs in the balance. There is already evidence that abuses by Nigeria's security services have facilitated radical recruitment.
> (cited in Oriola and Akinola 2017: 14)

One of the co-signers of the report also stated in a private correspondence with the author that they were concerned that the 'FTO designation would strengthen the hand of the hardliners' within Boko Haram. Some Boko Haram members who were reaching out to negotiate with the government asked General Buhari to serve as mediator. Therefore, the US academics 'felt that it was important for those talks to go ahead so that the government could pull away the "doves" in the movement, and isolate the hardliners, and that the FTO designation would just give the hardliners an additional tool to consolidate their hold'. State repression exacerbated the Boko Haram crisis and silenced leaders within Boko Haram who were clamouring for negotiations to end the conflict between 2011 and 2012 (Oriola and Akinola 2017). The heavy-handedness of Nigerian state forces provided the much-needed 'stories of injustice and repression' coveted by terrorists (Demant and de Graaf 2010: 409). This is reflected in the injustice framing of Boko Haram, which is deployed via four main dimensions. They include a challenge to the image of an 'irrational and blood-thirsty terrorist entity' that had begun to stick, casting the Nigerian state and its security forces as the aggressor responsible for extermination of 'innocent' preachers, assuring the *Ummah* that Boko Haram was engaged in a mission to avenge attacks on fellow Muslims, and generating public sympathy.

Boko Haram deploys the war against the infidel master frame to justify its use of violence as a routine aspect of a cosmic war with unbelievers. This master frame encompasses five dimensions. These include 'the war is a defensive war, the war is intended to propagate Islam, purification of Islam from within, elements of Manicheanism and predestined victory' (Oriola and Akinola 2017: 15). What the foregoing suggests is that Boko Haram's ideology is not homogenous, monochromatic, or inelastic. Besides, the exclusive focus on religious dogma implicit in Boko Haram's ideology neglects the fact that the organization exists within a specific social context that has shaped the texture and internal fidelity of its ideology.

Boko Haram's grievances and objectives

Boko Haram killed 2,053 persons in 95 attacks within the first 6 months of 2014 (Human Rights Watch 2014). A report by Amnesty International (2015c) indicates that Boko Haram attacked over 300 villages and towns and killed at least 14,000 people between 2009 and April 2015. Kashim Shettima, who was governor of Borno state, the main theatre of Boko Haram's operations, claimed, in February 2017, that Boko Haram had killed 100,000 persons (Tukur 2017a). The United Nations Development Programme (UNDP) estimates that nearly 350,000 people had been killed in the Boko Haram conflict in the Northeast at the end of 2020 (Reuters 2021a). These huge casualty figures and the use of suicide bombings have led to questions about Boko Haram's objectives and grievances.

Boko Haram seeks to destroy the Nigerian state. It rejects the secularity of the Nigerian state, has no respect for its laws, and considers the state illegitimate (Onapajo et al. 2012). Boko Haram insists that Nigeria is a country of unbelievers or *kafirs*—non-Muslims, Christians, and idolaters—who have to be put under Islamic rule (Oriola and Akinola 2017). Boko Haram's initial objectives focused on the introduction of a puritanical version of Sharia law in Northern Nigeria. It began to establish structures of governance thereafter until it started to lose territory from early 2015. Boko Haram pledged allegiance to ISIS on 7 March 2015. This move put it firmly at the epicentre of global concerns over the rise of violent religious extremism as well as gender-based violence against women.

Boko Haram articulated its main grievances and objectives in its 9 August 2009 official statement, 'We speak as Boko Haram'. Boko Haram argued,

1. That we have started a Jihad in Nigeria which no force on earth can stop. The aim is to Islamise Nigeria and ensure the rule of the majority Muslims in the country. We will teach Nigeria a lesson, a very bitter one.

2. That from the Month of August, we shall carry out series of bombing in Southern and Northern Nigerian cities, beginning with Lagos, Ibadan, Enugu and Port Harcourt. The bombing will not stop until Sharia and Western Civilisation is wiped off from Nigeria. We will not stop until these evil cities are tuned [sic] into ashes.
3. That we shall make the country ungovernable, kill and eliminate irresponsible political leaders of all leanings, hunt and gun those who oppose the rule of Sharia in Nigeria and ensure that the infidel does not go unpunished.
4. We promise the West and Southern Nigeria, a horrible pastime. We shall focus on these area which is the devil empire and has been the one encouraging and sponsoring Western Civilisation into the shores of Nigeria.
5. We call on all Northerners in the Islamic States to quit the follower ship [sic] of the wicked political parties leading the country, the corrupt, irresponsible, criminal, murderous political leadership, and join the struggle for Islamic Society that will be corruption free, Sodom free, where security will be guaranteed and there will be peace under Islam.
6. That very soon, we shall stir Lagos, the evil city and Nigeria's South West and South East, in a way no one has ever done before. Al Hakubarah

The statement ends with the ominous sentence 'ITS EITHER YOU ARE FOR US OR AGAINST US' (emphasis original) and was signed by one Mallam Sanni Umaru, 'Acting Leader of Boko Haram'.

To summarize, Boko Haram aims to Islamize Nigeria, remove all traces of Western civilization from Nigeria, kill anyone who opposes Sharia law, implement a bombing campaign in major Nigerian cities, teach the Nigerian state a lesson (purportedly for the death of its leader and hundreds of members), ensure a corruption-free society, and institute the rule of God.

Recruitment into Boko Haram

There are various factors responsible for Boko Haram's ability to recruit followers. Mustapha's (2014: 166) 'multidimensional evidence-based approach' to Boko Haram is instructive for understanding Boko Haram and its recruitment. Mustapha offers five dimensions in his framework: religious doctrines, poverty and inequality, the political context of post-1999 electoral competition, personal agency of young people engaged within Boko Haram, and the interplay of the geographical and international context of Boko Haram. A study conducted by the CLEEN Foundation at the behest of the US Institute for Peace investigated why young people were radicalized in select towns in Borno, Gombe, Kaduna, Kano, Sokoto, and Yobe states. The range of participants in the study included youth, women, and faith groups; traditional leaders; religious leaders from various groups; security personnel; political leaders; and heads of women's groups. The results demonstrated a mix of 'causative factors', which included political, religious, social, and economic issues (Onuoha 2014: 5). The factors included ignorance of religious teachings against violence, unemployment and poverty, hardship in early socialization, low literacy rates, excess of state forces, and corruption (Onuoha 2014: 5–7). The findings showed that these factors—to varying degrees—made young people susceptible to violent extremism. Similarly, Akinola (2015) argues for a multifactorial approach to understanding the emergence of Boko Haram. He finds that the 'interaction of politics, poverty, and Islamic fundamentalism' contributed to the rise and continued operation of Boko Haram in Nigeria (p. 2). The decline in the influence of moderate Sufism has intensified religious extremism in Nigeria, while other West African countries with larger proportions of Muslims have embraced moderate Sufism and therefore experience lower levels of jihadi fundamentalism (Akinola 2015).

The role of politics is pivotal to scholarly analyses of the emergence and spread of Boko Haram. Rather than the simplistic North–South dichotomy often associated with analyses of Nigeria, local politics 'provides more useful explanations of Boko Haram's emergence and continued existence' (Akinola 2015: 2). Local politicians such as Modu Sheriff patronized Boko Haram for purposes of winning elections and failed to stop the group during its infancy. The role of poverty in the rise of Boko Haram has also been acknowledged. Akinola (2015: 12–13) argues that the increase in Nigeria's absolute poverty rate from 29% in 1980 to 62% 'puts the socioeconomic factors driving the Boko Haram insurgency into perspective'. The lack of employment opportunities for young people who are migrating from rural to urban centres further contributes to the ranks of Boko Haram. Interviews granted by Boko Haram members have confirmed the salience of unemployment and poverty in their decisions to join the group. One report (Francis 2018) quotes a 20-year-old member: 'My job as a member of Boko Haram since 2014 was to take young girls, who are to be used for suicide bombings to target locations. I'm usually paid N200, 000 (approximately $550 [US]) for each operation.' While the whole of Nigeria has fared poorly on most social indicators, Northern Nigerian has been severely impacted far more than the South.

Consequently, the idea that poverty or relative deprivation has played a huge role in the spread of Boko Haram is widely acknowledged in the literature (Osumah 2013; Agbiboa 2014; Olaniyan and Asuelime 2014). Agbiboa (2013: 164) speaks to the fact that it is 'no coincidence that the worst forms of collective violence in Nigeria today originate in the most socioeconomically deprived parts of the country'. Aghedo and Osumah (2012) note that Boko Haram's members are drawn from persons who dropped out of school and those enrolled for Quranic education. However, not all members of Boko Haram are necessarily socially marginal. Aghedo and Osumah (2012) note that Boko Haram draws its members from other sources, such as Islamic clerics, the working class, professionals, and post-secondary students from institutions of learning such as the University of Maiduguri; Ramat Polytechnic, Maiduguri; and Federal Polytechnic, Damaturu—all in Borno and Yobe states. The involvement of well-placed individuals depicted by the indictment of two of Nigeria's former military heads of state and a former vice-president, as well as sympathetic members of state security forces, have also been noted (Aghedo and Osumah 2012).

Boko Haram's recruitment activities have been catalysed by the motivation of its members to fight against social injustice, the ideology of its founder, revenge for the 2009 security crackdown, financial benefits, the failure of the Nigerian state, currents of global jihadi terrorism, and resistance against perceived Western cultural domination and wars in Muslim countries such as Afghanistan and Iraq (Stern 2003; Onapajo and Uzodike 2012; Onapajo et al. 2012).

Divisions within Boko Haram and Islamic State—West Africa Province's (ISWAP's) June 2021 consolidation of power

There are ideological divides within Boko Haram. Zenn (2012: i) highlights three 'ideological strands' within the organization. These include an ideology to impose Sharia law on Nigeria; another strand that purports to be connected to the transnational goals of al-Qaeda; and a criminogenic ideological strand focused on kidnapping, among other crimes, for various state, non-state, and/or transnational entities (Zenn 2012). This characterization is now insufficient but remains one of the earliest indications of schism within Boko Haram. Boko Haram had at least three major factions until June 2021.

Ansaru (or the Vanguard for the protection of Muslims in Black Africa), which broke ranks with Boko Haram on 1 January 2012, was one of the three known factions. Led by Khalid al-Barnawi, the organization's main objective is to 'defend Muslims throughout all of Africa by fighting against the Nigerian government and international interests' (Smith 2016). Ansaru appeared to have left Boko Haram partly on doctrinal grounds—it criticized Boko Haram for killing Muslims and attacking security forces without provocation. Ansaru has strong ties with al-Qaeda in the Islamic Maghreb (AQIM), despite Boko Haram's pledge of allegiance to ISIS in 2015 (Smith 2016). Ansaru gained notoriety for several kidnapping incidents involving Western hostages shortly after its formation.

Another faction splintered from Boko Haram in August 2016 when ISIS named Abu Musab al-Barnawi, the son of the late Boko Haram leader, Muhammed Yusuf, 'Wali' (custodian) of ISWAP. The pronouncement by ISIS undermined Abubakar Shekau. Shekau criticized the appointment in an audio statement. Abu Musab al-Barnawi declared an end to attacks on Muslims in his first statement after his appointment. There was a crisis within Boko Haram on who ought to be in charge and who had deviated from the course of Islamizing Nigeria. The legitimacy of attacks on Muslims was one of the main ideological differences between ISWAP and Boko Haram. ISWAP's approach courts public support by minimizing attacks on civilians, particularly Muslims (Stoddard 2019).

The ties between the al-Barnawi faction (ISWAP) and ISIS influenced the decision to release all but one of the over 100 school girls kidnapped in Dapchi, Yobe state on 19 February 2018. The faction planned to use the kidnapped victims to obtain ransom and release of its fighters from state custody. One Abu Bashir, who led the Shura of the al-Barnawi faction, noted that the girls were freed because of its allegiance to the leadership of the Islamic State in Iraq and the Levant (ISIL) or ISIS (Sahara Reporters 2018b). He claimed that ISIL believed the kidnapping of Muslim girls 'cast the group in bad light' at a time when ISIL was having a hard time winning over Muslims in West Africa (Sahara Reporters 2018b).

Mamman Nur, one of the key leaders of the al-Barnawi faction, was killed by some of his closest commanders on 21 August 2018 (Idris and Sawab 2018). Nur was killed partly because of his 'soft approach' and perceived closeness to Nigerian government officials (Idris and Sawab 2018). Abu Musab al-Barnawi was removed as the leader of ISWAP in 2019 and replaced by Abdullahi Umar Al Barnawi (Ba Idrisa). Internal strife over how to share revenue led to killings of 'scores' of ISWAP members on 26 July 2019 (Sahara Reporters 2019b). This was a prelude to a serious cycle of violence within ISWAP. Ba Idrisa was removed as head of ISWAP in February 2020 and replaced by Ba Lawan. The struggle for power within ISWAP led to internal killings in the top echelons. Ba Idrisa and four other top ISWAP leaders (Mohammad Bashir, Mustapha Jere, Ali Abdullahi, and Baba Mayinta) were killed (al-Hussaini 2020a). The killings 'triggered the mutiny' which occurred between Wednesday 26 and Thursday 27 February 2020 by fighters loyal to Ba Idrisa (al-Hussaini 2020b).

The series of fratricidal struggles within Boko Haram and ISWAP further complicated attempts to destroy them militarily or engage in negotiations, given the emergence of multiple nodal and lethal centres of power. Each autonomous faction executed attacks against targets and prolonged the military's fight against Boko Haram. The power struggles also signalled a decline in doctrinal emphasis or 'clerical tones' (al-Hussaini 2020b) and greater preoccupation with combat. This has had the tendency to harden the position of the surviving factions and their key actors.

The most consequential factionalization of Boko Haram is arguably the separation of the original Boko Haram from the Islamic State-backed ISWAP in 2016 (Stoddard 2019). ISWAP announced, in June 2021, that Abubakar Shekau, the leader of the original Boko Haram, had killed himself by detonating a suicide vest during a battle between the two factions (BBC 2021). ISWAP consolidated its power in late June 2021 when several Boko Haram fighters pledged allegiance (Reuters 2021b). This merger has potentially grave consequences for the war against terrorism in Africa.

The kidnapping of the Chibok girls

On 14 April 2014, 276 girls were kidnapped at Government Secondary School, Chibok, Borno state.[8] The kidnappers claimed that their mission was to rescue the girls from ongoing violent incidents in Chibok. A report by Human Rights Watch (2014: 22) describes the night of the incident as narrated by an 18-year old female student:

> Two men told us we should not worry, we should not run. They said they had come to save us from what is happening inside the town, that they are policemen. We did not know that they were from Boko Haram. The rest of the men came and started shouting 'Allahu Akbar' and at that moment we realized, they were Boko Haram.

---

[8] A version of this section appears in my article 'The exploitation of Nigeria's Chibok girls and the creation of a social problem industry' (Oriola 2023).

Security at the school premises was poor. The school had only one guard—a civilian—who fled on realizing that Boko Haram operatives were on their way to the school (Human Rights Watch 2014). The lack of security provided a huge opportunity for Boko Haram as they encountered no resistance. Boko Haram members called for back-up trucks to take as many girls as possible as they had arrived unprepared for such a volume of young women (Human Rights Watch 2014). Several of the girls escaped by jumping off the trucks of their abductors, while three girls were released because there was no space to fit them into any of the trucks (Human Rights Watch 2014; Matfess 2017). Fifty-seven girls are believed to have escaped on the night of the incident by running into the bush.

A Boko Haram commander who was arrested along with 21 others in July 2018 contradicted the account of the Chibok girls as regards the real mission of Boko Haram at the school on 14 April 2014. The Commander Maita Alhaji, nicknamed Abu, argued that

> one of our commanders, who received direct orders from our leader, Abubakar Shekau, Bana Chungoru, called out over 100 of us and we all assembled at the Sambisa forest. He told us that our leader, Shekau had ordered that we should all go to Chibok Local Government and kidnap some girls at the school. We couldn't ask questions, because it was a direct order from Shekau and we all mounted our trucks, three Toyota Hilux vans and two Isuzu pickup trucks. We left Sambisa Forest around 5 pm that evening and arrived the school around 10 pm. We surrounded the school when we arrived and when we were certain that there woud be no resistance . . . We kidnapped many of them and took them away in our trucks.
>
> (cited in Okolie 2018)

The Boko Haram commander's account corroborates reports about lack of security at the school. It is plausible that the calls made by the Boko Haram operatives (and emphasized by the girls) had to do with the number of girls, which necessitated calling for more vehicles. Abu claimed to have received approximately $83 (US) on the day of the kidnapping and $166 when ransom was paid for some of the girls (Okolie 2018). Boko Haram confirmed, in a video released in May 2014, that they were behind the mass kidnapping, as had been widely suspected. The incident was a spectacular criminal act even by the standards of a country in which kidnapping had become relatively routine since the late 1990s, particularly in the oil-rich Niger Delta region (Oriola [2013] 2016).

Why did Boko Haram carry out the kidnapping? Drawing on the context and evidence before, during, and after the kidnapping, various explanations are considered. These are Boko Haram's quest for revenge against the government, ideological fidelity (specifically, opposition to Western education and the 'place' of women), and the quest for finances for its activities. Other explanations include the need to have a negotiation tool for prisoner exchange and to meet the domestic and sexual needs of male fighters. This section also considers the idea that the Chibok kidnapping was purely accidental.

First, there is evidence to suggest that Boko Haram was motivated by a desire to seek revenge for the arrest and illegal detention of hundreds of wives and children of its members (Human Rights Watch 2014). Since at least 2012 (two years before the Chibok kidnapping), Abubakar Shekau, the leader of Boko Haram, 'routinely accused the Nigerian government of kidnapping the wives and children of suspected militants' (Cummings 2014). There were also reports that some of Shekau's family members were among those who had been detained. Shekau issued warnings between 2012 and 2013 that security agents were engaged in widespread sexual and physical abuse of detainees and that 'the same fate would await the wives and children of government officials and soldiers alike' (Cummings 2014). Therefore, the Chibok kidnapping could be reasonably inferred as being part of a 'bloody campaign' announced by Boko Haram in 2013 as retaliation for the arrest of wives, children, and other family members of Boko Haram (Duthiers et al. 2014). The release, in 2016, of 566 family members of Boko Haram operatives appears to support the notion that the government had engaged in large-scale imprisonment of Boko Haram family members without necessarily ensuring due process (Sahara Reporters 2016).

Second, the Chibok kidnapping feeds into Boko Haram's ideological stance on two issues: its opposition to Western education and perspective on the 'place' of women in society. Boko Haram began to attack schools in 2010. Its most infamous attack prior to Chibok was at the Federal Government College, Buni Yadi, Yobe state on 25 February 2014. As noted earlier, Boko Haram killed 59 boys in the incident. Boko Haram's instruction to the female students at Buni Yadi has implications for the rationale behind the Chibok abduction. Boko Haram operatives, as earlier noted, told the female students to abandon their education and get married. Therefore, kidnapping the Chibok girls operationalized Boko Haram's belief that Western education pollutes the minds of young people, and young girls ought to get married and have children rather than acquire education. Abubakar Shekau was unequivocal about why the girls were kidnapped. He declared, in a video after the incident in 2014,

'Just because I took some little girls who were in western education, everybody is making noise. Let me tell you: I took the girls. Girls: Go and get married. We are against western education and I say "stop western education."' (Shekau 2014).

The incident has had harmful effects on the education of young girls and their right to education (Maiangwa and Amao 2015). Given pre-existing challenges to female education, the Chibok kidnapping increases the possibility that parents may prevent their children from going to school for fear that they might be abducted. Concerns over safety may also compel some students to seek other options outside school. For example, one of the Chibok girls who escaped on the night of the abduction was so traumatized by the experience that she never returned to school and got married despite objections from her family.[9] Another Chibok girl, Lugwa Sanda, who was among the 21 girls released in October 2016, attempted suicide in September 2017 as a protest against being sent to Abti Academy, a high school in Yola, Adamawa state, one of the areas most affected by Boko Haram. Sahara Reporters (2017) notes,

> three sources said some of the Chibok schoolgirls were opposed to going to the school. One of the sources said the girls' resistance owed to recent attacks in parts of Adamawa State by the Islamist terrorist group, Boko Haram. 'Many of the girls have expressed fear that they could be abducted for a second time. Yet, they are afraid to go against the decision of the (education) minister to enroll them in Abti Academy'.[10]

Lugwa Sanda preferred to die than return to school in Boko Haram's area of operation. Sanda's case and that of the Chibok girl who got married against her family's wishes and never completed high school demonstrate the impact of the abduction. The impact is synchronous with Boko Haram's ideology.

Third, the Chibok girls could have been kidnapped for purposes of being used for prisoner exchange in negotiations with the government (Human Rights Watch 2014). At least one kidnapping incident prior to Chibok had demonstrated the utility of taking captives to make demands on the government. Boko Haram attacked a police barracks on 7 May 2013 in Bama, Borno state. Shekau released a video in which he demanded the release of women

---

[9] Interviewee 13; female #BBOG member and aunt of a Chibok girl who escaped on the night of the abduction: personal interview, July 2015.
[10] This account was corroborated by an uncle to one of the freed girls and an activist from Chibok, both of whom were interviewed for the study.

connected to Boko Haram who were in state custody. Boko Haram released several hostages on 24 May 2013 during the period in which the military freed several detained Boko Haram wives (Cummings 2014). About 90 Boko Haram members and their wives and children were released in May 2013 (Zenn 2014) in exchange for Boko Haram's captives. Five top Boko Haram commanders were released in exchange for 82 Chibok girls in 2017.

Fourth, and as a corollary to the third point above, Boko Haram's use of the Chibok girls to generate revenue is arguably part of a broader plan by the organization, given its previous experiences with negotiations for the release of captives. The 2013 prisoner exchange involved a ransom payment by the government (Zenn 2014). Besides, there is evidence that Boko Haram earned over $70 million between 2006 and 2011 from its collaborative activities, including kidnapping alongside al-Qaeda in the Arabian Peninsula (AQAP) and AQIM (Ajani 2014). The release of 82 Chibok girls in May 2017 involved a ransom payment of €3 million (Parkinson and Hinshaw 2017). One Associated Press report notes that a '"handsome ransom"—in the millions of dollars' was also paid to Boko Haram to secure the release of 21 Chibok girls in 2016 (cited in Patience 2016).

In addition, Boko Haram considered taking captives a legitimate part of warfare. Boko Haram argued long before the Chibok abductions that each kidnapped person would be turned into a 'servant' (Duthiers et al. 2014). Servitude, in this case, includes sexual enslavement of young women. Therefore, the Chibok girls could have been kidnapped to fulfil the sexual needs of the predominantly male fighters. Given that most of the fighters are from poor socio-economic backgrounds and are largely isolated, capturing such a huge number of young women was an avenue to provide 'wives' to the fighters—a kind of earthly reward for heavenly pursuit. University of Birmingham Professor Paul Jackson argues that Boko Haram's operatives are mainly young men who live in isolated areas and have a 'particular set of needs that they want fulfilled. They view themselves as on some sort of religious journey, so they want to be accompanied and rewarded at the same time' (cited in Sputnik International 2018). This is supported by evidence from the diaries of some of the released Chibok girls: Boko Haram fighters pressurized several of the girls to get married. A BBC report notes one of the entries in a joint diary kept primarily by one Naomi Adamu and Sarah Samuel during their captivity. The diary notes,

> We saw the people come in two Hilux [vans]. Then they came asking for those who want to get married. They asked us and said anybody who accepts

Muslim religion ... must get married if truly she holds the religion with two hands. They gave us 30 minutes to give them their answer but we kept quiet. Then we stayed for an hour but nobody answered.

(BBC 2017)

Naomi Adamu confirmed that 'those who refused to get married were treated as slaves: "Every day, they beat us. They tell us to marry and if you refuse, they will beat you. We will wash cloth, fetch water, do everything for their wives. We were slaves"' (cited in BBC 2017).

Finally, there is also evidence demonstrating that the Chibok kidnapping was purely accidental. Human Rights Watch (2014: 23) notes that the 'primary objective of Boko Haram's attack was the theft of a brick-making machine as well as food and other supplies'. Therefore, the lack of resistance and access to the girls were critical variables in the incident. Adaobi Tricia Nwaubani, a prominent Nigerian journalist, who has had unfettered access to many of the released Chibok girls and their families, corroborates the report by Human Rights Watch. Nwaubani notes that the Chibok kidnapping was not planned—Boko Haram had gone to the Chibok school to steal an 'engine block' (BBC 2017; Nwaubani 2017). Nwaubani has in her possession multiple diaries from a number of Chibok girls.[11] The joint diary notes that, on the day of the kidnapping,

They [Boko Haram fighters) started argument in their midst [sic]. So one small boy said that they should burn us all and they said, 'No let us take them with us to Sambisa.' Another person said, 'No let's not do that. Let's lead them ... to their parent homes.' As they were in argument, then one of them said, 'No, I can't come with empty car and go back with empty car ... If we take them to [Abubakar] Shekau [Boko Haram's leader], he will know what to do.'

(cited in BBC 2017; see also Nwaubani 2017)

The immediate aftermath of the kidnapping incident revealed fundamental fissures in Nigeria's toxic politics. The army's claim, within days of the abduction, that the girls had been rescued was based on false information. There was reluctance within the Jonathan administration to admit that the girls were truly missing. President Goodluck Jonathan did not speak in public

---

[11] The author saw the diaries in the course of interviewing Nwaubani in July 2018 in Abuja, Nigeria.

about the kidnapping until nearly three weeks after the incident. The kidnapping quickly became mired in politics and contestation for presidential power between the ruling People's Democratic Party (PDP) and the opposition All Progressives Congress (APC). The two parties began to accuse each other of 'playing dirty politics' with the Chibok kidnapping within a few days of the incident.[12]

Any doubt that Chibok had been fed to the machinery of Nigeria's toxic politics was dispelled by September 2014. The APC released a statement in which it accused the government of President Jonathan of engaging in 'manipulation of the girls' release' (Vanguard 2014) to assist the ruling party in winning the 2015 presidential election. The APC argued,

> This is most unconscionable, most exploitative and blatantly shameless. It confirms what we have been saying all along that the Jonathan Administration knows more about the Boko Haram insurgency than it has admitted, and that the Administration is exploiting the insurgency for the President's re-election.
>
> (Vanguard 2014)

An article in *This Day*, a national newspaper, noted two years after the abduction that the incident

> ran straight into the web of local politics and through the sheer mismanagement of that critical security matter, the fate of the innocent girls were sealed—sadly, in bad taste. Unfortunately, for former president Goodluck Jonathan, the mood of the nation at the time did not give room for fair hearing. He had already been crucified before the girls were even delivered to the den of their abductors.
>
> (Oyeyipo et al. 2016)

However, President Goodluck Jonathan and the ruling party were not innocent bystanders or victims of the kidnapping, as they attempted to cast themselves. The slow response and focus on political optics rather than immediate and pro-active efforts to secure the girls demonstrate the positionality and investment of the Jonathan administration in the toxic political environment. This meant that a country with one of Africa's most decorated militaries could not swiftly act to secure its kidnapped citizens.

---

[12] See Vanguard (2014).

The Chibok kidnapping as a prism for understanding terrorism and human rights advocacy in Africa

The Chibok kidnapping sparked a series of events, crises, and one notable social movement—the #BringBackOurGirls (BBOG) movement. The Chibok kidnapping and the rise of the #BBOG movement provide an empirical context for understanding human rights advocacy in Africa. The fact that such large-scale kidnapping happened five years after Boko Haram had become established as a threat to security in West Africa, the failure of the government of President Goodluck Jonathan and other leaders of the Lake Chad Basin countries (Niger, Chad, and Cameroon) to work together within the period, and the reality that scores of the girls are still missing speak to broader issues about the nature of the African state, the dynamics of its military, regional cooperation in Africa, and the relationship with Western powers. The issues also speak to regional efforts aimed at combating global jihadi terrorist footprints in Africa, given Boko Haram's ties with al-Qaeda (specifically, AQIM),[13] its declaration of formation of an 'Islamic State' in 2014, its pledge of allegiance to ISIS in 2015, and the June 2021 consolidation of power by ISWAP.

Several studies have analysed the rise of Boko Haram (Onuoha 2010; Waldek and Jayasekara 2011; Loimeier 2012; Gray and Adeakin 2015), the role of socio-political and economic factors in its emergence (Brinkel and Ait-Hida 2012; Akinola 2015), Boko Haram's relationship with the global system (Onapajo and Uzodike 2012), particularly global jihadist groups such as al-Qaeda (Forest 2012; Onapajo et al. 2013), its challenges for the 'war on terror' (Oyewole 2013), and its historical ties to local fundamentalist religious groups such as Maitatsine (Adesoji 2011; Loimeier 2012). Others have considered the relationship between failed/failing states vis-à-vis Boko Haram's insurgent terrorism (Brinkel and Ait-Hida 2012), the implications of Boko Haram's ascendance for democratic governance (Igboin 2012), the capacity of the state to deal with the crisis (Akinola and Tella 2013; Osumah 2013; Udounwa 2013), and the consequences of Boko Haram's insurgency for national integration efforts (Osumah 2013). The framing strategies of Boko Haram (Roeflofs 2014; Sändig 2015; Oriola and Akinola 2017) and the ethno-religious fissures created by its operations have also garnered attention (Langer et al. 2017).

However, there is scant attention paid to the activities of social actors who are providing a counter-narrative to Boko Haram's atrocities. A few studies

---

[13] A document seized from Osama Bin Ladin's Abbottabad, Pakistan reveals that Shekau sought 'to be under one banner' with al-Qaeda (see https://www.dni.gov/files/documents/ubl2016/english/Praise%20be%20to%20God%20the%20Lord%20of%20all%20worlds.pdf. Accessed 23 March 2020).

have focused on the use of social media by #BBOG and its combination of online and offline activism (Chiluwa and Ifukor 2015). No study has attempted a comprehensive investigation of the rise of #BBOG, its tactics, mobilization, framing, internal issues (such as decision-making) and external challenges (such as state repression), and the overall implications of the #BBOG experience for human rights advocacy in Africa. This book aims to fill this vacuum.

Studying #BBOG has potential to reveal lessons for other social movements in postcolonial societies vis-à-vis human rights advocacy and the challenges confronted by activists. This book contributes to scholarship on social movements in Africa. How activists surmounted challenges, such as state repression, counter-framing of the movement's objectives, attempts at co-optation, and ethno-religious divide within membership, among others, are particularly useful for other social movements in Africa and the developing world in general. The study contributes to theory-building on sources of oligarchization within social movements and the impact of emergence of activist 'superstars' on movement activities, internal divisions, and movement outcome. The book offers evidence on the need for grassroots movements in the developing world to be wary of internationalizing their framing or overall movement activities in an age of internet activism. Global attention may not necessarily generate the desired change or intervention.

The study draws on, and contributes to, the transhistorical lineage of women-led protest movements in Africa. Women-led movements in Africa often do not have the benefit of protection by the law or a Weberian ideal-type state *qua* state with established structures to address grievances. Therefore, the contours of feminist praxis in Africa are shaped by factors related to the facticity of gender and macro-sociological variables arguably unique to the postcolony. It is 'counterproductive in the African setting to single out gender . . . as the primary source and focus of political agitation' (Oyewumi 2003: 2). Therefore, the book explores the role of the intersection of women's multifarious identities, embeddedness in the life of society, relations with others, and particularities of their cultural context.

The book enhances understanding of the engagement of the elite (specifically, female elite) in grassroots advocacy in Africa. The role of elite women in movements advancing women's rights in the Middle East and North Africa is recognized in the literature. Such movements were generally 'coopted by the state' by the end of the twentieth century and turned into large bureaucracies (Gheytanchi and Moghadam 2014: 3). State-sponsored feminism was also common in West Africa (Mama 1995), South America (Noonan 1995), and North Africa (Allam 2018). State feminism catapulted select elite women into international prominence, with the wife of the head of state as indisputable leader. However, such beneficiaries of state-sponsored feminism (or 'first-ladyism') as Egypt's Suzanne Mubarak and Nigeria's Maryam Babangida consolidated their position in the national imaginary on the backs of women. But what happens when a movement refuses to be co-opted, despite private and public overtures by the state? How does the state fight back? What are the consequences for such a movement?

The social class and gender dimensions provide a fascinating backdrop in states that are intolerant of political dissent: how do state actors respond to agitations by some of their own, for example former cabinet members or their spouses and children of highly revered former leaders? Elite involvement in local struggles plays a catalytic role in legitimizing and enhancing the visibility of the cause. Elite involvement also has the potential to attenuate the severity of state repression but comes with significant baggage that may imperil movement goals.

The research process

This book uses a mixed methodological approach: an exploratory qualitative research and a survey of #BBOG members. An exploratory research is a fundamentally 'broad-ranging, purposive, systematic prearranged undertaking designed to maximize the discovery of generalizations leading to description and understanding of an area of social or psychological life' (Stebbins 2001: 3). Exploratory research helps to garner insights regarding the contours of a problem (Marlow 2005). This approach is flexible and pragmatic (Van Maanen et al. 2001). Therefore, in addition to meaningful understanding of the phenomenon (i.e. the #BBOG movement), following Stebbins (2001: 6), the book focuses on 'potential generalizations' that the data speak to that may help formulate theories and policy. Nonetheless, any generalization within the book is (a) limited in scope and (b) delimited by the data. These are fundamental caveats to the arguments of the book.

Research for this book was conducted during five field exercises in Nigeria between 2015 and 2019. A short survey of #BBOG activists was also conducted in 2015 and 2016. The survey was aimed at gathering data to ascertain the demographics of the activists as well as their response to questions about the objectives of the organization, motivation of members, assessment of public support for the movement, and evaluation of the political process and its key state actors. Multiple qualitative methods of data collection were deployed. These included interviews, focus group discussions (FGDs), participant observation, and document analysis. Interviews were conducted with #BBOG activists, senior military officers, rank-and-file soldiers, journalists, and political leaders. Over 170 persons were involved in primary data collection. In addition, the author exchanged emails with six US academics who were part of the group of American scholars who wrote to Secretary of State Hillary Clinton not to designate Boko Haram as an FTO. Several leaders of the #BBOG movement, such as Obiageli Ezekwesili and Aisha Yesufu, among others, were interviewed multiple times over the course of the research. Senior military officers were also interviewed multiple times as the rescue of the Chibok girls dragged on.

This book also benefits from three summers (2015–2017) of extensive embeddedness of the researcher in the activities of #BBOG through participant observation of the daily sit-out. The number of persons at each sit-out ranged from 6 to 47 in the course of fieldwork. The lower end of the spectrum was observed in 2017. This method was used in a manner that prioritized observation and interrogation over participation. The author chose to remain in the background and did not contribute to discussions over 95% of the days that he attended the sit-out during the summer months of 2015–2017. This was an intentional decision that required enormous discipline. The aim was to observe the proceedings; make sense of the interactions from the actors' perspective; and take note of how the movement was shaped by the discussions, arguments, and decisions at the sit-out.[14] There were occasions when members of #BBOG explicitly invited the author to contribute to discussions. It was often difficult to decline to participate on such occasions, but there were few such. There were times when the author volunteered to speak on issues that were germane to the research interests, especially when discussions centred on insurgency, terrorism, or crime in general.

The author's insider–outsider approach enabled concentration on understanding the dynamics of the group, taking extensive notes, and avoiding choosing sides in the internal politics of the movement. This approach also enabled the author to become acquainted with opposing perspectives and personalities on various issues in the movement. That created room for further interrogation as the author was able to request interviews from individuals

---

[14] The #BBOG movement's WhatsApp groups were also immensely useful. I was added to the platform in 2017. The discussions on this forum provided key information that served as a starting point for further exploration.

who expressed views that warranted follow-up. Therefore, participant observation helped to identify key interview participants and informants.

Six research assistants transcribed the interviews and focus group discussions. The study themes emerged from a grounded theoretical orientation. There are six major considerations in this regard. These are engaging in collection of data and analysis at the same time; developing categories and codes for the data rather than any 'preconceived logically deduced hypotheses'; developing theory in the process of collecting and analysing data; rigorous note-taking as a step between data-coding and first draft-writing; non-representative sampling and conducting the review of literature after independently analysing primary data (Glaser and Strauss 1967; Charmaz and Mitchell 2001: 162). The book utilizes process-tracing for data analysis. This involves systematically selecting and analysing distinctive symptoms or 'diagnostic evidence' vis-à-vis research questions (Collier 2011: 823). Special attention is given to the description of patterns of change and constellation of events, episodes, encounters, crises, and other variables (George and Bennett 2005). This method of analysis helps to identify social or political phenomena, links among episodes, and insight into underlying social mechanisms. This process requires significant prior knowledge of the context to ascertain critical junctures, events, and variables as well as how situations unfold 'over time' (Collier 2011: 824). This involves drawing on multiple sources of data for an informed process-tracing. Primary data from a diverse selection of key actors who were on the front lines of the political events is cross-articulated with secondary data (such as newspapers and reports produced by human rights organizations like Amnesty International and Human Rights Watch) on those events, perspectives of various parties, observations during the multi-year field work, and the author's prior knowledge of the socio-political context. The study also draws on secondary data, particularly newspaper and human rights non-governmental organization (NGO) reports, on the war against Boko Haram and literature produced by the #BBOG movement. Hundreds of newspaper reports were collected in the course of the study.

Scope and limitations of the book

This book focuses on the 'original' #BBOG movement organization located in Abuja, Nigeria. Therefore, the analysis excludes other organizations by a similar name in Lagos, New York, Toronto, and other parts of the world. The Abuja #BBOG was the epicentre of the movement's activities, and its leadership was globally recognized. Publicity documents (such as press releases and strategies) and overall coordination of the movement came from the Abuja organization. The decision was also partly a matter of pragmatics: researching all, or even most of, the organizations within the movement was nearly impossible, given their geographic spread and the resources and time required to undertake such an endeavour. Therefore, the focus of this book is the pioneer #BBOG group that formally began its activities on 30 April 2014.

Beyond pragmatics, there are also theoretical considerations necessitating focusing on the Abuja group. The Abuja group, as pioneer, embodies the 'spirit' of the movement and generally enjoys global legitimacy[15] in ways that others do not, although they continue to make significant contributions to the movement. Although the name '#BringBackOurGirls' is widely used by other groups around the world, there is, in fact, no associational charter binding the various groups to the original organization in Abuja. Therefore, despite the similarity in name and the temptation to consider the internal micro-mechanics of other locations, these are independent organizations albeit fighting for the same cause. This is not necessarily an aberration in social movements.

This study is limited by the inability to interview Boko Haram members. This was initially contemplated but was dropped because of the legal risks inherent in being seen to be 'associated' with the organization. For instance, there have been cases of arrest of journalists who were conducting research or had direct contact with the terrorist organization.[16] There were also enormous security risks, given Boko Haram's killing of humanitarian workers, for instance. In addition, while reference is made to the 19 February 2018 kidnapping of 110 students at the Government Girls Science and Technical College (GGSTC), Dapchi, Yobe, this book's focus is the movement that developed following the 14 April 2014 kidnapping in Chibok, Borno state.[17] The Dapchi kidnapping appears similar to the Chibok kidnapping but is not the central theme of this book. Kidnapping of students at schools has become the 'norm' in Nigeria since December 2020 (Yusuf 2021). These incidents have been blamed

---

[15] The Abuja #BBOG received a human rights award on behalf of the movement in Argentina in 2016.
[16] For example, one Simon Ateba was arrested by Cameroonian authorities on suspicion of espionage at the behest of Boko Haram (Mojeed 2015). Ahmed Sarkida, who had helped to release to the public videos of proof of life of kidnapped Chibok girls provided to him by Boko Haram, was declared wanted by the Nigerian army in August 2016 and arrested the following month (Punch 2016a).
[17] #BBOG had begun to take up the issue of the Dapchi kidnapping as of 13 March 2018 with a march to the presidential villa. It also signified its intention to sue the federal government of Nigeria over the February 2018 abduction (Opoola 2018). Boko Haram released all but one of the Dapchi girls on 21 March 2018.

on 'bandits' rather than Boko Haram. There is growing concern that collaboration between bandits and Boko Haram is a distinct possibility as the former seeks to expand its operations (Samuel 2021). While the growth in kidnapping in Nigeria and the alliance between bandits and Boko Haram are disturbing, they are not the focus of the book.[18]

Chapter 2 analyses the formation of the #BBOG movement, factors responsible for the movement's global spread, its objective, and movement strategies on rescue of the Chibok girls. The chapter also focuses on the organizational structure of #BBOG and its repertoires of protest.

---

[18] The current wave of kidnapping by bandits at educational institutions in Nigeria since December 2020 warrants a dedicated study.

2

'The fight for the soul of Nigeria and the world'

The #BringBackOurGirls movement

Introduction

On 23 April 2014, Dr Obiageli Ezekwesili ('Aunty Oby'), former World Bank Vice-President for Africa and Nigeria's former Minister of Education, addressed a United Nations Educational, Scientific and Cultural Organization (UNESCO) forum in Port Harcourt in the Niger Delta region. Ezekwesili used the platform to criticize the reluctance of the Nigerian government to acknowledge that 276 girls had been kidnapped from Government Secondary School, Chibok 9 days earlier by Boko Haram. Ezekwesili requested that those at the event demand that the government should 'bring back our daughters' (Ibeh 2014). One Ibrahim Abdullahi, who was watching the event on television, began to tweet about it. Abdullahi created two hashtags—'#BringBackOurDaughters' and '#BringBackOurGirls'—drawing on Ezekwesili's speech.[1] Ezekwesili retweeted Ibrahim's '#BringBackOurGirls' tweet after her presentation and encouraged her followers on Twitter ('X') to draw attention to the kidnapped girls' plight by using the same hashtag. This marked the start of the social media dimension of the movement.

Another concerned member of the elite, Hadiza Bala Usman,[2] had begun to engage a number of women leaders. Email exchanges and other in-person contacts initiated by Usman began among a select number of female leaders (including Ezekwesili) to mobilize Nigerian women to demonstrate against President Goodluck Jonathan's government's failure to act. A plan to start a 'physical movement' (Interviewee 30)[3] was broached. A mass protest in Abuja

---

[1] The erroneous report in 2014 that a US citizen, Ramaa Mosley, coined the hashtag has since been corrected. There is no longer any debate about who created the hashtag.
[2] Daughter of popular Marxist historian, Bala Usman.
[3] Female member of the #BringBackOurGirls strategic team; personal interview, Abuja, July 2015.

was announced on social media, therefore bringing together the terrestrial efforts of Usman and the social media agitations led by Ezekwesili. Over 2,000 people gathered in Abuja on 30 April 2014, despite the heavy rainfall. Banners proclaiming 'Rescue our Chibok girls' were displayed. Ezekwesili was one of those who addressed the gathering. She led the crowd to chant: 'Bring back our girls.' Thus, the #BringBackOurGirls (#BBOG) movement was born. Several participants at the protest insisted that the demonstration had to continue until the government responded. Chants of 'everyday' filled the air. The group decided to meet daily until the girls were rescued. The presupposition was that the rescue would take a few days or weeks in the worst-case scenario. #BBOG spread to major cities around the world.

There are two emerging trajectories in scholarly work on the #BBOG movement. The first body of work focuses on the immanent problematic of the manner in which the agitation for the rescue of the girls is being framed (Loken 2014: 1). The second problematizes the 'imperialist appropriations' (Maxfield 2015: 1) of the #BBOG movement. The locus of these concerns (particularly the linguistic iteration of the movement between 2014 and 2015) is threefold.

First, the discursive machinery of the #BBOG movement relies on emphasizing that the missing girls were 'daughters' and 'sisters' and therefore privileges 'narratives of women as rights-deserving only through the capacity to be claimed' (Loken 2014: 1). Second, the use and disuse of the hashtag by various actors, especially in the geopolitical West,[4] is criticized as constituted by, and constitutive of, the limitations of social media activism or 'slacktivism' (Tandy 2014) or 'hashtag activism' (Scott 2014)—a convenient (computer-based), vociferous agitation that generates little to no praxiological results. The third dimension is the ostensible intricate entanglement of the movement in the labyrinth of imperialist discourse (Maxfield 2015)—or 'the white savior industrial complex' (Cole 2012; cited in Maxfield 2015: 2). #BBOG is criticized for providing an avenue for colonialist discourses and another non-committal 'cause' for Western subjects who have since moved on.

These are serious criticisms. The potency of the criticisms is symptomatic of the failure to rescue *all* the girls (at the time of writing) over seven years after their abduction. However, there is a tendency to conflate the globally diffused narratives surrounding the rescue of the Chibok girls with the much more strategic and painstaking *framework* of the original #BBOG social movement organization in Abuja. The former is a consequence of the latter.

---

[4] Northern and Western European countries as well as Canada and the United States.

#BBOG as a contemporary, African women-led social movement

The #BBOG advocacy is a social movement with external and internal dynamics, opportunities, and constraints. The Abuja #BBOG 'family' is its flagship social movement organization (SMO). The literature on *what* a social movement means is quite eclectic but accentuates certain thematic. One perspective argues that a social movement comprises 'collective challenges based on a common purpose and social solidarities, in sustained interaction with elites, opponents, and authorities' (Tarrow 1998: 4). Another perspective holds that a social movement refers to 'strings of more or less connected events, scattered across time and space . . . (and) consist(s) of groups and organizations, with various levels of formalization, linked in patterns of interaction which run from the fairly centralized to the totally decentralized, from the cooperative to the explicitly hostile' (Diani 2003: 1). What this suggests is that no single event or organization, in and of itself, however pivotal, constitutes a social movement. A social movement includes multiple political actors (with similar or divergent identities and loyalties); a series of events linked to a broader common theme (for instance, environmental justice) that challenge or defend an existing order—political, religious, ideational, etc. (Oriola [2013] 2016). A social movement 'comprises several SMOs in collective interactions: synergistic, antagonistic or mutually reinforcing' (Oriola [2013] 2016: 12).

Zald and Ash (1966: 329) define a social movement as 'a purposive and collective attempt of a number of people to change individuals or societal institutions and structure'. This definition is instructive. Herbert Blumer, one of the pioneers of scholarship on social movements, notes that social movements are

> collective enterprises seeking to establish a new order of life. They have their inception in a condition of unrest, and derive their motive power on one hand from the dissatisfaction with the current form of life, and on the other hand, from wishes and hopes for a new scheme or system of living.
> (Blumer 1969: 99)

Zald and Ash's (1966) and Blumer's (1969) description is particularly apt for engaging with the #BBOG movement. The #BBOG movement developed because of consternation and grievance over governmental degeneracy, which made the kidnapping of the Chibok girls possible, and the inertia that circumscribed efforts to rescue them, a poignant critique of present circumstances of under-privileged citizens and hopes for a more effective system of governance. The tactics and framing of #BBOG reflect these grievances and aspirations for a new kind of society.

#BBOG continues a legacy of involvement of African women in resistance against oppressive structures. Historically, women's struggles in Africa have targeted colonial governments, neocolonial states, transnational corporations, and patriarchal institutions. Women-led social movements have influenced the dynamics of social change in various African states. For instance, women were active in the struggle against colonialism. Women organized against economic exploitation and challenged colonialists, who saw colonized peoples as avenues for profit. In countries like Kenya, Nigeria, and Ghana, women challenged British colonialists. Women in Mozambique and Guinea Bissau, among others, challenged Portuguese colonialists, while French colonialists faced resistance from women in the Republic of Benin, Senegal, Togo, Burkina Faso, and Cote d'Ivoire, among others. This form of colonialism and its indigenized version in South Africa were generalized but also fundamentally gendered (Oriola 2020). Land grab undergirded both forms of despoliation. This reduced the capacity of the colonized to meet basic needs and led to organized resistance. Women organized as exclusively female-only social movements or part of a mixed resistance movement. The Aba women's war and the Kikuyu women in the Mau Mau revolution exemplify women's variegated trajectory in resistance against colonialism.

Women in Aba in Southeast Nigeria began a series of demonstrations on 18 November 1929, which lasted for three months (Van Allen 1975; Ukeje 2004). The source of grievance of the women was a proposed taxation targeting women after a similar tax in 1928 had been successfully imposed on men by British colonialists. Women also had grievances over official corruption, use of unpaid labour, harsh sentences for offences, under-pricing of agricultural produce, and over-pricing of imported commodities (Afigbo 1972). The new tax regime was abandoned as the protests proved popular and well organized (Mba 1982; Adler 1999).

Kikuyu women played a crucial role in the Mau Mau revolution for 'land and freedom'. They gathered and disseminated intelligence; transported supplies (such as weapons, food, and clothing) to the male fighters; and facilitated movement of recruits to the forest. There were also female Mau Mau fighters on the front lines. Although officially regarded as the 'passive wing' of the Mau Mau, they were 'treated as a serious force by the British' (Presley 1988: 504). Women's involvement in the Mau Mau occurred within the context of changing traditional roles of women. More women had begun to receive formal education and employment and had also established small businesses (Gachihi 1986). The British colonial government established a department with the responsibility to disengage women from the Mau Mau. A series of policies targeted at women who supported the Mau Mau was implemented. This included propaganda to curb what the colonial government considered fanaticism that was more virulent than men's (Kanogo 1987; Presley 1988) and villagization, a programme to herd people into villages so as to cut off linkages with fighters or 'Itungati' in the forests (Gachihi 1986).

Women's engagement in social movement activities continued in the early post-independence period, particularly from the late 1960s to 1970s. However, several of the organizations involved were affiliated to the ruling or opposition party and therefore had limited autonomy. State and/or party influence played a major role in selection of leaders for such movements. They depended on the state for funding, and their fortunes were therefore tied to the ruling party. A new wave of women's movements emerged in the 1990s. Contemporary women's movements in Africa were unmoored from dependence on the state, had agendas for women's emancipation (rather than as colonial subjects or ruling-party appendages), and had sources of funding independent of the state and autonomy to elect their leaders. Such movements in Africa emerged due to multiple factors and influences. These included developments in the international arena in relation to women's rights, availability of funding opportunities, greater political space through democratization (Tripp et al. 2009), and opportunities in the post-conflict period in several African countries. Laws and policies regarding land rights, inheritance, divorce, and domestic violence, among others, have been impacted by women's movements in several African countries.

These changes occurred within the context of the expansion of education and greater labour market involvement. The participation of African women in politics has grown tremendously since the 1990s. In several African countries, the level of participation of women in politics and their share in parliamentary and executive portfolios is high by global standards. For example, as of December 2018, Rwanda (61.3%) ranked first, Namibia (46.2%) ranked sixth, Sweden (46.1%) ranked seventh, South Africa (42.7%) ranked tenth, Finland ranked eleventh (42%), and Senegal ranked twelfth (41.8%) in the world in terms of representation of women in the lower house of parliament (Thornton 2019). One key lesson that may be gleaned from the South African example (and, to a lesser extent, from women in the anti-colonial struggle in Mozambique) is that engagement in the gunfight of the political process (literally and figuratively) is fundamental to securing women's rights.

The political process approach is apt to investigate the #BBOG movement. The political process approach captures the interplay of social movement organizations with existing realities—constraints and opportunities—in their domain of operation. The political process approach is concerned with the relationship between social movements and their socio-political context (Meyer 2004). This deals with the interactions between institutional political actors, such as the state and its agents, on one hand, and protest groups on the other (della Porta and Diani 1999: 9). This approach places emphasis on the political opportunity structure or the constellation of actors—antagonists, protagonists, and bystanders—and the political and socio-economic and cultural context of their interactions (Kriesi 2004; Oriola [2013] 2016).

The concept of political opportunity is fundamental to the political process approach. Political opportunity refers to 'consistent—but not necessarily formal, or permanent—dimensions of the political environment that provide incentives for collective action' (Tarrow 1998: 76–77). This refers to the relative openness of the institutionalized political system, the (in)stability of elite alignments inherent in the polity, and the presence or absence of elites (McAdam 1996: 26; Goodwin and Jasper 1999). State capacity and the apparatus of repression are considered a problematic dimension of political opportunity (McAdam 1996: 26; Goodwin and Jasper 1999).

Women's movements in Africa continue to utilize opportunities offered by international developments, technological advancement, and national context. #BBOG is a prime example of what Manuel Castells calls a 'networked social movement' (2015: 3). Networked social movements 'spread by contagion in a world networked by the wireless Internet and marked by fast, viral diffusion of images and ideas' (p. 2). The wireless networks and the social connections that they engender render time and space virtually irrelevant. They have led to the ascendance of the 'network society' (Castells 1996: 469) wherein grievances can be expressed in real time (Castells 2015). The role of the internet in the Arab Spring in North African countries such as Tunisia and Egypt is well documented. The spread of social media platforms such as Facebook, Twitter ('X'), and Youtube, among others, has led to a nodal and rhyzomatic communication network marked by instantaneity, interpenetrativity, and fluidity. This network is a spatial location for transcending—albeit symbolically and temporarily—the powerlessness that accompanies social marginality. The rise of an army of Twitterati and users of other social networks necessitates a reconceptualization of the idea of voice. For instance, everyday individuals with access to the internet and a smart phone, tablet, or laptop, can tweet to a political leader or challenge governments and demand answers.[5]

---

[5] The revelations about the use of social media (see Pileggi 2018) to manipulate the electorate in countries as diverse as the United States, Nigeria, Kenya, and the United Kingdom highlight the extent

In Kenya, social media brought down a bank and created panic among the governing elite (Nyabola 2018). Nyabola (2018: 7) notes that 'Social media is making it impossible to pretend not to notice anger or claims of disaffection.' Nyabola emphasizes the agency of Kenya's Twitterati and the opening of new spaces of political engagement, particularly for those whose voices were drowned out offline. Nonetheless, Nyabola acknowledges the double-edged sword of social media—the possibility of reproduction of unfavourable offline conditions.

There are genuine concerns over slacktivism or hashtag activism, as stated earlier. One of the earliest accounts of the synthesization of the capacity of social media with on-the-ground grassroots organizing is the account of the anti-corporate globalization movement in Spain. Juris (2008) notes the political and cultural changes that networked actors are capable of catalysing when backed with offline social engagement. In other words, without grassroots mobilization, internet-based activism is mainly an avenue to vent.[6]

Several factors have contributed to the rise of #BBOG. These are the patriarchal ideational infrastructure, specifically the normative articulation of gender, the social and cultural capital of the co-conveners of #BBOG, political elite fragmentation, and the movement's positive transformation (among a section of the masses) from a struggle to free kidnapped girls to a symbol for fighting for human rights in Africa.

Gender and Nigeria's patriarchal ideational infrastructure

The normative articulation of gender in a highly patriarchal environment has played a role in the rise of #BBOG. Two major issues are involved. First, the hetero-normative environment, its social interpretation of the vulnerability of teenage girls, and the facticity of being female constitute a salient factor. This is evident when juxtaposed with Boko Haram's attack on the Federal Government College, Buni Yadi, Yobe state on 25 February 2014—nearly two months before the Chibok girls were kidnapped. Boko Haram killed 59 boys in the attack, as noted earlier. The massacre generated comparatively little attention from the Nigerian government and civil society. As Ezekwesili pointed out, only a few women were involved in protesting the killing of the 59 Buni Yadi

---

of the malleability of social networks. The use of social media as political echo chambers and virtual spaces of intolerance (rather than democratic spaces of citizen engagement at the local, national, and international levels) also suggest that this is a powerful tool without a user-specific manual.

[6] I return to use of social media later in this chapter.

boys. The 'society simply moved on ... With the Chibok girls, I wasn't going to move on as we did in the past' (Ezekwesili 2015). The silence on the Buni Yadi case might have been a result of fatalistic acceptance that the boys could not be brought back and therefore demonstrated an insouciant attitude to human life.[7]

However, the sheer scale of the Chibok incident as an act in and of itself—kidnapping rather than outright slaughter—and the gender of the victims played a role in the advocacy that followed. This is demonstrated in the discourse around the 'pollution of the girls', consequences of the kidnapping for female education in Northern Nigeria, and marginalization of women in general (Interviewees 06, 08, 12, and 13).[8] Therefore, the gendered performativity of the #BBOG movement was an attempt to harness the conscience collective. Consequently, it was constituted by, and reflective of, the patriarchal ideational infrastructure of the society: the construction of females as the 'weaker' gender in need of protection. This is evidenced in the focus of #BBOG framing (analysed in Chapter 4) on the missing girls as 'daughters' and 'sisters' rather than irreducible bearers of inalienable human and citizenship rights. Therefore, large banners displaying slogans such as: 'Would you be silent if your daughter was missing?'; 'Protect the future of Nigeria' speak to two intertwined issues: on one hand, a relational dynamic between the missing girls and those being pressurized to find them; and, on the other hand, the gendered ideation of women as the bearers of the society's future, whose fecundity and chastity must be conserved (for future use) and normatively channelled.

The 6 May 2015 editorial in the *Leadership* newspaper articulates society's concerns about the well-being of the girls:

> The insurgents may have decided to literally sow seeds of discord that will ultimately take on a life of their own and haunt the nation sometime in the not too distant future. To the scum, polluting the blood of these women and siring in the process their kind who will inexorably become thorns in the flesh of future generations could be their way of having a laugh at the expense of decent Nigerians. ... Taking them away from their homes, familiar environment and dear ones was harrowing enough. Now they are unwilling cocoons of the seeds of those who defiled them.
>
> (Leadership Editors 2015)

---

[7] The Buni Yadi massacre was not acknowledged by the federal government of Nigeria until civil society groups led by #BBOG marked its first anniversary in February 2015.

[8] Female members of #BBOG; personal interviews, Abuja, 2015.

The epicentre of the concerns is the potential for serving as 'cocoons' for Boko Haram and the likelihood of raising progeny who might become terrorists. This embodies the problematique of canvassing for the rescue of the missing girls on the facticity of their being *females* (therefore, potentially capable of reproduction) rather than as simply natural *persons*. Given the 'logic of masculinist protection' (Young 2003: 1) and the traditional role of men as supposed defenders of society, such sloganeering is intended to mobilize women (as fellow sanctuaries of society) and provide a rationale for spurring into action the lethargic, male-dominated government.

The second dimension concerns the symbolic and emotive value of the group of well-placed elite women organized as *mothers* fighting for the return of the kidnapped high-school students. The core group of #BBOG women utilized their identity as mothers to mobilize other women, the media, and other bystanders. For instance, Hadiza Bala Usman noted why she was involved in the #BBOG movement:

> As a mother, I have experienced the trauma of not knowing where my child is for few minutes; does it then surprise many why I would be moved to act on behalf of mothers who are yet to see their daughters for over 189 days?
> (cited in Isine 2014a)[9]

The ethno-religious diversity of the core group of #BBOG co-conveners also broadened the appeal of the organization. This was crucial in a politically toxic society, where religion and ethnicity were lenses through which social action was distilled. The person of Obiageli Ezekwesili, a Christian Igbo Southerner, leading a movement to rescue girls kidnapped in the Muslim-dominated North represented powerful symbolism. Having Ezekwesili as leader enhanced the appeal of #BBOG, particularly in Southern Nigeria, where the media was concentrated. This speaks to the need for movement activists in multi-ethnic countries of the Global South to be sensitive to local political sentiments and symbolic representation when choosing leaders. While gender was important, ethnic and religious diversity was also critical. #BBOG leaders overwhelmingly emphasized the salience of their status as mothers, but social class, evident in the social and cultural capital of the co-conveners, was also fundamental to the rise of #BBOG. This is analysed below.

---

[9] While Ms Usman also mentioned the relevance of being a 'human being', 'Nigerian', and 'African' in the agitations for the girls' rescue, she stressed the salience of being a mother. The significance of the motherist frame is further explicated in chapter 3.

Social and cultural capital of co-conveners

Pierre Bourdieu's (1986) work on the forms of capital analyses the impossibility of accounting for the 'structure and functioning of the social world unless one reintroduces capital in all its forms and not solely in the one form recognized by economic theory'. Bourdieu's widely celebrated work explicates the importance of cultural capital and social capital. Social movement activism has long involved much more than economic capital, a fact that has been widely recognized in social movement scholarship. This is reflected, for instance, in the attention paid to networks and interpersonal ties in social movement recruitment and mobilization.

#BBOG has benefited from the social and cultural capital of its co-conveners. This core group of women includes Obiageli Ezekwesili, Hadiza Bala-Usman, Maryam Uwais, Saudatu Madhi, Ireti Kingibe, and Aisha Oyebode, among others. A quick overview of the pedigree of three of these women provides a glimpse of the extraordinariness of the group.

Obiageli Ezekwesili is the most widely recognized among the co-conveners. She was educated at the University of Lagos and the Kennedy School of Government, Harvard University. She served in the administration of President Olusegun Obasanjo, first as the head of the budget monitoring and price intelligence unit. She gained a reputation as a strict and incorruptible public official, embodied in her *nom de guerre* 'Madam Due Process'. She also served as minister of solid minerals and minister of education in the same administration. She served as World Bank vice-president, Africa after leaving government. Ezekwesili's speech in Port Harcourt led to the coinage of the popular hashtag, and her followership on Twitter ('X') provided the initial thrust of individuals who began the #BBOG movement.[10] Her connections within and outside the Nigerian government, as well as around the world, contributed to the appeal of the movement.

Hadiza Bala-Usman has degrees from Ahmadu Bello University, Zaria—widely recognized as a major training ground for a significant number of Northern Nigerian elite—and the University of Leeds. Her father, Yusufu Bala Usman, was a respected post-colonial Marxist historian and progeny of the daughter of a former Emir of Kano, the second most important traditional royal position in Northern Nigeria. Ms Bala-Usman has brought the uncommon privilege of a highly revered family name to the movement. She served as

---

[10] Ibrahim Abdullahi, who first tweeted using the hashtag, had about 1,765 twitter followers as of 11 March 2016.

chief of staff to the governor of Kaduna state, the first woman to serve in that capacity following Nigeria's return to democracy in 1999 and also served as chair of the Nigerian Ports Authority.

The third person in the triumvirate, Maryam Uwais, has LLB and LLM degrees from Ahmadu Bello University, Zaria. She is principal partner at Wali Uwais & Co. Her spouse, Mohammadu Uwais, is a former chief justice of Nigeria. Ms Uwais served as special adviser for social protection plan to Nigeria's president, Muhammadu Buhari.

The pedigree of the co-conveners—a combination of academic prowess, political connections, experiences in various public bureaucracies, the private sector, and non-governmental organization (NGO) involvement—gave #BBOG considerable latitude and innervated the movement. The background and integrity of the conveners are didactic for movement actors. This is important, given the cynicism of Nigerians about the integrity of their leaders. Support from male elites such as Dino Melaye (who had lost his seat in the Senate at time of writing) and Jimoh Ibrahim (a wealthy businessman) was also an important component of the struggle at the initial stage. The conveners have been able to transform their impressive profiles into strong support from international players such as lawmakers from the United States, and the European Union parliament, among others.

Besides the international connections and personal accomplishments, the #BBOG elites worked in a context that qualified as an 'old society' and a 'new state' (Geertz 1963). This facilitated camaraderie, elite circulation, and navigation of bureaucracies through informal ties, familial connections, and friendships. As Charrad (2001: 17) notes in her comparative analysis of the state and women's rights in Tunisia, Morocco, and Algeria, the 'important similarity among many old societies and new states is that loyalties and foci of solidarity rested with the collectivities themselves rather than with nationwide institutions' (Charrad 2001: 17). The co-conveners and elite supporters of #BBOG had tremendous kinship networks, which enhanced the status of the movement. For example, Ireti Kingibe comes from an ethnically diverse background. Her father is Muslim and of mixed Yoruba and Fulani origins. Her mother is a Christian with roots in the Niger Delta region in Southern Nigeria. Ireti Kingibe's background connects her to the axis of power in Nigeria. She speaks all three of Nigeria's major languages. Her older sister, Ajoke Mohammed, is the widow of Nigeria's former Head of State General Murtala Mohammed. Her spousal connection is also strong. Her ex-husband, Babagana Kingibe, is a three-times federal minister and former vice-presidential candidate. Ireti Kingibe contested a Senate seat in Abuja. The robust ties of the

#BBOG elite women to major players in the system was helpful to the rise of the movement.[11]

The nature of the Nigerian state and political opportunity

The ascendance of the #BBOG movement was also catalysed by factors intrinsic to the context of the movement's operations—the Nigerian context. Several factors within the polity have played a role in the ascendance of #BBOG. First, the Nigerian political terrain is concurrently closed and open to movement actors. This is common in newly democratized states in Africa. Movement actors are generally tolerated, although there is always the risk of co-optation or elimination, as evidenced in the schism within the Ogoni movement and the hanging of nine Ogoni activists by the regime of General Sani Abacha (Oriola [2013] 2016). The Nigerian state has been neither fully authoritarian nor totally democratic since 29 May 1999, when democracy was restored after years of military rule, but perception of protest as a regime threat is prevalent. Nonetheless, space does exist for movement actors to organize, albeit with some risks. Groups such as the Nigerian Economic Summit Group (NESG), Enough is Enough (EiE), BudgIT, and Occupy Nigeria (c. 1993, 2009, 2011, and 2012, respectively) were formed as part of movements for a range of issues focused on economic development and transparency in government (Williams-Elegbe 2015). The non-violent Niger Delta movement, which reached a climax in 1995 and transmuted into an armed insurgency in the early 2000s, is another example. The Nigerian terrain has a rich history of social movement activities, in part because of opposition to military rule, environmental degradation, minority rights, and a perpetually depressed economy.

Second, the Nigerian state functions as a 'private indirect government' (Mbembé 2001: 66) consistent with postcolonial spaces. Widespread ineptitude is the centrepiece of such a social milieu. While this poses several challenges, it also provides political opportunity for movement actors. This assertion is fundamental to understanding the realities surrounding the #BBOG movement. For instance, toxic politics influenced attitudes to the rescue of the kidnapped girls and drew widespread attention towards #BBOG during the first few weeks of protest. This is embodied in the fact that, on 16 April 2014,

---

[11] I argue, in Chapter 4, that these social networks, connections, and political affiliations, while fundamental to the ascendance of the movement, enmeshed #BBOG in partisan politics.

Director of Defense Information Major General Chris Olukolade released a statement indicating that all but eight of the Chibok girls kidnapped two days earlier had been rescued by the military. Olukolade retracted his statement moments later as it turned out the information he was provided by field commanders was inaccurate vis-à-vis the identities of persons the military had found (Interviewee 04).[12] In addition, President Goodluck Jonathan publicly acknowledged the kidnapping incident three weeks after it happened. The thinking in government circles was that the government of Borno state, where the incident occurred, was merely playing politics with the issue in order to embarrass the federal government (Ezekwesili 2015). This meant that from the onset, the #BBOG movement had a strategic advantage over the framing of the incident. The #BBOG movement was quick to point out that it was merely asking the state to perform its constitutional responsibilities. The government's initial response to the daily protests by #BBOG handed another major advantage to the protesters. Olajumoke Akinjide, the minister of state for the Federal Capital Territory, was deployed to speak with the #BBOG protesters as they marched to the presidential villa on 22 May 2014. She read a prepared statement arguing that 'protests should be directed at the terrorists who have abducted our innocent daughters ... We must be careful not to politicize the campaign against terrorism. When a bomb goes off in Kabul, Afghanistan, the people of Afghanistan do not blame the government, they blame the terrorists.'

The attempt to deflect responsibility further damaged the government's credibility. #BBOG's response was that it was 'not acceptable because, we never voted for any party called Boko Haram, we did not give authority to anybody called Shekau so why should we go to him and demand for our girls?' (Interviewee 30). Nonetheless, the government's response helped to fine-tune pre-existing debates regarding the messaging of the movement. There had been internal debates in #BBOG over how to articulate the group's demand, the locus of responsibility, and therefore what entity to focus on. There were deliberations on two major slogans: 'Release our girls' and 'Bring back our girls'. The debate was on the question of responsibility:

when we say Bring Back Our Girls, we are simply placing that responsibility on constituted authority you say that you have the power, the mandate, and the authority to ensure that these girls are protected not to be abducted in the first place. And then having been abducted, we still have that confidence

---

[12] Major General Chris Olukolade, Director of Defence Information; personal interview, July 2015.

in you to ensure that you put the apparatus together to make sure that those girls are rescued.

(Interviewee 30)

The hashtag 'ReleaseOurGirls' appeared to place responsibility on Boko Haram and was dropped.[13]

The ineptitude of the Jonathan administration had become widely known, thus rendering the administration unpopular among large sections of Nigerians. Some of President Jonathan's major allies, such as former President Olusegun Obasanjo, who was instrumental in Jonathan's ascendance to the presidency, had begun to publicly complain about the government's poor performance. The schism among the elite provided political opportunity for #BBOG. The political situation helped to generate support from elite across the political divide. Members of the ruling party, including senators and state governors, publicly supported the objectives of #BBOG. Opposition party apparatchiks were quick to lend a voice to the movement's objective.[14] This meant that a notable elite such as Nobel laureate, Wole Soyinka, who was often at loggerheads with the likes of Obasanjo, found themselves supporting the #BBOG cause. #BBOG actively sought and used support from political elites who belonged to different parties to promote the cause. The political catholicity of #BBOG won allies among governing and non-governing elites at the start of movement activities in 2014. Grassroot movements in African states may find support from unusual sources, given the ubiquity and centrality of the state to distribution of resources in particular and social life in general.

The #BBOG movement's positive transformation

The #BBOG movement quickly evolved from a struggle strictly established to demand the rescue of the Chibok girls to a symbol for human rights advocacy. For example, a variety of workers often came to the sit-out to seek the group's help on the non-payment of their salaries (Focus group discussion

---

[13] This was the slogan that was used by a government-sponsored group of women and men who attacked #BBOG members on 28 May 2014 at the Unity Fountain, Abuja: Interviewee 10, #BBOG strategic team member; personal interview, Abuja, August 2015.

[14] The concluding section discusses the consequences of such relatively broad support for #BBOG among opposition party politicians and some members of the ruling party.

(FGD 1).[15] Some police officers deployed to curtail the protest of the movement would often whisper to #BBOG members that they supported what they were doing and that 'your activities have made them to consider increasing our salary' (Interviewee 30). The membership of the group reflects its broad appeal as it transcends ethnic and religious affiliation. This is particularly significant given the ethno-religious dynamics of Nigeria. The location of the #BBOG sit-out also became symbolic ground for social mobilization. Several groups with varying grievances began to use the Unity Fountain as a centre of collective action (Interviewee 09).[16]

This is not to suggest that support for the movement was universal. However, many sympathizers of the #BBOG movement began to view the group as a symbol of the trans-generational quest for social justice. #BBOG members also began to view the movement as transcending the struggle for the rescue of the Chibok girls. For instance, its signature slogan evolved to include the statement: 'The fight for the Chibok girls is the fight for the soul of Nigeria and the world' (Interviewee 12).[17] The addition of the last three words in the slogan was at the suggestion of a senior European Union (EU) official, who visited #BBOG and suggested that their cause was beyond social justice in any particular country. The EU official's visit, as well as those of government officials and NGO representatives from the United States and several African and European countries, indicated the growing interest in the cause of the movement and its acceptance as a critical legitimate actor in human rights advocacy in Africa.

The slogan drew on prevailing global concerns over sexual and gender-based violence (SGBV) against women and girls. Boko Haram had assured the world that the girls would be forced into marriage and sexual servitude. The slogan therefore tapped into issues relating to human trafficking, sexual exploitation, denial of education to the girl-child, blocked socio-economic opportunity, and femicide. The African Union, Amnesty International, and the United Nations Children's Fund (UNICEF), among several other organizations, supported the campaign. World leaders and celebrities held #BBOG placards to show their support. Protests were held in New York, London, Accra, and Johannesburg, among other places. The underlying tenet of the movement was therefore construed as a global rather than a mere Nigerian or African problem.

---

[15] Two female #BBOG members, July 2015, Abuja.
[16] Male member of #BBOG in charge of publicity; personal interview, July 2015, Abuja.
[17] Female member of the #BBOG strategic team; personal interview, August 2015, Abuja.

A 'single-issue' movement?

#BBOG strongly considers itself a 'single-issue' movement (Ezekwesili 2015). An internal document, 'The Strategic Angle to #BringBackOurGirls', states that the objective of #BBOG is to 'ensure the over 200 abducted Chibok schoolgirls are brought back safe, sound, and within the shortest possible time'.[18] A statement on #BBOG movement's website reiterates the demand: 'That the 219 Chibok schoolgirls abducted on April 14, 2014 be rescued by the government. Improve government's accountability to Nigerians on security issues, particularly in the northeast.'[19] The web page provides five paths to meeting its objective:[20]

1. Improved communications on Nigerian security happenings with daily briefings on the rescue of the abducted girls.
2. Create communication channels that help inform the public on safety measures being taken to protect Nigerian citizens.
3. Provision of rehabilitation services, such as counselling and healthcare, as well as witness protection, to all abducted girls who have escaped or been rescued.
4. Take measures to ensure the protection of children of school age to curb future abductions and sexual violence.
5. Passage of the Violence Against Persons Prohibition Bill (VAPP Bill) that protects girls to ensure persecution of those responsible for sexual violence once captured.

#BBOG believes that its associated demands on the Nigerian government are connected to its single objective—the rescue of the Chibok girls.

Strategizing on how to 'rescue' the Chibok girls

#BBOG commenced discussions during the first 100 days of the abduction on options for the rescue of the Chibok girls. The discussions began within the strategic team and later included members of the sit-out (see the #BBOG organizational chart below). #BBOG arrived at three major options (Interviewee 30).

---

[18] #BBOG Internal Document # 3. Provided to the author by #BBOG.
[19] See 'Our demand', http://www.bringbackourgirls.ng Accessed 21 December 2017.
[20] Ibid.

First, #BBOG considered that a kinetic approach or a series of military operations was the most viable option during the first 100 days. There was cautious confidence within the group that the military could get the job done, given the exploits of the Nigerian army in peacekeeping operations in Liberia, Sierra Leone, and other countries. Second, #BBOG believed that a non-kinetic approach would be more appropriate if military operations might endanger the lives of the girls. #BBOG believed that this non-military option would entail a combination of ransom payment to, and prisoner exchange with, Boko Haram. The third option, articulated within #BBOG, entailed a composite of the first two options—a mix of both military and non-military approaches. This would imply weakening Boko Haram militarily and therefore compelling them to engage in negotiations with the government.

#BBOG's thinktank agreed to be 'absolutely careful' not to suggest any of the approaches to the government and to refrain from making such recommendations in their engagement with the media. The latter was not always successful. However, #BBOG members claim that they recognized their limitations on the rescue of the girls. They were cognizant that they were not experts on the matter and knew that there could be information available to the government to which #BBOG was not privy.

#BBOG began a process of evolution in its assessment of appropriate strategies for rescuing the Chibok girls as the matter became prolonged. An internationally orientated discursive strategy (see Chapter 3) was a major part of the shift in orientation of #BBOG. #BBOG was hopeful that if all the options failed, or the Nigerian government was unwilling or unable to rescue the girls, the international community could be persuaded to step in to provide the required assistance to secure the girls. #BBOG also envisaged a situation in which the government would be implored to grant foreign state actors access to its territory to rescue the girls. This approach was not necessarily viewed as an independent strategy, given that state sovereignty meant that the Nigerian government would have to endorse such plans (Interviewee 30).

#BBOG believed that the United States, the United Kingdom, and other international partners had the technical expertise and experience to handle the rescue. For instance, the United States had experience dealing with al-Shabaab on the African continent. There was also a distinctive belief within the top hierarchy of #BBOG that the 'Nigerian government seems to respond to the language of international embarrassment' (Interviewee 30). Therefore, #BBOG's discursive framing began to emphasize state failure (see Chapter 3). #BBOG utilized several local media organizations in Nigeria but realized that the advocacy would gain greater traction in international media. This was also partly shaped by the fact that several local media organizations owned by or reliant on the government chose not to 'respond to anything that had to do with the rescue of the Chibok girls' (Interviewee 30). These factors contributed to the internationalization of #BBOG's framing.[21]

Data from this research indicates that four major factors were behind #BBOG's reorientation on how the Chibok girls could be rescued. First, Boko Haram began to demonstrate willingness to murder women and children. For instance, Boko Haram killed a woman who was in labour when they invaded Baga, a town in Borno state, in January 2015. An eyewitness noted that 'Half of the baby boy [was] out' when the woman was killed by Boko Haram (The Telegraph 2015). This was one of a number of reports about gruesome killings by Boko Haram. #BBOG came to terms with the reality that Boko Haram could, indeed, kill the Chibok girls.

Second, #BBOG members were concerned that time was running out. They were worried about the possibility of some Chibok girls beginning to bond with their captors and pledge allegiance to Boko Haram. That could translate to joining Boko Haram's fighting forces. Indeed, reports began to emerge in June 2015 that some Chibok girls were observed killing people on behalf of Boko Haram. A BBC report quoted a 17-year-old girl who had been a Boko Haram captive for 6 months. The girl argued that 'the girls had been "brainwashed" and that she had witnessed some of them kill several men in her village. "They were Christian men. They [the Boko Haram fighters] forced the Christians to lie down. Then the girls cut their throats"' (Mazumdar 2015). Although the girl's claim could not be corroborated, the BBC cited Amnesty International's research, which indicated that some of the girls had been 'trained to fight' (Mazumdar 2015). Another former Boko Haram abductee, a 60-year-old woman, also claimed that 'she had seen some of the Chibok schoolgirls commit murder' (Mazumdar 2015).

Third, a change in #BBOG's notion of mechanisms for the rescue of the Chibok girls was influenced by a video released by Boko Haram in which 13–17 young girls were shown lying dead in the Bush. Boko Haram claimed that the girls were Chibok girls who had died in the course of aerial bombardment by the Nigerian military. This was a clear message to the government that attacking Boko Haram had led to loss of lives of the girls (Interviewee 30).

Fourth, #BBOG realized that military operations in the Northeast did not lead to the rescue of a single Chibok girl. It was also evident to #BBOG that the

---

[21] This was a qualified transnationalization, as articulated in Chapter 3. #BBOG refused to accept funding from or institutional affiliation with transnational NGOs that offered support.

December 2015 claim by President Buhari, who had campaigned vigorously on rescuing the Chibok girls that Boko Haram had been 'technically defeated' (BBC 2015) was a ruse. No Chibok girl returned from captivity until after two years. Amina Nkeki, the first Chibok girl to regain freedom, fled with her Boko Haram 'husband', who decided to leave with Nkeki and their son because he had fallen out of favour with the organization and worried that he might be killed by his comrades.

Consequently, a #BBOG strategic team member argued, 'we tilted unconsciously to the second and third options' (Interviewee 30). #BBOG began to favour negotiations and attempted to avoid openly calling for negotiations with Boko Haram for the release of the girls. However, #BBOG gradually embraced negotiations following the release of two batches of Chibok girls (21 girls in October 2016 and 82 girls in May 2017).

Core values of #BBOG

Social movements devise core values to signpost their identity, intentions, and common creed (Haenfler 2004). Core values serve as insignia of the aspirations of a movement, a genre of poetry in the prosaic grind of activism. They embody the ideals of a movement couched in a narrative to serve as compass for members. Core values are fundamental to membership recruitment, retention, and public support (Stern et al. 1999). Crafting core values presents an opportunity for movement activists to co-produce a guiding set of principles, philosophy, and world view to shape their engagement in socially meaningful actions.

The #BBOG leadership divided members into various task teams to work on various themes in the early days of the movement. The product is a co-constituted emblem of the movement. The #BBOG movement's core values are represented by the backronym 'HUMANITEEDS'.[22] This term stands for

- H—Hope
- U—Unity
- M—Motivation
- A—Affability
- N—Nationalism
- I–Integrity

[22] See 'The Bring Back Our Girls?', http://www.bringbackourgirls.ng/?page_id=1604 Accessed 21 December 2017.

- T—Transparency
- E—Empathy
- E—Equity
- D—Discipline
- S—Sacrifice.

Visual symbols and symbolism of the #BBOG movement

Colours are part of broader political performances, one in a collection of paraphernalia within an economy of political contestation. Colours serve to symbolize visually a movement's cause and are significant to the 'emotional life' of social movements (Chesters and Welsh 2004; Sawer 2007: 39). The performativity inherent in movement activities means that specific colours are selected for easy identification of the movement. Therefore, the decision on specific colours of a movement is a major political exercise—an engagement in symbolism. A movement's colours must be socially meaningful, evocative, and iterative to a broad range of entities and actors within a sphere of contentious politics. This includes movement activists, the cause of the movement (in and of itself), its primary constituency, potential allies, bystanders, and opponents. This necessarily means that colours have political denotative and connotative meanings. These meanings are also culturally, historically, and spatially delimited (Fine et al. 1998). Colours are culturally powerful and socially significant (Luckiesh 1938). While political parties have always adopted specific colours (Fine et al. 1998; Sawer 2007), social movements also find a sense of shared identity, communicative praxis, and self-expression in their colours.

For instance, the use of the colour orange in the Ukrainian Orange Revolution (2004–2005); red by the socialist movement as far back as the nineteenth century; black by anarchists in the 1880s; a potpourri of colours in the rainbow flag of the gay rights movement; and green, white, and purple of the women's movement in the late twentieth century (Sawer 2007) is socially meaningful. To wear specific colours is to literally, figuratively, and performatively identify with a particular cause, ideology, beliefs, and principles. This is what Sawer (2007: 39) calls 'wearing your politics on your sleeve'.

The #BBOG movement's colours are red and white. For #BBOG, red denotes two things—'danger' and 'passion'. Danger within #BBOG's universe of meanings represents 'that in which our missing Chibok schoolgirls are and have been', while passion epitomizes the 'love and conviction that drives the call for their rescue and safe return.'[23] The colour red has historically emerged as a symbol of radicalism (Sawer 2007)—although not acknowledged by #BBOG. The colour white within #BBOG's ideational construct signifies 'Innocence: Our girls are innocent and were only seeking knowledge through education, in spite of the odds, in order to better their lots and that of their families and community.'[24]

Chants/slogans of the #BBOG movement

Social movements often create anthems, slogans, chants, and songs as a mark of solidarity, identity, emotion, work, and motivation. The words therein may draw on existing and easily identifiable chants and slogans but may also be unique to the movement. The words and messages in chants and songs are carefully selected or composed. Songs, chants, and slogans are part of the aesthetics of a social movement and serve as a reminder of its creed or call to action. These performances may also involve speech and dance that form part of 'oppositional expression' (Downing 2001: 105). They constitute part of the 'cultural politics' of social movements and have been in use as long as groups have been formed to challenge authority (Eyerman 2002: 443). Examples of such radical expressions in public spaces abound in social movement studies. They include speech acts by Moroccan women street traders, the Mothers of the Plaza de Mayo in Buenos Aires, African American song and dance during and after slavery, and use of songs in the German labour movement.[25] These forms of expression help with group solidarity, communalism, belonging, and encouragement in periods of tribulations (Eyerman 2002). They help a movement 'objectify itself and its history, making itself visible to others, as well as creating and establishing a sense of continuity' (Eyerman 2002: 447).

#BBOG has modified a popular chant in Nigeria that signposts the cause, expresses the demand of the movement, and motivates members through its emotional appeal. The chant serves as a reminder of the worthiness of the objective of the movement and the need to remain steadfast. Members raise their right hand to shoulder level and clench their fist. The chant begins with a popular Nigerian song:

---

[23] Ibid.
[24] Ibid.
[25] See Downing (2001) for a fascinating analysis of these case studies.

Soli, soli soli
Solidarity for ever
Solidarity for ever
Solidarity for ever
We shall always fight for our girls
All we are saying
Bring back our girls
Now and alive!
All we are saying
Bring back our girls
Now and alive!

The song is followed by a series of one-liners led by whoever is coordinating the daily protest. The coordinator's lines in the chant are formulated in the form of questions to which members respond with pre-composed answers. The #BBOG chant is stated below:

CALL: What are we demanding?
RESPONSE: Bring Back Our Girls now and alive
CALL: What are we asking?
RESPONSE: The truth, nothing but the truth!
CALL: What do we want?
RESPONSE: Our girls back now and alive!
CALL: When shall we stop?
RESPONSE: Not until our girls are back and alive!
CALL: When shall we stop?
RESPONSE: Not without our daughters!
CALL: Where are we from?
RESPONSE: Chibok
CALL: Where are we from?
RESPONSE: Nigeria
CALL: What is our core value?
RESPONSE: HUMANITEEDS
CALL: What are we fighting for?
ALL: The soul of Nigeria! The fight for the Chibok girls is the fight for the soul of Nigeria and the world!

The chant continues to evolve and demonstrates the dynamism of movement activities. New lines were added to the chant to reflect the political context and mood of the movement following the delay of the Buhari administration to secure the release of the girls. The new lines are:

CALL: Mr President!
RESPONSE: No more excuses!
CALL: Mr President!
RESPONSE: No more delay!
CALL: Mr President!
RESPONSE: Decide now!
CALL: Mr President!
RESPONSE: Act now: we want more results!
CALL: Three years too long!
RESPONSE: No more excuses!
CALL: Three years too long!
RESPONSE: No more excuses!
CALL: Three years too long!
RESPONSE: No more excuses!

Organizational structure of #BBOG

The organizational structure of the #BBOG movement is made up of five major parts (see Fig. 2.1). These are (a) the #BBOG leader, (b) the strategic team (ST), (c) the strategic communication team (SCT), (d) ad hoc committees, and (e) general membership or 'sit-out'.

The #BBOG leader

Dr Obiageli Ezekwesili is the indisputable leader of the #BBOG movement. Such has been her influence in the movement that some leading members consider her the 'spirit' of #BBOG. Her name, recognition, reputation, and influence were critical to the establishment and spread of the movement. Ezekwesili was one of the founding members of Transparency International, Nigeria and served in various capacities in government as noted earlier. Nasir El-Rufai, a former federal cabinet colleague and governor of Kaduna state, describes Ezekwesili in his autobiography:

> Oby is one of the most honest people I know ... Oby does not play games, what you see is what you get. Oby is an amazingly talented woman. She is hardworking and focused on problem solving. She is one of those rare

Fig. 2.1 The #BBOG organizational structure
Source: author.

persons who combine skills in numeracy, literacy and oratory. She is also very forthright and courageous. Oby's only clear weakness is inadequate 'people skills'—she can be impatient and brusque with people she considers of low standards, either ethically or professionally.

(El-Rufai 2013: 184–185)

El-Rufai notes that President Obasanjo was fearful of Oby's tongue and direct approach to issues. Ezekwesili went to President Obasanjo during his quest for an unconstitutional third term in office and told him: 'Why have you allowed the devil to take you over? This third term attempt will fail!' (El-Rufai 2013: 185). Movements reflect their leaders (Nepstad and Bob 2006; Bob 2007). These personality traits would play out in the movement's approach, as articulated later in this chapter.

The strategic team

This is the highest deliberative organ of the #BBOG movement. It is the think tank of the movement and the final arbiter. It comprises the co-conveners and a number of individuals selected from the general membership. The co-conveners are largely influential women whose efforts—online and offline—led to the rise of #BBOG. They vary in terms of their life's work prior to the movement—NGO sector, private sector, and governmental bureaucracies. They include Obiageli Ezekwesili, Hadiza Bala-Usman, Maryam Uwais, Saudatu Madi, Hosea Tsambido, Dauda Iliya, Aisha Yesufu, Jubril Ibrahim, Ireti Kingibe, Bashiru Ibrahim, Florence Ozor, Bukky Sonibare, Tunji Baruwa, Sesugh Akume, Abubakar Abdullahi, Rotimi Oluwale, Fati AbbaKaka, Emman Shehu, Maureen Kabrik, Jeff Okoroafor, and Manasseh Allen, among others.[26]

The strategic communication team

As shown in Fig. 2.1, the SCT immediately follows the ST in the #BBOG organizational structure. The SCT was formed due to the need to interface with traditional media organizations. The interest of traditional media was intense when the BBOG hashtag went viral. The level of media attention was so high that members of #BBOG—literally anyone who showed up for the daily sit-out, given that there was no formal procedure for membership—were routinely approached by media organizations for comments. Some members made such outlandish and inaccurate comments that leaders of the movement began to worry that 'they could get us killed' (Interviewee 30). Therefore, the leaders formed a 'Strategic Communication Team' with responsibility (among other things) for media engagement. The SCT took over this role from the ST, which had performed an identical role prior to and after the first protest on 30 April 2014.[27]

Ad hoc committees

#BBOG often relies on members drawn from the sit-out as well as the ST and SCT to execute specific assignments. These include research, garnering information, and preparation of policy documents, among others. The ad hoc committees constitute a vital yet minor organ of the #BBOG movement as they are occasional and orientated towards relatively narrow tasks. Nonetheless, their fluidity and temporality make them avenues for utilizing the divergent pool of talents in #BBOG.

---

[26] Membership of the ST has been relatively non-static over the past four years. New ST members have been added while some (such as Ireti Kingibe and Saudatu Madi) have since become inactive in the movement.

[27] The following were members of the SCT as of 30 May 2017: Sesugh Akube (Head), Abubakar Abdullahi, Tunji Baruwa, Chinwe Madubuike, Jeff Okoroafor, Nifemi Onifade, Rotimi Olawale, Emman Shehu, and Edith Yassin.

The general assembly of members at the 'sit-out'

The sit-out refers to the #BBOG re-coinage of the term 'sit-in' (discussed below) and represents the general membership of the #BBOG movement. The sit-out comprises an amalgam of local activists from different parts of Nigeria, parents, families, and community members of the kidnapped girls; and other concerned persons and groups. Membership of the sit-out (and, by implication, #BBOG) is open-ended. A #BBOG publicity document articulates eligibility for joining the movement. It states that the movement is 'open, democratic and free for all Nigerians and people who are concerned for the safe return of our girls and the peaceful future of our country. We welcome people from all ethnic groups, tribes, religions, geographic origins and political persuasions.'[28] This recognizes the transnational nature of the cause of the movement. New 'members' are, therefore, welcomed daily at the sit-out.

Overall, there is synergy among all the organs of #BBOG. For example, issues discussed at the sit-out are often taken to the ST for final resolution. Conversely, several decisions taken by the ST are put to vote at the sit-out. Ad hoc committees are often formed at the sit-out and draw from the expertise of members. The committees submit their report to the ST and provide feedback to the general membership at the sit-out. Nevertheless, there have been internal debates and conflicts regarding the organizational structure of #BBOG, as demonstrated later in this chapter.

Snapshot of #BBOG members' profiles

Figs 2.2–2.6 present the demographic profile of a sample of #BBOG activists from a survey conducted by the researcher in June/July 2015. The activists represent a broad spectrum of Nigerian society: 8% are Igbo, 14% are Yoruba, and 24% are Hausa-Fulani while 18% are Kibaku.[29] The movement also comprises several other minority ethnic groups, as shown in Fig. 2.2. Fig. 2.3 shows that most of the members surveyed (34%) are aged 30–39 years, while persons aged 23–29 (16%), 40–49 (13%) and 50–60 years (9%) are also represented in the movement. Fig. 2.4 indicates the religious affiliation of the surveyed members. Members are largely affiliated with Christianity (60%) and Islam (38%). Most #BBOG members are highly educated. Of those surveyed, 55% had a

---

[28] See 'Who are #BringBackOurGirls?', document made available to the author by #BBOG. The problematic that this catholicity poses is interrogated below.

[29] The people of Chibok, where the 14 April 2014 kidnapping occurred, are largely Kibaku people. This partly explains the relative overrepresentation of the Kibaku people in the ranks of #BBOG.

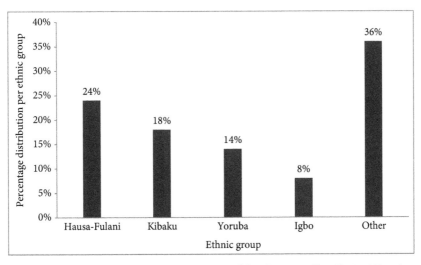

Fig. 2.2 #Bringbackourgirls members, sample's ethnic profile, Abuja, Nigeria. What is your ethnic group?/N = 50

Note: The category 'other' includes the following ethnic groups: Bajju, Berom, Ebika, Edo, Etsako, Ibibio, Idoma, Igala, Ikwerre, Ishan, Oko, Sayawa, Suku, and Tiv.
Source: author.

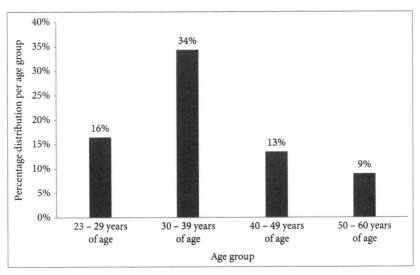

Fig. 2.3 #Bringbackourgirls members, sample's age profile, Abuja, Nigeria. How old are you?/N = 50

Note: The other participants (28%) did not indicate their ages.
Source: author.

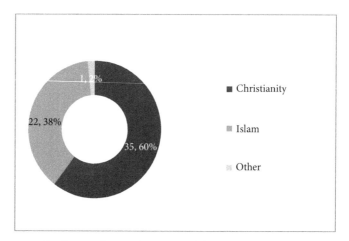

Fig. 2.4 #Bringbackourgirls members, sample's religion, Abuja, Nigeria. What is your religion?/N = 58

Note: The category 'other' reflects a single case and refers to traditional African religion.
Source: author.

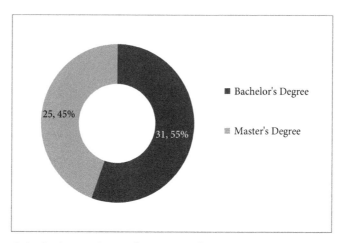

Fig. 2.5 #Bringbackourgirls members, sample's educational profile, Abuja, Nigeria. What is your highest education qualification at this moment?/N = 56
Source: author.

bachelor's degree while 45% had master's degrees (see Fig. 2.5).[30] The marital status of the #BBOG members who were surveyed is presented in Fig. 2.6. Fifty-four per cent of members are married and 42% are single, while 4% are separated or divorced.

---

[30] It is probable that members with lower levels of education deselected themselves from the survey by not completing or returning the questionnaire.

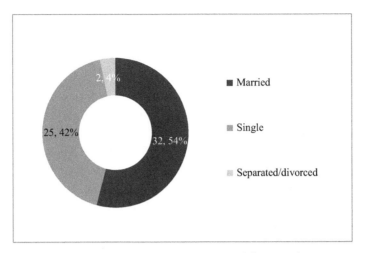

Fig. 2.6 #Bringbackourgirls members, sample's marital status, Abuja, Nigeria. Marital status/N = 59
Source: author.

Tactics of #BBOG protests

Social movement organizations develop a variety of tactics of protest. These tactics help define a movement. Given that grassroots activists often lack institutionalized mechanisms for being heard, particularly in neocolonial societies, they resort to non-conventional tactics of protest.[31] Tactics are contentious performances (Tilly 1999) in an amphitheatre encompassing movement activists, the state (and/or other institutionalized entity), audience, and bystanders. Tactics reflect the identity of the movement and draw on its cultural context.

A movement may, in fact, be remembered for its tactics rather than goals (Wilson 1973; Taylor and Van Dyke 2007). For instance, the Niger Delta women who organized a nude protest against Chevron in 2002 (Turner and Brownhill 2004) are largely remembered for their tactic of protest rather than their objectives. Nudity as a protest tactic has been used in Cameroun, Togo, Uganda, and Kenya. It is based on cultural shaming and the instrumentalization of nudity of female bodies. Nude protests in Africa are similar to protests in India against brutality of state agents (Misri 2011) but qualitatively different

---

[31] See McAdam and Snow (1997).

from nude protests by women in Western contexts, such as FEMEN (the Special Force of Feminism) in Europe.

The #BBOG movement signposts the growing *tactical divide* between educated urban (women) and rural-based activists in Africa. The #BBOG movement is an example of the new trajectory of women-led movements in Africa that are deploying sophisticated, internationalized framing and tactics. Rural-based women, on the other hand, rely on naked protests for grievances on socio-economic conditions and food prices, for instance. The continued use of nude protests concurrently symbolize empowerment and conditions of powerlessness. Naked protesters deploy the cultural symbolism, contextual intersubjectivity, and power in the insignia of their bodies as women, seniors, mothers, and grandmothers, but resorting to nude protests signifies that the protesters have no other options to address their grievances. A study on Kenya and Nigeria finds that the 'symbolic resonance' of nakedness is a key factor in its persistence (Fallon and Moreau 2016: 323).

Nonetheless, social class shapes the use of protest tactics and is at the heart of the tactical divide among women-led movements in Africa. Nude protesters and those who use more sophisticated means rarely share social circles. Their priorities and goals also tend to be different. For instance, the Soulaliyate movement in Morocco emerged as land became increasingly commodified (Berriane 2016). The movement was a coalition of individuals from different socio-economic backgrounds: rural and largely uneducated women and the Democratic Association of Women in Morocco (ADFM), which was championed by urban-based, educated elite. While the ADFM favours a broad, long-term institutional approach such as advocating for legislative changes, members of the the Soulaliyate movement have one immediate priority—to have a share of the land (Berriane 2016). The food protests in at least 14 African countries between 2007 and 2011 (Sneyd et al. 2013) also revealed issues relating to goals and tactics. Protests occurred in African countries as diverse as Algeria, Burkina Faso, Cameroon, Côte d'Ivoire, Egypt, Guinea Conakry, Madagascar, Mauritania, Morocco, Mozambique, Senegal, Somalia, Tunisia, and Uganda. Protest tactics varied from burning cars in Senegal to national strikes in Guinea Conakry. Protest tactics are shaped by internal factors within movements in interaction with the external environment.

#BBOG has adopted several tactics since its inaugural mass protest in Abuja on 30 April 2014. The tactics include daily sit-out, days of action, periodic marches to symbols of governmental power, media engagement, and the annual Chibok lecture. The tactics are analysed below.

The daily sit-out

The 'sit-out' is the #BBOG movement's term for *sit-in*. It shows the transnational influences on the movement. #BBOG drew on the use of sit-ins in the civil rights movement, the Vietnam War protests in the United States, and the anti-apartheid movement in South Africa. The term 'sit-out' was preferred over the much more common term 'sit-in' because the latter could generate confusion. 'Sit-in' in the Nigerian context sounded like a stay-at-home action and was therefore avoided in favour of the more linguistically, and culturally appropriate *sit-out* (Esekwesili 2015). The majority of those who participated in the inaugural protest were committed to daily protest until the Chibok girls were secured. Therefore, the movement leadership acceded to the determination of the demonstrators to meet daily. The daily protest or sit-out began 16 days after the Chibok abduction. There have been multiple attempts to end the daily sit-out. In particular, leaders were concerned about state-sponsored violence against #BBOG. The ST's decision to end the daily protest was communicated, but members insisted on continuing the daily protest (multiple interviewees).

The daily sit-out serves as a forum for members to solidarize and obtain the latest information on the cause. The sit-out is a public space for generating, incubating, and interrogating ideas and practices. It begins with a call to stand for rendition of the second stanza of Nigeria's national anthem. This rendition is a political act. The stanza states:

> Oh God of creation
> Direct our noble cause
> Guide our leaders right
> Help our youth the truth to know
> In love and honesty to grow
> And live in just and truth
> Great lofty heights attain
> To build a nation where peace
> And justice shall reign.

The anthem is significant. It speaks to the quest for justice, truth, and nation-building. It also invokes the name of God in a highly religious society. The aptness of the anthem to the #BBOG cause cannot be overemphasized. It is difficult for authorities to cast #BBOG as enemies of the state, given that they begin their daily protest with one of the nationalistic rhetorics of the country. The brilliance of using the anthem is that it discursively ties #BBOG to Nigeria's self-avowed creed while concurrently engaging in a *noble cause* that is shared by the members of # BBOG, albeit an irritant to the government. In other words, it suggests that #BBOG activists are citizens too and share the aspirations of the country's founders. Movement activists' use of narratives, symbolisms, and syllogisms favoured by the state is not new. It serves as an ideational instrument for connecting the movement with the widely shared aspirations of the nation state. This mitigates accusations of subversion against the movement by authorities. Chilean women, for instance, tapped into the entrenched ethos of Catholicism and patriarchal ideations to construe activists as people who share similar sentiments as the state under the brutal regime of Augusto Pinochet (Noonan 1995).

The anthem is followed by an opening remark by the sit-out coordinator. While there is a designated person for this role, any member may be asked to coordinate a sit-out. The opening remark is generally intended to be inspirational and serve as a reminder of the reason for the daily protest. Media updates follow the opening remark. Everyone present is given an opportunity to present to the group any issues in the news that concern the Chibok girls, the #BBOG movement, and efforts (or lack of) by the government to rescue the girls. Therefore, the sit-out is a forum for sharing information about the movement's cause. The media update segment also provides an avenue for members to give their perspective on issues affecting the cause. The 'Any other business' or 'AOB' follows the media update. Discussions about internal and external matters, controversies, member grievances, and the direction of the movement, among others, are aired. Announcements about upcoming activities are made after AOB.

Afterwards, the group rises upon hearing the statement 'Who is standing for our Chibok girls?' A one-minute silent prayer is observed for the Chibok girls, those affected by Boko Haram, and the Nigerian armed forces. Given that members are drawn from diverse religious backgrounds, praying in silence helps to avoid the pitfalls of appearing to favour one religion over another or spending time praying in ways favoured by the two dominant religions in Nigeria. The chant discussed above is used to conclude the daily sit-out.[32]

The sit-out takes place at the Unity Fountain in Abuja, a prime location adjacent to the Transcorp Hilton Hotel. The Unity Fountain is a national monument. It has the names of all 36 states of Nigeria etched on concrete around a fountain. This was designed to symbolize the unity of Nigeria. The location

---

[32] Members regularly spend an hour or more after the official end of the day's protest to socialize.

has since become the epicentre of expression of dissent in Nigeria. Various advocacy groups have used the Unity Fountain as the spatial location of their struggle.

Days of action

The #BBOG movement designates specific periods for days of action. These periods are created to coincide with landmarks in the abduction saga. For instance, the movement announced a 'Global Week of Action to mark #Day1000' in January 2017. It presented an opportunity to join forces with and coordinate #BBOG spin-offs in other parts of the world. This particular landmark was used as an avenue to highlight issues that were germane to the cause. The week was used to address seven issues (one per day): #ChibokGirls—#Day1000, internally displaced persons (IDPs), military welfare, corruption/poor governance, endangered education, girl-child vulnerability, and insecurity. The themes have 'connections with and are relevant to our Chibok girls and the #BringBackOurGirls advocacy'.[33] These carefully organized events ensure membership, media, and public engagement in the cause. They are occasionally tied to internationally recognized thematic events such as the International Day of the Girl Child.[34]

Periodic marches

#BBOG also organizes occasional marches to symbols of state power. Members congregate at the Unity Fountain at an agreed time and march to spaces like the presidential villa (Aso Rock) or the National Assembly. The march to the location of protest generates public interest, given the number of participants. Members are often joined by bystanders, who are fascinated by the movement, the resplendent red colour of #BBOG members, and the messages on the banners. The most iconic of #BBOG messages on its banners states: 'Would you be silent if your daughter was missing?' Two or more members, who appear at the head of the march, hold the banner during periodic marches.

The periodic marches are used strategically. For instance, #BBOG held no march for nearly three months after 82 Chibok girls were secured in May 2017. The movement marched to the State House on 1 August 2017 to demand the

---

[33] See 'Schedule of activities for #Day1000 Global Week of Activities', http://www.bringbackourgirls.ng/?p=2773. Accessed 22 December 2017.
[34] See http://www.bringbackourgirls.ng/?p=2851. Accessed 24 October 2023.

rescue of the remaining 113 girls. #BBOG announced that it was not acceptable to provide no updates to the parents and guardians of the missing girls. The march was 'intended to wake the federal government up and prevent it from relapsing and sinking into inertia and complacency' (cited in Obike 2017). The protests sometimes involve sealing the mouths of participants with tapes. This speaks to the theme of symbolism in social movement protest. Certain words, banners, clothes, and other paraphernalia (such as stickers and lapel pins) are selected or designed by social movement activists for their evocative quality.

The 'silent marches' are meant to portray the helplessness and silencing of the Chibok girls. They also convey the non-violent nature of #BBOG as activists march through the streets. The marches have often spurred authorities to action as their significance is understood in the corridors of power. For instance, the Inspector General of Police criticized #BBOG for '*overdramatisation of emotions*' (Bada 2016). The marches pose a conundrum to the authorities: ignoring them means that the public may perceive the authorities as inept while disrupting them often leads to accusations of human rights abuses. Either way, the movement garners more attention to its cause.

The Chibok girls' ambassador tactic

#BBOG introduced the Chibok girls' ambassador idea as a tactic to engage young school girls all over the world. Each participant is given the name and number of a missing Chibok girl and encouraged to imagine being in the position of a missing girl. The refrain in the public exercise is 'It could have been me.' This tactic simultaneously engages the girls and parents who convey their daughters to the venue of the protest. It raises awareness among young people about the responsibility of the state and human rights issues. One Chibok girl ambassador notes,

> I feel sad that I live in a country, where 219 girls would be abducted and kept in captivity ... and yet nothing is done, yet no attempt is made to rescue them, and everyone just moves on as if nothing ever happened. Why? They are kept in the hands of monsters that go around killing people ... What if it were I that was abducted? Will everyone just move on and forget about me? Bring Back Our Girls Now And Alive.[35]

---

[35] See 'Chibok ambassadors', http://www.bringbackourgirls.ng/?cat=35. Accessed 22 December 2017.

Annual Chibok girls' lecture

The annual Chibok girls' lecture is a more recent tactic within the #BBOG movement's repertoire. It was introduced on 14 April 2017. The inaugural lecture was delivered by the Sarkin (Emir) of Kano, Muhammad Sanusi II. Sanusi's speech was entitled 'Chibok and the mirror in our faces: Some reflections on gender in our society'. The Emir focused on the social positionality of the girl-child and women in Northern Nigeria. He drew widespread commendation for analysing the social conditions that led to the rise of Boko Haram and the terrorist organization's maltreatment of female persons. The event marked the third-year anniversary of the Chibok kidnapping. The fact that it attracted the head of a major traditional institution in Northern Nigeria further bolstered the legitimacy and credibility of #BBOG and its cause.[36] The lecture generated huge publicity and laid bare the struggle between forces supporting and negating women's rights, particularly in Northern Nigeria. The 2nd annual Chibok Girls' lecture (14 April 2018) was themed 'Towards a just and good society: Renewing our commitment to the girl-child in Nigeria'. Tunde Bakare, a popular Pentecostal pastor and former vice-presidential candidate, was the guest speaker. The annual lecture by influential persons keeps the movement's cause in the public focus.

Media engagement

This is one of the most consequential tactics of #BBOG. #BBOG engages in occasional press conferences, press releases, interviews, and speeches by key leaders to raise awareness about its cause. These closely aligned tactics have been streamlined since the formation of the SCT. The early days of rhetorical overkill by virtually any member has been replaced with greater attention to detail. While a lot of attention has been accorded to the #BBOG movement's use of social media, the section below argues that the movement has, in fact, deployed an approach in which both new and traditional media are seamlessly blended for communicative efficacy.

---

[36] Sanusi was represented at the event by one of his daughters, apparently due to political pressure. This marked the first time an Emir of Kano was represented by an individual who was not on the Emirate Council or was female. The latter factor in particular generated huge controversy in the Northern establishment. Sanusi was dethroned in March 2020.

The #BBOG communication process

The use of social media by social movements has generated tremendous scholarly attention (Howard et al. 2011; Bennett 2012; Gerbaudo 2012; Fuchs 2017). Scholars are fascinated by the use of multiple social media platforms for information dissemination, organizing, and mobilizing activists for protests. The political tremors in the Arab world (the Arab Spring) from 2009 to 2011 embody the increasing use of social media by activists to challenge authority. Social media platforms have become important spaces and tools for organizing protest, particularly in repressive environments. For instance, the collapse of the regime of Hosni Mubarak has been linked to the use of Facebook as a mobilization tool by activists (Lim 2012).

Gheytanchi and Moghadam (2014) investigate Iran's Green Protest movement and its feminist wing, the political revolutions in Egypt and Tunisia and attendant women's movement, and the movement for women's rights in Morocco. The findings show that women's cyberactivism contributed to changes in those contexts, and their involvement as citizen journalists led to changes in the political opportunity structure, thereby undermining state power (Gheytanchi and Moghadam 2014). This is particularly impressive in the Middle East and North Africa, given the absence of a strong civil society and open media (Khondker 2011). In Tunisia, social media produced a crop of 'digital elite' which mobilized people partly by displaying the most gruesome televisual evidence of state repression of protesters and disseminated information despite state-imposed blackout of traditional media (Breuer et al. 2015).

Similarly, social media continues to have strong influence on protest in Southern Africa. Mare (2014: 332) investigates cycles of protests in South Africa, Malawi, Mozambique, and Swaziland and finds that netizens in Southern Africa 'creatively appropriated social media platforms to disseminate information, pass on solidarity messages, and exchange mobilization tactics across space and time'. This was part of a transnational process. For instance, the global 'Occupy' movement began in September 2011 at Zuccotti Park in the Wall Street financial district of New York City to protest economic inequality. There was a 'demonstration effect' across Africa as activists in the Occupy Grahamstown movement learned key lessons from the Egyptian uprising and other protests around the world (Mare 2014: 331). One of the organizations that participated in Occupy Grahamstown notes, on its website, that they were 'inspired by this global rebellion because the comrades in Tahrir Square showed the world the strength of a united and determined people' (cited in Mare 2014: 331). Uwalaka and Watkins (2018) examine the role of social media in the 2012 Occupy Nigeria movement. They find that mainstream media initially refused to cover the protests due to pressure from the government. Social media became the 'Fifth Estate' as it fostered 'interaction, socialisation, collective engagement, and liberation that was not present in the mainstream media' (Uwalaka and Watkins 2018: 22). The deployment of social media by activists in Africa has broadened the political space and inspired challenges to authority in a way that departs from culturally imposed silence as people question the social conditions and actors affecting their lives (Mabweazara 2015). Therefore, from Northern to Southern Africa, there is cross-fertilization of protest ideas, tactics, and ideation with social media as the epicentre of engagement.

Social media platforms are particularly relevant to activists, in part because of their interpenetrative capacity. Mason (2012: 75) argues,

> Facebook is used to form groups, covert and overt—in order to establish those strong but flexible connections. Twitter is used for real-time organisation and news dissemination, bypassing the cumbersome 'newsgathering' operations of the mainstream media. YouTube and the Twitter-linked photographic sites—Yfrog, Flickr and Twitpic—are used to provide instant evidence of the claims being made. Link-shorteners like bit.ly are used to disseminate key articles via Twitter.

Social media has been described as 'liberation technology' (Diamond 2012: xi) due to its role in the struggle for human rights, economic justice, and democratization. However, Chiluwa and Ifukor (2015: 286) caution that 'practical offline actions' must be part of social media activism in order to be effective. While many movements that began on social media have been criticized for their slacktivism or failure to lead to any concrete social action, some have, in fact, led to physical or offline movements. For example, an online movement was formed in Guatemala following the assassination of a lawyer, Rodrigo Rosenberg. One of the organizations within the broader movement to find the killers of Rosenberg, *Movimiento Cívico Nacional*, has since transmuted to a physical social justice advocacy group concerned with ending violence (Harlow 2011). The Egyptian revolution also utilized social media for mobilization and organizing protest (Gerbaudo 2012).

The #BBOG movement has become synonymous with the potency and utility of social media in grassroots advocacy. This is a rather uncritical position. Besides analysing the communication strategy of the #BBOG movement, this section advances two main arguments. First, while social media was integral to the formation of the #BBOG and its global spread, the movement's approach is a hybridized communication process that seamlessly combines the immediacy and global tendrils of platforms such as Twitter ('X') and Facebook with the credibility of traditional print and electronic media. Second, #BBOG held several marches in late 2014 and early 2015 that received scant media coverage. This frustrated the activists and necessitated a change of strategy. Consequently, #BBOG activists realized the salience of traditional media coverage of their activities. Sesugh Akume, who leads the SCT, highlights the logic behind the #BBOG movement's engagement with traditional media. He explains that the name of the communication arm was changed from 'media team' because

> what we do is beyond media. It is not just media; it is the whole gamut of strategic communication, about how the advocacy is perceived; about how our Chibok girls' issue is always on the front burner, deflecting attacks, everything that has to do with strategic communication. That is why we renamed it 'strategic communication team'.
>
> (Sesugh Akume, SCT leader)

Therefore, #BBOG activists who formed the nucleus of the group's strategic media engagement are bemused by the widespread perception that the movement simply walked into the global media spotlight. In reality, a lot of *media sense* was involved. #BBOG assembled an email list of journalists, media organizations, and bloggers and sent electronic copies of the group's statements. One SCT member argues that 'we tailor our message towards people that may have reasonable doubt.[37] We craft our messages, when there are issues, we respond to them by way of press statements.' The SCT set up an exclusive WhatsApp account for its members. The account is known as the 'situation room' and serves as the virtual space in which statements meant for public release are fine-tuned prior to being sent to the ST.

The SCT put together a weekly compendium—a comprehensive report and analysis of issues relating to the missing girls, efforts of the military, (mis)steps by the government, comments from the international community, and #BBOG activities, among others. This was done for six consecutive weeks following the first #BBOG march. The compendium was sought by traditional media and posted on social media. The SCT also invited the media to a briefing every Sunday. Journalists could obtain hard copies of the compendium

---

[37] This was particularly important in 2014, when the government was reluctant to acknowledge that the girls were kidnapped, which led to widespread doubt about the incident.

and ask questions. Sesugh notes, 'That is how we kept them (the media) and sustained that relationship.'

The #BBOG movement is social media-savvy. This has been particularly relevant in creating awareness for the movement among middle-class Nigerians, the Nigerian diaspora, and the international community. The first #BBOG demonstration on 30 April 2014, for instance, received 3.3 million mentions on Twitter ('X') within 48 hours (Interviewee 30). However, only 37.59% of Nigerians had internet access in 2014,[38] at the peak of #BBOG activities. Traditional media was therefore the main avenue by which the majority of Nigerians learned about #BBOG activities. It is didactic to recognize that, as of 6 April 2020, the official Twitter ('X') handle of BBOG had slightly over 35,000 followers and 24,000 tweets.[39] As demonstrated below, the echoing of the #BBOG movement's message on traditional media has been central to the global attention it has garnered.

Consequently, it is surprising that in an attempt to frame #BBOG as a social media-led movement, the role played by traditional media remains largely unacknowledged. While the #BBOG movement was launched on social media, traditional media—print and electronic—has been fundamental to generating momentum for the movement. For instance, Channels Television—ranked number 1 in Nigeria in the past 10 years—provided daily coverage of the sit-out of #BBOG. The *Leadership* newspaper, a popular publication in Northern Nigeria, also dedicated its second page to activities of the #BBOG movement, in addition to stationing a member of staff to report on activities at the daily sit-out. A mimetic process was set in motion, as is common in institutional fields (Zucker 1987)—several media organizations began to cover the activities of #BBOG to keep up with the competition and the market that was rapidly formed.[40]

---

[38] See 'Nigeria internet users', http://www.internetlivestats.com/internet-users/nigeria. Accessed 14 March 2014. Recent estimates suggest that the number has increased to between 47% and 54% (see Premium Times 2015).

[39] These numbers represent an increase rather than a decline. As of 30 September 2018, the official Twitter handle of #BBOG had less than 30,000 followers and 4,357 'likes', although it had posted over 22,000 tweets.

[40] Traditional media coverage of #BBOG activities was intense until Channels television withdrew coverage following a fall-out between #BBOG de facto leader, Obiageli Ezekwesili and the organization over the comments of one of the station's guests on live television (Interviewee 30). Support for the #BBOG movement was not universal in Nigeria's traditional media. There were media organizations, such as the government-owned Nigerian Television Authority (NTA), which largely ignored the #BBOG movement and the privately operated Africa Independent Television (AIT), which appeared to have been deployed to discredit #BBOG (Interviewee 30). The latter's activities were so biased against groups opposed to the government that the media team of President Buhari briefly prevented them from covering the newly sworn-in president in summer 2015.

Traditional media played a huge role in the internationalization of the grievance and framing of the #BBOG movement. Global media hegemons such as CNN, the BBC, and Al Jazeera covered #BBOG activities by interviewing leaders of the movement or asking world leaders questions about #BBOG. Most of the members of the ST, such as Obiageli Ezekwesili, Hadiza Bala Usman, and Bukky Sonibare, among others, have made multiple appearances on virtually all the major media organizations broadcasting in English and, in some cases, the Hausa language. A co-convener, for instance, noted on Al Jazeera that 'the media propelled a lot of support around the world' for #BBOG's cause (Ogene 2014). Multifarious personalities, such as US President Barack Obama and his spouse, Michelle Obama and Nobel prize winner, Malala Yousafzai, among other opinions and world leaders, also played a significant role in drawing global attention to the #BBOG cause. In 2014, British Prime Minister David Cameron was handed a '#Bring Back Our Girls' sign by CNN's Christiane Amanpour on BBC's Andrew Marr Show. Cameron discursively 'joined' the campaign by arguing, 'this is not just a problem in Nigeria' (BBC 2014c).

#BBOG also regularly received several personalities at the sit-out whose presence attracted significant press coverage. Such persons included leading clergy in Nigeria, the President of the EU, the US Ambassador to the United Nations, and members of the US Congress (such as Frederica Wilson), among others. The SCT ensured that such solidarity visits were given adequate coverage on traditional and social media. Images from such visits, in addition to videos and pictures of world leaders, entertainers, etc., were shared on social media. Social media was also used to make announcements about marches and 'Days of Action'. Such visits and announcements were amplified by traditional media organizations, thus leading to an interactional, iterative, and co-productive process. Consequently, *while social media played a central role in the #BBOG movement's take off, the key variable in the propagation of the group's activities was the cyclicality of social media and traditional media coverage.*

Fig. 2.7 shows the #BBOG communication process. The chart demonstrates the interactional dynamic analysed above. Information flows from the various publics to the sit-out. Members can learn about issues in the news through media updates during the daily protest. That generally encourages members to attempt to stay informed in order to have something to share at the sit-out. Members serve as a feedback mechanism to the public in which they are embedded. Many #BBOG members have social media accounts and often share information about activities, pictures, and videos about the movement.

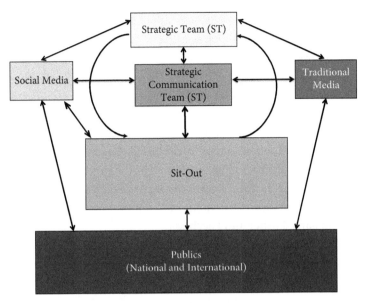

Fig. 2.7 The #BBOG communication process
Source: author.

These are taken up by their contacts or 'friends' on social media, thus generating greater reach. In turn, members report criticisms and other potentially useful information at the sit-out. The sit-out is therefore a major source of intelligence for the SCT and the ST.

Members of the SCT have individual social media platforms, for example the SCT Head's handle @Sesugh_Akume and Edith Yassin's @Ecyassin. They utilize these in addition to the official handles of #BBOG, for example @BBOG_Nigeria. The information disseminated by the SCT is concurrently made available to traditional media organizations. Journalists from radio, television, and print media organizations have direct access to the SCT. The SCT's WhatsApp group is used as a platform to disseminate information to local, national, and international media organizations. The WhatsApp group has over 100 journalists who represent organizations as diverse as the Associated Press and *Premium Times*. This shows synchronous use of social and traditional media. The journalists are able to pose questions in real time to the SCT to seek clarification or more information. Journalists often provide information (sometimes inadvertently given questions that they pose) on what they are working on prior to going public with their reports.

Conversely, members of the ST have individual handles that are used to disseminate movement-related activities. The most prolific and closely followed is Ezekwesili's handle, '@obyezeks', which had 1.2 million followers and had posted 113,000 tweets as of 4 October 2021.[41] ST members receive feedback from their followers. The tweets by Ezekwesili in particular have become major staples of political life in Nigeria.[42]

The ST and SCT work together on drafting press releases. The coordination is facilitated by the fact that some SCT members are also on the ST. The head of the SCT, for instance, is also a member of the ST. That smoothes the communication process as coordination is enhanced. The SCT prepares drafts of press statements. Drafts have to be sanctioned by the ST prior to being formally released. The statements are concurrently released on social media and traditional media. Instantaneous reactions and comments are garnered on social media, particularly Twitter and Facebook.

The symbiotic relationship between #BBOG (specifically, the SCT) and the media is based on trust and accuracy of the information provided by #BBOG. Sesugh Akume notes that there has never been a single statement put out by #BBOG that was found to be inaccurate or false because 'we crosscheck our facts; we double-check. We check the context, we are not in a hurry to put out anything.'[43] The SCT head also notes the team's background preparation. The speed with which they supply useful sources to journalists has made them indispensable in the coverage of the Chibok girls' matter. He notes that the team has resources such as contact numbers of Chibok parents. Therefore, within minutes, such contacts are provided to journalists, who are amazed at the efficiency of #BBOG. Such journalists often attend #BBOG's media briefings.

Over time, the public and the media began to rely on the credibility of the statements put out by #BBOG. Such has been the legitimacy and credulity of #BBOG statements that journalists routinely send text messages or emails to the SCT to ask for confirmation of statements put out by the government. For instance, when the government announced that 82 girls had been secured in May 2017, several journalists contacted #BBOG, arguing that 'they don't believe (the government), even when they saw pictures. They said they don't believe, they have to get confirmation from the BBOG' (Sesuge Akume, SCT leader). What the foregoing analysis suggests is that traditional media has been

---

[41] These numbers are up from 776,000 followers and 44,000 'likes' and 96,000 tweets as of 30 September 2018.
[42] Traditional media organizations often rely on her tweets to formulate news stories. Her tweets routinely receive official reactions from the presidency and, inevitably, traditional media coverage; for example, see Daily Trust (2017).
[43] This is difficult to verify but media organizations, NGOs, and the public began to rely on the veracity of #BBOG claims a few days after #BBOG's first public mobilization in April 2014.

just as critical as social or new media to the global tendrils of the #BBOG movement. An interview with a #BBOG SCT member (Interviewee 33)[44] accentuates the salience of traditional media in publicizing #BBOG activities:

INTERVIEWER: If somebody were to say that #BBOG to a significant degree is a massive media operation, would you agree?
SCT MEMBER: I would agree. #BBOG, you may not believe it but active #BBOG members around the world are not up to 100.
INTERVIEWER: Wow!
SCT MEMBER: The Abuja family, active people in Abuja, we are not up to 50. Then we have Lagos, then we have New York, and some other places where people do activities ... how many are we? If it were not for a skilful use of the media and how we go about it, we are just a spec somewhere.

#BBOG protest mobilization

#BBOG leverages the networks and contacts of its elite leaders to attract other elites who bring significant cultural and social capital to the protests of the movement. #BBOG engages in three types of street-level protests. These are (a) *the daily sit-out*, (b) *solo or small-scale celebrity marches*, and (c) *street marches or mass protest*. The daily sit-out is the #BBOG movement's signature within its repertoire of protest. The solo celebrity march is a personality-driven protest geared towards enabling famous, respected, and influential individuals to demonstrate their concern for the Chibok girls and support for the #BBOG movement. Such marches involve only one celebrity or two to three celebrities marching in tandem with two or three #BBOG leaders. This tactic garners significant media attention as (one or more) non-conventional protesters march on the streets. The celebrity march demonstrates the mixture of #BBOG's internal resources and opportunities provided by the fractionalization of the elite within the Nigerian political process.

For instance, #BBOG utilized a celebrity march on 11 April 2017 during its Global Week of Action on the third-year anniversary of the Chibok abduction. John Onaiyekan, the Catholic Archbishop of Abuja diocese, and Mouhammed Khalid, the Chief Imam of the Apo legislators' quarter's Juma'at Mosque, marched with representatives of #BBOG (Ibrahim and Yesufu 2017). The march concluded with a press conference near the State House. Besides

---

[44] Male #BBOG SCT member; personal interview, Abuja, July 2017.

the publicity given to the cause, the march was a hugely symbolic exercise as it strongly indicated that key actors from the two dominant religions in Nigeria solidarized on a common objective. It also drew the attention of power-holders in a way that marches by regular citizens may not (Isa and Himelboim 2018).

Street marches or mass protests are the most intricate of the #BBOG movement's demonstrations. They are collaborative exercises between #BBOG and multiple organizations.

As shown in Fig. 2.8, four major sets of actors are involved in #BBOG's mass protests. These include (a) all the organs of #BBOG, (b) NGOs and civil society organizations (CSOs), (c) community (development) organizations, and (d) the media. Law enforcement agencies are often in the background to maintain order while the public plays the role of bystander. The ST often conceives the need for a mass protest or march based on developments outside the control of #BBOG. A member of the ST notes that the 'factors are usually extraneous, totally outside our control. It could be an attack on a community; it could be any information about the Nigerian military retreating.' This suggests

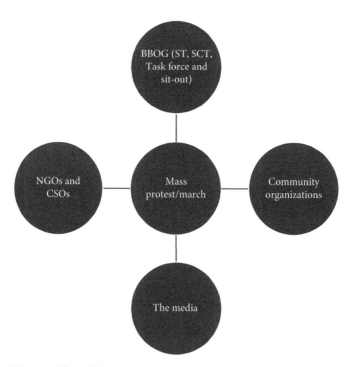

Fig. 2.8 The #BBOG protest mobilization matrix

Source: author.

that #BBOG organizes mass protest based on changes or development in its larger political context.

Mobilization for mass protests has evolved within #BBOG. There was a mobilization task force led by one member, Mariam Okunaye, within the first year of #BBOG activism. The team's activities included distribution of flyers and other publicity materials and coordination of partner organizations (explained below). However, the mobilization team 'faded away naturally' once its leader was absorbed into the ST (Interviewee 10).[45] Subsequently, ad hoc committees were set up to coordinate mass protests. Multiple steps are involved.

First, a theme is coined for the protest. Themes vary according to the circumstances #BBOG wishes to highlight. For instance, a march may be held specifically on the plight of the troops deployed to fight against Boko Haram or conditions of victims of Boko Haram bombings. Second, the ST informs members at the sit-out about the protest. Ideas are solicited from members about what organizations to invite and specific issues to highlight in public communication about the impending protest. #BBOG members are mobilized through the group's WhatsApp account, Facebook, and other social media handles. The SCT also sends text messages to the over 800 mobile phone numbers of #BBOG supporters (Interviewee 10). Reminders about the protest are sent multiple times on various platforms. It is routine practice for members to receive reminders via regular text message about a protest up to 30 minutes before it starts.

Third, the theme of the protest determines the stakeholders who are invited to participate. These generally include those most closely associated with the focus of the struggle, such as parents of the Chibok girls, the Kibaku Area Development Association (KADA), and the Yobe–Borno Forum. KADA is the umbrella association for the Kibaku-speaking peoples, including the people of Chibok, Borno state. The Yobe–Borno Forum is an organization of the peoples of Yobe and Borno states, two of the three states that constitute the epicentre of Boko Haram's operations. Some members of both KADA and the Yobe–Borno Forum are members of #BBOG. Therefore, such members are tasked with the responsibility of ensuring the representation of their respective associations at the marches. For example, Dr Manasseh Allen is a member of #BBOG's ST and serves as the spokesperson of KADA. Such dual roles held by specific individuals ensure relatively smooth coordination between #BBOG and its constituency.

---

[45] Male #BBOG ST member; televisual interview, 4 January 2018.

Fourth, multiple interest groups (NGOs and CSOs) are also involved in #BBOG mass protests. These are generally associations formed by, or representing, military wives or widows of soldiers killed in the fight against Boko Haram, victims of bombings, and persons displaced from the Northeast by Boko Haram's terrorist activities. Organizations focused on girl-child advocacy, women's causes (such as prevention of violence against women), youth-centric organizations, and CSOs concerned with education issues are mobilized by #BBOG. This implies that the theme of the protest must accommodate the goals and objectives of NGOs and CSOs.

#BBOG draws on existing networks and contacts of members to mobilize relevant organizations. For example, a #BBOG member is a central player in YouthHub Africa and helps in mobilizing young people to #BBOG mass protests. #BBOG also has multiple members who were involved in advocacy issues on education, girl-child advocacy, and prevention of violence against women prior to the movement. Such members are central to the mobilization efforts of the movement. #BBOG communicates with such interest groups through official emails and letters of invitation. #BBOG members with networks in any of the interest groups ensure follow-up. Therefore, mobilization involves both formal and informal channels.

Journalists are also mobilized. #BBOG issues press releases several days before each march and circulates them to its contacts in traditional media. The WhatsApp account set up by #BBOG to coordinate with and pass on information to journalists has been pivotal in this area. Journalists publish stories about imminent #BBOG marches and therefore help to generate attention.

Law enforcement agencies are an important part of the #BBOG mass protests. #BBOG applies for a protest permit from the Nigerian police force 48–72 hours before each protest. Each protest is an interagency operation for law enforcement. The Road Safety Commission, Department of State Security (DSS), Nigeria Intelligence Agency (NIA), and the Nigeria police force are involved in each protest for various reasons. The police deploy, on average, 100–400[46] personnel (depending on number of participants) to each protest to protect law and order. Security agents from the stated agencies are deployed to the Unity Fountain, where each protest kicks off. A few officials remain at the Unity Fountain while others are deployed along the routes—streets and major intersections—of the protest. Two police vans lead the protesters. A line of police personnel is formed to serve as a cordon to ensure protester safety. Trucks and police vans also remain at the rear of the protesters.

---

[46] The estimate is based on activists' recollections.

#BBOG members realized that some of the personnel deployed by law enforcement agencies were intended to infiltrate their ranks. Operatives from the NIA and DSS, in particular, have attempted to camouflage as #BBOG members in order to gather intelligence about #BBOG.[47]

#BBOG internal discipline vis-à-vis mass protests

A protest can make or mar a social movement. Consequently, movement activists deploy measures to ensure that their messages are passed on to the intended audience while minimizing distractions and incidents that may impugn the integrity of the movement and its cause. Movements tend to attract persons who may differ in their view of preferred tactics, location of protest sites, stakeholders to engage with, and how to engage. One of the early issues #BBOG dealt with was the notion that the movement was too careful in challenging the state. One ST member notes that

> We had a hard time in the early days trying to persuade people that we have to be law-abiding even as we want to engage the state. Some people would say that we should go to the airport road and block the road and that will get attention from the government. People would say that all the formal notification was playing into their hands; we should just block a major road and go and sit down somewhere. Those were serious arguments. People were making suggestions. They were emotional.
> (Interviewee 10)

Members who wanted more 'action' did not take into cognizance the consequences of impeding traffic on a major road and hence risking public disapproval.

#BBOG mass protests are carefully contemplated and rigorously planned events. There has been only one spontaneous protest in the annals of #BBOG. The unplanned protest occurred in 2014. The daily sit-out was being observed. A member argued that there had been no activities from the movement (apart from the daily sit-out, which was already routine by then). A member of the ST assured the gathering that #BBOG was not afraid to march at any time, including right there and then. The statement was intended to rhetorically assure members that the leadership had no fears about being engaged in marches. However, someone immediately suggested 'yes let's go and march. And before

---

[47] See the section on state repression in Chapter 4.

you know it, people got up and we were marching.'[48] More members supported the idea of marching to the State House to prove that the group was not afraid of the government. Florence Ozor, who was coordinating the sit-out at the time, argues that the spontaneous march

> wasn't too well received (by #BBOG leadership) because we went out of our modus operandi. Many things could have happened because normally when we are going on marches, we have people designated for certain roles. We know those whose emotions can flip, and we know those who to put around them to manage those emotions so that you don't get aggravated by the security forces who are looking for a reason to say we have become a riotous group . . . This was totally out of what we used to do, totally unplanned and at very great risk. Anybody could have misbehaved and it couldn't have gone the way it did. But it was the only spontaneous march we have done in the movement.

Other mass protests or marches by the movement have followed a strict disciplinary regime. All protest participants must converge at the Unity Fountain. No one else may join after the group leaves the starting point unless they are positively identified as a member of #BBOG. A flyer containing a 'Don't do list' is handed out to each protester at Unity Fountain. The list includes prohibitions aimed at ensuring orderliness. These include, 'Don't throw stones or any objects', 'Don't get angry during protest', 'Don't talk rudely to security agents', and 'Don't litter'. Protesters are informed about what to expect. This includes the possibility of aggression by law enforcement officers, name-calling or mockery by some bystanders, counter-protest by government supporters, and provocation, among others. The protesters are also informed about information dissemination by #BBOG. No one is permitted to speak with the media; only designated persons within #BBOG leadership are allowed to do this.

The core values of #BBOG are stressed before marches (see the earlier analysis). Jibril Ibrahim, a professor of political science from Ahmadu Bello University (ABU), Zaria, often provides intellectual support and rationale for the approach of #BBOG. He gives short lectures on the philosophy of Martin Luther King (Jr) vis-à-vis the power of peaceful protests. Members believe that such an ideational framework helped during a particular repressive episode.[49]

---

[48] Florence Ozor, #BBOG ST chair; personal interview, Abuja, July 2017. Ozor was sit-out coordinator when the incident happened.
[49] See Chapter 4 on state repression.

There are specificities to being part of a march. Six persons are lined per row, starting with those holding a large banner. Everyone stays behind the persons holding the #BBOG banner. #BBOG ensured that the 'mixed crowd'—a collection of representatives of NGOs, CSOs, and community development organizations among other miscellaneous interest groups—is fully informed about the character of #BBOG protest. One ST member argues that the key variable in the success of #BBOG marches is 'organization'. #BBOG is generally wary of mixed crowds and goes to great lengths to ensure that participants from partner organizations conform to the ethos of #BBOG. More experienced members of the group, or 'senior citizens', are also deployed to manage emotions before and during mass protests. The presence of prominent elite in the movement plays a role in ensuring compliance with protest rubric.

This section demonstrates the mobilization of a typical #BBOG protest. #BBOG protests are generally a disciplined and highly coordinated affair. The level of organization and attention to detail by #BBOG is instructive for grassroots activists challenging authority in authoritarian or quasi-democratic contexts.

Funding the #BBOG movement

Funding is a critical issue in movement activities. Movement funding sources include movement constituents, government, foundations, transnational NGOs, and corporations. Corrigall-Brown (2016) analyses the three major trajectories in scholarly literature on the nexus of movements and funding. These include the texture of the relationship between funders and groups that are funded. The main concern centres on how funders may influence movement actions. The second concern accentuates the impact of a movement's social context on its funding. Scholars are also concerned about the implications of corporate funding for movement activities (Corrigall-Brown 2016). One major finding in research on movement funding is that funders may engage in channelling movements away from more controversial or contentious actions to moderate goals, projects, and provision of services (Jalali 2013; Corrigall-Brown 2016). Over time, this may lead to loss of vitality in a movement (Zweigenhaft and Domhoff 1997). A movement may gradually abandon its main objective as it engages in widening its focal concerns (Minkoff and Powell 2006).

While government funding for social movements fighting for social justice in the Global South is virtually non-existent or considered anathema to movement objective and survival due to concerns about co-optation, some grassroots movements in the Global North actively seek state funding. Foreign donor support provides a source of funding for movements in the Global South. However, the impact of foreign aid on social movements and NGOs in the Global South has been found to be largely inimical due to its three-pronged 'unintended effects' (Jalali 2013: 60). These include resource dependency. Such grassroots movements may reject local political alliances in favour of foreign ones and may become fragmented, bureaucratized, and self-perpetuating and preoccupied with the fear of losing funding. They may also become infected with 'projectitis' disease—becoming concerned with being seen to be 'doing' or executing projects rather than seeking to influence key actors (Jalali 2013: 60–61). Besides, the capacity of such movements to engage in mass mobilization declines over time as the free-rider problem sets in. Jalali (2013): 55) draws on evidence from Brazil, Pakistan, Uzbekistan, India, Romania, Uzbekistan, and South Africa, among others, and argues that international support decouples movements from their constituents' support and transforms 'conflict movements into consensus movements that follow an institutional, resource-dependent, non-conflictual strategy with no deep roots in the community'.

For #BBOG, state funding negates what the movement represents and feeds into the government's narrative, which impugns the integrity of the movement. Therefore, *#BBOG takes enormous pride in being a self-funded grassroots movement.* In its early days, the movement made a decision not to accept any form of donation or assistance because #BBOG did not require a lot of money for its activities. The direct financial cost of running the movement centres on the cost of posters, banners, stickers, t-shirts, and other insignia of the movement. These are relatively low-cost. Members contribute money for these materials. Some more affluent #BBOG members routinely pay for materials needed by the group.

Foreign NGOs, foundations, and agencies funded by foreign governments have made numerous efforts to provide financial assistance to #BBOG, particularly between 2014 and 2015 (multiple interviewees). The movement has consistently turned down such offers of assistance. #BBOG's argument is that it wishes to remain autonomous and self-funded. The refusal to accept funding has enhanced the authenticity and legitimacy of #BBOG. It earned the movement tremendous respect even among the ranks of its opponents. General Chris Olukolade, Director of Defence Information and the face of the military's war against Boko Haram during the Jonathan administration, noted, in summer 2015, that #BBOG was 'With due respect . . . noble . . . and commendable'.⁵⁰ This was a remarkable statement from someone who had been publicly criticized on numerous occasions by #BBOG.

The decision to not accept funding was unacceptable to some members. Ezekwesili notes that some members who did not have altruistic intentions left after quickly realizing that there was no money to be shared by being part of the group. The decision to not accept funding was also predicated on the need to avoid providing fodder to the government's narrative about being funded by entities that were opposed to the government. #BBOG was concerned that accepting funding from any sources was a slippery slope that could ultimately destroy the credibility of the movement (Ezekwesili and Yesufu, #BBOG leaders).

#BBOG is far from a monolithic movement. The decision not to accept funding from donors was one of the issues that threatened the cohesion of the movement between 2014 and 2016 in particular. Some #BBOG members who have remained committed to the movement since it began strongly disagree with the movement leadership's refusal to accept donations. They believe the movement could have more direct and immediate impact on the families and communities of the kidnapped girls. They argue that funds offered by donors could be used to support the poor, rural-based families of the kidnapped girls and displaced community members and provide counselling and educational services in the areas that have been affected by Boko Haram (Interviewees 07 and 36).⁵¹ Some members also argue that #BBOG prioritized the image and integrity of its leaders to the detriment of providing concrete support for victims of Boko Haram (Interviewee 32 and several others).

However, Ezekwesili believes that the movement's stance on funding has been vindicated. For instance, one organization, Africa Support and Empowerment Initiative (AFRISEI), led by Hadiza Buhari-Bello, a daughter of President Muhammadu Buhari, and the Peace Corps of Nigeria organized a fundraiser in Abuja in October 2016. The event had the theme 'Official inauguration and signing of memorandum of understanding (MOU) on the Chibok Girls Endowment Project'. The #BBOG insignia formed the backdrop at the event. #BBOG released a statement arguing that

> We are shocked, perplexed and completely dumbfounded to see the bold inscription of our hard-earned name, #BringBackOurGirls, on the event's

---

⁵⁰ General Olukolade did complain about some individuals in the group, whom he accused of being job-seekers. His perspective, and those of other participants on #BBOG vis-à-vis the rescue of the girls, is analysed in Chapter 5.

⁵¹ Interviewee 07: female #BBOG member; personal interview, Abuja, June 2016. Interviewee 36: female #BBOG member; personal interview, Abuja, June 2016.

backdrop. We state categorically that we are not party to the said event and have absolutely no information of its origin. We urge the general public to disregard attempts at linking our movement to this highly suspicious event.

#BBOG threatened legal action on the attempt to 'smear our movement'. Ezekwesili also tweeted to the president's daughter, 'What's hard to understand? From the outset in 2014, DECIDED that the Movement shall NEVER be mired in DONATIONS. Simple . . . WE DON'T RAISE FUNDS. If your organization is RAISING FUNDS, don't call it "BBOG STAKEHOLDERS". ETHICS matter, not so?' (cited in Ogbeche 2016, emphasis original). She informed the researcher that some members who were opposed to the idea of not accepting funding have seen the wisdom of the decision and are glad that the group took the decision and can categorically state that they have no funders and are not beholden to anyone or organization. She believes that the refusal to transmute into an NGO funding model is a fundamental part of the legitimacy and credibility of the movement. This is a major philosophical difference and source of contention in the movement. Prominent members of #BBOG in Lagos, such as Aisha Muhammed Oyebode, daughter of former Head of State General Murtala Mohammed, have partnered with the government of President Buhari to provide humanitarian services in the Northeast. This has put social distance between leaders of #BBOG in Lagos and Abuja.[52]

The #BBOG experience regarding funding has important implications for grassroots advocacy. First, accepting funding might, in fact, necessarily refocus the objective of a grassroots movement to a service delivery organization. Over time, tactics such as street protests, days of action, and marches would be replaced by specific donor-driven projects. Second, opponents can be handed a strategic victory if external funds are accepted by a social movement organization. Given the politically charged nature of the Chibok kidnapping, the efforts of the Jonathan government to cast #BBOG as an opposition tool, and the president's belief that Western powers conspired to make him lose the 2015 elections, the movement could be enormously tainted by accepting funding from donors.[53] These issues demonstrate the importance of a movement's socio-political context in decisions about funding. Movement activists must make hard decisions about the consequences of accepting funding, analyse each avenue of funding, and consider its implications for their legitimacy and credibility. The third implication of #BBOG's stance on funding concerns the

---

[52] I return to this theme in Chapter 4.
[53] However, the decision of the movement to maintain its stance despite the change in government in May 2015 provides an interesting variable (see Chapter 5).

question of whether it could have done, or could be doing, more for its constituency. One #BBOG activist argues that 'one mistake that we keep making is that we keep saying Bring the Girls Back (i.e. through protest), we are not interested in if they come back, what next. Do we have the capacity or means to rehabilitate these girls? We don't' (Interviewee 36).[54]

The #BBOG decision on funding was influenced partly by the stance of its leaders on its core objective (the need for transparency), the realities of Nigeria's patrimonial system, and toxic political climate. Funding is a major issue for social movements all over the world. However, funding of social movements in developing societies tends to be far more politically charged—whether from international or national, governmental or non-governmental sources. Each social movement must evaluate its cause, core values, and social position within a given socio-political, cultural, and economic context in making such decisions.

Conclusion

The #BBOG movement continues a contemporary wave of women-led social movements in Africa. The contemporary, women-led social movements emerged in the 1990s as relatively autonomous entities concerned with human rights and change in the structures of society affecting women's lives in Africa. This chapter situates #BBOG within the political process of its external environment. It also provides insight into how the movement coordinated protests with relevant NGOs, CBOs, and social and traditional media, as well as its constituency. The chapter unpacks the backstage of the #BBOG movement that had not been previously considered in available literature on #BBOG. #BBOG protests are extremely well-coordinated events. There has been only one unplanned or spontaneous #BBOG protest since 2014. This chapter contributes to understanding the #BBOG movement: its formation, core values, symbolisms, organizational structure, and how activists strategized for the rescue of the Chibok girls. The chapter also highlights #BBOG protest tactics—the daily sit-out, days of action, the Chibok girls' ambassador tactic, and the annual Chibok girls' lecture. The chapter unpacks the rigour, choreography, and backstage of #BBOG's protest tactics.

The chapter also contributes to the literature on social movement communication process in an age seemingly dominated by internet activism. While a lot

---

[54] Female #BBOG member; personal interview, Abuja, June 2017.

of attention has been focused on #BBOG's use of social media, in reality, the movement relies on a hybridized communication process—which combines the credibility of traditional media with the instantaneity and social media's time–space transcendence. #BBOG's on-the-ground mobilization efforts and use of traditional media speak to the need for scholars and activists to carefully approach the utility of social media in movement mobilization. This is not to downplay the utility of social media. Rather, it is intended to offer more nuance on the use of social media by movements which deploy physical mobilization. Scholars and activists need to view social media as part of social movement toolkit. The chapter ends with an analysis of funding issues and the challenges movements, particularly in the developing world, may face. Chapter 3 interrogates the ideational framework of #BBOG, the internationalization of its framing, and the consequences.

3
Framing of the #BringBackOurGirls movement

Lessons for grassroots advocacy

Introduction

Framing is central to social movement activities. Social movement activists invest time and resources to strategize on particular ways in which their cause should be portrayed, analysed, and meaningfully represented. In essence, activists seek to depict reality in intelligible and relatable ways. This privileges a particular genre or rendering of reality. Framing is a process—a becoming rather than a being. Activists and their opponents, such as the state or rival movements, engage in an ideational battlefield. This may include contestations over events, situations, social facts or problems, and their meanings and implications for a specific constituency or wider society. Framing makes participation in collective action meaningful and helps to achieve movement goals and objectives (Snow and Benford 1988; Klandermans 1997).

The outcome of a movement is influenced by how activists and their organizations effectively frame their grievances. Framing helps to mobilize people with grievances over a particular issue, garner attention, and potentially secure support of bystanders and may serve as a counter-narrative against those construed as opponents of a movement (Snow and Benford 1988: 198). Overall, framing must have cultural resonance in the social context in which it is deployed in order to be successful. Therefore, activists must use diction, symbols, values, creed, and ethos that are relatable and appropriate within their socio-cultural context.

The stakes are high for social movements in developing countries. They are engaged in an environment in which institutions are weak and human rights protections are tenuous. The state may resort to repressive measures if movement framing is deemed too critical or aggressive. Movements in authoritarian contexts attempt a balancing act, deploying language that is intelligible to the audience and has sufficient sharpness to meaningfully convey their grievance, yet is carefully crafted to avoid unnecessarily provoking state repression. This balancing act is not always successful.

Social movements in the developing world often draw on the grammar of movements in the developed world in their attempt to make demands concerning human or women's rights, sexual or ethnic minority rights, and environmental rights, for example. Local struggles in the Global South draw on human rights, injustice, and environmental justice framing, among others. Großklaus (2015: 1255) captures the intricate nature of framing in social movements in developing countries:

> Local struggles may be transferred to the international level by appropriating the respective language. In so doing, local politics can be dealt with in 'universal' terms without having to fall back on the traditions of Western societies at the same time. It becomes possible to challenge local social realities in a language bearing foreign roots that has yet become one's own. It is local while still maintaining a semantic relation to international ('modern') frameworks of reference.

Human rights movements in Africa often strategize on, and frame their grievance to generate, international attention and intervention. For instance, the anti-apartheid movement in South Africa and diaspora deployed framing that relied on universal notions of human rights. This was catalysed by the dissemination of the images of horror of the apartheid regime. Anti-colonial movements in Africa also deployed the language of universal human rights.

Post-independence governments in Africa tend to be intolerant of demands for respect for, or expansion of, human rights, despite international norms and conventions. This creates tension between the local context and developments in the international arena regarding human rights. Bob (2002: 398) cautions, 'international developments will not affect domestic politics so obviously and directly. Instead, the national opportunity structure will dominate. This is particularly true in highly repressive states and in poor communities of the developing world.'

This chapter is concerned with one main question: *why did the #BringBackOurGirls (#BBOG) movement attract significant attention both nationally and internationally but achieve only moderate success on its goal—the release of all the school girls kidnapped by Boko Haram?* There are two main arguments in this chapter. First, the internationalization of the framing of #BBOG and the attention it generated hindered efforts of national institutional actors to rescue the girls. This means that #BBOG became the victim of its own success.

The internationalization of #BBOG framing alienated key national actors and shut avenues for collaboration. Therefore, the emphasis of #BBOG on internationalizing its framing rather than work with local actors was a strategic blunder. The chapter articulates the broader implications of the findings for social movements in the developing world.

Second, while #BBOG framing was internationalized, the core movement was not. #BBOG refused to have formal associational ties with international organizations, despite #BBOG spin-offs in other parts of the world. These operate as autonomous and organizationally loose entities concerned with occasional and ceremonial advocacy for the Chibok girls. The chapter demonstrates that the refusal to transnationalize the entire #BBOG in a conventional sense was an astute strategy that was cognizant of the movement's national political context.

This chapter is divided into four parts. The first part articulates how #BBOG conducts its core framing tasks—diagnostic, prognostic, and motivational framing (Snow and Benford 1988). The master frames of the #BBOG movement are analysed in the second section. #BBOG publicity materials, internal documents, and interviews with leaders and members are used to identify and elucidate four master frames deployed by the movement. This is the first attempt to identify and analyse the full spectrum of #BBOG framing beyond the motherist or maternalist framing. The third section focuses on the social consequences of #BBOG's framing. The final part emphasizes the need for movement advocates in Africa and other developing countries to focus on engaging with local political processes and actors rather than seeking to create global awareness and potentially internationalize their framing and/or struggle. The chapter contributes to social movement theory regarding the political process, framing, and implications of interactions of international opportunity with local context.

#BBOG and core framing tasks

Snow and Benford's (1988) conceptualization of three core framing tasks is an analytically useful tool for interrogating the ideation of a social movement organization. The first core framing task is *diagnostic framing*, which is intended to identify the problem and assign blame. The second—*prognostic framing*—creates space for explicating solutions and mechanisms for solving the problem, while the third core framing task—*motivational framing*—provides rationale for collective action (Snow and Benford 1988). This section considers how the #BBOG movement conducts the three core framing tasks.

Diagnostic framing

The #BBOG movement is unequivocal in its assessment of the locus of blame for the abduction of the Chibok girls. The #BBOG movement made a decision early on in the struggle to focus on asking the Nigerian government to 'rescue' the girls from Boko Haram rather than asking Boko Haram to 'release' the abductees (Interviewee 30). This is beyond mere semantic difference; it constitutes the nucleus of #BBOG's framing and focus of movement activities. The logic, following several intellectual debates within the #BBOG movement, is that the state has the primary responsibility to protect the lives of its citizens. Therefore, as Boko Haram is a non-state and illegitimate actor, movement activities are not directed towards the organization.

There are three individual and institutional actors within the Nigerian political process held responsible for the abduction and failure to rescue the Chibok girls. These are the presidency; the security architecture, comprising the military, police, and State Security Services; and the Borno state government. These three entities are examined to explicate why the #BBOG movement holds them responsible for the abduction and failure to rescue the Chibok girls.

The presidency of Nigeria

#BBOG articulated its stance on the Nigerian presidency within the first month of movement mobilization. #BBOG believes that 'the institutional response to their [kidnapped girls'] fate was indifference'.[1] The government's indifference is believed to be partly because of the class background of the kidnap victims and party politics.[2] Ezekwesili argues that

> to immerse the girls in the politics of contestation for power was a colossal abuse of the power of the state. You denied citizens rescue because you thought that they were taken to embarrass the state. An effective and functional nation-state would first go after whoever took the girls and then come back to the issue of the motive for taking the girls.
>
> (Ezekwesili 2015)

This speaks to the refusal of President Goodluck Jonathan to acknowledge that the Chibok girls had been kidnapped until after three weeks; the failure to

---

[1] Obiageli Ezekwesili, cited in Ibekwe (2014a).
[2] The salience of social class is discussed in the section on master frames.

order an immediate rescue, particularly within the critical first 48-hour period following the abduction, and news reports that the thinking at the presidential villa was that the opposition party in control of Borno state, where the girls were kidnapped, was merely trying to embarrass the government as the president prepared for re-election. #BBOG was disappointed that the government did not act on the Chibok issue until Chibok women marched on 29 April 2014 and #BBOG on 30 April 2014. President Jonathan began a series of media engagement from 22 May 2014 to inform the public that it was 'wrong and most unfair to suggest that there has been slow reaction' to the kidnapping incident (Elebeke and Akinboade 2014). The reaction of the president and his handlers was testament to the effectiveness of the mass mobilization of #BBOG as a lot of Nigerians did not initially believe that an abduction had taken place (Interviewees 09, 10, 12, and 30).

#BBOG blames President Goodluck Jonathan and his administration for the lax security that enabled the mass kidnapping in a zone that had been ravaged by Boko Haram since 2009, failure to protect all schools following several attacks on similar sites in the Northeast region and the assumption that the president was the victim of criminal political mercenarism[3] rather than the abductees, and, ultimately, the lackadaisical attitude towards securing the girls.

The security architecture of Nigeria

The #BBOG movement also blames the security establishment for the abduction and failure to secure all the Chibok girls. Boko Haram had begun to challenge state monopoly of force since at least July 2009. The confrontation between the police and the group led to the killing of 30 police personnel. Boko Haram's leader, Mohammed Yusuf was extrajudicially executed as retaliation for the fatalities recorded by the police. Yusuf's death occurred in 2009. Boko Haram returned in a more virulent form a year later. The organization began spectacular waves of violence targeted at schools, religious buildings, police stations, and army barracks, among others, as noted in Chapter 1.

Therefore, there was a period of at least five years between the watershed moment in the Boko Haram phenomenon—the killing of its leader—and the

---

[3] See Godwin (2015).

kidnapping of the Chibok girls. Boko Haram showed signs of its new wave of violence in 2010. Consequently, the security machinery would seem to have had ample time to secure sites and symbols of the organization's angst against the state. #BBOG blames the military, the police, and the Department of State Services (DSS) for not fully recognizing and dealing with the threat posed by Boko Haram. They are also blamed for intelligence failure. This includes the 16 April 2014 announcement of the girls' rescue, which turned out to be inaccurate.

Reports about widespread corruption, poor equipment, desertion, mutiny, sabotage, non-payment of allowances, and loss of territory as the fight against Boko Haram intensified firmly ensconced the security apparatus, particularly the military, in the diagnostic framing of the #BBOG movement.[4]

The Borno state government

The political dynamics of the Borno state government contributed to the rise of Boko Haram (Iyekekpolo 2020). This includes the patronage afforded Boko Haram in order to secure votes for the former Governor of Borno, Ali Modu Sheriff (Akinola 2015). The alleged sponsorship of Boko Haram and subsequent falling out of the former governor with Boko Haram over the failure to implement a puritanical version of Sharia law played a major role in the violence perpetrated by the organization (Oyewole 2013).[5] The Jonathan administration insisted that the 'Governor of Borno State is culpable, and have [sic] questions to answer about the abduction of the Chibok girls. This is because he broke his promise to guarantee the security of those girls and he allowed them to be abducted' (*Premium Times* 2015a). While the facts are difficult to verify in the toxic political theatre, #BBOG blames the government of Borno, particularly the Modu Sheriff administration, for promoting religious zealotry in the state and lack of security at schools.

Prognostic framing

The #BBOG movement's diagnosis of the Chibok issue includes suggestions of mechanisms for solving the problem. The solutions proffered by #BBOG

---

[4] See *Daily Post* (2014). See also the trial of the former National Security Adviser Sambo Dasuki for embezzlement and illegal disbursement of arms procurement funds (Tukur 2015b).
[5] Sheriff's successor, Kashim Shettima, was also embroiled in allegations of using Boko Haram operatives to kill his political rival for the nomination of his party as governor.

are intertwined with its demands. The group's document, 'The ABC of our demands', states 13 related issues.[6] These demands are summarized below:

1. rescue of the 219 Chibok girls by the federal government of Nigeria;
2. an apology from the government for the failure that led to the abduction;
3. an apology for the failure of governance that caused failure to rescue the Chibok girls for over 400 days;[7]
4. a demand for the government to device strategies for dealing with the emergence and growth of various religious sects in Nigeria;
5. a demand for a 'structured feedback and communication system that is composed of the Federal and Borno State Governments through designated security and ministerial authorities, the parents of the abducted girls. the Chibok (KADA) community, and citizens, through the #BringBackOurGirls group';
6. a demand for the implementation of a 'global best practice system of Verification, Authentication and Reunification System (VARS) abducted citizens who are rescued';
7. a demand for the establishment of a Commission of Inquiry for 'Accountability on Abduction and Rescue of our #ChibokGirls';
8. a request that all Nigerians join the #BBOG movement to continue the advocacy for the rescue of the 219 Chibok girls as well as rescue and rehabilitation of other missing persons in Nigeria;
9. a demand for the establishment of a 'Missing Persons Bureau' [sic];
10. a demand for the government to '(f)ormally re-affirm the legitimacy and relevance of the #BringBackOurGirls campaign as a purely citizen contribution';
11. a demand for the government to 'adopt and utilize BBOG Citizens' Solution document to counter insurgency efforts';
12. a demand for the government to 'adopt the #BringBackOurGirls *Accountability Matrix*' in order to ensure effective communication between Nigeria's security apparatus and citizens;
13. a demand for the government to put into consideration the adoption of 'Community/Proximity Policing'.

---

[6] See 'The ABC of our demands', http://www.bringbackourgirls.ng/downloads. Accessed 16 March 2016.
[7] At the time the document was written.

Several of these demands/panaceas transcend the struggle to rescue the Chibok girls and reflect the growing accommodation of related human rights issues in the #BBOG movement's mono-focal objective. The demands encompass three categories. First, there are central demands—numbers, 1–4, 7, and 8. These demands are directly related to the rescue and rehabilitation of the Chibok girls. Second, policy-related demands are contained in numbers 4–6, 9, and 13.[8] These are policy suggestions aimed at engendering structural changes. The third category comprises institutionalizing demands: 10–12. This category of demands concerns attempts to legitimize and institutionalize the #BBOG movement.

All categories of demands have been channelled almost exclusively to the Federal government of Nigeria. Questions such as 'Why are they not taking their protest to Boko Haram to release the girls?'[9] have been asked by opponents of the movement. The movement organization's framing in this regard is articulated in legal terms. The movement's position is that directing their demands to the government

> recognizes the constitutional responsibility, power, and mandate of government as enshrined in Section 14(2) of the Nigerian Constitution wherein it is stated '... *the security and welfare of the people shall be the primary purpose of government*'. By directing its campaign to the government, the group is invariably communicating that it has reposed its confidence in government's ability to live up to that responsibility.
> (#BBOG publicity material; italics original)

Providing answers to such questions with reference to the government's responsibility under the Constitution provides a discursively powerful way to remind opponents that the government does have primary role for security. Such reference to the Constitution serves as a relatively incontrovertible way to challenge the movement's critics to deny that the government is the right entity to focus on rather than terrorists.

#BBOG produced a 'Citizens' solution to end terrorism: The voice of Nigerians' manual through crowdsourcing on social media. The manual contains 10 solutions to the problem of terrorism in Nigeria. These include placing citizens

---

[8] Demand no. 8 may also be embedded in this category as it relates to rehabilitation of all missing persons in Nigeria.

[9] #BBOG publicity material. This has been one of the major questions posed to #BBOG by its opponents. The material contains 12 questions and answers on #BBOG, members, *modus operandi*, etc.

as key actors in the war against terror, financing and rebuilding the security apparatus, local security governance, successful prosecution and ensuring that the trail of budgetary allocations is followed (or 'follow the money'). Other solutions concern cross-border movements and citizens' identification, risk assessment and mitigation, counter-radicalization and the promotion of peace education, and social welfare.[10]

Motivational framing and mobilization of #BBOG members

#BBOG has devised various speech acts to motivate members. First, #BBOG members are reminded daily at the sit-out that innocent young girls are still missing. The presence at the sit-out of family members of the missing girls and occasional visits by some who managed to escape constitutes a major motivational technique. Such young girls and their families are often given the opportunity to speak about their experiences. Such testimonies by persons directly affected have played a huge role in helping members continue with the struggle. One of the strategic team members stated that, as attendance at the daily sit-out waned,

> one of the things we usually say to ourselves when we stand up was that if I will be the only one standing for the Chibok girls, I will ... So for some reason, everybody took up that sense of individuality, that should anything happen, and no one wants to stand, I will be here standing. And those people who usually will stand up to say that are the ones still standing till today. A lot of people have fallen by the way side.
>
> (Interviewee 30)

Therefore, members interpreted continuing the #BBOG struggle as coterminous with symbolically 'standing' for the missing girls. The symbolic act also became increasingly individualized as each member was encouraged to be the only one standing if nobody else did.[11]

Second, performative chants and slogans at the sit-out have played a role in generating excitement for the struggle. Each sit-out begins and ends with the following 'call- and-response' chants:

---

[10] See the #BBOG movement, Abuja, 2014, 'Citizens' solutions to end terrorism', http://www.bringbackourgirls.ng/citizens-solution-to-end-terrorism. Accessed 17 March 2016. This chapter uses a revised (hard-copy) version which is not available online.

[11] Participant observation at the sit-out, July–August 2015, Abuja.

CALL: What are we demanding?
RESPONSE: BringBackOurGirls Now and Alive!
CALL: What are we asking?
RESPONSE: The truth, nothing but the truth!
CALL: What do we want?
RESPONSE: Our girls back now and alive!
CALL: When will we stop?
RESPONSE: Not until our girls are back and alive!
CALL: When will we stop?
RESPONSE: Not without our daughters!
CALL: What's our core value?
RESPONSE: HUMANITEEDS!
ALL: The fight for the Chibok girls is the fight for the soul of Nigeria and the world![12]

Any member who indicates interest in addressing the group, asking a question, or making a comment would begin with 'What are we demanding?' before stating their contribution. While this may have become stale after several years, it ensures that each member is reminded of the reason for the gathering.

Third, the daily sit-out also involves a media report period when every member is encouraged to inform the gathering on news reports about the missing girls, activities of the military vis-à-vis the rescue of the girls, and coverage of the movement in the media. This ensures that members are kept up to date about the struggle. This also gives members the sense that they are part of something extremely important given the extensive national and international media coverage (Focus group discussion (FGD) 2).[13]

The relatively open atmosphere—freedom to ask questions, make comments, critique the leadership (including a former federal minister), and opportunity to contribute to the direction of the movement[14]—also engenders a sense that everyone is important.[15]

Furthermore, the core values developed by the movement and its iteration have contributed to mobilizing members. The backronym 'HUMANITEEDS'

---

[12] Most of the slogans were composed by Obiageli Ezekwesili while Aisha Yesufu, the former ST chair of the #BBOG movement, added the line on the fight for the soul of Nigeria (Interviewee 30).

[13] Two male members of #BBOG; July 2015, Abuja.

[14] There were concerns in late 2014 that decision-making was being monopolized by the strategic team. That led to the expansion of the strategic team and more robust discussions on directions and strategies of the movement organization.

[15] The reputation of the likes of Obiageli Ezekwesili was instrumental in the decision of many to join and remain in the #BBOG movement (Interviewee 01, male member of #BBOG and ethnic Kibaku from Chibok, where the girls were kidnapped; personal interview, July 2015, Abuja).

was developed to provide the philosophical underpinnings of the movement, as stated in Chapter 2. The core values of Hope, Unity, Motivation, Affability, Nationalism, Integrity, Transparency, Empathy, Equity, Discipline, and Sacrifice are reiterated at every sit-out to motivate members.

#BBOG places emphasis on the shared humanity of all and the need to overcome ethnic and religious divisions. This is extremely important, given the composition of the movement. Several members indicated the importance of the core values of the group. One member from the Chibok community, where the girls were kidnapped argues that

> this group has shown human feeling, what we call humanity, the real definition of humanity you will find in this group. Because there is no group that would face these kind of challenges and yet is standing. I doubt you would get such group in Nigeria. But because people from various background ... come together, then they encourage one another ... If not for this group, I would have fall back but because of the encouragement I got from this group and because of what this group preaches, they preach humanity, they preach equality, they preach change ... This group is so wonderful.
> (Interviewee 01)

In summary, speech acts, performative chants, regular media reports, the processes of deliberation and decision-making, the sheer force of personality of Ezekwesili and other co-conveners, and the core values of the group constitute some of the major mobilizational tools for the #BBOG movement. The following section interrogates the master frames of the #BBOG movement organization.

Master frames of the #BBOG movement

A frame defines a situation vis-à-vis the principles of organization of the social and how an individual or group subjectively experiences events (Goffman 1973: 10–11).[16] A frame is an 'an interpretive schemata that simplifies and condenses the "world out there" by selectively punctuating and encoding objects, situations, events, experiences, and sequences of actions within one's present or past environment' (Snow and Benford 1992: 133–155). The intrinsically complex interplay of political actors—state and non-state—guarantees

---

[16] An abridged version of this section was first published in my piece in Third World Quarterly (see Oriola 2021a).

that framing involves competing assessments, definitions, and understandings of a situation (Oriola [2013] 2016). Framing is *contentious* because it may challenge existing frames and/or radically differ from them (Benford and Snow 2000: 611–639). #BBOG has engaged in a fairly sophisticated framing of the abduction for multifarious audiences. The audiences include the Nigerian government, security apparatus, religious communities, and the public. The audience also includes transnational non-governmental organizations (NGOs) such as the Malala Fund; multilateral organizations such as the United Nations (UN); and state actors such as the United States, the United Kingdom, Canada, China, and influential global elites. Framing has played a fundamental role in the international attention #BBOG has garnered. This has produced serious consequences, as demonstrated in this chapter.

This section draws on #BBOG publicity materials, internal documents, and interviews with several leaders and members of the movement to identify and analyse four major master frames in the #BBOG movement. These are the *motherist, human rights, girl-child's right to education*, and the *state failure framing*. These master narrative techniques are analysed below.

The motherist or maternalist framing

The motherist or maternalist framing 'refers to elements of motherhood, mothering, and maternal identity deployed to evoke meanings within a given context and elicit participation and/or support of collective action' (Carreon and Moghadam 2015: 19). Motherist framing has a long history in social movement activism. Anti-war protesters, pro-democracy groups, and anti-poverty/austerity activists, as well as movements challenging or supporting the status quo, have used the motherist or maternal framing for collective mobilization (Carreon and Moghadam 2015: 19). The *Madres de la Plaza de Mayo* is one of the most notable motherist social movements (Howe 2006: 43–50). The *Madres* accentuated their role as mothers of victims who had been kidnapped or killed to challenge oppressive structures and state-organized terror in Argentina. The *Madres* 'reinterpreted' motherhood and transformed it from its traditional garb to a force for social praxis (Howe 2006: 43).

Scholarly analyses of movements utilizing motherist framing have engaged conceptually with its use for 'strategic gender interests' and/or 'practical gender interests' (Valiente 2003: 241). Strategic gender interests relate to demands that challenge structural bias against women (2003: 241). Practical gender interests concern more immediate demands such as improvement in the health sector, well-equipped and affordable schools for children, and lower food prices (2003: 241). These demands are intertwined with the centrality and primary care-giver role of an overwhelming number of women. #BBOG's use of maternalist framing is nested in practical gender interests. The rescue of the Chibok girls is the sole objective of #BBOG, as stated earlier. Therefore, #BBOG does not necessarily challenge entrenched structures of society holding back women and girls. Rather, it emphasizes the facticity of the *motherhood* experience. Motherist framing is used to demand that women in general, and mothers in particular, want the Chibok girls rescued.

As previously noted, the mothers of the abducted girls in Chibok organized the first protest for the rescue of the Chibok girls on 29 April 2014. However, factors such as social class, minority status, geographic location, and limited media coverage ensured that the Chibok mothers' maternal identity did not generate any momentum. This is congruent with research on the role of class and ethnicity in the ability of maternal identity to serve as a cultural resource (Milman 2014).

Mothers who were well placed in society soon intervened. Hadiza Bala Usman, who led the efforts for the first physical #BBOG protest a day after the Chibok mothers' protest (30 April 2014) 'started it from the angle of... mothers that are agitating for other mothers whose children have been taken' (Interviewee 30).[17] The #BBOG movement's mobilization of women through their social positionality as mothers strongly resonated in the population. Such cultural resonance is a fundamental characteristic of successful framing. The success of this framing was demonstrated in the estimated 2,000 persons who attended the first protest in Abuja, despite inclement weather. This was a major accomplishment, given that the protest occurred prior to the formation of a coherent group.

Motherist framing was used as the nucleus of #BBOG ideation at the start of mobilization. Large banners bearing a central message have been part of the aesthetics of #BBOG protests. A publicity material titled 'Would you be silent if your daughter was missing?' contains a paragraph which articulates this framing:

> The girls could have been our sisters, daughters, cousins and nieces. Our ability to imagine the unfortunate position of the girls and their families drives us to rise and act in the manner that we would, if the girls were our own. What if your daughter, sister, niece or cousin was among the girls? How would you feel? What would you want someone to do in the name of such grief? Would you appreciate it if someone was there for you?

[17] This view is widely shared by participants.

This framing approach interpellates the audience and urges them to walk in the shoes of the parents, particularly mothers of the kidnapped girls. The evidence indicating the efficacy of this approach is overwhelming. Its appeal to parents is striking. One participant notes that she joined the movement because of the 'fact that I have a daughter and what later kept me is the fact that I was just like them 24 years ago' (Interviewee 12). Maternalist framing makes people connect the predicament of the girls with their own lived experiences. This narrative ensures that the audience views the kidnapped girls as, or sees in them, their own children. Michelle Obama, for instance, states that 'In these girls, Barack and I see our own daughters. We see their hopes, their dreams, and we can only imagine the anguish their parents are feeling right now' (McVeign 2014).

Maternal framing is anchored on, and reflects, patriarchal ideational presuppositions about gender roles and the 'nature' of motherhood. It reinforces and yet strategically calls to question the traditional role of men as protectors of society. This framing relies on traditional gender constructions to cast the kidnapped girls as victims and 'our girls' or 'our daughters' as worthy of being rescued. It draws attention to the facticity of *femaleness* and the increased risks that the victims are exposed to because of their gender identity. This has several tactical advantages that are connected with the normative articulation of gender: vulnerability, innocence, fecundity, bearers of society's future, beauty, youth, peace-loving women, and purity. The frame's micro-mechanics is that vulnerable young girls are missing, and mothers are demanding their release from the men, who are the protectors of society. Mothers tend to enjoy greater 'discursive opportunity structure' than other women and men in general (Valiente 2003: 258). Making claims on the Nigerian government through the prism of motherist framing provides a strong basis of legitimacy, particularly because they are acting on behalf of others. This 'social motherhood' identity (Di Marco 2009: 53) is further enhanced by the social class status of the conveners of #BBOG—powerful and well-connected women from the top echelons of society with activist leanings. What is unique is that these women are acting in support of poor and underprivileged members of society.[18]

One notable problematic of motherist master framing is that it is constituted by, and reflective of, existing gender relations. Its propagation naturalizes the man–woman divide and its attendant gendered sociological ideals and realities. Therefore, as noted in Chapter 2, #BBOG has been criticized for

---

[18] This is not without contradictions, given that some of them had either served in cabinet positions at the highest level or had spouses who had held high office.

advocating for the missing girls on the basis of their relationship with other natural persons (e.g. mothers, fathers, etc.), that is as claimable beings rather than focusing on the girls as right-bearing persons.[19]

However, the #BBOG framing language in this regard is the grammar that the society understands. It is one that aligns and resonates with societal beliefs. This framing is pragmatic rather than revolutionary. Lacking the luxury of feminist analysis, pedagogy, or critique, the #BBOG movement's use of motherist framing puts into cognizance the male-dominated, heteronormative, and non-egalitarian nature of the society. Such framing does not turn patriarchy on its head but *instrumentalizes* patriarchal notions about gender roles and hence engages in relatable gender performativity. The use of maternalist framing by #BBOG is neither feminist in orientation nor traditionalist (Michel 2012: 22–37; Carreon and Moghadam 2015). It is a pragmatic response to a particular social problem.

The human rights framing

Perspectives about the origins of human rights differ. There is a school of thought that believes human rights 'are the rights that one has because one is human being' (Donnelly 2008: 123). Another school of thought considers 'human rights as claims upon society' (Henkin 1990) or 'reasonable demands (or claims) against humanity' (Shue 1980; cited in Sjoberg et al. 2001: 25). Sjoberg, et al. (2001: 25) argue that human rights are 'claims made by persons in diverse social and cultural systems upon "organized power relationships" in order to advance the dignity of . . . human beings'. #BBOG argues that the Chibok girls have human rights because they are 'human beings and are bequeathed with inalienable right to life' (Ezekwesili 2015). This demonstrates #BBOG's approach to human rights—people have human rights by virtue of being human simpliciter.[20]

Human rights framing was gradually included in the repertoire of the movement as #BBOG sought to raise global awareness about the missing girls. This requires symbolically appealing to a common denominator—humanity. #BBOG adopts a universalistic human rights discourse nested in the idea of global citizenship. #BBOG argues that their members are 'not all from Chibok but our sense of shared humanity makes it legitimate to connect with the

---

[19] See Loken (2014).
[20] I return to this theme later in the chapter.

missing girls and their people'.[21] #BBOG also emphasizes that the 'key element of human rights is the dignity of human life' and that 'regardless of differences in geography, culture, race and other markers of difference, we must dignify each other's right to life' (Ezekwesili 2015). This framing therefore emphasizes a sense of collective responsibility for what may not directly concern the audience. Framing local issues as international problems is not new.[22] It draws actors from different parts of the world into the issue in order to pressurize governments and organizations into intervening or assisting to make changes. This globalized rights narrative is meant to construe the issue as a transnational matter regarding a shared humanity, which therefore must not go down as just another African crisis.

This framing is used in several interrelated dimensions. First, it is deployed to justify and legitimize the existence of the #BBOG movement. Questions were being raised about why #BBOG was 'crying more than the bereaved'[23] and whether or not the movement existed (in late 2014 and early 2015) as a political tool of the opposition party, the All Progressives Congress (APC). The latter issue was particularly problematic, given that some key leaders of the movement were politically active in the opposition party.

Second, #BBOG used human rights framing to highlight the insouciant attitude of the Nigerian government vis-à-vis the kidnapping of the girls. There had been varieties of opportunistic kidnappings all over Nigeria apart from oil insurgency-related kidnappings in the Delta region (Oriola [2013] 2016). The kidnapping of parents of some government ministers, spouses of legislators, and other celebrities had increased (BBC 2012b). A fairly standard social matrix had also been established: families of victims quietly paid ransom to kidnappers. The police intervened predominantly in cases where the kidnap victim was a member of the elite. Therefore, #BBOG's argument is that the Chibok girls' rescue was not a government priority because they were the 'daughters of the lowest income group of the society' (Ezekwesili 2015). The group's argument hinges on the idea that 'when consideration is given to people's socio-economic or political status in the enjoyment of rights, such a human rights framework is no longer consistent with the unalloyed interpretation of the fact that every human being has a right to life and a right to freedom' (Ezekwesili 2015). Consequently, a social class dimension is introduced to the narrative to emphasize that the Chibok girls are also bearers of

---

[21] #BBOG publicity material no. 1.
[22] See Bob (2005).
[23] #BBOG publicity material no. 1.

human rights and deserve the deployment of the appurtenances of state power for their rescue.

Third, the global community was interpellated in the human rights framing. Leaders of the movement granted series of media interviews and delivered speeches around the world to ensure global engagement on the issue. This has helped ensure that efforts to rescue the girls are not abandoned.[24] Global days of action are regularly organized by #BBOG to keep alive the memories of the girls. The focus of this trajectory in the human rights framing is to provide a rationale for the involvement of entities who are not necessarily connected to sub-Saharan Africa.

The argument centres on the fact that the Chibok girls have the right to life 'simply because they are human beings; not because they are men or women, rich or poor, black or white' (Ezekwesili 2015). Framing the narrative this way provides a liberal democratic, gendered, and race-conscious perspective, which Western audiences are familiar with. Western audiences are positioned by #BBOG as entities that can make a huge difference in putting pressure on the government. For instance, while presenting her keynote at the 2015 International Week at the University of Alberta, Ezekwesili informed her predominantly white Canadian audience that 'As people of this same planet, this [the Chibok girls' issue] is a symbol for us and it is one that we must not be careless with.' This framing also serves to legitimize external assistance or intervention by other states. It suggests that any intervention aimed at rescuing the girls was justified, given that human lives were at stake.

The girl-child's right to education framing

The use of the girl-child's right to education framing by the #BBOG movement draws on the lessons from Boko Haram's massacre of 59 boys at the Federal Government College, Buni Yadi, Yobe state, on 25 February 2014. As previously stated the incident was momentous for issues relating to the education of the girl-child: 'Teachers at the school in Buni Yadi said the gunmen gathered the female students together before telling them to go away and get married and to abandon their education' (BBC 2014a). Boko Haram's approach to the female gender was revealed in the incident: women existed in the ideological universe of the terrorist organization for purposes of marriage and procreation. Therefore, for Boko Haram, female education was incompatible with true religion and was a waste of women's reproductive capabilities.

---

[24] #BBOG publicity material no. 1.

Consequently, #BBOG's use of the girl-child's right to education framing spotlights (a) the symbolism of the space in which the girls were kidnapped, (b) the significance of the efforts of the girls to acquire education, (c) the #BBOG movement's counter-narrative to Boko Haram's perspectives on female education, (d) the subliminal message the kidnapping sends to girls in Northern Nigeria and other developing regions of the world, and (e) overall implications of the incident for the girl-child's education.

The education of the girl-child in Northern Nigeria has been particularly challenging. Cultural bias (e.g. prioritization of male children), poverty, and inadequate access to education, among other factors, have led to low enrolment of girls in schools. Early marriage has also played a major role (Erulka and Bello 2007). #BBOG recognizes that the kidnapped girls (aged 14–21 years) represent a small number among many who may never go to school. Therefore, the Chibok kidnapping has the potential to concretize the resolve of parents against sending their female children to school. It can also become emblematic of the risks of going to school in a culture that places low value on female education. One speech act explicates the scope and use of the girl-child's right to education:

> As global citizens we have to realize that if we allow the story of the Chibok girls to end without a concerted determination to solving it, we would lose our credibility in telling the girl-child anywhere in the world that the best thing they can do is to get an education. We would have failed the girl-child hugely. If 219 of them that listened to us and agreed with us that education is the most effective tool for social and economic mobility . . . If we move on without seeing the end of this as positively as possible, we lack the credibility to advocate for the education of the of the girl-child anywhere in the world.
> (Ezekwesili 2015)

The construction of the girl-child's right to education framing demonstrates that the location of the kidnapping is symbolic, and the girls showed resolve to have gone to school against all odds. It also emphasizes that the kidnapping episode feeds into, and draws on, the cultural bias against the education of the girl-child.

This framing encourages the audience to consider that the kidnapping incident has broad consequences. It draws attention to the Chibok kidnapping as an affront on the global efforts to educate the girl-child. This framing aligns with well-established concerns in the UN and other global organizations about the impediments to the girl-child's education (UNICEF 2016). The girl-child's right to education framing is therefore founded on an ongoing global narrative.

The state failure framing

Nigeria is 'characterized ... by a ruling class without vision or will and a populace not yet awakened to its power and density (Marenin 1988: 222). The unwillingness and incapacity of the state to meet the massive expectations placed upon its shoulders have undermined its standing, power, and legitimacy' (Marenin 1988: 222). This speaks to state failure. Scholars have examined factors such as incapacity to monopolize the means of violence, breakdown of authority, the law and the political order, and endangering the lives of citizens as some of the basic characteristics of a failed state (Helman and Ratner 1992; Zartman 1995; Ignatieff 2002). While the debate over state failure remains unsettled, failed states demonstrate certain characteristics. The 'capacity to execute any form of policy has quite simply evaporated and its place has been taken, at least to some extent, by churches and religious solidarities, a burgeoning informal economy, and military organizations and militias or other armed movements' (Bayart et al. 1999: 19). The state is reduced to a 'legal fiction' (Bayart et al. 1999: 21) because state bureaucracies are rendered ineffective by personalization of political power and the rise of extra-state machineries. The incapacity of the Nigerian state is exacerbated by what Ake calls the 'the overpoliticization of social life'. Ake argues that the 'Nigerian state appears to intervene everywhere' Merenin (1988: 221).

Ake presupposes that overpoliticization is coterminous with interventionist overreach. The Nigerian state, however, often adopts a matrix of non-intervention when the *talakawa* ('the poor') are the actors in harm's way and/or state interests are not directly threatened. This appears to have been the case with the Chibok girls' kidnapping. The government over-politicized the Chibok kidnapping without intervening. The Jonathan administration was initially unconvinced that the Chibok girls were missing. The thinking was that the Borno state government, which was headed by a member of the opposition party, was merely playing politics. As it became clear that the girls were genuinely missing, the standpoint of the Jonathan administration was that (a) the girls were kidnapped to embarrass the government and make it look incompetent in an election season, while (b) #BBOG was established to 'internationalize the embarrassment' (Godwin 2015).

#BBOG activists were displeased at the failure of the state to perform its basic responsibility to protect lives. The framing of the grievance of the #BBOG movement began to change to a more critical narrative as the rescue of the girls failed to materialize. Movement activists had envisaged a swift return of the girls and therefore became increasingly frustrated by the inaction of the government (Interviewees 06, 07, 08, 09, 10, and others).[25] The government set up a fact-finding team on 2 May 2014 (18 days after the kidnapping) to ascertain the number and identity of the girls who were kidnapped, how many had escaped, why their school remained open to boarding students when other schools had been shut and to 'articulate a framework for a multi-stakeholder action for the rescue of the missing girls' (Channels Television 2014). This was perceived as mere bureaucratese and lack of urgency.

Consequently, the framing of the movement became increasing dominated by a failed state narrative. The earlier motherist framing technique gradually became de-emphasized as activists became frustrated by the inertia of the Jonathan government. The language, diction, and tone of the messaging turned increasingly non-diplomatic and confrontational. #BBOG began to engage its audiences on the ineptitude, corruption, and degeneracy of the Nigerian state.

There are four key elements in the use of state failure framing by #BBOG. First, it is a poignant critique of the Nigerian government (hence, the—predominantly—men who run it). Second, it is aimed at compelling the government to act through a 'language of international embarrassment' (Interviewee 30), and third, it is directed at the international community to put pressure on its Nigerian counterpart to act. This framing is centred on a structured and strategic appeal to the international community. It hinges on the hope that the international community would help with the rescue if the Nigerian government failed to act.

Consequences of the #BBOG movement's framing

Transnationalization assists local struggles to benefit from networks and resources. Such transnationalization has at its epicentre ties with international NGOs in the United States and Western Europe. Tarrow (2005) articulates the short-term nature of opportunities for coalition-building, externalization of claims by local actors and problems such as cultural differences, entrapment in local conflict situations when a transnational movement seeks to become domesticated, and disputes that may occur regarding the direction of the movement (Tarrow 2005: 59). Tarrow problematizes Naomi Klein's idea of 'two activist solitudes'—the local that may not necessarily be connected with the global—in transnational contention (2005: 53). Tarrow notes that despite

---

[25] The activists were initially convinced that the movement would exist for only a few days or weeks.

a decade of protests against global injustice, 'many of their themes, tactics and organizational preferences have failed to penetrate the global south' (2005: 55).

The lack of penetration may be the appropriate approach within certain national contexts. *Local activists in the Global South may be better served by tactics and strategies that are neither ideologically puritanical nor align with global or transnational discourses and practices.* The crucial element is that the tactics, ideation, and framing adopted by local activists take cognizance of their social context and are consistent with the values of the movement. Only the motherist and the girl-child's right to education framing were suited to the conditions in the Nigerian political process, although #BBOG focused on the state failure framing, particularly after the first six months of the advocacy.

Transnationalizing local struggles produces mixed results at best. For instance, Schmitz (2001) finds that the reliance of local activists on transnational networks and support helped with protests against the Arap Moi government in Kenya but left them ill equipped for the peculiar challenges of local politics (Schmitz 2001). Transnational ties and networks did 'bind' and 'blind' local activists (2001: 150). Similarly, Widener (2007) investigates four oil struggles in Ecuador and finds that the move towards transnationalization simplifies complex issues and pivots towards the priorities of the international partners (Widener 2007). In Quito and Mindo, local environmental justice campaigns were relegated while global environmental protectionist advocacy became preponderant (Widener 2007: 28).

However, the original #BBOG organization in Abuja has had little formal institutional arrangements with transnational advocacy networks (TNAs), despite the spin-off #BBOG protests in major world cities such as New York and London. The #BBOG organization declined offers of financial support from European and US-based foundations and organizations, as noted in Chapter 2 (Interviewees 12, 30, and many others). The strategic team of #BBOG was concerned that accepting financial support would play into the 'franchise' and 'political tool' narrative made famous by Doyin Okupe, the spokesperson of President Jonathan. Some members of the public were also sceptical about the motivations of the movement. One #BBOG activist notes that 'Many Nigerians could not just in their minds conceptualize that there was a group that was sitting out in the (Unity) Fountain everyday come rain or shine, and weren't getting paid, and up till today, people believe that we were getting foreign aid' (Interviewee 17).[26] The People's Democratic Party (PDP) government was sensitive to its reputation and how #BBOG framing was

---

[26] #BBOG 50-year old female activist; personal interview, Abuja, July 2015.

affecting its electoral chances and tried to discredit the movement.[27] Therefore, accepting financial support would have delegitimized the movement, tainted its leadership, and caused rancour among members.

Consequently, the #BBOG movement did not become 'transnationalized' in the conventional sense, but its framing (specifically all but the maternalist framing) merely adopted a transnationalist and globalist approach. This might have been expected to be effective because of several seemingly favourable factors:

- The movement began at a time of tremendous focus on international terrorism. Hence, the international community could be expected to act on the objective of the movement in a post-9/11 environment.
- The movement was established as a countervailing force against the activities of a violent non-state actor.
- #BBOG is a single-issue movement and therefore ought to avoid the pitfalls of movements with multiple and irreconcilable objectives.
- The movement's sole objective directly concerned a recognized state actor, the government of Nigeria.
- The focus on young girls and impediments to their education connected with the priorities of the UN system and several global bodies.

Contrary to Großklaus (2015), movement objectives may be negatively affected when activists, particularly in the Global South, adopt universal terms or *global-speak*. Framing local struggles using global-speak has huge potential to popularize and internationalize such struggles. However, this may not necessarily mean that assistance is offered to accomplish movement objectives. Such universalistic framing may distantiate key national actors and ultimately become self-defeatist for local activists.

The #BBOG framing was bifocal in orientation. The maternalist framing was directed locally to Nigerian women (in terms of micro-mobilization) while the girl-child's right to education framing was also well received in Nigeria. It won an influential ally in the Emir of Kano, who encouraged #BBOG to expand its focus beyond the Chibok girls to all young girls and women in Northern Nigeria (Sahara Reporters 2017a).[28] However, the human rights and state failure framing were externally orientated to the international community. The underpinnings of the state failure framing in particular alienated the wielders of political and military power in Nigeria who could have rescued

---

[27] See Godwin (2015).
[28] As stated earlier, Sanusi was dethroned in March 2020.

the girls. It also inadvertently enmeshed the movement in toxic presidential politics, which had strong ethno-religious colorations.

The #BBOG experience is instructive for movement actors the world over but particularly in authoritarian or quasi-democratic contexts. First, the #BBOG movement symbolizes the limits of transnational awareness and mobilization in attainment of movement objectives. Despite worldwide concerns over jihadi terrorism at the time of the Chibok kidnapping, heads of states who held placards with the #BBOG slogan on global television did little to rescue the girls during the Jonathan administration (Interviewee 04).[29] News about US deployment of surveillance drones for intelligence-gathering to secure the Chibok girls emerged on 12 May 2014 (Reuters 2014). However, the drones were withdrawn before any progress could be made. The reason for the withdrawal varies. The American side argues that they were frustrated by the lack of cooperation of their Nigerian counterpart, while the Nigerian military has questioned the motive of the assistance. A Nigerian army general argues,

> the whole world felt that they [the United States] had the answer. They gave the impression that within three days they would bring back the girls. After six months there was no clue . . . Some of the questions they asked were not related to the issue at hand. What was the motive of coming in the first place? As for assistance, it has never been rejected . . . Also, by virtue of training, we are very sensitive about the sovereignty of our nation . . . and our nation's security . . . We need weapons, we need intelligence. We open up our needs but how far have they been met with sincerity? We are ready to pay. We are not asking for them to be donated which is what a helper should do. Even when we are ready to procure and you still put stumbling block on our way, how does that translate to assistance?
>
> (Interviewee 04)[30]

The general stated that the leaders of the US forces asked questions they were uncomfortable with and came off as 'spies'. The military was also frustrated by the refusal of the United States and its allies to sell arms to Nigeria. The US government cited concerns about the Nigerian military's human rights record for the refusal to sell arms to Nigeria (Amnesty International 2015b). The government lost valuable time between May 2014 and early 2015 while waiting to purchase arms from the United States and other major Western countries

---

[29] Army general; personal interview, Defence Headquarters, Abuja 2015 and multiple activists.
[30] Defence Headquarters, Abuja, July 2015.

(Interviewee 04). The government decided to use clandestine means to purchase arms in South Africa as soldiers began to flee from the superior firepower of Boko Haram (Tukur 2015a). There were no plans by the United States to sell arms to the Nigerian military to fight Boko Haram until mid-August 2015, following the inauguration of a new president in Nigeria (*The Punch* 2015).

A distinction can be made between humanitarian support to deal with the disaster caused by Boko Haram and military support for the Nigerian government to fight Boko Haram. Publicly available evidence suggests that while donations have been pouring in to deal with the humanitarian crisis, little military support—in the form of hardware and intelligence-gathering—was made available. The US government did not approve the sale of 12 Embraer A-29 Super Tucano aircraft until 3 August 2017, despite assurances of support by the Obama administration (Lederman 2017). The sale was approved by the Trump administration. This arguably shows the level of assistance received by the Nigerian government in the war against Boko Haram. The August 2017 interview granted *Leadership*, a Nigerian newspaper, by the Chief of Air Staff, Air Marshal Sadique Abubakar sheds light on the matter:

JOURNALIST: You have been sold aircraft by countries hitherto unwilling to sell planes to Nigeria. How do you plan to maintain them?

AIR MARSHALL ABUBAKAR: I am not sure I understand which countries you are referring to here, but what I can say here and now is that we have acquired Mi 35M helicopters. These are functional helicopters.

The government bought the Mi 35M helicopters from Russia in January 2017 (Tukur 2017b). In July 2021, Nigeria received 6 of the 12 attack helicopters ordered from the United States. Some US lawmakers attempted to block the remainder of the order due to Nigeria's human rights record (Gramer 2021).

Movement members were frustrated that the international community's engagement with their grievance was to state their 'condemnation' of Boko Haram's atrocities without any further 'action' (Interviewee 01). The group had begun to feel abandoned by October 2014. Hadiza Bala Usman argued,

> People need to remember that 219 girls remain in captivity... We appreciate the fact that the media propelled a lot of support around the world, but that support has not translated into any rescue. For us, if whatever is said and done doesn't translate into the rescue of the girls, it hasn't really achieved anything.
> (Ogene 2014)

The movement seemed to have put a lot of stock in the international community—the notion of a rescue by concerned Western powers. The involvement of Switzerland and the International Committee of the Red Cross (ICRC) in the May 2017 release of 82 Chibok girls suggests that the #BBOG movement's interpellation of Western powers had not been futile. However, the clarification provided by the Swiss government and the ICRC about their roles in the release of the 82 girls is didactic. The Swiss government indicated that it acted at the request of the Nigerian government; major roles were played by local individual actors such as Zannah Mustapha and Asiha Wakil, who had 'pre-existing relationships with one or more factions (of Boko Haram)' and 'the principles of strict neutrality and non-interference' guided the involvement of the Swiss government (Ukpong 2017). The ICRC also confirmed that it was 'not involved in the negotiation for their [the girls'] release, as negotiations often imply a political process which is contrary to the political and neutral nature of ICRC work' (Tukur and Agency Report 2017). While the idea that solutions to local problems cannot be completely outsourced should be immediately clear from the foregoing, the fact that none of the traditional superpowers (such as the United States and United Kingdom—countries with extensive ties to, and interests in, Nigeria) were involved in the negotiations is an indication that non-militaristic, middle-level powers and humanitarian NGOs arguably engender more confidence among belligerent non-state actors. Both the Swiss government and the ICRC emphasized the roles played by both sides in the crisis (the Nigerian government and Boko Haram) as well as local individual actors in Nigeria.

Given the largely symbolic support given by the United States and the United Kingdom, movement activists need to properly articulate what *support* means to their specific objective(s), understand that support offered by some entities may not go beyond symbolisms and rhetoric, and appreciate that there is no monolithic international community. Also, while raising awareness about an issue may be, in and of itself, part of solution to a problem (e.g. awareness about HIV/AIDS), there are cases where generating international publicity about a cause is not necessarily the same as actual action to solve a problem. Placards, pictures, and video uploads on social media demonstrating support are mere insignia of the times: such symbolic support may arguably mean little in terms of a movement's cause. Movement activists should be wary of struggles that become popularized in such manner.

Motherist framing was largely abandoned within the first six months of the advocacy, despite the fact that only the motherist and the girl-child's right to education framing were suited to the local context. This was interesting because of the success of the motherist framing as a mobilization tool. The girl-child's right to education framing continues to be useful in a national discourse on education and gender. However, the emphasis on the failed state framing in particular did not take into cognizance the realities of the national context and the quality of the state. The narrative excessively relied on human rights discourses from the geopolitical West. Such discourses are suited to environments where an effective Weberian ideal-type state exists. As #BBOG framing got closer to the grammar of the internationalist/transnationalist language, the group got farther away from local institutional actors who could have helped. The #BBOG approach spoke 'above the heads' of major players in Nigeria and ultimately prolonged the realization of the movement's objectives. The real 'institutional sovereigns' (Matusiak 2014: 1) in the movement's social milieu, the Nigerian government and the military, were antagonized by the state failure framing and the extremely negative attention it attracted.

The tremendous attention generated on the Chibok kidnapping by the internationalization of #BBOG framing made it more difficult for the military to find the girls. General Olukolade, Director of Defence Information under the Jonathan administration, argues that the 'bad side' of the movement is that it is 'one reason why these girls are still being held because the captors realize that they are important and decided to keep them'. This narrative goes beyond a mere 'official' standpoint. Some other rescued survivors have confirmed that the Chibok girls were put under stricter security control at Boko Haram's camps (Ross 2015). All but two #BBOG members interviewed for this study also believe the advocacy inadvertently prolonged the captivity of the Chibok girls.[31]

State failure framing brought the movement closer to international actors but foreclosed any opportunities to work with major local actors at the institutional level. This speaks to a lack of strategy about the minutiae of how to secure the girls. #BBOG's framing was viewed as oppositional and disrespectful. The Nigerian government and military leaders felt humiliated by the approach of #BBOG (Interviewee 04). The state failure framing succeeded in its quest to cause international embarrassment, but drawing on what, in essence, constituted oppositional framing rather than discourses that would not antagonize a government noted for its rather deviant status in an illiberal, quasi-democratic context was a strategic error by #BBOG. State-friendly narratives and framing may be used to generate desired results in an authoritarian

---

[31] Further analysis of this issue appears in Chapter 5—'Outcomes of the #BBOG movement'.

context, as demonstrated in the Chilean women's movement under Augusto Pinoche (Noonan 1995).

Some members of #BBOG had wanted a conciliatory and diplomatic engagement with the government. The texture of the (internationalized) framing was not universally accepted within the movement. There were serious divisions over the tone and language being used. #BBOG began to haemorrhage influential elite members a few months into its existence, partly because of its framing (Interviewee 30 and others). The military, particularly the Chief of Defence Staff, Alex Badeh, indicated interest in 2014 in engaging #BBOG, but that avenue was closed as #BBOG's framing gained momentum in the international media. A member of the #BBOG group's strategic team argues that

> The language, the approach of engagement would have been different if we had done proper analysis and profiling of our stakeholders right from the beginning. At the time we developed the strategic document, we had gone too far, and the narrative of we being against them had been formed. It was too late to be redeemed. But I wish we did that right from the beginning because ... they have a reputation to protect ... they became defensive and not collaborative.
>
> (Interviewee 30)[32]

The framing of #BBOG became the movement's most formidable strength and yet its greatest weakness.

A particularly damaging trend began to emerge in the autumn of 2014: the movement began to be perceived as an opponent of the government—a political tool in the hands of the APC designed to wrest power from the PDP government. Hadiza Bala Usman was an APC member who had contested and lost a seat in the federal parliament. She was part of the strategic team of the APC while also serving #BBOG in an equally significant capacity. Ezekwesili had delivered a keynote speech at an event of the opposition party, as noted earlier. #BBOG was perceived as part of the opposition party as some regular members openly wore APC publicity materials to the daily sit-out prior to the 2015 presidential elections (Interviewee 30).

The perception was reinforced by a rhetorical slip by Audu Ogbeh, the national chair of the APC, when Muhammadu Buhari formally declared his interest in running for president. Ogbeh stated that 'We commend the

---

[32] There were also members who felt that #BBOG was too soft and needed to be tougher in its approach.

#BringBackOurGirls movement led by members of this party; we thank them for their commitment to Nigeria because they remain the only living evidence that Nigeria has a conscience' (Isine 2014b). One civil society group argued that 'People feel betrayed and hoodwinked into believing that the BBOG movement was in the interest of the innocent parents of the abducted Chibok girls, whose pain and anguish have been floundered on the altar of partisan politics' (Isine 2014b). Ogbeh apologized for his comments, but the damage was done.

The 'narrative that a #BringBackOurGirls leader ha[d] been rewarded' for her efforts emerged when the APC governor of Kaduna state appointed Hadiza Bala Usman as chief of staff in June 2015 (Interviewee 30). The optics were unseemly. It reinforced presidential spokesperson Doyin Okupe's rendering of the perspective of the Jonathan Government: 'One of the reasons the Chibok girls were kidnapped was to present Jonathan's administration as incompetent and hold it to ransom against 2015 elections ... One of the reasons the BBOG was formed was to sustain and internationalise the embarrassment' (Godwin 2015).

Dietz (2000: 76) argues that 'the institutionalized recognition of a political category at the level of international organizations is an indicator that—for better or worse—it has acquired some degree of status as an "international problem" rather than a domestic matter of the state'. The critical term is 'for better or worse'. The #BBOG movement rapidly became the darling of international organizations, such as the UN, the European Parliament, and several Euro-American governments. Its leadership began to receive speaking invitations across the globe. These provided platforms for articulating the demands of the movement. The worldwide visibility and framing of the issue as an international, rather than national, problem and one that required international intervention, however, further alienated Nigerian state actors, who felt humiliated by the speeches of the #BBOG spokespersons.

The attitude of the Nigerian state towards #BBOG also began to work against the international profile of the movement among institutionalized organizations, particularly within the UN establishment. Although the movement had relied on support from the UN, the UN began to avoid being seen as supporting #BBOG. For instance, UN Secretary General Ban Ki Moon did not attend a meeting scheduled with the activists on Monday 24 August 2015 in Abuja. Ezekwesili informed the #BBOG members who gathered for the meeting that '(u)nfortunately, he is attending a dinner with the president. Otherwise, he would have passed through to say hello to the rest of the group' (Ibeh 2015). The UN relies on the cooperation of states. Therefore, some #BBOG activists read Moon's non-appearance at the meeting as an attempt to avoid irking the new Nigerian government. The imagery of the #BBOG movement as an opposition platform had gained momentum at the UN (Interviewee 30). The #BBOG experience in this regard suggests that although 'certification' by major international actors helps to validate non-state actors (Tarrow 2005), it is a double-edged sword for a movement's objectives and should therefore be approached with caution.[33]

#BBOG has also been confronted by a major problem encountered by movements purporting to fight for others—authenticity (Valiente 2003). This concerns who has the right to speak for whom and why. #BBOG movement activists have been criticized for 'crying more than the bereaved' and engaging in activism for material profits and political gains (Interviewees 08, 09, and 10). One activist notes that 'there was so much hostility and so many questions asked about the group' (Interviewee 17). The criticisms concerning political motives were fuelled by the political activities of some of the key leaders prior to the start of movement activities, as noted earlier.

The international arena versus local political process

#BBOG's framing was well intentioned and mostly theoretically sound. However, its immanent problematic was fivefold: (a) non-recognition of the refraction of the framing of the movement across local political power conflicts, (b) interpellation of the movement leaders in the toxic political environment, (c) the presupposition that the Nigerian government could be forced or shamed into taking action on an issue in which it had little interest, (d) the notion that the international community would help to rescue the girls if the Nigerian state was unable or unwilling, and (e) not thinking through the step between mobilizing opinion and how the girls would be rescued. The #BBOG framing could not overcome two major obstacles: the salience/absolutism of geopolitical interests and the low priority in the global imaginary of the lives of poor high-school girls in the Northeast corridor of Nigeria.

These factors concern the utility of human rights framing vis-à-vis the centrality of the character of the state and overall socio-political context. Although '(h)uman rights has gone global' and nurtures struggles of the oppressed

---

[33] President Muhammadu Buhari hosted #BBOG activists in July 2015 and called them the 'conscience' of the nation. By January 2016, relations had deteriorated. Buhari accused unnamed leaders of the #BBOG movement of using their international connections and grammatical ability to embarrass the government. This shows that, like the Jonathan administration, the Buhari government was offended by the internationalist nature of the advocacy.

against powerful forces, as Ignatieff (2001: 7) argues, the reality is that the latitude afforded to human rights and their basic enjoyment are a matter of social context. This should resuscitate spectres of the debate over the origins of human rights. While that is not the focus of this book, suffice to state that the debate is not settled.[34] The level of organization of society matters. Therefore, the socio-political context and the nature and exercise of power is salient on issues regarding human rights. Human rights framing may lose its persuasive power in social contexts with democratic deficits, where organized civil society and state institutions are weak.[35]

While human rights framing is fast becoming 'hollow rhetoric' in the West (Brean 2015), claims to human rights that have not been won in an illiberal, quasi-democratic context is more tenuous. Human rights are 'not self-executing' (Sloss 1999: 131). Clement has warned that human rights are 'a sociological rather than a legal fact … [and] a product of human interaction [which] derive from society and the state rather than an abstract pre-social individual' (cited in Brean 2015). Therefore, the #BBOG movement's human rights framing resonated in other parts of the world, but only a relatively small, middle-class and well-educated segment of Nigeria was engaged in the movement beyond the first few months.[36] Many #BBOG activists have been disappointed in not only the government but also regular citizens as regards the attitude towards the lives of the Chibok girls (Interviewees 12 and 17).

This is not to suggest that humans rights advocacy is absent in non-Western contexts (Sen 1999; Ibhawoh 2018). Anti-colonialist movements in Africa, for instance, were framed around universal norms and conventions on human rights, but the reality is that post-independence African states often stifle dissent, limit individual freedoms, and repress attempts to expand the frontiers of human rights (Ibhawoh 2018). The internationalization of human rights discourses expresses a future possibility rather than subsisting empirical reality. Merry (2006) analyses how human rights discourses are transnationalized and become widely shared in non-Western contexts. She argues that rights discourses are 'vernacularized' or adapted to suit local meanings and practices (p. 39). However, the process of vernacularizing human rights is problematic in at least two ways. It may not be understood by the local public, on whose

---

[34] See Gutmann (2001) for a collection of excellent essays on the question of human rights.
[35] See Mbembé (2001) and Bayart (2009) on the nature of the state in Africa.
[36] A survey of #BBOG activists conducted in 2015 indicated that all participants who indicated their level of education (100%; $N = 56$) had at least a bachelor's degree. The leadership of #BBOG has, however, indicated that non-degree holders might have either been absent when the survey was conducted or had deselected themselves from completing the questionnaire.

behalf a struggle is being fought, and it may be misunderstood by powerful forces within the local political process. In the case of the #BBOG movement, the human rights framing sounded like an elitist utopian vision to the Nigerian masses, given the concerns of the majority of the people with basic survival.[37] The global-speak therefore seemed too remote and irrelevant to their daily concerns—it had limited cultural resonance in Nigeria. The state interpreted the universalized framing as politically motivated and an embarrassment.

Concerns about the idea of universal human rights have long been noted. For example, Hafner-Burton and Tsutsui (2005: 1378) problematize the global regime of human rights treaties as a 'paradox of empty promises'. The institutionalization of human rights around the world, they argue, constitutes a 'double-edged sword' (p. 1,378). The lack of strong mechanisms of enforcement allows states to engage in superficial adherence after signing treaties, while activists use the treaties as a framework for challenging states to improve their human rights records.

Activists often appeal to humanity using human rights framing. Appeals to 'our common humanity' is necessarily indicative of abject conditions and does not imply that a favourable intervention would occur. Arendt (1951: 298) highlights the problematic of evoking humanity for the 'right to have right'. Douzinas (2006: 55) emphasizes that '(h)umanity has no foundation and no ends, it is the definition of groundlessness'. The sea-washed lifeless body (Smith 2015) of a three-year old Syrian boy, Aylan Kurdi, accentuates the limits of appeals to humanity and, by implication, externally orientated human rights framing. Retired US major general, James 'Spider' Marks, offered a candid perspective during a CNN interview on Boko Haram and inadequate international efforts to rescue the Chibok girls:[38]

> What is happening in Nigeria is barbarous, it is horrible, it is complete madness, yet it's not a priority. The United States unilaterally could do anything it needs to do to root out Boko Haram ... But it's not a priority. We're committed elsewhere in the world. Black West Africa is not a priority.

Former CNN journalist, Isha Sesay (2019), was surprised at how the girls' abduction had *become stale news two years after their abduction. A New York*

---

[37] The poverty rate in Nigeria is estimated at 62.6%, human development Index (HDI) 0.47, and per capita income $1280 (see UNDP 2016a).
[38] See 'Black West Africa and Boko Haram are not a priority to the West—CNN Military Analyst', https://www.youtube.com/watch?v=XBCYN6ijgEI. Accessed 17 March 2016. The Syrian refugee crisis is another instance.

Times review of Sesay's book, *Beneath the Tamarind Tree: A Story of Courage, Family, and the Lost Schoolgirls of Boko Haram*, highlights how

> Far too much effort is put into explaining why this story matters. This is a common pitfall for authors who are trying to chronicle the lives of others to Americans, and it's unfortunate. Sesay pleads with her readers to pay attention because the story is about terrorism and therefore a threat to the 'global strategic interests of the United States'. There should be no such imperative.
> (Sengupta 2019)

The focus on the international community (i.e. the United States, Canada, the United Kingdom, and other Western European countries) is common among movement activists and other civil society actors from the Global South. The results are, in fact, underwhelming.

Critics may correctly note that there have been successful transnational rights campaigns in the Global South. However, the long-term impact of such campaigns tends to produce mixed results (Rodrigues 2011). One example is the Ogoni struggle against environmental injustice in Nigeria in the 1990s. Any assessment of the outcome of the movement depends on how *success* is defined. The transnational support the movement received ensured that the Ogoni plight acquired global recognition. The struggle eventually went to a federal court in New York. An out-of-court settlement was reached in 2009. Shell Petroleum Development Corporation agreed to pay a compensation of $15.5 million to the families of the nine activists who were executed by the regime of General Sani Abacha on 10 November 1995 (Pilkington 2009). It is one of a handful of cases in which a transnational corporation paid compensation for human rights violations.

However, it is worth noting that the Ogoni movement began as an ethnic minority struggle against 'cultural genocide' (Saro-Wiwa 1992) but was *marketed* as an environmentalist issue to garner international support (Bob 2005). Transnational advocacy, including clamours by the Commonwealth heads of governments, did not prevent the execution of the nine Ogoni activists, including Ken Saro-Wiwa. The Movement for the Survival of Ogoni People (MOSOP), which led the Ogoni struggle, has since suffered fractionalization and is in steady decline (Nyiayaana 2018). The internal divisions and power struggles within MOSOP come from two major sociological sources: the dynamics of oil politics in Nigeria and competition for financial support from international organizations. Some Ogoni refugees still remained in dire economic straits in the Republic of Benin as of May 2016 (Nyiayaana 2018). The clean-up of the Ogoni environment, one of the major grievances of the transnationalized non-violent protest of the Ogonis, did not commence until 5 June 2016—over 20 years after the death of Saro-Wiwa (Edosie 2016). The clean-up began at a time of a generally recognized lull in protest activities in Ogoniland and negligible transnational support for, and advocacy on, Ogoni grievances. A change in the national political process—the election of opposition politician Muhammadu Buhari—was the main catalyst for the clean-up, although a United Nations Environment Programme (UNEP) report was widely cited in the build-up to the clean-up exercise.[39] The movement for environmental justice in the Niger Delta has, since the late 1990s, taken on an explicitly violent turn (Oriola [2013] 2016). This trajectory is led by the Ijaws rather than the Ogonis (Okonta 2006).

Overall, #BBOG framing and attendant consequences provide invaluable lessons for movement actors around the world. International support for causes in developing countries in general, and sub-Saharan Africa in particular, is arguably unreliable. Movement actors in such societies will do well to look inwards rather than outwards by engaging with their internal political processes. Widener (2007: 33) concludes her investigation of four oil struggles in Ecuador by suggesting that results 'may be better achieved through grassroots efforts that target the state, rather than through transnational actors'. Seidman (2005) has offered similar conclusions as regards labour struggles in South Africa. This book aligns with the conclusions of Widener and Seidman.

Conclusion

The #BBOG framing was internationalized but the movement elected not to become transnationalized. The latter was appropriate for its political context; the former was not. The experience of #BBOG regarding internationalized framing and its consequences provides invaluable lessons for movement actors around the world, particularly those in postcolonial societies ensconced within the interstitial space between authoritarianism and democracy. These include conscientiously working with local actors to achieve movement objectives. Movements in developing societies also need to avoid framing and repertoires of protest that may be deemed oppositional by the state. Such movements need to strategize and publicize very early on in their advocacy what (transnational) 'support' means for movement objectives. Activists in the Global South should also ensure that movement activities do not become entangled in toxic politics.

---

[39] The clean-up exercise has become mired in corruption (see Munshi 2019).

The #BBOG movement, given the antecedence and ambitions of some of its co-conveners, could not avoid the latter.

This chapter analyses the framing of the #BBOG movement. It contributes to the literature by unpacking the diagnostic, prognostic, and motivational framing of the movement. It also identifies and interrogates the four master frames of #BBOG. This expands the scope of what was previously known about #BBOG's ideation—a focus on the full picture of #BBOG framing beyond maternalist framing. By emphasizing the salience of social class in the #BBOG maternalist framing, this chapter also contributes to our understanding of the efficacy of the use of motherist or maternalist framing in social movements. It matters what mothers are advocating, where, and when. The differential reaction to protests by the biological mothers of the Chibok girls and the #BBOG elite women demonstrate the significance of social and cultural capital of those deploying maternalist framing.

The findings contribute to social movement theory. The effects of internationalized framing are refracted through a range of variables within the local political context. These include

- closeness of movement mobilization to a major event (particularly elections) in the political calendar,
- the nature of the cause,
- primary beneficiaries of movement activities,
- the social positionality of key movement leaders—political affiliation and ambitions—before and during movement activities.

These four variables are critical to the efficacy of framing within the context of human rights movements in Africa and other regions of the world, where elections are matters of life and death.

The 2015 presidential election influenced how #BBOG framing was perceived within the national context. The opposition party, APC, weaponized #BBOG framing; the presidency and the ruling party perceived #BBOG framing as part of a political plot. This was complicated by the political antecedents of the co-conveners of #BBOG, the cause (human rights advocacy in an institutionally weak state) and primary beneficiaries, the *talakawa* from the most marginalized part of Nigeria. These four variables above are crucial to make framing theory more nuanced and sensitive to realities in developing countries.

The findings also show that social movements using social media for their advocacy need to distinguish between raising awareness about their cause and *practical* steps to achieve the objectives of the movement. The two are neither necessarily coterminous nor mutually exclusive.[40] Movements that enter the limelight on social media, with thousands or millions of clicks, posts, likes, shares, or tweets, should be wary of their movement becoming popular without tangible, on-the-ground efforts to accomplish their objectives. This does not detract from the utility of social media but merely urges caution, particularly among activists in the postcolony.

The findings of this chapter have other implications for framing theory and practice. This chapter contributes to the empirical literature on the relationship between developments in the international arena and the local political process or opportunity structure, on the one hand, and framing on the other. Framing does not occur in a social vacuum. The local context predominates despite opportunities that may be provided by engaging international actors or language. Consequently, social movement activists in developing societies should be careful about adopting transnationalist language. Overall, *the findings demonstrate that when it comes to certain local struggles, particularly in the Global South, activists should think local and act local.*

---

[40] To use a peculiar 2020/2021 example, given the widespread shutdown across the globe, raising awareness about how to prevent contracting COVID-19 is not the same as developing a vaccine to prevent it or developing medication to help those who have the ailment recover. One must not be conflated with the other.

4
#BBOG, members' social positionality, and politics

Introduction: The 'mascot' and acrimony within the #BBOG

> I do not like Labels. I am ME. I say it as it is. My mum says in my court nobody wins. You would either love me or hate me and either one is perfectly okay!
>
> (Aisha Yesufu, #BringBackOurGirls activist, Twitter [X] background information)

Her powerful voice and the confluence of her identities as a middle-class, veil-wearing, educated, vocal, and opinionated businesswoman and human rights activist have made her one of the most recognizable members of the #BringBackOurGirls (#BBOG) movement. Aisha Yesufu is widely regarded among #BBOG members as the 'mascot' of the movement. The term is not derogatory in any way—#BBOG protests have become synonymous with Yesufu's distinctive red hijab. Yesufu has served as the coordinator of the sit-out and chair of the Strategic Team (ST). Yesufu made a video in May 2017, following President Buhari's weeks-long health-related vacation in Europe. Yesufu stated in the video, 'We need to take our country back. Let the president resign. If he can't resign, let the National Assembly do the right thing and let's have another president.' In a country sharply divided along ethnic and religious lines, she posed a conundrum as a fluent Hausa speaker (with a peculiar Kano inflection) and practising Muslim woman criticizing the Muslim president of a politically toxic country.[1] Simply put, the intersectionality of Yesufu's identities and political activism are a rare combination.

The video went viral. It received tremendous coverage in both traditional and social media. The terms 'BBOG' and 'co-convener' were used in several

---

[1] Aisha Yesufu grew up in Kano, although her parents were originally from Edo state in the Niger Delta region. This fact appeared not widely known at the time by the public and could have been used to delegitimize her critique of the president, given the toxicity of Nigeria's political atmosphere.

Terrorism, Politics, and Human Rights Advocacy. Temitope B. Oriola, Oxford University Press.
© Temitope B. Oriola (2024). DOI: 10.1093/oso/9780198886976.003.0005

of the headlines and main text of news reports. The headline of *Premium Times*, a leading investigative online newspaper, for instance, was 'Resign now, Buhari—BringBackOurGirls co-convener, Aisha Yesufu'. Yesufu was not a co-convener of #BBOG. However, the media consistently referred to her as co-convener. There was a missing crucial detail in the media coverage: Yesufu made the video in her personal capacity and never mentioned #BBOG. Nonetheless, the video created divisions that came dangerously close to destroying the movement. Several members believe that the Yesufu video controversy remains the most significant internal crisis ever experienced by the movement.

There were concerns among some members that Aisha Yesufu had politicized the movement and should resign her position as ST chair. However, some #BBOG members supported Yesufu's right as a citizen to express her concerns over the situation in Nigeria. They argued that being chair of the ST did not mean that she had no right to criticize the government. Others felt that Yesufu's personal perspective on any political issue could not be distinguished from that of the movement and, therefore, her position was taken by the media as the stance of #BBOG on the president's health. They demanded a formal rebuttal by #BBOG so that the media would realize that Yesufu's comments did not reflect #BBOG's stance.

Heated arguments ensued. Some members nearly engaged in physical altercations at several sit-outs after the video went viral. One member argued,

> As BBOG chair of ST, you have a responsibility to the BBOG ... if you drive against traffic today, people would say BBOG co-convener is driving against traffic. Nobody would separate you from BBOG. So once you have taken up a responsibility ... the public would see it as if you are representing the organization.
>
> (Male #BBOG sit-out participant 01)[2]

Another member suggested that '(t)here is no way you can lead a group like this, have very strong political feelings and air them and still lead this group. It is not possible' (Female #BBOG strategic communications team (SCT) member and sit-out participant 03).[3] This was countered by a member who pointed to the slogan of #BBOG concerning asking for the truth and nothing but the truth. She argued, 'are we saying that because someone is a leader here, there is something we need to express, we wouldn't be able to express

[2] Abuja, May 2017.
[3] Abuja, May 2017.

it the way we want because we are leaders?' (Female #BBOG SCT member and sit-out participant 02).[4] Some members were also concerned that Yesufu had out-grown her position as ST chair and needed to step down. Several other members argued that Yesufu's voice was essentially #BBOG's voice as her public recognition emanated from the advocacy.

Yesufu insisted, 'I lent my voice to BBOG . . . You either love me or you hate me, but from the beginning I said I don't have the political whatever to be a leader. I don't want to be a leader because I hate that label' (Yesufu 2017). Yesufu's stance was that she was merely expressing her mind like everyone else, and she did not wish to sound politically correct, hence her initial reluctance to be ST chair. She also highlighted the contradiction in the fact that she was not perceived as being 'too political' when she led a protest in support of the government's anti-corruption efforts in 2016 but was being castigated because of her criticism of the government.[5]

The ST fixed 10 June 2017 as a meeting date to discuss the matter. Some members interpreted that as a delay tactic and claimed that the ST did not need to have a physical meeting to issue a press release in an age of electronic communication. The meeting was held as scheduled, and major decisions were made. Aisha Yesufu stepped down from her position as ST chair effective August 2017.[6] The ST elected Florence Ozor as the new chair. Bukky Sonibare was elected deputy ST chair, a new position created at the meeting.

Aisha Yesufu continues her personal advocacy against poor governance. She offers her perspectives on issues ranging from fuel scarcity, wrangling among media aides of the president and vice-president, and issues regarding religious holidays (what she coined 'competitive religiosity') in Nigeria. Her tweets and other public statements continue to make headlines. Yesufu's tweets concerning the fuel crisis in Nigeria in December 2017 generated tremendous attention. Yesufu's tweets were directed to the president's personal handle and noted,

> What type of president are you? You have not the decency to address the Nation on the crippling effect of the fuel scarcity that many are suffering . . . At your age one would have expected you have seen it all and not be

---

[4] Abuja, May 2017.
[5] Debates on the #BBOG WhatsApp group ('#BringBackOurGirls') were so vitriolic that some members were summarily deleted from the platform. Those deleted quickly set up another WhatsApp group ('BBOG'). The newly created WhatsApp group remained active as of the time of writing, while the older one was moribund.
[6] Yesufu had indicated willingness to relinquish her position as ST chair at least a year before the video controversy.

swayed by the temporary insanity of power but alas age does not mean wisdom, integrity, values and character . . . Be warned one day we would no longer take it.

One #BBOG member noted, on the group's WhatsApp platform, that

> This anger by Aisha is rather abnormal, I feel a deep sense of frustration and hatred that sounds more personal than a citizen demand in her words [sic] . . . I now believe those rumors about not being considered for appointment . . . It's very sad that our Mascot has let loose; loosing all sense of decorum [sic] and core values in her public comments.

Yesufu's criticisms of the person and administration of President Buhari have led to acrimony and major schisms in the movement. This is, in part, because there are #BBOG members who are supporters of President Buhari. Buhari's supporters are largely from Northern Nigeria, the president's region of origin. Buhari's supporters in the movement openly wore to the sit-out campaign materials of then opposition party All Progressives Congress (APC) prior to the 2015 election. The victory of the APC in the 2015 presidential election brought Buhari to power. Supporters of President Buhari in #BBOG prefer a conciliatory approach towards the Buhari government and appear offended by any criticisms of the administration. Such members expect the movement to accommodate the lapses of the Buhari administration, given that it had already helped to secure over 100 of the girls. The official position of #BBOG, however, is that the movement is 'administration-blind' or 'regime-neutral', and therefore, no government is spared criticism.

The contentiousness of the political engagement of the #BBOG mascot raises several questions, given that activists do not lose their right to freedom of expression or association when they sign up for movement activities. Censorship is hardly an option for movements that seek to advance the frontiers of human rights. Therefore, how does a movement regulate the personal advocacy of members, particularly those who are extremely committed to the cause and have acquired significant name recognition? How does a movement balance its official position on an issue with the right of a (leading) member to express their opinion? How should a movement respond to media and public conflation of its official standpoint with the personal opinion of one of its leaders? Is a public rebuttal in order? How should a movement handle internal divisions from such episodes? Can grassroots movements whose activities are directed against a government remain apolitical? How does a movement resolve divergent political views within its ranks?

There are no easy answers to these questions. Therefore, the #BBOG mascot's vocal personal advocacy provides a fascinating case study on balancing the right of a movement member to express their opinions and the movement's right not to be dragged into toxic politics. Movements may toil to transcend the personal politics of their members because movements constitute a microcosm of the societies in which they are formed. Despite all good intentions, ethnic, religious, and political loyalties and allegiances may boil over occasionally and spark divisions in the ranks of a movement. These issues suggest that social movements are embedded in national politics (Tilly 1979).

The antecedents, proclivities, and/or personal ambitions of some well-placed #BBOG members have embedded the movement in Nigeria's toxic politics. For instance, Oby Ezekwesili served in the People's Democratic Party (PDP) government of President Olusegun Obasanjo, as previously noted. Dr Ezekwesili was a high-profile minister. There was an initial perception that her activities under #BBOG were influenced by the fact that her political mentor, President Obasanjo, had fallen out with President Jonathan. Conversely, her keynote speech at an APC convention also drew widespread criticism even though she used a significant part of the speech to criticize the political elites and their poor performance in office. Ezekwesili was also criticized on the grounds that her vigorous campaign for the release of the Chibok girls after the Buhari government took over presidential power in May 2015 was intended to secure a ministerial appointment.

Several elite women have been unequivocal that Ezekwesili has succeeded in repudiating her social class through #BBOG advocacy. Some of the elite view as rather extreme and antagonistic to the political class that Ezekwesili belonged to the idea of a two-time minister dressed in red and engaging in street demonstrations to fight for the release of girls from the Northeast corridor.

While Ezekwesili remains outside of government and engages in regular critique of governmental ineptitude, some of the elite women who assisted in convening #BBOG have accepted positions in the APC government. This has led to concerns about the 'real' intentions of such individuals and their motives for founding the movement. Hadiza Bala Usman became chief of staff to Nasir El-Rufai, the APC governor of Kaduna state, in 2015. She was appointed managing director of Nigerian Ports Authority (NPA) by the APC-led federal government in July 2016. The NPA position was considered significantly beyond the expertise and experience of Usman.[7]

---

[7] Usman was suspended as MD of the NPA in May 2021 (Mojeed 2021), although there had earlier been indications she had been outstanding in the position (Ogunyemi 2018).

In 2016, another co-convener of #BBOG, Maryam Uwais, the spouse of a former chief justice of Nigeria, was appointed special adviser for social protection plan by President Buhari. The backgrounds of the elite women, their acceptance of positions offered by a government that replaced another they indirectly helped to defeat (see Chapter 5), has been a source of division in #BBOG and arguably a stain on the reputation of the movement. Some #BBOG members believe that the Chibok incident was weaponized by #BBOG for the benefit of the political aspirations of some of the movement's leaders.

The fact that some elite women who have accepted political appointments from the APC government are no longer publicly campaigning for the rescue of the Chibok girls is viewed as indicative of having used the movement to secure political positions and circulate within the political class. However, several of the elite women were politically active long before the Chibok girls were kidnapped. Ms Usman, for instance, had worked with Governor El-Rufai in Abuja when he was minister of the Federal Capital Territory. Usman was also already active in the APC prior to the Chibok kidnapping. Therefore, this raises the question of appropriateness of involvement in partisan politics during movement mobilization.

Besides, some members of #BBOG have criticized the fact that all the #BBOG elite women who have received political appointments in the APC government are from Northern Nigeria. One female #BBOG member, who comes from the Northeast, believes that the appointments are capable of destroying the movement, given the lopsidedness (Interviewee 37).[8] This is another indication of the politically toxic environment, where every activity, policy, law, appointment, and routine act of governance is evaluated through ethnic, religious, and political lenses.

The multiple roles undertaken by other prominent #BBOG members has also embedded the movement in Nigeria's toxic politics. For instance, Sesugh Akume leads the SCT of #BBOG. He is also the national spokesperson of Abundant Nigeria Renewal Party (ANRP), a political party formed after the 2015 presidential elections. A #BBOG strategic team member who opposes the involvement of leaders of the movement in politics argues that the optics are terrible: 'How more political can we be? How more political can people see us? Of course, political parties are competitive in nature so definitely, we are in the political party' (Interviewee 10). This demonstrates a level of unease

---

[8] Female #BBOG sit-out member; personal interview, Abuja, June 2016.

within the movement that key members are involved in partisan politics and yet expect to be viewed as human rights advocates.

These issues have generated major divisions within #BBOG. Ideological blocs have emerged within #BBOG. The evidence garnered suggests five categories of #BBOG members. These are 'regime-neutral die-hards', 'regime-change emergency activists', 'committed pragmatists', 'non-committal advocates', and 'totemic elite members'.

Regime-neutral die-hards are those who have continued the advocacy at the street and/or intellectual level despite the change of government. They are not necessarily members of any political parties. They have continued the quest to have #BBOG maintain its ideological puritanism by abstaining from any form of collaboration with the government. Regime-neutral die-hards believe #BBOG must remain in the trenches until all the Chibok girls are back. They also believe that #BBOG must not transmute into a non-governmental organization (NGO model) as that would lead to its demise.

Regime-change emergency activists (or 'Buharists') are members of #BBOG who take offence at any form of criticism of the APC government of President Buhari. They believe that #BBOG's tactics, such as street protests, are outdated and ought to have been replaced by collaboration with the government. They strongly believe in the person of President Buhari and often engage in social media vitriol against any #BBOG member who criticizes the Buhari government. Such persons make little to no distinction between legitimate criticism of the Buhari administration and dislike for the person of the president. Any criticism of the Buhari government is largely viewed as political and/or personal animosity towards President Buhari. A large number of such persons share markers of identity such as ethnic, religious, and linguistic affiliation with President Buhari. The affinity demonstrates the politicization within the movement and its situatedness within a particular socio-historical and cultural context.

Committed pragmatists are individuals who are non-partisan and believe in a practical approach to rescuing the Chibok girls. They believe in working with intent, caution, and diplomacy with the government to achieve the objective of #BBOG. Committed pragmatists are wary of aggressively engaging the government in a war of words in the media. They believe #BBOG ought to tap into its numerous 'back channels' to engage with the government and avoid direct confrontations. Such persons believe #BBOG should not hesitate to sit with the government on the way forward, appreciate the government when and if warranted, and criticize only when absolutely necessary. Committed pragmatists have a radically different vision of advocacy, in contradistinction to regime-neutral die-hards. They believe #BBOG is suitably positioned to do more than it currently does. They envision a #BBOG that renders concrete assistance to rescued women and girls and provides educational opportunities in war-ravaged areas. Committed pragmatists are interested in changing the strategic direction of #BBOG towards an NGO model.

Non-committal advocates are akin to passers-by in the movement. They show up to the #BBOG sit-out when major events have been scheduled or a dignitary is being expected. Non-committal advocates utilize #BBOG images as bragging rights about the quality of individuals they are associated with and are excited by their images on pages of newspapers or television broadcasts. Such persons make up the numbers and are crucial to protest activities but are only occasionally involved in the advocacy.

Totemic elite members are well-placed individuals who continue to discursively associate with #BBOG but have evidently moved on to other things. They grant occasional media interviews on issues relating to the Chibok girls, although they rarely show up for any movement activities. Totemic elite members also tend to have major issues with how the #BBOG leadership is running the affairs of the movement. As elite, they are conscious of their class position and are not particularly fond of street protests. Therefore, they remain indoor members who brandish their #BBOG identity largely in the media. This category of #BBOG members demonstrates the divisions in the movement regarding tactics and overall strategy.

The Sambisa tour and the risks of acceptance of a movement

A movement's acceptance as a legitimate actor in a field or cause opens up political opportunities but also portends risks. While collaboration between social movement organizations and the state in Europe and North America may not necessarily lead to loss of legitimacy, the situation is different in Latin America and Africa. The #BBOG's advocacy against the Buhari government was unrelenting. In response, in early 2017, the federal government of Nigeria organized a tour of the Sambisa forest, where the girls were believed to be held by Boko Haram, to show #BBOG activists the efforts of the government to rescue the Chibok girls. The controversy over the Sambia tour demonstrates the need for activists in the Global South to be careful about political opportunity, particularly when delivered on a platter.

This section argues that the Sambisa tour episode exemplifies the need for a movement to be acutely aware of its environment and assess the intentions of opponents, even when they offer an olive branch. This section raises several critical questions. Should a movement be part of orchestrated efforts by the government or refuse to participate? Would participation risk the legitimacy and credibility of the movement? Such collaboration influences the internal dynamics of a movement. However, movements must endeavour to prepare for consequences of efforts to work collaboratively with the entity to whom their claims are made, particularly in the Global South. The intrigues surrounding such collaboration may entangle a social movement in toxic national politics. The context of the Sambisa tour, its effects on #BBOG and the implications for grassroots activists in Africa are analysed below.

Lai Mohammed, Nigeria's minister of information and culture, sent a letter, dated 11 January 2017, to Obiageli Ezekwesili. Mohammed asked Ezekwesili to select three members of the group to join her on a 'guided trip' of the Northeast on 16 January 2017. He stated that the 'trip will avail the BBOG of the opportunity to witness and better understand the effort being made by the Nigerian military to secure freedom for the abducted Chibok girls and all other victims' of Boko Haram. The chiefs of the army and air force, as well as the ministers of defence and information, would be on the tour. #BBOG had five days to prepare. Ezekwesili informed members about the invitation. The minister's letter was leaked to the press before #BBOG could respond. #BBOG sensed an ulterior motive—a political stunt by the government at best and an attempt to create a public relations disaster for the movement at worst.[9]

The Sambisa tour invitation led to a major crisis in the movement. There were fears that #BBOG would splinter if the issue was not properly handled (Interviewee 10 and several others). Two factions quickly emerged as debate ensued on whether #BBOG should accept the invitation. Some members felt that it was a ploy to 'decapitate' the movement. Others (regime-change emergency activists and committed pragmatists), who wanted a closer working relationship with the government, felt that #BBOG should accept the invitation and assess the military's activities in the Northeast. Most members of the ST wanted #BBOG to accept the invitation with certain conditions, such as a pre-tour meeting and a list of journalists going on the tour, among others. Only one member of the ST (Bukky Sonibare) voted to accept the invitation without any conditions. Ezekwesili said she would consult with her family and make a

---

[9] Lai Mohammed's reputation contributed to the concerns within the movement. His first name had been framed to the epithet 'Liar' on social media because of his spin on reality on behalf of the APC and the government. Such was the potency of the epithet that Mohammed informed the Senate, while being screened for a second term as information minister, that 'I used to ignore it until my seven-year-old grandson asked me, "Why do they call you 'Liar Mohammed?'"' (Sahara Reporters 2019a).

decision. The deliberative pace of #BBOG was widely read as indication that they would not accept the invitation. The tour invitation quickly became an existential issue for #BBOG. There were rumours within the movement that a faction of #BBOG would nominate four representatives if Ezekwesili and the ST declined the invitation. There was a real possibility that an autonomous faction of #BBOG could emerge in Abuja.

#BBOG sent a letter, dated 13 January 2017, to the minister of information. The group requested postponement of the tour, a pre-tour meeting with government officials, and retraction of comments made by the chief of army staff against #BBOG. The minister responded a day later. He said the conditions set by #BBOG were 'at best tangential' to the tour and that he hoped that #BBOG 'will drop the conditions and join the trip, which shows the commitment of the Federal Government to securing freedom for the Chibok girls and its transparency in handling the issue of the girls'. The correspondence was put in the public domain. The press and the public began to criticize #BBOG for not promptly accepting the invitation. #BBOG realized that a political game was in progress, which it would be calamitous to lose. Social media was already awash with stories that #BBOG had refused to go on the tour.

Some members feared for the life of Ezekwesili, given her high profile and Nigeria's history of suspicious accidents, particularly plane crashes, under military rule.[10] Others felt such sentiment was ridiculous as the Minister of Information, who invited #BBOG, and heads of the army and air force would be part of the tour. Those who wanted #BBOG to decline the invitation argued that the information minister and military chiefs were not indispensable to the government in a country like Nigeria. Emotions were high. Tears flowed freely during discussions on the matter as many read sinister motives to the tour. Some members believed that the end of #BBOG had arrived. There were suspicions that those who wanted #BBOG to accept the invitation were sympathetic to the government and were 'deliberately pushing aunty Oby to danger' (Interviewee 10).[11]

Ezekwesili and her family decided that she would go on the tour. The next step was to nominate three members. Aisha Yesufu, as ST chair, was a definite candidate. Ezekwesili made a strong case for ensuring adequate representation of all key stakeholders on the tour team. The Chibok community association,

---

[10] The crash of the Hercules C-130 aircraft in Ejigbo, a suburb of Lagos, on 27 September 1992, is one example. The crash led to the death of 163 middle-level officers from all three arms of Nigeria's military. The crash is believed to have happened three minutes after take-off of the aircraft. See *Reuters* (1992).

[11] Male #BBOG ST member; personal interview, July 2017.

the Kibaku Area Development Association (KADA)[12] Abuja branch, was asked to select a nominee to represent the people of Chibok on the tour. The association nominated #BBOG ST member, Allen Manasseh, a veterinary doctor, and the spokesperson of KADA.[13]

The final slot would be filled at the sit-out through an open contest. Three persons were nominated to compete for #BBOG members' votes. The sit-out voted overwhelmingly for a young journalist, Ibrahim Usman (known as 'Morocco'). The #BBOG team on the tour therefore comprised Ezekwesili, Yesufu, Manasseh, and Ibrahim Usman. There were mixed feelings on the team. At least two members thought that it might be the end of their lives. Aisha Yesufu discussed her concerns during a 2017 interview.

INTERVIEWER: Were there fears that this might have been a set up to kill somebody like Dr Oby Ezekwesili?
AISHA YESUFU: Absolutely! There was that fear. It really traumatized some of our members. Some were fiercely against us going, and it was a very traumatizing period ... It is just like going to war and leaving your loved ones behind. Some felt it would be a set up to take Dr Oby out and then, probably, myself. Because some have the notion that the moment the two of us are out, then you could play ball ... The fear was quite there.
INTERVIEWER: Did you feel personally that they could try to kill you?
AISHA YESUFU: That was already at the back of my mind; it could be a possibility. I might go on this trip and not come back. I went anyway. No matter what, when it's time die, it's time to die, there are no two ways about it.

The government's travel arrangement was to have journalists and #BBOG on one aircraft and the service chiefs and minister on another. The #BBOG team insisted that the service chiefs and minister of information had to be on the same aircraft with them.[14]

The tour was successful and without incident. The #BBOG delegation was impressed by what they witnessed. #BBOG issued a report on the tour. The report stated,[15]

---

[12] KADA represents the Kibaku-speaking peoples, including Chibok, where the girls were kidnapped.
[13] The Chibok community association reached out to several parents of the kidnapped girls, but all either declined or claimed they could not make it to Abuja, given the short notice (Interviewee 10).
[14] The #BBOG team was initially at a wrong wing of the airport.
[15] See 'Special report by the #BringBackOurGirls movement following the return of four of its members as part of the federal government, local and foreign media guided tour of the Sambisa war zone', http://www.bringbackourgirls.ng/?p=2793. Accessed 26 December 2017.

We can confirm that the air component of the counter insurgency war is being prosecuted by a highly professional, capable, motivated and committed team of the Nigeria Air Force (NAF). Furthermore, the presentation by the Chief of Air Staff on the training and human capital development strategy of the NAF enabled us to appreciate its plans for the future.

Some supporters of #BBOG criticized the movement for the positive report on the military's activities in the Northeast. The movement was accused of having been compromised during the tour.[16] The criticisms were reinforced when, two days after the tour, the NAF accidentally bombed an internally displaced persons (IDP) camp in Rann, a village in Borno state. The camp was purportedly mistaken for a Boko Haram location. Over 230 persons died in the incident. Dr Manasseh Allen said #BBOG began to receive comments that the 'Air force that you have just been praising . . . has bombed an IDP camp and aid workers with the same state of the art facilities that you said they have acquired'. #BBOG demanded a probe of the bombing.

The Sambisa tour and its aftermath offer lessons for movement advocates, particularly in contexts with weak institutions. First, although the tour was a political opportunity for the movement, it needed to be deftly and expertly managed. #BBOG would have become splintered, lost a level of public support, and be construed by bystanders as a purposeless movement if it had declined the invitation. Therefore, social movements must strategize painstakingly about accepting such political opportunities. What are the circumstances surrounding the political opportunity? What actors are providing the opportunity? Are they credible or reputable? What do those actors stand to gain?

Second, movement activists must realize that they risk alienating some members and losing a measure of public support if they utilize such political opportunity. The invitation was political genius on the part of the government. Accepting the invitation and the tour, in and of itself, tilted the positionality of #BBOG nearer to the government. Movement activists must consider the question 'What might the movement lose?' Activists must weigh the benefits of taking up a political opportunity against the disadvantages of rejecting it. The calculation within #BBOG was that the movement would lose the public relations battle if it declined the invitation.

Third, movement activists in toxic political environments must be measured in tone when they need to commend the efforts of their opponents.

---

[16] Allen Manasseh, a member of the #BBOG team to Sambisa.

Activists should consider giving themselves latitude by qualifying commendations unless there is a structural positive change in their cause—full realization of their objectives. #BBOG offered an arguably objective and fair assessment of the military hardware they saw in the Northeast. Their assessment was enthusiastic in praise of the military. However, the assessment quickly boomeranged as the air force blundered by bombing an IDP camp.

Fourth, a political opportunity can be used by activists to enhance democratic participation in the movement. The decision to have members elect a representative at the public sit-out and allow the Chibok community to nominate its preferred candidate was functional in giving disenchanted members a sense of belonging. Finally, it is worth reiterating that the political opportunity presented by the Sambisa tour invitation signifies the need for activists in countries with weak institutions to be mindful of their political contexts. The legitimacy and credibility of their movement is always at stake whenever they collaborate with the government. This is not to suggest that activists in the Global South must not work with the government. Rather, political opportunities must be analysed, various scenarios contemplated, and the consequences of available options carefully calculated.

Challenges of contemporary women-led social movements in Africa

Social movements grapple with issues that threaten to derail their objectives, polarize members, and generate ossification. Social movements, as a microcosm of societies in which they are formed, are riddled with various challenges peculiar to their environment. Therefore, while social movements everywhere face certain generic challenges, some issues are specific to postcolonial societies. The contemporary women's movements that began to emerge in Africa in the early 1990s had significant political opportunities that earlier women's movements did not have (see Chapter 2; Tripp et al. 2008). However, comparative analyses of women's movements in Africa indicate major challenges. These include fractured relationship with African states, engagement in explicitly political rather than developmental issues favoured by earlier women's movements, the overweening influence of donors within a patron–client relationship, accusations of diffusion of inappropriate Western feminist ideals and priorities, and poor internal bureaucratic mechanisms (Tripp et al. 2009).

In South Africa, for example, the involvement of major women's organizations, such as the African National Congress Women's League (ANCWL) and the Federation of South African Women, which provided a racially inclusive atmosphere during apartheid, contributed to a strong women's movement which made South Africa 'the African country with the most politically organised women's movement, that made a significant input in the negotiations that established a new political system' (Mkhize and Mgcotyelwa-Ntoni 2019: 10). This created major breakthroughs in politics for South African women. The representation of women in the lower house of parliament in South Africa as of December 2018 was 42.7% and ranked tenth in the world (Thornton 2019). Despite the political inroads, parliament remained largely impervious to women's issues, and female parliamentarians engaged in another round of struggle (Britton 2005). Major challenges remain with respect to racial identities, disabilities, and social class (Albertyn 2003; Mkhize and Mgcotyelwa-Ntoni 2019). Besides, the education, income, occupation, and racial demographics of the women in post-apartheid South Africa who adjusted well to the challenges of lawmaking are not fully representative of the Rainbow nation (Britton 2005).

What constitutes women's or human rights is also another challenge for contemporary women's movements in Africa. North Africa provides an interesting case. For example, evidence on engagement of women in the revolution that toppled the regime of Hosni Mubarak is strong. Women at Tahrir Square made up 20–50% of protesters (Hafez 2012). However, 'secular' and 'Islamic' feminism were paradigmatic camps in the Egyptian women's movement (Allam 2018: 11) prior to and after the fall of Mubarak. These camps have shaped outcomes. The ensuing political changes have unearthed major challenges to the women's movement in Egypt. Many educated and urban-based women voted in favour of emancipation of women, while the rural, non-literate and deeply religious women supported Islamists. The Islamists have rolled back several of the rights won by women. The Egyptian experience raises critical questions about how various groups of women across religious, social class, and ethnic lines perceive the 'place' of women in society and what constitutes women's rights.

Contemporary women's movements in Africa also face challenges regarding strong differences of opinion on movement's goals, repertoires of protest, strategic direction, and framing. Besides, international organizations, agendas, and norms (Bouilly et al. 2016) as well as language or discourses (Urkidi and Walter, 2011; Großklaus, 2015) influence the trends and complicate women's movements in Africa.

#BBOG has faced numerous challenges related to questions around bona fide members, internal democracy, and decision-making as well as the strategic direction of the movement. The most significant problems the #BBOG movement confronted and the implications for human/women's rights advocacy in Africa are analysed below.

Who is a #BBOG member?

The stance of #BBOG on the question of membership is that a #BBOG member is someone who cares about the Chibok girls, advocates anywhere in the world for their return, and is concerned about humanity generally. The response is in line with the democratic ethos of #BBOG. However, it leaves membership of the more strategically sophisticated Abuja #BBOG flagship open-ended. That, in and of itself, is not a problem. However, there have been instances when the universalized approach to membership created uncertainty, raised expectations (that led to belligerence when unmet), and, in some cases, created genuine befuddlement.

For instance, do people have to be present at the sit-out to qualify as members? Is membership affected by inability to attend the sit-out for an extended period of time? Is virtual membership (via social media) allowed? Are people who rarely attend the sit-out and occasionally participate in marches allowed to be part of the decision-making process at the sit-out (virtually or in person)? These questions have remained unsettled within #BBOG.

A movement may adopt a tiered approach to membership: general members and registered members. In the case of #BBOG, anyone who advocates for the return of the Chibok girls is a #BBOG member. Such a person is always welcome at the sit-out and may join any of the #BBOG marches. A registered member (delineated by fulfilling a set of criteria the movement may wish to map out and completion of a short form for documentation purposes) is someone who can vote in the decision-making process of the movement. A registered member would agree to a code of conduct wherein obligations and rights are clearly articulated. #BBOG has stayed committed to its 'free entry and free exit policy'. This has contributed to rancour in the movement, which often puts more consistent members against those who show up on special occasions yet expect to have the same level of authority over the activities and direction of the movement. This is the quintessential freerider problem. However, freeriders, in this case, have latitude to demand that their views shape the activities of the movement, in part because of the policy on membership. Social movements need to comprehensively resolve at the onset issues relating to bona fide membership. Failure to resolve such issues after mobilization of a movement may lead to unnecessary conflict. The #BBOG ST chair, Florence Ozor, admits,

> we could have put this structure in to say, this should be a criterion to be a member. But you know the funniest thing it is out of our hands; it is a global movement, so how do you put criteria on the embassy of another person in Brazil, who decides to get to the street and call on their government to do something about the girls who were taken?

The lesson for activists is that the longer a social movement organization takes to articulate the criteria for membership, the more difficult and divisive it is to do so in the future. This can be costly in terms of time, energy, and potential loss of membership on such matters.

Oligarchization and decision-making in the #BBOG movement

Robert Michels' ([1911] 1962) work on the *iron law of oligarchy* explicates the intrinsic nature and tendency of organizations towards oligarchization. Oligarchization means the 'concentration of power, in the Weberian sense, in the hands of a minority of the organization's members' (Zald and Ash 1966: 328). Michels demonstrates that oligarchic tendencies in organizations are inevitable, and true democracy—in the sense of collective decision-making—is impracticable even in organizations that begin with a fierce commitment to democratic ideals. Michels argues that delegation of authority in organizations develops for reasons related to technical and tactical requirements of specific roles. Therefore, oligarchization is a natural part of complex organizations: 'Who says organization, says oligarchy?' (Michels [1911] 1962: 365).

Bureaucratization is an aspect or 'form' of oligarchization (Zald and Ash 1966: 328). Bureaucratization implies growth of hierarchical structures, layers of authority, and formalized rules and regulations (Zald and Ash 1966). An organization may develop oligarchization without necessarily becoming bureaucratized. In other words, an oligarchy may function outside of a formal organizational structure (Leach 2005).[17] However, bureaucratization develops with the increasing complexity of an organization and specialization of roles. Both bureaucratization and (in particular) oligarchization suggest an inexorable shift away from the type of face-to-face, no-fuss, direct democracy

---

[17] Leach (2005) provides a compelling engagement with the work of Michels.

that social movement organizations pride themselves in. Both terms also connote increased conservatism in organizations, and for Michels, oligarchization is perceived as somewhat ethically or morally inappropriate (Zald and Ash 1966).

Social movements are generally auto-critical and reflexive about their democratic credentials (della Porta 2005, 2013). With the exception of 'awkward' social movements such as terrorist collectivities (Poletta 2006: 475), social movements often aim to increase levels of social inclusion and expansion of the frontiers of belonging. Therefore, an ambiance of autocracy, exclusivity, and elitism is antithetical to most social movement organizations and repulsive to the individuals therein. Given that social movements' reward or incentive systems are rarely materially orientated (Zald and Ash 1966; della Porta 2013), a social movement that purports to change the society but remains non-inclusive will engender non-participation and/or low levels of commitment of members, which may lead to its demise. Consequently, internal democracy is a fundamental issue within social movement organizations (della Porta 2013). While there are at least four models of internal democracy in social movement organizations (associational model, deliberative representation, assemblary model, and deliberative participation: p. 3), several studies show that movement members prefer models of decision-making that enhance consensus and deliberation, particularly assemblary and deliberative participation (della Porta 2013: 3). The assemblary model denotes decision-making in open gatherings, while deliberative participation involves decision-making in open gatherings where consensus is reached (della Porta 2013).

The #BBOG movement is extremely careful about its democratic credibility and fidelity. Nevertheless, there are issues relating to internal democracy and decision-making in #BBOG. There are concerns about growing oligarchization—concentration of power in the hands of a small number of members in the ST, thereby leading to reduction in internal democracy and majority participation in governance and decision-making. These issues are centred on three questions regarding the movement's organizational structure:

- What is the relationship between the sit-out and the ST vis-à-vis decision-making?
- What is the process for determining ST membership?
- Is there a delimited tenure for ST membership?

#BBOG members have radically divergent perspectives on the first question. Some members presuppose that the sit-out and the ST are equals; others maintain that the ST is the final decision-maker, while many sit-out members believe that a decision made by the ST lacks legitimacy unless it is ratified by the sit-out. These variegated views on such a salient question are a major source of internal conflict in the movement.

Grassroots social movements often construe themselves as self-governing entities with equal rights and responsibilities for every member. This is a noble ideal. However, the daily grind of movement activities means that, over time, some members demonstrate more commitment than others. Those who devote more time, energy, and resources to movement activities acquire symbolic and/or real powers. Such persons are more likely to have their suggestions and ideas accepted and implemented. Besides, socio-economic status and other social divisions also find expression, even in some of the most fiercely democratic non-hierarchical movements. This often leads to criticism of lack of, or diminishing, internal democracy. This issue remains a major source of division in #BBOG.

#BBOG has no policy document that spells out its organizational or governance structure. Interviews with key leaders of the movement suggest that (in theory) the sit-out and the ST are regarded as equal partners. Suggestions are often made by members at the sit-out for consideration by the ST. The ST deliberates on such ideas and tries to reach a consensus if there is disagreement. Ezekwesili has been insistent on the need to reach a consensus rather than putting an issue to vote, although voting does take place when no consensus can be reached. The emphasis on consensus allows all sides to articulate their views in the hope that everyone understands the perspective of the other. This approach has been immensely beneficial to the movement, particularly at the level of the ST. Heated arguments often result in agreeable denouement, with members hugging one another after hours of meeting on contentious issues. Members leave meetings—for the most part—convinced that they made their case and the decision represents the collective will even if it is contrary to their views.

Decision-making at the level of the ST, however, sits uneasily with the positionality of the sit-out. The sit-out is a much larger and broader collection of people—all #BBOG members. It is literally a coalition of everyone who cares about the Chibok girls and shows up at the Unity Fountain. This means that diverse opinions may be heard but also makes deliberations somewhat tedious, given that there is no codified methodology for becoming a member. The leadership has therefore had to coordinate deliberations with tact, skill, and diplomacy. The sit-out coordinator endeavours to give everyone an opportunity to contribute to discussions. Despite this openness, the ST has earned the image of 'the place where ideas go to die' in the opinion of some of the most vocal sit-out members (Interviewee 10). This speaks to grievances about (a) a subtle tendency towards bureaucratization, leading to major decisions being made outside the sit-out, and (b) a quest for democratic participation or having a voice. It also unearths a basic governance issue: the relationship between the sit-out and the ST. This question was posed to the ST chair, Florence Ozor:

INTERVIEWER: There seems to be a very significant number of sit out members who feel they have the final authority when it comes to #BBOG and that whatever happens at the ST is mere conversation towards reaching a decision. Is that true?

FLORENCE OZOR: We are equals. No organ is greater than the other; our roles are different. The role of the ST does not diminish the importance of the sit-out, neither does the role of the sit out diminish the value of the ST. In the beginning, it was how it was done . . . At what point did it change if it has changed? At what point did we become competitive? You know, one time, we were two sides of a coin, still one coin. *But now we don't even see ourselves as part of the same body.* So, it becomes a competition to say, even if ST has a conversation on a decision, we would not endorse it . . . The ST was never the implementing arm of the movement. It was the sit-out. The ST was responsible for strategy . . . It is not a competition; there is no greater arm. People have to be reminded that it is a relationship of equals [italics added].

In practice, the most serious decisions affecting the movement are made by the ST and ratified or announced at the sit-out. Many topics regarding tactics and miscellaneous issues are openly and freely deliberated at the sit-out and decisions reached by consensus or vote. The 10 June 2017 decisions of the ST provide a compelling example. The ST elected Florence Ozor ST chair as Aisha Yesufu prepared to step down. The ST also created a new position, deputy ST chair, as stated earlier. Ezekwesili announced the decisions to the sit-out on 11 June 2017. Several vocal members of the sit-out—colloquially known as the 'strategic cabal'—staunchly opposed the two key decisions of the ST. They argued that the decisions were 'undemocratic'. Following intense arguments, the sit-out was asked to vote on endorsement of the decisions.

An individual within the sit-out raised a point of order on the voting eligibility of ST members. His argument was that those who decided on the issues being deliberated ought to be prevented from voting. Ezekwesili (rhetorically) asked, 'Should they be disenfranchised?' Up to eight members of the ST were part of the electorate at the sit-out. The result was 8 to 19 in favour of those who endorsed the ST's decisions.

There were several procedural issues during the process besides the question of whether ST members should have been part of the general electorate. First, the sit-out had gone beyond 4–5 p.m., the scheduled time. No motion was moved to prolong the meeting; the meeting simply continued. Second, a member of the sit-out suggested that members be allowed to mull over the decisions and vote later. A voice vote was taken, which overruled the suggestion. Third, the atmosphere did not appear conducive for the election. There was heavy rainfall, and some members had returned to their cars. A few could follow proceedings but several could not. This was infuriating for those on the opposing side. Fourth, the adoption of the decisions of the ST also spoke to the problematic of who was/is a #BBOG member and the hierarchical structure of #BBOG. There were concerns about the turnout of people from the Chibok community, who otherwise did not participate in #BBOG activities but were visibly present whenever a major vote was scheduled at the sit-out.

A spontaneous celebration occurred as the results were announced. The 'strategic cabal' and others, who disagreed with the decisions and/or wanted the ST chair popularly elected at the sit-out, construed this as insulting triumphalism. While a majority of members accepted the decision of the ST on new leaders, aggrieved members raised concerns about the process and timing. They argued that it was 'orchestrated' and mocked the notion of democracy. A #BBOG sit-out member (Interviewee 32) expresses her frustration at decision-making and internal democracy in the movement:

INTERVIEWER: So tell me about why you are tired?

RESPONDENT: I think we have lost our path and we are not willing to trace our steps back. *I think we are just, something like, will I say puppets in the hands of a few.* It is what they want that goes on; nobody listens to anybody. It is just like, you against me. *If someone has an opposing view it is just that the person doesn't like you.* Nobody seems to listen to, I don't know and I think it all has to do with the leadership. The leadership of #BBOG, I think they have taken us to where they can and the level we are in now, we can't go further unless we retrace our steps and when we were larger, we were more united and now we are fewer we are not as united as we used to be.

INTERVIEWER: That is counter-intuitive to the smaller . . . [interviewee interrupts]

RESPONDENT: Yes, when you are smaller, you are supposed to be more united but unfortunately we are not. There is too much bickering, too much back and forth, and then some people think they have sacrificed more than others so they should have a say, it has to be their way. And it's just crazy. When we were a larger group if something comes up, it would be discussed at the sit-out, task teams would be created to go and search and then come back then give their results. Everything was done in the open. Now there is so much secrecy.

INTERVIEWER: So less democracy?

RESPONDENT: Yes. Not less; there is no democracy at all.

The #BBOG member's comments above suggest conflation of disagreement with personal attack or animosity (Freeman 1978), a belief that a few people control the organization and others have no voice over decisions in the movement. It also indicates that the perceived decline of internal democracy happened over time and negates the decision-making process of the early days of the movement. The second and fourth points are congruent with oligarchization. Several regular members who were interviewed claimed that decision-making in the early days of the movement was a lot more open and democratic. Some members claimed to have canvassed for a system to periodically replace or replenish ST members. A small number criticized the enormous influence of the leader of the movement. They argued that the movement is cast in her image and there was a need to envision the movement without her leadership for the purposes of continuity.

However, several members noted that those agitating for greater openness in decision-making rarely participate in some of the most demanding aspects of the movement and are content to raise frivolous issues at the sit-out.[18] The election of specific persons as new leaders seemed to be a minor part of a much broader concern of some members. The lack of process was the issue. The process seemed whimsical, and persons with opposing views felt they were barely heard. The lack of specified, clear-cut criteria as regards ST membership and tenure has also been a contentious issue within the movement. Some sit-out members believe that membership of the ST has excessively been by a tap on the shoulder after the initial burst of activities of the movement.

The ST chair, Florence Ozor, explains that the ST engages in rigorous discussions before bringing anyone on board. Specific reasons have to be provided for why the person merits a place on the ST. The nominee for ST membership is also brought before the sit-out for discussions. No nominee

---

[18] They cited an example of a day of action in 2017 when members of the sit-out were asked to come up with ideas. The ST took over the planning and implementation when no response was received from the sit-out.

presented to the sit-out has ever been rejected by the members.[19] Other members argue that a reasonable tenure is difficult to establish, given the fluidity of the struggle. There is also a strong belief that some of those agitating for more clarity on procedures wanted to be part of the ST as a pedestal for working with the government (Interviewee 01).

Overall, oligarchization has inadvertently crept into the #BBOG movement. The sources of oligarchization in the #BBOG movement are fourfold: *level of commitment, resources, regime-neutrality, and interpersonal relations with top leaders of the movement*. The level of commitment of members is reflected in the time devoted to the advocacy, despite the lack of material incentives. Given the fact that #BBOG is self-funded, members who make significant financial contributions appear inadvertently privileged over others. Those who are regime-neutral (a position favoured by the leadership) are more likely to influence the movement. Regime neutrality concerns the division over whether or not #BBOG ought to change its approach following the election of President Muhammadu Buhari. Those who have good rapport and regularly socialize with top leadership also have greater opportunities for shaping the direction of the movement.

Oligarchization in #BBOG presents lessons for grassroots social movements. There is a need to consider, as early as practicable, the governance structure, decision-making process, selection of members to the social movement organization's (SMO's) highest decision-making body, tenure of office, and leadership succession in a movement. Discussing and resolving these issues early in the life of a movement organization would help to prevent governance issues that may cause internal fragmentation, alienation, and diminished sense of belonging. Grassroots movements tend to rely on setting up structures as they go on. This is sometimes inevitable, but movement activists must be aware of the potential pitfalls of such an approach to governance.

Debates over the strategic direction of #BBOG

#BBOG continues to experience major internal debates over the strategic direction of the movement. The key issue centres on what the movement *ought* to be doing. This concerns a fundamental critique of the value of continuing the daily protest to bring back the Chibok girls at a time when over 100 of the girls have already been secured. There is a legitimate philosophical and

---

[19] #BBOG chair (effective 1 August 2017); personal interview, July 2017.

ideological divide within #BBOG on this issue. Two schools of thought have emerged. The first believes that #BBOG is a pressure group, therefore its role is to ensure that *all* the Chibok girls are brought back and alive. This means that any changes to that single goal constitutes mission creep and may cost the movement its credibility, especially if it metamorphoses into an NGO. This is the position of the top leadership of #BBOG. The stance denotes a resistance to 'goal transformation' (Zald and Ash 1966: 327). The second school of thought holds that the advocacy should transmute into a pragmatic structure in which tangible services can be offered to the Chibok girls who have returned from captivity, their families, and other victims of Boko Haram. This school of thought argues that #BBOG has the organizational capacity and expertise to make meaningful contributions in this area through active collaboration with the government and donor agencies. This would necessitate a change in #BBOG's approach, tone, tactics, and strategic direction, as well as transformation of its original goal. One #BBOG member notes,

RESPONDENT: I heard that one of the girls that escaped even came to the sit-out and she said she didn't want to be quoted. You see we have made ourselves enemies of the government unnecessarily. What we should be doing is find a way to work with the government but, unfortunately, we have burnt our bridges when it comes to that. The only thing we can keep doing is just to keep demanding.

INTERVIEWER: So you would have wanted a more pragmatic approach?

RESPONDENT: Yes . . . There has to be a point where you have to say, the fight is enough. Even divorced couples when they are fighting for custody, after a while, they will have to say, it is enough, it is not about me and you. It is about the kids. Let's find a way so that these kids will not be affected. And you see, now we are completely shut out. None of the girls that have come back has ever even acknowledged. Even the parents themselves have not acknowledged #BBOG. They acknowledged #BBOG before the girls were back; as soon as the girls are back it is the government. There was even a set of parents that were even saying that #BBOG should stop the sit-out, that we are a hindrance to the rescue of the girls because we are fighting with the government. It is the government that can bring back the girls, not us.

However, both schools of thought agree that #BBOG has come to stay. The question remains *what the BBOG movement ought to be or become*. Florence Ozor, the ST chair, argues that #BBOG 'would evolve' if the girls were rescued but #BBOG would not go away. Ozor notes that

It is beyond all of us. We all came in to form #BBOG but it has taken a life of its own. We are only implementing them. If you and I leave #BBOG today, #BBOG is not going. Even if all the members of #BBOG in Nigeria decide that #BBOG is gone, they are not doing anything anymore; #BBOG isn't gone. Because there is probably somebody in America who has followed the story everyday and is still tweeting to the government and saying that there are still 15 girls left, where are they? Because we are the foot soldiers, doing the groundwork doesn't mean that we constitute the whole of #BBOG. When the girls come, it will naturally evolve into what's next. But for now, we can't be thinking of evolution when the objective has not been reached. We must totally meet that objective, otherwise we are deemed to have failed, and I do not think failure is on the agenda of any #BBOG member anywhere in the world.

Consequently, the strategic direction of #BBOG remains unresolved. The leaders of #BBOG believe that the movement will continue in one form or the other, but the silhouettes of that remain unclear. The lack of clarity over the direction of the movement is a source of division among members. Movements must strategize and be clear about the direction of their struggle.

The #BBOG movement's engagement with the Nigerian military

This section focuses on the relationship between #BBOG and the Nigerian military vis-à-vis the rescue of the Chibok girls.[20] As previously noted, #BBOG was initially optimistic about the capacity of the Nigerian military to rescue the Chibok girls. The inability of the military to rescue the girls led to a gradual change in the relationship between the movement and the military, particularly after the first six months. The evolving dynamics of the relationship began to affect the public image of both the military and #BBOG. To understand the texture and evolution of the relationship, this section provides a brief analysis of why the Nigerian military was unable to rescue the Chibok girls, how that contoured the relationship, and the implications for the broader socio-political context.

Decades of studies in the sociology of the military in newly independent African states indicate that problems in the military, particularly the army, are always broader and speak to deeper societal issues than it would first seem

---

[20] A version of this section was first published in my 2021 article on 'Nigerian soldiers and the war against Boko Haram' (Oriola 2021b).

(Luckham 1969: 1). The dynamics, actions, and predilections of key actors in the military have an overbearing influence on the trajectories of such societies. Besides the particularities of the Nigerian state, the dynamics of its military, elite politics, and civilian–military relations are crucial to understanding the handling of the rescue of the Chibok girls and the relationship of #BBOG with the military. As Luckham noted concerning Nigeria over 50 years ago, a 'careful analysis of the process of fragmentation in the army will be a way of raising a number of more general issues' (1969: 1). Many of the issues in the Nigerian military have miniature equivalents in several other West African countries. Therefore, an informed analysis of the Nigerian military vis-à-vis the Chibok girls and #BBOG would help to understand the military architecture in West Africa; its embeddedness in the life of society; and how it influences and, in turn, is shaped by wider socio-political, economic, and cultural forces in its external environment.

Despite significant media and public attention on the performance of the Nigerian military in the war against Boko Haram, scholarly analysis has been meagre and sporadic. There are several reasons for scholarly reticence on this matter. The issue may seem too 'obvious' as problems in relation to corruption, poor welfare of troops, and obsolete equipment (among others) are already in the public domain. Military officers and troops are difficult to access for research. Besides, where access is granted, researchers may consider conducting research in a war theatre as too dangerous to justify to themselves, their families, and/or research ethics boards.

Two of the few studies on the Nigerian military's war against Boko Haram focus on the political process (Amao and Maiangwa 2015; Bappah 2016). They attribute the failure to defeat Boko Haram to ineffective national leadership during the Jonathan presidency (2010–2015), the role of politics in the national security architecture, and the decline in military professionalism since 1999. Using data from senior military officers, Iwuoha (2019) argues that the failure to defeat Boko Haram may be explained by the multifaceted disconnection between countries like Nigeria seeking counterterrorism support and their superpower sponsors, such as the United States. Consequently, the support provided is uneven and fragmented.

Why has the Nigerian military not been able to defeat Boko Haram and rescue all the Chibok girls? This study finds evidence in support of 10 major factors. These are (a) corruption, (b) intelligence leaks/sabotage, (c) alienation of the public, (d) shortage of arms and ammunition, (e) inadequate coordination of security operations, (f) 'strategic blunders' of political leaders, (g) the rise of actors benefiting from the problem, (h) nepotism, (i) toxic politics in the military, and (j) troops' perception of the war against Boko Haram as a 'rubbish mission'. A select number of these factors is analysed below to understand the context of the change in the relationship between #BBOG and the military.

The ways in which corruption serves as tool for political mobilization are evident in Nigeria's arms procurement scandal, known as 'Dasukigate'. The scandal was revealed in December 2015 (20 months after the kidnapping of the Chibok girls) by a committee set up by the Muhammadu Buhari administration to audit arms procurement in Nigeria's defence sector from 2007 to 2015.[21] The committee found that $2.1 billion had been illicitly disbursed by former National Security Adviser (NSA), Colonel Sambo Dasuki (retired). Dasuki appeared to have had unbridled authority to use huge parts of the money to support the re-election of President Goodluck Jonathan. Those who shared the arms funds cut across politics, media, military, traditional institutions, and the clergy. The scandal began from the President, who appeared to have approved the funds without oversight. Categories of persons charged with receiving the arms money included 17 serving and retired senior military officers.[22] At least 241 companies were allegedly involved. These included companies owned by Nigerians and non-Nigerians. The arms procurement corruption also involved high-ranking civil servants.[23] Of the 12 indicted civil servants, 10 were from the Ministry of Defence (MoD). Three of the officials from the MoD had served as permanent secretaries, while five had served as directors of finance and accounts at the MoD.[24] In particular, the turnover in the Permanent Secretary and Director of Finance and Accounts were striking.

The media also benefited from the largesse. Daar Communications, which owns Africa Independent Television (AIT) was paid over two billion Naira in four instalments by the NSA through the Central Bank of Nigeria (Okakwu 2016b).[25] Sambo Dasuki gave ₦120 million to the Newspaper Proprietors

---

[21] See Shehu (2016).
[22] They include (a) Former Chief of Defence Staff, Air Chief Marshal A.S. Badeh (Rtd); (b) Former Chief of Air Staff, Air Marshal M.D. Umar (Rtd); (c). Former Chief of Air Staff, Air Marshal A.N. Amosu (Rtd); (d) Former Director General of the Defence Industry Corporation of Nigeria (DICON), Major General E.R. Chioba (Rtd); (e) Air Vice Marshal I.A. Balogun (Rtd); (f) Air Vice Marshal A.G. Tsakr (Rtd); and (g) Air Vice Marshal A.G. Idowu (Rtd), among others.
[23] They include former Director of Finance in the Office of the National Security Adviser, Shuaibu Salisu; former Permanent Secretary Ministry of Defence, Bukar Goni Haji; former Permanent Secretary Ministry of Defence, Haruna Sanusi; former Permanent Secretary Ministry of Defence, E.O. Oyemomi; former Director of Finance and Accounts Ministry of Defence, Josephine Okpara; former Director of Finance and Accounts Ministry of Defence, Abdulhahi Maikano; and former Director of Finance and Accounts Ministry of Defence, John Bamidele, among others.
[24] See Amaefule (2016).
[25] The AIT was accused of serious bias against the opposition APC during the Jonathan administration. See Nwabughiogu 2015.

Association of Nigeria (NPAN). This was supposedly meant to compensate proprietors whose newspapers were seized by security operatives in 2014 but was generally read as a bribe in the build-up to the 2015 presidential elections (Owete 2016b). Major newspapers such as the *The Sun, Leadership*, and *The Guardian* (Nigeria) were implicated in the scandal. The publisher of *This Day* newspaper, Nduka Obaigbena, was at the centre of the media angle of the scandal. Obaigbena admitted to the Economic and Financial Crimes Commission (EFCC) that he collected ₦120 million in March 2015. He claimed he was acting on behalf of NPAN and 12 of Nigeria's major newspapers.[26] Several newspapers returned the money they received after the scandal became public knowledge (Owete 2016a).

The Dasukigate scandal is one of several corruption cases involving serving and retired senior officers. For instance, former Chief of Air Staff, Air Marshall Mohammed Umar Dikko withdrew ₦558.2 million (approximately $1,545,660.00) per month over a two-year period (September 2010–2012) (Economic and Financial Crimes Commission 2018). Air Marshall Dikko is one of several retired senior officers who were sued for siphoning military resources in the course of the war against Boko Haram. Turning the war against Boko Haram into an avenue for raising personal or political campaign cash and corruptly disbursing such funds have been unhelpful to efforts to rescue the Chibok girls and defeat Boko Haram.

Intelligence leaks and sabotage have also hampered efforts to defeat Boko Haram. A statement by President Goodluck Jonathan in January 2012 signposted the level of concern about leaks and sabotage prior to the kidnapping of the Chibok girls. President Jonathan stated that

> (S)ome of them [Boko Haram members] are in the executive arm of government, some of them are in the parliamentary/legislative arm of government, while some of them are even in the judiciary ... Some are also in the armed forces, the police and other security agencies ... During the civil war, we knew and we could even predict where the enemy was coming from ... But the challenge we have today is more complicated.
>
> (BBC 2012a)

Although attempts were made by government officials to modify the statement, the comment reverberated around the world. Some serving and retired

---

[26] The claim was disputed by several newspapers. See Premium Times (2015c).

generals and non-commissioned soldiers interviewed for this study strongly corroborated President Jonathan's statement on the infiltration of the armed forces by persons sympathetic to Boko Haram. One general noted that prior to the Buhari administration, several of their colleagues were non-cooperative at the highest level of decision-making in the Defence Headquarters. Such officers refused to contribute to discussions on strategy and seemed unenthusiastic about the mission. Such officers would often say they 'concurred' or had 'no comment' when called upon to share their thoughts and ideas. This was a source of concern to officers who were committed to the cause and/or had major combat or associated responsibilities. They began to worry that many of the losses incurred by the military in the war against Boko Haram were due to intelligence leaks, sabotage, and disloyalty. Non-commissioned soldiers who fought against Boko Haram support the claim that senior officers were responsible for intelligence leaks. One soldier argued that the phones of non-commissioned soldiers were seized at the war theatre and there was 'no network but they used to connect wifi for the officers. So, if information used to leak, it is from them not the other ranks. The gap between the officers and the other ranks is high. We don't even mingle with them' (Interviewee S01).

A pattern began to emerge: military bases were attacked shortly before pre-planned operations against Boko Haram or a few days after receiving supply of arms and ammunitions. The routing of troops at Baga, the headquarters of the Multinational Joint Task Force in January 2015, was particularly troubling for the think-tank at the Defence Headquarters. One general noted that it was an 'insider job'—someone privy to high-level deliberations provided intelligence to Boko Haram (Interviewee 04). In June 2014, 10 generals and 5 other officers were found guilty of selling arms and providing intelligence to Boko Haram (Wienner-Bronner 2014).

There were also particularly disturbing political, religious, and ethnic dimensions to the issue. The level of distrust increased as some senior officers began to suspect that some of their Northern colleagues did not want the mission to succeed because failure would be politically favourable to their kinsman, opposition candidate Muhammadu Buhari. This shows the level of toxic politics in the military.

There were soldiers who received monetary inducement to switch sides. Tank drivers were particularly highly prized. One general notes that

> they [Boko Haram] use money because it will take more than six months of training for an average soldier to drive a tank, and the way these people do our tanks that they captured, the way they drove it against us to massacre us,

shows that they are being driven by expert drivers, Nigerian army trained drivers. Actually, there was a time when we surprised their camp, and one of the people we killed in their camp happened to be a warrant officer who was training our tank drivers in Kotangora.

The warrant officer was killed by troops in 2014 while fighting in support of Boko Haram. A Nigerian journalist also reported that 'the SSS [State Security Service] members who were sent to spy on the sect members soon became more Boko Haram than the sect members they were detailed to spy on' (Agekameh 2014). The combination of intelligence leaks, sabotage, and disloyalty led to the hiring of mercenaries, largely from South Africa. A retired general notes that 'if we were to reverse the situation . . . the degree of sabotage, the degree of disloyalty we were getting . . . we could not depend on the army of that period'.

Alienation of the public also played a role in the inability to defeat Boko Haram. The relationship of the Nigerian military with Nigerian citizens has been widely noted as 'extremely complex' (Hill 2009: 290). In particular, the incessant interventions of the military in the polity and years of military rule continue to divide public opinion on the military. Everyday Nigerians also resent the brutality with which they are treated by the military in public spaces. For instance, excessive use of force and killing of civilians by members of the armed forces occurred during special operations in the Niger Delta, the invasion of Odi (Oriola [2013] 2016; Adeakin 2016) and the lockdown in 2020 due to COVID-19.[27] Such incidents and their regularity have negatively affected the military's relationship with the public.

The December 2015 killing of Shi'ites in Kaduna and lethal violence against pro-Biafra activists are further examples of the egregious approach of the military. A report by the Kaduna state government notes that 347 persons were killed and given secret burial by the military (Premium Times 2016a). Amnesty International notes that Nigerian security forces, led by the military, killed 'at least 150 peaceful pro-Biafra protesters' between August 2015 and November 2016 (Amnesty International 2016c).

The invasion of communities where soldiers had been attacked and ensuing arrest, beating, or killing of males of military age have also led to fractured relationship with the military (Amnesty International 2015b). In '"Stars on their shoulders. Blood on their hands": War crimes committed by the Nigerian

---

[27] There were more deaths of citizens (13 persons) in the hands of security forces enforcing the lockdown than deaths due to COVID-19 (6 persons) as of 8 April 2020.

military', Amnesty International (2015b) argues that over 7,000 men and boys have died in military detention, while over 20,000 males have been illegally detained by the military since 2009. Amnesty International (2015b: 11) recommended that five senior military officers 'be investigated for the war crimes of murder, enforced disappearance and torture'.[28]

These human rights abuses have led to a loss of legitimacy, and lack of trust in the military. The implication of the broken relationship between the military and the citizens is that the latter are reluctant to provide information to the military. The systematic maltreatment of civilians by the military, coupled with a lack of basic means of subsistence, has also contributed to the decisions of some young women and men to join Boko Haram.[29]

Toxic politics in the military has also contributed to the inability to rescue the Chibok girls and the deterioration of the relationship between #BBOG and the military. As one general argues,

> The military is a microcosm of the society and so there is no ill of the society you don't find in the military because we are not cocooned from the larger society. And it is a society that has lost its value system; the military has followed suit.
>
> (Interviewee 03)[30]

The war against Boko Haram became embroiled in political theatrics and opportunism long before the Chibok girls were kidnapped. Outgoing Chief of Army Staff (COAS), Lieutenant General Kenneth Minimah, accentuated the lethality of the toxic political atmosphere in August 2015. General Minimah argued that the situation in Nigeria vis-à-vis the war against Boko Haram would have been different 'if we had all stood against the terrorists at the onset through public condemnation of their activities and active collaboration with the military to confront them . . . (r)ather than use it as a tool to advance

---

[28] These were Major General John A.H. Ewansiha, Major General Obida T. Ethnan, Major General Ahmadu Mohammed, Brigadier General Austin O. Edokpayi, and Brigadier General R.O. Bamigboye. Amnesty International (2015b: 12) recommended that four other senior officers (Lt General Azubuike hejirika, Admiral Ola Sa'ad Ibrahim, Air Chief Marshal Alex Badeh, and Lt General Ken Minimah) be

> investigated for their potential command responsibility for crimes committed by their subordinates, on the basis that they knew or should have known about the commission of the crimes and failed to take adequate action to prevent the commission of war crimes, to stop the commission of war crimes and to take all steps necessary to ensure the alleged perpetrators are brought to justice in fair trials.

[29] The military received scant intelligence from the public until the Civilian Joint Task Force (CJTF) was formed.

[30] A general in the army.

sectional, tribal, religious and political interests' (cited in Mutum 2015; italics added). General Minimah was COAS between January 2014 and July 2015. His comment speaks to the politicization of the Chibok issue as well as the war against Boko Haram.[31]

Multiple military officers emphasized the idea that some influential politicians, military officers, and other security agencies actively or passively worked to ensure that the Jonathan administration failed militarily as a way to ensure the electoral success of Muhammadu Buhari. One retired general, who served in a prominent capacity in the Jonathan administration, stated that

> We operated at a time that nobody wanted to sell arms to us. We operated at a time that there was serious sabotage within the system ... And what are the things that compounded the desperation? The attitude of our soldiers, attitude of our politicians, attitude of the media, everybody. It was as if they wanted to watch us fail and we were determined not to fail.
>
> (Interviewee 04)[32]

The rhetoric of the Jonathan administration and the zeal with which opposition politicians sought to garner political capital from the pre-existing North–South dichotomy created an atmosphere of widespread toxic divisions. Boko Haram began to be perceived as a Northern tool for acquiring political power, while the military's efforts in the Northeast, which were in any case riddled with gross human rights abuses (Amnesty International 2015b), were perceived as a deliberate effort to decimate the North to ensure that voting could not occur in the Northeast, where Buhari had overwhelming support.

Overall, efforts to fight Boko Haram and rescue the Chibok girls were caught in the toxic presidential politics, ethno-religious divisions in Borno state and across Nigeria, and the attendant contagion in the military. Relations among military personnel at the Army and Defence Headquarters in Abuja and the barracks all over Nigeria were negatively affected. For instance, some officers openly branded themselves 'PDP officers' while others identified as 'APC officers'. The 'PDP officers' received lucrative postings. Several 'PDP officers' were handed assignments related to efforts to rig the 2015 elections.

---

[31] However, General Minimah was subsequently indicted for corruption. The EFCC indicated that he refunded 1.7 billion Naira stolen through '"phoney" arms contracts' (Alli 2018). Minimah's candid assessment, while helping himself to funds meant to equip the military, demonstrates the doublespeak and plunder that have characterized the failure of the military to release all the Chibok girls and effectively curtail Boko Haram.

[32] Retired army general; personal interview, Abuja, July 2016. This participant was interviewed multiple times between 2015 and 2016.

Officers also fell into a familiar ethno-religious quagmire. Several Southern officers were displeased about President Jonathan's electoral loss because it meant they would lose their positions or fail to receive portfolios for which they had lobbied the PDP government. Some Northern and largely Muslim officers were ecstatic when Buhari became president-elect. The degree of polarization became evident in military barracks all over Nigeria. Private parties were organized by several senior Northern officers within and outside the barracks. Some of the senior Southern Nigeria officers who held prominent positions in the Jonathan administration heaved a sigh of relief when Jonathan lost the election as they feared outbreak of violence if Buhari had lost the 2015 presidential election. An interview with a general who was in the nucleus of the strategic efforts against Boko Haram during the Jonathan administration underscores the triumphalism of officers who were aligned with the APC, the level of toxicity within the military, and concerns by insiders about its consequences:

GENERAL: [T]he polarization is widening. Do you know that we got information that if Jonathan had insisted on staying; the polarization in the North was such that some people had already marked some of us they would eliminate. And there would have been a lot of killing in the military.

INTERVIEWER: From within?

GENERAL: From within. Do you know that when Buhari won election, some soldiers were doing barbecue in the barracks? They were celebrating and jumping all over the place. This is against military ethics. The army headquarters had to write a letter warning against such attitude, but it didn't stop some of them from running to politicians to run down their superiors. So, the polarization within the military is a dangerous thing that would not serve anybody any good.

Although the Nigerian military has had problems such as indiscipline, nepotism, and incapacity since inception (Luckhan 1969; Miners 1971), the evidence suggests that these fissures have widened. Former Chief of Air Staff and Chief of Defence Staff, Air Marshall Alex Badeh warned, during his farewell ceremony in 2015, that 'divergent interests coupled with political, religious and tribal affiliations often conflict with national interest' and made managing the military challenging (cited in George 2015).[33] Badeh spoke to the toxic

---

[33] Air Chief Marshall Badeh faced a 10-count corruption charge related to arms procurement for the military (Okakwu 2016c). He is estimated to have stolen at least $20 million (BBC 2016). Some officers who served alongside Badeh during the Jonathan administration claim that Buhari's war against

political atmosphere that weakened the military. The Nigerian military was a major victim of the struggle for power between the two major political parties prior to the 2015 presidential elections. This impeded its operations against Boko Haram. Both the PDP and APC exploited the subjectivities of officers and soldiers. These included their ethnic, religious, and regional affiliations. Simply put, officers' and soldiers' identities were politicized (Szeftel 2000). The two major political parties weaponized these pre-existing predilections and the overweening ambitions of some officers to turn the military into a political battleground. Loyalty to political patrons was rewarded with undeserved promotions and favourable postings, while political neutrality was severely punished. Professionalism of the military was sacrificed as many officers took sides in the political game. The consequence was a dangerously weakened military.

These issues manifested in the level of morale of troops and their attitudes to, and experiences in, the war theatre in the Northeast region. The war against Boko Haram began to be perceived as a 'rubbish mission'. All rank-and-file soldiers interviewed demonstrate antipathy towards the mission—the defeat of Boko Haram. The soldiers do not believe in the mission. The discourse espoused by participants about the mission has four interrelated elements. These are (a) suspicions about the sponsors and political god-fathers of Boko Haram, (b) the notion that Boko Haram is a conspiracy involving the government and top brass of the military, (c) anger over the patronage system involved in deployment into key positions on the war front, and (d) the belief that the war is being deliberately prolonged because it is a money-making machinery for the political and military elite (Oriola 2021b). One of the interviewees exemplifies the perspective of participants:

> The integrity of the system is no longer there . . . If you don't belong to their own group, their own caucus, you can never become GOC [general officer commanding] of anywhere. So, that's why you see people were dying at that period because the more we die, the more money they make.
> (Interviewee S07)[34]

The participant also describes the process for appointing commanders and the general conduct of the war as 'rubbish'.

---

corruption (in the military) is selective, given that Lt General Tukur Buratai (Chief of Army Staff) and Lt General Abdulrahman Dambazau (retired; Minister of Interior, 2015–2019), among others, who are also alleged to have corruptly enriched themselves, served in the Buhari administration without prosecution.

[34] Male soldier; personal interview, 2018.

Consequently, #BBOG responded to its external environment as the rescue of the Chibok girls was hampered by the factors analysed above. As noted, #BBOG initially expressed cautious optimism that the military had the capacity to rescue the girls. The military reciprocated by engaging #BBOG in discussions following a protest at the defence headquarters in Abuja. Key leaders of the movement were invited for a briefing. Interviews with some of those at the meeting (#BBOG leaders and the army general serving as the director of defence information, who put together the briefing) indicate that the meeting was cordial. However, as rescue failed to materialize and political leaders seemed to not prioritize the Chibok girls, the tone of #BBOG towards the Nigerian government and, invariably, its security architecture, particularly the military, changed. The state failure master frame (see Chapter 3) gained traction nationally and internationally and embarrassed the military and the government.

News about corruption in the war, poor performance, and intelligence leaks also became ubiquitous. Despite internal disagreements about how to relate with the military and the Nigerian government, #BBOG representatives began to emphasize the corruption, incompetence, and seeming lack of motivation of the military to rescue the Chibok girls. This fundamental change emerged in the autumn of 2014, as noted in Chapter 3. The PDP government of President Jonathan and the top echelons of the military began to regard #BBOG as a tool of the opposition APC, which was determined to win the 2015 elections. Therefore, the relationship between #BBOG and the military deteriorated. Avenues for mutual engagement had reduced by late 2014.

The relationship between #BBOG and the military became further complicated during the APC government (May 2015–May 2023), led by President Buhari. #BBOG's first visit to the presidential villa in summer 2015, following President Buhari's inauguration, was celebratory and friendly. However, the second visit, in 2016, damaged the rapport of #BBOG with the government and all its organs, including the military.[35] The relationship between #BBOG and the military appeared to improve immediately after the tour of Sambisa forest. However, the military's bombing of a camp of IDPs led to criticisms of #BBOG for offering praise about the 'highly professional, capable, motivated' air component of the counter-insurgency efforts of the military. This created a dent in #BBOG's reputation and affected its relationship with the government and the military.

---

[35] See details in Chapter 5.

Nonetheless, there is evidence demonstrating that the pressure from #BBOG led to direct instructions from military leaders and commanders to troops to prioritize the Chibok girls as they began to rescue thousands of women and girls from Boko Haram's camps.[36] Finally, the complicated relationship between #BBOG and the military frustrated both sides. For example, it exacerbated internal divisions within #BBOG. The military perceived the stance of #BBOG as disrespectful and unhelpful towards their efforts to rescue the girls. The military's image was further damaged as #BBOG's state failure master frame reached international audiences and reinforced the military's pre-existing poor relationship with the Nigerian public. The military also believes that #BBOG advocacy compelled the Buhari government to negotiate with Boko Haram. As previously stated, the government paid millions in hard currency and released several commanders of Boko Haram in state custody in exchange for the Chibok girls. #BBOG believes it had no choice than to act in the way it did in order to stand a chance of securing at least some of the girls.[37]

State repression against #BBOG

There are multiple empirical examples from both Western and non-Western contexts on the social movement–state repression nexus. The pre-eminent explanation is the 'threat' perspective (Earl 2003; Chang and Vitale 2013). The threat perspective holds that the level of threat posed by activists to governing elite interest is a major predictor of state repression. Larger threats to elite interests attract more severe and more frequent acts of repression by the state (Earl and Soule 2006). Political elites perceive threats in multifarious dimensions. These include large-scale protests and broad movement mobilization, use of nonconventional and seemingly abrasive tactics, and pursuit of revolutionary goals or radical objectives, among others (Davenport 2000; Earl and Soule 2006). There are also scholarly works that focus on the weakness of social movements vis-à-vis state repression (Gamson 1975). Gamson's (1975) weakness approach presupposes a bi-dimensional reasoning on the part of political elites: a social movement has to pose relatively significant threat to warrant repression but adequately weak enough to guarantee a decisive victory for the state in order to avoid any embarrassment for state actors. However, Duvall

---

[36] The Nigerian military rescued 28,150 persons (mainly women and girls) between 19 January 2015 and 27 February 2018 (Oriola 2023).

[37] See Chapter 5 on 'Outcomes of the #BringBackOurGirls Movement'.

and Stohl (1983) present an arguably unilinear framework that suggests that weakness attracts a variety of opportunistic repressive state actions.

Earl et al. (2003) have proposed a more robust weakness-centred framework. This approach encompasses weakness-from-within and weakness-from-without (Earl et. al 2003). The former speaks to lack of access of movement actors to institutional powers and the actors therein, such as politicians. Therefore, the cost of repression against such movement activists is minimal from the perspective of state actors. Weakness-from-without presumes that movements depend on external entities to monitor the activities of state actors vis-à-vis treatment of protesters. Therefore, groups that are externally weak lack the support of entities—NGOs, influential business and political elites, and foreign governments and multilateral international organizations—to forestall repression.

Earl et al.'s model (2003) provides a useful way of examining state repression against #BBOG, albeit with slight modification—an emphasis on strength rather than weakness. #BBOG has both *strength-from-within* and *strength-from-without*. The core nucleus of #BBOG is a group of powerful and influential women from the government, NGO, business, and political sectors of Nigeria (see Chapter 1). To reiterate, Ezekwesili is a Harvard-trained, two-time federal government minister and former vice-president of the World Bank; Hadiza Bala-Usman unsuccessfully ran for a seat at the House of Representatives; while Maryam Uwais is a lawyer and spouse of a former chief justice of Nigeria. In addition, Ireti Kingibe is a former Senate candidate and spouse of a three-time federal government minister and secretary to the federal government of Nigeria. Another co-convener of #BBOG, Aisha Oyebode, is the chief executive officer (CEO) of the Murtala Mohammed Foundation and daughter of a former head of state, General Murtala Mohammed. The kinship and social networks of the co-conveners offered protection to #BBOG. Besides, given the particularities of gender relations within a highly patriarchal environment, state repression against (such extremely well-connected and powerful) women would seem improbable.

The #BBOG movement is also evidently strong-from-without. The United Nations (UN) system routinely issued statements backing the cause of #BBOG. Representatives from parliaments as diverse as the United States and the European Union regularly visited the Unity Fountain to solidarize with the #BBOG movement. The likes of Malala Yousafzai also identified with the cause of the movement. This is in addition to the widespread #BBOG placard held in full view of global cameras by the likes of Michelle Obama, David Cameron, and numerous artistes and celebrities. Consequently, #BBOG also has tremendous external strength. Any act of repression against the movement would attract stern transnational condemnation.

Nevertheless, repression is shaped by regime type and other situationally dependent variables. Nigeria presents a fascinating case study, given that it is, in theory, a democratic state (since 29 May 1999) but has had a long history of military rule. Extreme state repression was ubiquitous during military rule. The 1995 extrajudicial hanging of the Ogoni Nine, a group of environmental justice and human rights activists from the oil-rich Niger Delta region, is one example of the price of social movement activities under military rule (Ikelegbe 2005; Oriola [2013] 2016). Nigeria remains heavily militarized, and human rights abuses and repression of protest by police and military authorities are frequent (Amnesty International 2015a, 2015b, 2016a, 2016b; Adeakin 2016). Some of the most recent episodes of repression include the brutal suppression of #EndSARS protests in Lagos in 2020, the abuse of Biafran secessionist agitators in the Southeast and the Shi'ites in Kaduna. The Nigerian government banned Twitter ('X') in June 2021, partly because of its use as a mobilization tool by young Nigerians.

The influence of the military on a nation state is fundamentally related to its deployment of repression (Davenport 1995; Noonan 1995). This is shaped by the type of political system in a nation state (Hanneman 1985) and the connections of the nation state to the international order or political economy (Cardoso and Faletto 1979).[38] Nigeria occupies an interstitial space between military-style authoritarianism and democracy. It is neither completely authoritarian nor democratic. The internal and external strengths of #BBOG have attenuated repressive acts directed at the movement, given its arguably provocative protests and ideations. As demonstrated below, due to its claims to a democratic ethos and the fact that #BBOG is both strong-from-within and strong-from-without, state repression against #BBOG has been largely (with one exception) subterranean and subversive rather than full-blown overt, life-and-limb assault. Covert forms of repression sow seeds of discord in social movements and hasten decline through internal decadence (Davenport 2015).

Available evidence indicates that repression against #BBOG has five major dimensions. These are attack by state-sponsored thugs, bomb threats, smear campaigns, attempts to sponsor chaos and leadership change in the movement, and intimidation through false arrests.

---

[38] Consider a self-contained pariah state versus one that is export- or aid-dependent, for instance.

Attack by state-sponsored thugs

On Wednesday 28 May 2014, #BBOG activists arrived at the Unity Fountain to find another group of women occupying their usual spot. The new group called itself '#ReleaseOurGirls'. The name was suggestive of the group's sense of the locus of responsibility as regards the Chibok girls: Boko Haram kidnapped the girls and therefore agitations needed to be directed to Boko Haram to free the captives. #BBOG found another spot and began the day's protest. Members of the #ReleaseOurGirls group surrounded #BBOG members. They began to dance and sing 'holy ghost fire, pursue Boko Haram' (Ibekwe 2014). The song appeared to be an intimidation tactic against #BBOG members. It fed into the ethno-religious and political divide in Nigeria, given that the position of the Jonathan administration was disbelief and perception that the girls were kidnapped to wrest power from the PDP. It had a subliminal message as well—a discursive invocation of the power of the Judeo-Christian God of President Jonathan, a Southerner, against the forces of the Muslim North, where Boko Haram originated.

A group of male thugs soon arrived in about 30 federal government Subsidy Reinvesetment and Empowerment Programme (SURE-P)[39] buses. *Premium Times* reports that the '(b)ottle-wielding thugs . . . attacked the #BringBackOurGirls protesters . . . breaking their seats and forcibly confiscating their phones and cameras while a group of policemen ostensibly deployed to maintain order looked on' (Ibekwe 2014). The handbags of female #BBOG members were seized and cameras of journalists from local and international media organizations were seized and destroyed. A #BBOG statement on the incident noted that the 'police, at a point, arrested two of the ringleaders, but before our very eyes, released them barely 10 minutes after' (Ibekwe 2014). This incident marked the first public act of repression against the #BBOG movement.

Bomb threats

The security situation in Nigeria was generally alarming in 2014. Large gatherings were being targeted as Boko Haram rapidly gained ground in the Northeast and expanded its operations to the North-central region. On 25 June 2014, a bomb blast occurred near Banex plaza shopping complex, a popular shopping area in Abuja. News reports indicated that 21 persons died and

---

[39] The Subsidy Reinvestment and Empowerment Programme, set up in 2012 by the Jonathan administration as a platform to invest government savings from removal of fuel subsidies.

52 were injured in the blast (BBC 2014b). The security task force of #BBOG, comprising former officials from the military and SSS, warned of a possible bomb attack against #BBOG. Some of the #BBOG security task force members still had access to insider information in appropriate circles and believed the threat of an attack against #BBOG was credible. #BBOG leaders suggested cancelling the sit-out altogether to prevent loss of lives and in order 'not to have the blood of anyone on their heads'. #BBOG members insisted that the daily protest must continue. The group began to hold the daily sit-out at different locations. One of the locations was a public park. A suspicious bag was found at the location as #BBOG members gathered. At a time of sporadic bombings in Nigeria, members believed the bag was a bomb and quickly left the location. The suspicious bag turned out to be the property of a young National Youth Service Corp (NYSC) member. While the episode turned out to be a hoax, it highlighted the real sense of danger felt by members of #BBOG.

While such existential threats diminished after the Buhari administration took over power, multiple marches by #BBOG began to be impeded. The police, under Inspector General Ibrahim Idris Kpotum, who was appointed by President Buhari, had set a pattern of preventing #BBOG from marching to the State House by September 2016. The police spokesperson for Abuja released a statement concerning #BBOG protests, arguing that the 'indiscriminate actions which are carried out in disorderly and sometimes riotous manner create unwarranted tension and apprehension among law abiding citizens and in the process obstruct legitimate business activities' (Punch 2016b). However, the Minister of Information, Lai Mohammed, continued to emphasize that the administration was willing to work with #BBOG. At the time the police were routinely preventing marches by #BBOG, Lai Mohammed stated, 'I want the Bring Back Our Girls to understand that this government appreciates what they are doing. We are battling on the same side . . . I do not see the objective of the BBOG group as different from ours.' This suggests a two-pronged response by the Buhari administration to #BBOG: suppression of dissent while simultaneously holding out an olive branch. This approach caused discord within #BBOG as some members began to worry that the #BBOG strategy towards the Buhari administration was unreasonable.

Smear campaigns

The Jonathan administration embarked on a systematic series of attempts to discredit #BBOG. The smear attacks had five main dimensions. They were intended to (a) cast #BBOG members as terrorist sympathizers; (b) demonstrate that the activists were merely using the Chibok girls as a money-making machine; (c) show that #BBOG was intent on creating breakdown of law and order; (d) destroy the image of #BBOG members, particularly its leaders, as unpatriotic citizens; and (e) construct #BBOG as a tool in the hands of the opposition party, APC. For example, Marilyn Ogar, spokesperson of the Department of State Security (DSS), 'disparaged the #BringBackOurGirls movement and referred to it as a franchise, and suggesting that the movement is affiliated to terrorists' (Premium Times 2014a). Ogar argued that

> security forces know about all the activities of the group. We know that they have a bank account ... We know that they visit prominent individuals to solicit funds; we know that they have split themselves into groups; we know that they want to simulate a protest march in Abuja to make it look like they went to Chibok.[40]

Such was the seriousness of Ogar's campaign to destroy #BBOG (and any entity critical of the government) that a *Premium Times* editorial on 20 August 2014 demanded that the DSS sack Ogar on the basis of the 'serious allegations (against #BBOG) without citing any evidence and without subsequent follow-up, clearly demonstrating that they are political statements' (Premium Times 2014a).

The official stance of the Nigerian military on #BBOG during this period was more nuanced and sophisticated than that of the DSS. The Defence Headquarters' stance was that #BBOG was attempting to lure the military into partisan politics and create unnecessary turmoil in the political arena.

#BBOG had a temporary reprieve when Buhari was sworn in as president on 29 May 2015. The movement was feted by the new president at the State House in July 2015. #BBOG once again visited the presidential villa on 14 January 2016 but the meeting turned sour and heralded a decisive change in the relationship between the Buhari administration and #BBOG. #BBOG had recommenced occasional marches to the presidential villa to demand the rescue of the Chibok girls. A national newspaper captured the deteriorating relationship:

> an indication of the souring love story emerged when against the advise [sic] of the police, the BBOG pressed on to protest the failure of the administration

---

[40] See 'Attacks on #BringBackOurGirls by security forces must stop', http://www.bringbackourgirls.ng/?p=2276. Accessed 28 December 2017.

to make remarkable progress in rescuing the Chibok girls. *For an administration that came to power with the silent goodwill of the BBOG and its supporters around the world, the clash ... was a dramatic change of tone in the communication* that had developed between the group and the Buhari administration

(Ajayi 2016; italics added)

Buhari's spokesperson, Garba Shehu, berated 'critics who are used to being settled by successive governments, with false claims to being so-called conscience of society popping out from the cupboard on and off to drive the country towards religious and ethnic polarization, they have no other motive but to rock the boat of good governance' (cited in The Cable 2017).

Attempts to sponsor chaos and leadership change in the movement

State House officials in both the Jonathan and Buhari administrations made efforts to sponsor a small number of #BBOG members to dismantle the group's leadership. A #BBOG member from the Northeast whom many members claimed had been approached by actors in government confirmed the efforts:

INTERVIEWER: I learned from a fairly reliable source that [name of National Assembly member withheld] approached you about what it could take to remove the leadership of #BBOG.
RESPONDENT: Not just him, so many people have approached me, especially because they are not comfortable with the leadership of Oby [Ezekwesili]. So, they cannot control her. That is why some of them, especially the people in government, are not comfortable with her leadership of the movement. Doing away with her by any means will weaken the movement. Therefore, the movement will not be 'antagonistic', as they put it, to the government in power.

(Interviewee 02)

The participant stated that the said National Assembly member indicated that three officials from the presidency had approached him on how to run the movement. The official noted the need to 'at least reduce this pressure coming from the movement ... [T]hey were asking him how he would help so that they can control the movement.' The government was interested in weakening the movement. He argued that 'Weakening the movement means changing Dr

Oby... if we get Dr Oby out... the remaining ones would be easy to control' (Interviewee 02). The participant emphasized that the idea emanated from the presidency, but the lawmaker was asked to serve as an instrument to make inquiry on how to get it done.

The experiences of #BBOG vis-à-vis its handling of state repression are useful for grassroots movements, particularly in the Global South. First, the decision of the leadership to shut down the sit-out and the determination of the members to continue was a critical moment that tested the democratic credentials of the movement. The followers essentially overruled the leaders. The leaders allowed the voices of the followers to determine the course of action. This may be an appropriate measure under certain circumstances. The movement could have splintered had the leadership overruled the majority of followers, who wanted the sit-out to continue. Consequently, movement leaders need to be sensitive to the *zeitgeist* among their followers: Be clear about what the options are and the implications of adopting any particular resolution. #BBOG rank-and-file members essentially agreed to absolve the leadership of responsibility if anyone got killed in bombings at the sit-out.

Second, the #BBOG leadership took major steps to prevent casualties. Bomb detection devices were brought to the sit-out to search items before anyone was allowed to participate. Parking arrangements were also overhauled. Vehicles of members had to be parked far from the sit-out to mitigate the likelihood of any car bomb attacks. Members of the #BBOG security task force were also deployed rotationally to guard the vehicles of #BBOG members during the sit-out. Leaders not only moved the sit-out to various locations, but also exact locations of the daily sit-out were not announced until an hour (or thereabouts) prior to the daily protest. This was done via text messages to members. This minimized the likelihood that the venue of the protest might be compromised.

Third, grassroots movements need to carefully manage repressive episodes. State repression can present a huge opportunity to movement activists if its aftermath is skilfully navigated. For example, #BBOG used the violent attacks against its members in May 2014 to position itself as a champion of human rights. The movement was only a few days old at the time; poor handling of the violent acts could have been the end of the movement. The government-sponsored thugs were seeking an equally violent reaction from the activists. They were ready to film outbursts of fisticuffs between #BBOG and the rented crowd. The optics would have been a public relations disaster had #BBOG members responded in the manner they were treated. However, #BBOG members huddled together and did not strike back. Taking a high moral approach drew sympathy towards the movement, and the attackers were cast as villains. It also bolstered the street credibility of the nascent movement. #BBOG passed its first major test through its dignified response. Social movement organizations must ensure that members are informed about how to act when under such attacks. The non-violent reaction of #BBOG to the provocation became a rallying point of support for the movement and further legitimized the new movement.

#BBOG immediately released a statement, which emphasized that the attacks were an affront on human and citizenship rights, which should be a source of concern to everyone, regardless of political affiliation. The attacks were therefore framed as an attack on everyone who believed in human/citizenship rights. #BBOG stated that 'We know that this is a violation of our fundamental right to peaceful assembly and freedom of association, but we remain resolute in standing with the Chibok girls. We invite every Nigerian with goodwill towards the abducted girls to our daily events.' #BBOG also emphasized the need for the government and the international community to take note of the 'descent to anarchy against our group, which simply emerged as a women-led civil society group driven by a response to the plight of the abducted Chibok girls and their families'.

The #BBOG official statement was delicately defiant and compelled several elites from the opposition party to strongly condemn the attack. The emphasis on the fact that the thugs attacked non-violent women protesters was socially meaningful. It set the tone for the response of politicians from rival political parties seeking to wrest power from the government. For instance, Bukola Saraki, a former state governor, went on Twitter ('X') to condemn the attacks on #BBOG. He said that 'Sending thugs to attack peaceful protesters acting within confines of our constitution is a new low even for this government. We should always put people over politics. Getting thugs to attack those protesting to #BringBackOurGirls is an act of cowardice.'[41] #BBOG also made effective use of social media to share images of the attacks. This drew more attention to the movement and cast the government in a negative light. Movements must take a proactive stance in shaping the narrative following episodes of repression.

Smear campaigns against a movement can be overcome through a range of actions, as demonstrated by #BBOG. These include remaining steadfast to the core values of the movement, avoiding co-optation by the government, proactively engaging the media through carefully crafted press releases and

---

[41] Saraki served as president of the Senate from 2015 to 2019.

conferences, and ensuring that the movement make available to the press the most up-to-date and accurate information. The latter ensures that, over time, the media begins to rely on the narratives of the movement as honest and beyond reproach.

Attempts to remove the leadership can be rendered ineffective by ensuring more democratic space for new leaders to emerge. #BBOG has adopted this approach by bringing on board several new faces to the ST. Ezekwesili stepped down as ST chair. Since then, multiple individuals, including Aisha Yesufu and Florence Ozor, have served as ST chair. The creation of the position of deputy chair of the ST also increases the number of leaders. This makes government attempts at removing legitimate #BBOG leadership more difficult, given the increasing number of members with leadership responsibilities. Therefore, decentralization of power and responsibilities is arguably a panacea to destruction of a movement through leadership removal or decapitation.

There are examples of movements in Africa that failed to decentralize leadership and began to decline once the lone leader was neutralized. The decline of the Movement for the Survival of Ogoni People (MOSOP) following the death of Ken Saro-Wiwa and eight of his followers is one example (Bob and Nepstad 2007).[42] The activists were framed for murder and executed (Rowell and Lubbers 2010). While Saro-Wiwa's deputy managed to escape, Saro-Wiwa was the epicentre of the struggle. The movement has not recovered from Saro-Wiwa's extrajudicial killing (Nyiayaana 2018). Repression in the form of arrests over phantom charges or, in extreme cases, assassination of activists is a real possibility in several African states. Movement leaders need to prepare for the worst-case scenario. This necessitates selecting several committed individuals, assigning responsibilities to them, and nurturing their leadership potential.

Intimidation through false arrest

On 23 January 2018, Oby Ezekwesili, Aisha Yesufu, Maureen Kabrik, Jeff Okoroafor, and several other members of #BBOG were arrested in Abuja. The protesters were marching to the presidential villa in Abuja. A detachment of predominantly female officers encircled the protesters at Unity Fountain and prevented them from leaving. The protesters were taken in police vehicles, first

---

[42] Bob and Nepstad (2007: 1370) argue that four factors internal to a movement shape the consequences of a leader's assassination. These are the 'type of leader, the movement's ideology of martyrdom, the leader's embodiment of a shared group identity, and the movement's preexisting unity'.

to a district station (the Maitama police station) and later to the Abuja Police Command. Sesugh Akume, the #BBOG spokesperson, notes that the police 'abducted' the protesters and 'locked us in and prevented us from leaving' (Adepegba 2018).

Ezekwesili live-tweeted the incident to the public and key state officials at the Unity Fountain. Ezekwesili tweeted to President Buhari that 'I have been ARRESTED along with rest of our BBOG members and NOW DETAINED without a charge by the @PoliceNG. WE are detained at the FCT command. The Police here has REFUSED to tell us why we are DETAINED' (Premium Times 2018). The crop of other persons in the movement with leadership responsibilities sprang into action. They used social media to raise awareness about the arrest and activated the impressive social capital of the movement. The internal and external strength of #BBOG was immediately evident. Ezekwesili was a respected public figure. The moment became a major embarrassment and public relations disaster for the government. Public discourses online and offline centred on the notion that Nigeria had returned to the dark days of the military and that President Buhari, a former military ruler, was back to his repressive best. The Socio-Economic Rights and Accountability Project (SERAP), a popular advocacy organization, issued a statement on Twitter ('X') demanding the immediate release of the activists (Premium Times 2018).

The Commissioner of Police released Ezekwesili and all the other protesters after about an hour. The police claimed that the protesters were not 'arrested' but had been taken 'to forestall a breakdown of law and order' (Adepegba 2018). The co-mingling of #BBOG's impressive external and internal strength had once again proven efficient against a government concerned with optics and in search of materiel and intelligence support from key global actors in its war against Boko Haram. The #BBOG spokesperson, Sesugh Akume, informed the media that 'We are going to take this up, we have already discussed with our lawyer, Femi Falana.' The statement by Akume speaks to the level of external support available to #BBOG. Femi Falana is a senior advocate of Nigeria, former president of the West African Bar Association, and a highly respected human rights advocate.[43]

---

[43] Falana has been offering his services *pro bono* to #BBOG since its inception.

Conclusion

This chapter contributes to understanding challenges confronting social movements in Africa. It analyses the interplay of oppositional politics of movement members with movement internal cohesion. There are consequences for movement unity when superstars emerge in the course of the struggle. Social movements are caught in the middle of efforts to curtail excesses of members while ensuring that they do not muzzle the rights of their vocal and visible members. This chapter raises questions about the notion of human rights-focused social movements remaining apolitical in developing countries. Social movements in Africa are inexorably drawn into politics. The political history of movement leaders and engagement in their personal capacities in the political process as electoral candidates, commentators, or keynote speakers have serious consequences for human rights advocacy. These variables embed activists in partisanship, particularly in politically toxic contexts. Such embeddedness in politics has both internal and external ramifications for social movements.

The internal divisions within #BBOG have led to fragmentation into five categories. These divisions shape how movement members perceive the (in)action of others. This weakens the movement relative to its opposition. The internal divisions of #BBOG offer important lessons for human rights advocates in Africa. A social movement needs to clearly establish membership criteria, periodically strategize on direction in the face of realities, and set a framework of governance. The vagueness of #BBOG regarding the flow of authority is a pitfall that movements must avoid. A clearly articulated governance framework needs to be crafted to address issues relating to appointment or renewal of leadership and hierarchy of authority.

This chapter contributes to theory on social movement leadership. Movements with decentralized leadership will fare better if their main leaders are neutralized through arrest or assassination. Despite criticisms of oligarchization, movements in Africa can learn from #BBOG's conscious effort to ensure diffusion of responsibilities by creating a crop of leaders to ensure that no single person's neutralization through arrest, injury, or death can destroy the struggle.

This chapter highlights how #BBOG became associated with human rights advocacy in Nigeria in its handling of repressive episodes. Repressive episodes present an opportunity to boost the credibility of activists but may be costly. #BBOG demonstrates *strength-from-within* and *strength-from-without*. This offers an important modification to the theoretical focus on weakness of movements. #BBOG's internal and external strengths—evident in the assorted pedigree (genealogy, accomplishments, and pre-existing coupling practices) of its co-conveners and its capacity to attract support from institutional and non-institutional national and international actors—have attenuated the level of state repression directed at the movement. This is fascinating, given the militarized structure of Nigeria's quasi-democratic state and widespread state violence against multiple movements, such as the Islamic Movement of Nigeria or Shi'ites (Amnesty International 2016b) and Biafran activists (Amnesty International 2016c).

The chapter contributes to understanding how social movements may be entrapped by political opportunity in Africa. The experience of #BBOG in the Sambisa tour saga suggests the need to be careful in accepting or rejecting political opportunity. Accepting political opportunity within an African context may be read as co-optation, while rejection of such opportunity may be a public relations disaster. Therefore, movements in authoritarian or quasi-democratic contexts must strategize about what the advocacy may lose in both scenarios. Questions must also be raised about the credibility of actors providing political opportunity. Movements in African contexts must be careful with messaging and wholesome 'endorsement' of state action or policy. This should not lead to unnecessary or insincere criticism. However, activists must be cognizant that the grounds may shift quickly and unexpectedly. Activists should create space to give the movement latitude in case the state reneges on a promise or policy, fails at implementation, or commits a blunder. #BBOG learned this lesson the hard way. Finally, political opportunities, including problematic ones, may be used to enhance democratic participation in a movement, as the Sambisa tour experience demonstrates.

5
Outcomes of the #BringBackOurGirls movement

Introduction: Social movements and contradictory outcomes

Social movements routinely produce contradictory outcomes despite painstaking efforts of activists. While activists may plan and strategize on tactics, framing, symbolisms, among other things, they have no control over the external environment, how their strategies are interpreted by interested institutional and non-institutional actors, as well as bystanders. Besides, the local context, and developments in the international arena may also affect movement outcomes in profound ways. Social movement outcomes have become a salient domain of inquiry, particularly since the late 1990s. There are two major schools of thought in scholarship on social movement outcomes. One school of thought explores resource mobilization and other organizational variables in movement outcomes (Gamson 1990). This focuses on the structure of social movement organizations, objectives, and tactics as key determinants of outcomes. The second school of thought emphasizes opportunities within the political process. The underlying assumption of this approach is that organizational characteristics and tactics have no effect on movement outcomes. Therefore, emphasis is on the role of structural factors, such as political context or process (Goldstone 1980). This is supported by arguments that not only are social movements shaped by their political contexts, but also their tactics and strategies are influenced by the context (Kitschelt 1986).

There are problems in the two major approaches to movement outcomes. The main critique of the two schools of thought centres on the failure to engage with (a) how the various sets of variables—organizational factors and political context—interact with one another to produce outcomes and (b) the idea that the factors that are important in producing outcomes depend on the *type* of outcome (Cress and Snow 2000). The two approaches have limited engagement with the role of framing in producing movement outcomes. Specifically, the two major approaches

Terrorism, Politics, and Human Rights Advocacy. Temitope B. Oriola, Oxford University Press.
© Temitope B. Oriola (2024). DOI: 10.1093/oso/9780198886976.003.0006

fail to consider how variation in outcome attainment might be influenced by cultural or ideational factors. One set of such factors that has been overlooked concerns the manner and extent to which the identification of targets or adversaries, the attribution of blame or responsibility, and the articulation of a plan of attack or resolution affects the attainment of desired outcomes. These factors take us to a consideration of framing processes.

Cress and Snow (2000: 1071)

An empirically and theoretically informed approach must consider the influence of a range of factors, including organization, tactics, political process, and framing, among others. Any linear approach to movement outcomes is ill informed (Cress and Snow 2000).

The need for a broad-based approach to movement outcomes is evident in social movements in Africa, particularly women's rights movements. For instance, in the women's movement in South Africa, 'a complex interaction of variables contributed to the achievement of certain positive gender outcomes' (Waylen 2007: 521). This included efforts by women's organizations, such as the Women's National Coalition (WNC), a political opportunity structure which was generally conducive to women's rights and the coalition building of influential women and their strategic actions (Hassim 2003; Witton 2005; Waylen 2007). The outcomes were therefore shaped by individual level, organizational, and structural variables. The women's movement in South Africa made significant gains in the representation of women in political offices, reproductive rights, land rights, legislation on violence against women, and many other gender-sensitive policies. However, the gains fell short of expectations, given the number of women in parliament. Despite being elite, women who were elected to parliament experienced personal and institutional problems (Witton 2005). Several of them decided not to run for a second term. It is instructive that while the political process provided an avenue for women to run for office, it also ensured that elected women were more accountable to party officials than the people they represented (Waylen 2007). Internal organizational variables, such as the decision of the WNC that women who had taken roles in government could not hold leadership positions in the organization, diminished WNC's capacity. Besides, the vitality of gender-related activism has reduced within the African National Congress (ANC) and government, which was at the epicentre of women's gains in post-apartheid South Africa.

The women's movement in Chile provides an interesting contrast to its South African counterpart. The gains in South Africa are more substantive than those made by the women's movement in Chile. The women's movement in Chile was aligned with the leftist party Concertacion, which, unlike the ANC, had limited openness to making gender-related changes. Fewer women were elected into office in Chile. The political opportunity structure available to the Chilean women's movement was further limited by two influential forces—the Catholic Church and the political conservatives (Noonan 1995; Waylen 2007).

Some authoritarian governments in Africa have promoted state-sponsored women's rights movements. This is interesting, given that the involvement of the government may provide an enabling political opportunity structure. In Egypt, Suzanne Mubarak was the symbol of state-sponsored feminism (1981–2011). Ms Mubarak arguably represented the advancement of women. She was perceived earlier in the regime as a sign of women's progress and an insignia of what was possible for young women and girls.

Suzanne Mubarak's approach to women's issues was highly centralized. Women's activism was organized around the National Council for Women (Azzi 2011). Suzanne Mubarak maintained close control of the organization and required non-governmental organizations to obtain approval before implementing any programme. Nawal El Saadawi, a popular Egyptian women's rights activist and former political prisoner, notes that 'Suzanne Mubarak killed the feminist movement so she could be the leader' (Azzi 2011). Those who criticized the organization were promptly removed. However, changes in the Egyptian political process has led to nostalgia towards the era of women's rights under the Hosni Mubarak regime. The so-called 'Suzan's laws' (Allam 2018: 116), which were associated with advances in women's rights and considered somewhat contaminated by those on the political left and right who held puritanical views, were gradually dismantled by the Islamist party, the Freedom and Justice Party of the Muslim Brotherhood (Coleman 2011). A year after Mubarak's regime, activists began to concede that the 'truth is that women were doing better under Mubarak' (cited in Ramdani 2012).

The examples above demonstrate that the outcomes of movements are shaped by factors within a social movement and external factors in the movement's socio-political and cultural context. Therefore, a social movement's outcome has to be examined vis-à-vis the movement's internal characteristics and structural variables over which the movement has no control. The outcomes of #BBOG provide an interesting space to evaluate the interplay of political context and organizational variables such as leadership, framing, tactics, and movement internal dynamics. The choices made by the #BringBackOurGirls (#BBOG) movement as regards tactics, funding, and framing were shaped by the dynamics of Nigeria's political context, which, in turn, shaped movement strategic actions. This intricate interplay influenced the outcomes of #BBOG.

Envisaging outcomes: The #BBOG movement's three scenarios

A #BBOG internal document, 'The Strategic Angle to #BringBackOurGirls', engages in *inter alia* 'scenario building' for the movement.[1] Three scenarios were envisaged: first, 'success—All our girls are brought back, safe and alive'; second, 'Failure—All or some of our girls are not brought back due to failed rescue operation, death, or being killed by the insurgents'; third, 'No Closure—The situation drags for months and beyond'. A hybrid of the second and third scenarios applies to the current situation—106 girls have been released and four have been found, while 113 are still missing.[2] However, movement outcomes are far more fluid and complicated than presupposed by #BBOG—the terms 'success' and 'failure' are increasingly problematized in scholarly literature (Amenta 2006).

Gamson calls for analysing movement 'success' 'as a set of outcomes' (Gamson 1990). His model on outcomes is dyadic: (a) '*acceptance* of a challenging group by its antagonists' as a legitimate representative of a particular interest and (b) 'new advantages' gained by a group's constituency during or after a challenge (Gamson 1990: 28–29). Kitschelt has suggested focusing on procedural impacts, substantive impacts, and structural impacts of movements (Kitschelt 1986). His approach enhances analysis of movement outcomes within specific political contexts (Guigni 1998). This approach bridges the superficial distinction between social movement organization (SMO) tactical characteristics, such as framing, and the influence of the political context. Both sets of factors are mutually reinforcing and co-constitutive.

This chapter analyses the outcomes of the #BBOG movement using terms such as *consequences* or *impact* in place of the highly problematic notions of *failure* or *success* (Amenta 2006). Overall, the chapter emphasizes the implications of #BBOG outcomes for social movements in the developing world.

The media attention on the #BBOG movement in the first six months (April–October 2014) has largely evaporated and membership—denoted by

---

[1] #BBOG internal document 02.
[2] See http://www.bringbackourgirls.ng. Accessed 26 October 2023.

attendance at the daily sit-out—has plummeted. World leaders and celebrities have moved on to other priorities. However, die-hard activists remain committed to the cause and the #BBOG movement remains synonymous with agitations for the rescue of the Chibok girls. #BBOG has gained widespread legitimacy as *the* entity to contact on issues relating to the Chibok girls. The recognition—despite the refusal of the government to involve the Abuja #BBOG organization, preferring to work with the Lagos #BBOG in the rehabilitation of the freed girls—cuts across the Nigerian government, multilateral organizations, and the international community. #BBOG's procedural impact or acceptance is evident in the regular visits, at its daily sit-out in Abuja, of representatives of various organizations and governments from all over the world.

The Nigerian government has come full circle as regards its stance on the #BBOG movement. The Jonathan administration initially ignored the movement and then reluctantly developed a bidimensional response: the military top brass demonstrated willingness to engage with the movement, while the presidency saw #BBOG as an opposition tool. The Buhari administration warmly embraced the movement, hosted the activists on 8 July 2015, and referred to the movement as the 'conscience' of Nigeria. This was a mere 40 days after taking office. The relationship between the movement and the Buhari government broke down early in 2016 because of the administration's perceived inaction over the rescue of the girls. The Sambisa tour in January 2017 (see Chapter 4) shows a significant degree of acceptance of #BBOG as a legitimate actor in the Chibok issue, although the Nigerian government continues to have a frosty relationship with the movement. This supports evidence that privileges new advantages provided through movement activities over acceptance of a movement by the state and other entities (Amenta et al. 1992). The next section examines whether the #BBOG movement has had one fundamental unintended outcome—delaying the rescue of the Chibok girls—and what this means for movements in the developing world advocating for the rights of others.

Did the #BBOG movement inadvertently prolong the Chibok girls' captivity?

The #BBOG movement raised the world's consciousness about the Chibok girls. However, that may have come at a huge price—turning the girls into prized assets in the hands of Boko Haram. For instance, Boko Haram leader,

Abubakar Shekau, mockingly told the #BBOG movement, in a July 2014 video, to 'bring back our army' (AFP News Agency 2014). The video demonstrated that Boko Haram was aware of the efforts being made by prominent women to rescue the girls. Top echelons of the Nigerian military believe the high profile of the #BBOG movement made it more difficult to find the girls (Interviewee 04). No Chibok girl was among the 28,150 people, mainly women and children, rescued by the Nigerian military, mainly from Sambisa forest, between 19 January 2015 and 27 February 2018. Some of the rescued women claimed that Boko Haram put the Chibok girls under a stricter security regime, as noted earlier. One of the army generals interviewed during research for this book illuminates how the top echelons of the Defence Headquarters views the #BBOG advocacy. He argues that, although #BBOG is 'noble',

> I don't think that putting undue pressure where it does not belong by bringing up issues where there are no issues in the name of wanting to keep the thing in discourse has helped the matter. That's one reason why these girls are still being held because the captors will say that they are important and decide to keep them.
>
> (Interviewee 04)

The general's response is antinomic. On one hand, he believes that the #BBOG movement was an important intervention, which helped to keep alive the issue of the Chibok girls, but on the other hand, the tenor and popularity of the advocacy has contributed to the prolonged captivity of the girls.

A May 2017 report in *The Guardian* notes the growing concern that the 'unintended consequence of the girls' sudden fame was that their value to the militants who held them was multiplied' (Maclean and Ross 2017). Movement members evaluate the outcomes of their advocacy and wonder, 'What have we done'? Only two of the activists interviewed for this study did not agree that #BBOG activities might have indirectly prolonged the girls' captivity. At one of the daily sit-outs, one activist asked the question, 'Supposing we #BBOG had not talked so much about our Chibok girls, would they, by chance, have been left behind by Boko Haram in Sambisa forest?' (Interviewee 17). No one had any response. The author asked Obiageli Ezekwesili, the movement's leader (Interviewee 32):[3]

INTERVIEWER: There is a belief in certain quarters that as crucial as the #BBOG was in raising awareness about the Chibok girls, #BBOG has inadvertently

---

[3] Personal interview, Abuja, May 2016.

raised the profile and the value of the Chibok girls. These girls have become prized assets in the hands of Boko Haram. How do you respond to that?

EZEKWESILI: I respond to that by saying: 'What's the counterfactual?' The counterfactual would have been to say, 'Don't say anything about the girls' so that they would forever be lost. By saying something about the girls, and enabling a focus on them, you stood a 50–50 chance on their rescue. By being quiet about the girls, you simply said they don't matter. So, which would you have chosen? In situations like this, the choices are seldom easy. All the choices are not good. So, it's the least bad one that you go for.

#BBOG's relentless advocacy compelled the government to negotiate the release of the girls by paying ransom and releasing some incarcerated Boko Haram suspects. This action worsened the overall war against Boko Haram in favour of short-term gains. Boko Haram used the ransom to purchase more sophisticated weapons and increased the intensity of its attacks. The headline of a *Wall Street Journal* article captures the sentiment: 'Two bags of cash for Boko Haram: Freedom for the world's most famous hostages came at a heavy price' (Parkinson and Hinshaw 2017). Parkinson and Hinshaw (2021) reach similar conclusions in their book *Bring Back Our Girls: The Untold Story of the Global Search for Nigeria's Missing Schoolgirls*. Several of the hostages were released only through unpublicized mediation.

This contradictory perspective on the impact of #BBOG on the struggle for the Chibok girls is widespread among a broad range of participants in the study. This is reminiscent of how the political system in South Africa promoted women's election into parliament yet ensured that female parliamentarians toiled to make changes and were largely accountable to party officials instead of constituents. It also brings to mind women's engagement in the political revolution in Egypt. Women played an active role to remove Hosni Mubarak, but successive democratically elected governments have gradually eroded the rights secured under the dictator.

Impacts of #BBOG

The #BBOG movement has had numerous impacts, despite inadvertently prolonging the girls' captivity. The negotiated release of 106 girls is a direct and substantive impact of the efforts of the movement. The activities of #BBOG had become so compelling that, in order to save face, the government had to negotiate with Boko Haram. For instance, a public spat between #BBOG and the government prior to the release of 82 Chibok girls in May 2017 sheds light on the level of pressure being mounted by #BBOG. Following the Nigerian air force accidental bombing of an internally displaced persons (IDP) camp in Rann, Borno state, in January 2017, Ezekwesili tweeted that President Buhari had failed to secure the lives of Nigerian citizens who were abducted or displaced by Boko Haram. Minister of Information, Lai Mohammed countered that the 'Federal Government has bent over backwards to carry the BBOG along and to show transparency in the conduct of the search for the girls ... We won't do anything to jeopardize these talks, irrespective of the pressure or provocation from any quarters' (cited in Odunsi 2017).

Eighty-two Chibok girls were released on 6 May 2017, less than six months after the Information Minister's public response to Ezekwesili's criticism. The negotiations involved the release of five Boko Haram commanders. The #BBOG movement's pressure on the government was effective in ensuring that negotiations were not abandoned, given multiple failed negotiations during President Jonathan's administration. Legitimate questions may be raised over whether or not the movement has inadvertently prolonged the captivity of the Chibok girls, but it is not inconceivable that the society would have simply moved on without serious efforts to rescue the girls.

Although the government has refused to acknowledge its indebtedness to #BBOG, the blueprint for psychotherapy, and other (educational) activities for the rehabilitation of the freed girls, was laid out by the movement long before the girls were released. The government's seemingly punctilious attention to the Chibok girls' welfare is unusual in the Nigerian political context. These 'new advantages' are direct effects of the #BBOG advocacy. They include

- the 'Chibok Girls Desk' in the Federal Ministry of Women Affairs and Social Development, responsible for (a) overseeing the rehabilitation and reintegration of the girls and (b) coordinating communication between concerned government agencies and family members of the kidnapped girls;
- accommodation for the freed girls in a hostel at the National Centre for Women's Development, Abuja;
- reintegration and rehabilitation programmes organized by the Ministry of Women's Affairs and the United Nations Fund for Population Activities (UNFPA), UN Women, and other donor agencies between January and September 2017;
- various instructions in English, Mathematics, Biology, Agriculture, and Civics given to the freed girls. They also received vocational and ICT training;

- psychosocial therapy and counselling to mitigate the effect of post-traumatic stress disorder (PTSD);
- medical care by doctors and nurses, provided by the government;
- sponsorship of parents of the girls by the government to visit their daughters in Abuja;
- on 27 November 2017, payment of ₦164.8 million by the government to the American University of Nigeria (AUN) in Yola for the second-semester school fees of the 106 Chibok girls who were released by Boko Haram (Ogunmade 2017).[4]

The government's uncharacteristic devotion to the rehabilitation of the Chibok girls has led to concerns about the neglect of the 'other victims' of Boko Haram (Baker 2017). *The Guardian* cautioned, 'less high-profile prisoners still held captive by the extremists would be forgotten' after the release of 82 Chibok girls in May 2017. Less than four months after the release of the 82 girls, *Time* Magazine noted that

> Humanitarian organizations estimate that there are anywhere from hundreds to tens thousands of victims who are suffering both the physical and psychological trauma of abduction, indoctrination, and savage maltreatment... *The world's attention, however, has been focused on just 276 of those victims*: the young women whose fate became a global concern after they were kidnapped from their boarding-school dormitory in Chibok on the night of April 14, 2014. The Nigerian activist group Bring Back Our Girls sprang up in the wake of the kidnapping, drawing international attention to their plight with celebrity-studded hashtag advocacy.
>
> (Baker 2017; italics added)

The substantive impact of the movement evident in the national attention to the kidnapping and the engagement of the international community on the issue is a major accomplishment, given other disasters around the world.

Other substantive impacts of #BBOG are reflected in the reinvigorated attention on the education and plight of the girl-child in Northern Nigeria. The Emir of Kano stated, during the first Chibok girls annual lecture in 2017, 'I would urge BBOG, while you keep this issue of Chibok on the table, to broaden your message to cover all girls and boys abducted by Boko Haram, and also

---

[4] There are conflicting reports about the exact number of girls enrolled as university students. Most of the students are in a remedial programme within AUN. Four Chibok girls formally registered as AUN undergraduates in September 2018 (Sahara Reporters 2018a).

draw attention to the condition of girls and women in our society in general' (Sanusi 2017). This led to widespread debates within the Northern establishment. It opened up public discourses on broader structural and cultural factors that undergirded the Chibok abduction and the rise of Boko Haram. Sanusi argued that 'after these girls are brought back, shall we ask ourselves as well: where are they being brought back to? What kind of society? How much better is the "normal" environment we all take for granted than Boko Haram camps?' (Sanusi 2017). The #BBOG advocacy opened up these critical conversations.

Resources are now being channelled towards rebuilding schools in the Northeast, due largely to the #BBOG advocacy. For instance, the African Development Bank (ADB) approved $1 million for rebuilding Government Girls Secondary School (GGSS), Chibok, Borno, the scene of the 2014 kidnapping (Musa 2017). Several other programmes, such as the Presidential Committee on the North-East Initiative (PCNI), were set up following #BBOG advocacy. The Safe School initiative led by former British Prime Minister Gordon Brown, clearly articulates the influence of the #BBOG movement in its implementation of the programme in Nigeria. The Office of Gordon and Sarah Brown (2014) notes that as 'part of the growing movement to 'Bring Back Our Girls, the initiative is an initial $10 million fund, challenging matching investments by the government, to promote schools as safe spaces'.

There are other indirect impacts of the #BBOG movement. These include support for IDPs in the Northeast region. Some members of the movement have set up non-governmental organizations (NGOs), such as 'Adopt-a-camp' and 'Girl-child Africa',[5] which provide assistance to those displaced by Boko Haram. Other NGOs, such as Citizens of Impact, are contributing to scrutiny of government ministries and agencies to enhance accountability. Sesugh Akume, the head of #BBOG's strategic communication team, is engaged in multiple lawsuits challenging the constitutionality of government actions. Although #BBOG has decided not to transmute into an NGO, the newly formed organizations suggest that #BBOG has nurtured the humanitarian drive and leadership skills of several members. The advocacy appears to have brought out leadership drive in several members. This is consistent with research indicating that 'distributed leadership' in movements has potential to nurture the capacities of participants (Brown and Hosking 1986: 65).

At a structural level, #BBOG has advanced the frontiers of non-violent protest in Nigeria. A lawsuit filed by #BBOG in Abuja in 2014 is one example. #BBOG's victory in the case made the police 'backtrack' over cancellation of

---

[5] Led by Bukky Sonibare and Tunji Baruwa, #BBOG strategic team members.

peaceful protests in Abuja and issue a statement in September 2016 that they were 'committed to the principles of democratic policing and adherence to international best practices in public order management' (Okakwu 2016a). This is a major accomplishment, given the reputation and mode of operation of the Nigerian police force. The #BBOG influence has impacted several other forms of human rights advocacy. #BBOG has played a catalytic role in sensitizing citizens to issues of governmental responsibility and state failure, as well as human and citizenship rights. Other social justice-orientated movements have been formed and have often chosen the Unity Fountain in Abuja, the venue of #BBOG's daily sit-out, as their meeting point.[6]

Furthermore, the #BBOG movement's indirect outcomes include its contribution to bringing about a major political change—the first electoral defeat of an incumbent president in Nigeria's history. The evidence demonstrating the contributions of #BBOG to the 2015 tectonic change in Nigeria's political landscape is overwhelming (Adeniyi 2017; Godwin 2015; Siollun 2015; Alli 2017). How the Chibok girls' case was handled—the focus of #BBOG—galvanized international support for political change (Vanguard 2017). Olusegun Adeniyi, a journalist and spokesperson to former President Yar'Adua, states in his book on the 2015 elections (Adeniyi 2017: 190) that Nigerians were 'riled' and 'the opposition used [it] to campaign against him'. The #BBOG movement's framing of the kidnapping of the Chibok girls (Ezekwesili 2015), the failure of the Jonathan government to rescue the victims, and the bungling of multiple opportunities to secure the release of the girls significantly eroded the credibility and legitimacy of the Jonathan government. This fed into the change mantra of the All Progressives Congress (APC), the main opposition party at the time (Adeniyi 2017).

Assessing the #BBOG movement's outcomes

#BBOG has been criticized for its seemingly narrow focus on the Chibok girls.[7] However, #BBOG has maintained that the Chibok girls are a symbol of the

---

[6] The groups include 'Our mumu don do' and 'Resume or resign', among others. Other groups fighting more immediate issues, such as salary and pension payment, have also begun to make use of the Unity Fountain. Such has been the symbolism and utility of the Unity Fountain that a detachment of police officers—ranging from 6 to 13 men—daily guard the location to prevent any 'trouble'. A conversation with a senior officer on duty provided an interesting angle to the police deployment. The officer insisted they were there to prevent 'copycat' groups from causing trouble. The police often left when #BBOG began its daily meetings.

[7] #BBOG was quick to join the struggle for the release of the Dapchi girls, who were killed in Yobe state on 19 February 2018.

clamour for a just society. Therefore, outcomes in other areas, such as funding for education and growth in human rights advocacy, are an indirect effect of the influence of #BBOG. Critics of #BBOG—including some of its own members—argue that the movement could have had more impact, given the enormous goodwill it garnered, especially internationally. For instance, the decision of #BBOG not to accept any form of financial assistance is criticized as a 'missed opportunity' (Interviewee 30). Several donor agencies approached #BBOG in its early days to find out how they could support the cause (Interviewee 30). However, #BBOG insists that accepting funds may feed into a government narrative, as noted in Chapter 4. This narrative purports (a) to cast #BBOG as a tool of the opposition party, (b) that it is sponsored by foreign agents to make the government lose its credibility, and (c) that leaders of #BBOG are motivated by money and fame (Ezekwesili 2015).

Social movements must adapt as circumstances change in their political context. #BBOG has been criticized for its framing and overall discursive tone and tactics. Some #BBOG members also share this perspective, as previously noted. Such #BBOG members believe that #BBOG's framing and tactics ought to have evolved when the APC government was sworn into office (Interviewee 19).[8] One #BBOG member argues, 'I am not surprised that we have been shut out because it was our process ... So I think we could have, instead of trying to fight, we could have tried to partner with the government for the benefit of the girls' (Interviewee 32).[9] Some #BBOG members believe that it was unnecessary to continue marches and public confrontations with the Buhari administration. Such members argue that the movement has always had 'back channels' of communication with, and access to, several individuals at the highest levels of government. Some government officials, such as Mariam Uwais, Hadiza Bala-Usman, and Saudatu Madi, are co-conveners of #BBOG but have largely distanced themselves from the movement. One #BBOG member argues, 'maybe because we are used to fighting the government we don't know how to grasp an olive branch when we see one' (Interviewee 32).

The government has maintained that #BBOG has been unnecessarily adversarial in its approach. For instance, Nigeria's Minister of Information, Lai Mohammed, felt disappointed that, after he had facilitated the government-sponsored Sambisa tour (see Chapter 4) to show #BBOG the government's commitment to ensure the release of the girls,

---

[8] Male #BBOG member; personal interview, Abuja, July 2015 and six participants in three focus group discussions, among several others.
[9] Female #BBOG member; personal interview, Abuja, July 2017.

it came to us as a surprise that in spite of its initial positive report on the tour, the BBOG has too quickly reverted to its adversarial role. BBOG should stick to its role as an advocacy group rather than pretending to be an opposition party... The synonyms of the word 'advocacy' do not include 'antagonism', 'opposition' or 'attack'. In fact, those words are the antonyms of 'advocacy'.

(cited in Odunsi 2017)

How #BBOG framing impacted the political opportunity structure is evident in the government's perspective regarding the 'impudent language' of the #BBOG leadership, with its regular ultimata and the notion that the movement would 'no longer tolerate delays' and 'excuses' over the release of the girls. The Buhari administration believes such language was suited to President Jonathan's government but 'not for a President who has presided over the liberation of all captured territory, the opening of shut schools and roads, the safe release of some of the abducted girls and the decimation of Boko Haram' (Odunsi 2017). Consequently, #BBOG antagonized the Buhari government, which led to its being shut out of the rehabilitation and reintegration of the rescued Chibok girls.

While #BBOG's framing impacted the political opportunity structure and its political context, as demonstrated in the government's response, it is pertinent to consider what alternatives were available to the movement. Given that Borno was in a state of emergency because of Boko Haram's attacks, the kidnapping in Chibok and the languid response demonstrate a level of governmental ineptitude that arguably left movement activists with little choice but to challenge the government on themes centred on state failure. Therefore, #BBOG's framing tactics, such as periodic marches and press releases during the Jonathan administration, were a direct response to the movement's political context. These, in turn, influenced the political context and opportunity structure in an unfavourable direction. It is debatable that a more conciliatory regime-placating approach could have been effective. #BBOG had two options when the APC took over presidential power. One was to be fully co-opted; the other was to remain outside and continue their agitation. One influential #BBOG member argues, 'I would have chosen to be fully co-opted and I say it with a sense of responsibility. We had people in government who are sympathetic to the cause and I believe ... the only reason for agitation is to get a seat at the table' (Interviewee 45).[10]

Contrasts may be drawn with Chilean women's approach, which drew on framing favoured by the Pinochet regime and therefore did not antagonize

---

[10] Male #BBOG member; personal interview, Abuja, July 2018.

the government. However, such comparisons omit factors such as the North–South divide on public opinion regarding the Chibok kidnapping. There was a lot of scepticism about the veracity of the kidnapping incident. This is a major factor within the political context that is rarely appreciated vis-à-vis its influence on the choices made by #BBOG. The #BBOG narrative included the need to convince sceptical members of the public, particularly in the South, that 219 girls were kidnapped in Chibok. President Jonathan continues to have serious questions about the incident even after leaving power. Olusegun Adeniyi, who interviewed President Jonathan for his book, notes that 'Jonathan does not seem able to resolve some questions about the incident in his own mind' (Adeniyi 2017: 190).

Keeping the Chibok issue in the news despite the election of Buhari as president appears to have been shaped by factors that the movement could not control. For instance, it is rarely acknowledged that President Buhari evolved in his attitude towards the threat posed by Boko Haram and the war against it. As presidential candidate in 2013, Buhari was opposed to the declaration of a state of emergency in Borno, Yobe, and Adamawa states. He was also displeased with the clampdown on Boko Haram (Akowe 2013). Buhari's party at the time, the Action Congress of Nigeria (ACN), also argued that designating Boko Haram and Ansaru terrorist organizations, 'desirable as it may be in tackling the terrorist organisations, violates the Constitution of the Federal Republic of Nigeria by stifling the press and tampering with the fundamental human rights of Nigerians.'[11] ACN transmuted to APC, which assumed power in 2015. Buhari backtracked on his views on Boko Haram during his inauguration speech on 29 May 2015. He acknowledged the threat posed by Boko Haram and argued, 'we can not claim to have defeated Boko Haram without rescuing the Chibok girls and all other innocent persons held hostage by insurgents'.

Nonetheless, although no Chibok girl had been rescued, President Buhari declared, on 24 December 2015, that Boko Haram had been 'technically defeated'. This negated his inauguration message and the overarching symbolism of rescuing the Chibok girls in the war against Boko Haram. On 30 December 2015, President Buhari stated that his administration had 'no credible information' on the Chibok girls' whereabouts. #BBOG viewed the idea that Boko Haram had been technically defeated without the rescue of any Chibok girl and the admission of the President, in December 2015, that he had no

---

[11] The statement could have been politically motivated but speaks to the complexity of the context in which #BBOG operates.

credible intelligence on the location of the missing girls as indication that the government was lax in its approach to the issue. #BBOG had a rancorous meeting with the President in January 2016 and expressed displeasure at the lack of results. #BBOG subsequently resumed its marches, convinced that the government was not prioritizing the rescue of the Chibok girls. #BBOG's return to the trenches further alienated the government.

The analysis above indicates the complicated maze the Nigerian political context posed to #BBOG movement activists. Movement outcomes must be considered within the political context of the movement (Goldstone 1980; Giugni 1998). The #BBOG experience demonstrates the link between framing and political context—both are intricately intertwined. Movement actors adopt specific framing and tactics in view of their appreciation or evaluation of the specificities of the political structure or context of their advocacy, and in turn, the political context is influenced by movement framing and tactics. One consequence is a hardening of positions, measures, policies, and affective dispositions of political actors, in part as a reaction to framing. This means that movement activists are somewhat in a double bind, especially in illiberal quasi-democratic contexts: they may want to respond appropriately to the context within which they operate, but such response also ends up shaping the political opportunity structure, the trajectory of their struggle, and its outcomes.

An informed understanding of movement outcomes needs to put into cognizance organizational variables such as SMO structure, objectives, framing, and tactics and opportunities or constraints within the political process. The two sets of variables are synergistic and mutually reinforcing. This finding contributes to the scholarly literature on how social movement tactics, framing, and overall organization are shaped by political context; the tactics and strategies, in turn, influence the context. The interlay of both sets of variables influences movement outcomes.

Theorizing social problems

One of the basic lessons of the social constructionist perspective in the sociology of social problems is that defining a social condition as a *social problem* is a game (Loseke 1999).[12] This game involves various contextually situated actors with particular values and interests, which shape how they view the

---

[12] This section was first published in my 2023 article on 'The exploitation of the Nigerian Chibok girls and the creation of a social problem industry' (Oriola 2023).

situation. Therefore, there are competing claims, claims-making, and claims-makers (Loseke 1999) in an ideational process of contestation and a battlefield over meanings, legitimacy, veracity, and authenticity. The interplay of actors, actions, and constructed meanings in multifarious audiences may lead to the rise of a social problem industry around a successfully defined social condition. Such industries are denoted by variegated nomenclature. They include the 'troubled persons industry', the 'helping professions', and the 'mercy industrial complex', among others. They count in their ranks occupational specialists and professionals as diverse as workforces in criminal justice, human services, social work, as well as NGOs and community-based organizations (CBOs). The social problem industry commands huge budgets and provides for its professionals an avenue for earning decent wages and a fine career path, despite the risks shaped by context.

Individuals are motivated to get involved in the social problems industry for different reasons. These include '*subjective values*, the moral beliefs we personally hold' (Loseke 1999: 32; italics original). Personal objective interests may also influence involvement in the social problem industry (Loseke 1999). This means that individuals may be involved due to benefits they may obtain. This is not merely limited to pecuniary benefits but may include benefits such as a new school for children or a safer neighbourhood. Individuals may also get involved in the social problem industry because it is simply fun to do so (Loseke 1999). This implies that their involvement neither reflects their values nor are their interests met by their engagement. Rather, a community of fun-seekers develops, which can be quite gratifying (Loseke 1999).

In reality, '[t]rying to separate interests and values often is a hopeless task' (Loseke 1999: 34). For instance, there is growing recognition that much NGO work in the developing world provides living standards unavailable to most people in the local community and beyond such professionals in their home countries. The experiences garnered overseas, particularly in poor countries, can also be parleyed into application documents for admission into prestigious institutions and well-paying positions in the public and private sectors and multilateral organizations. Therefore, such individuals may have rendered help to others just as much as they have helped themselves.

The idea that a social problem may serve positive functions for those who are not directly impacted is not new. Gans (1972), for instance, applies a Mertonian structural-functionalist approach to explicate how poverty and the poor as a social category perform 15 positive functions for US society. These include ensuring that menial and monotonous jobs are done, subsidizing the rich through low wages, and the army of occupational specialists and professionals that serve the poor. Oriola ([2013] 2016) adopts a dramaturgical perspective to articulate the entanglement of a web of state and non-state actors in the processual fabrication of kidnapping of oil workers in Nigeria's Delta region. These actors include oil-producing communities, 'interventionists' who serve as negotiators during kidnapping episodes, oil workers, transnational oil corporations, and insurgents, among others (Oriola [2013] 2016: 28). Oriola concludes, 'ending the insurgency is not in the interest of most of the actors involved. Many of them have become entrenched ... and will suffer considerable economic and/or symbolic loss' (p. 47).

Blumer identifies three 'central deficiencies' in the sociology of social problems (Blumer 1971: 301). First, sociology does not help to identify or discover social problems; recognition of a social problem by, and within, society precedes sociological detection. Second, sociologists typically assume that social problems are objective social conditions. Third, sociologists often presuppose that their diagnosis of the objective conditions of a social problem provides a panacea for solving the problem. Blumer proposes a thesis that 'social problems are fundamentally products of a process of collective definition instead of existing independently as a set of objective social arrangements with an intrinsic makeup' (Blumer 1971: 298). This thesis is anchored on a five-stage model regarding the life course of a social problem. The stages are: (a) emergence, (b) legitimation, (c) mobilization of action regarding the social problem, (d) crafting an official plan of action, and (e) implementation of the official plan of action.[13]

This is a useful theory for understanding how an undesirable condition becomes defined as a social problem. It calls attention to the fact that (a) there are numerous harmful social conditions in society, (b) the seriousness of harms experienced by a section of society does not guarantee that a social condition will be defined as a social problem, (c) there is a need to understand the underlying process by which deleterious conditions become defined as a social problem, and (d) social problems are not merely issues of structural strain, pathology, or dysfunction (Bossard 1941).

However, Blumer's theorization has limited applicability. There are four major weaknesses in Blumer's theory:

- It has limited applicability outside developed societies. It does not put into cognizance the peculiarities of non-Western, illiberal,

---

[13] Bossard articulated a 12-stage model in 1941. The weaknesses in Blumer's theory, discussed in the remainder of this section, are evident in Bossard (1941).

quasi-democratic societies, particularly in relation to the establishment or efficacy of an official plan of action to tackle a social problem.
- It is unilinear and deterministic by presupposing that once a condition is recognized as a social problem, it will proceed through all five stages and ultimately get resolved in a manner favourable to those affected.
- While the theory recognizes the contestedness of legitimizing a social condition as a social problem, it does not account for the role of (international) actors outside the immediate population and locality affected by a successfully defined social problem.
- It is limited in scope regarding the political economy that may arise within a social problem industry.

These four issues need to be considered when analysing social problems in a developing world context. This section proposes a contextual, seven-stage model that captures the career trajectory of the social problem industry around the Chibok girls' cause. This model avoids the weaknesses of Blumer's theory and arguably offers a more theoretically and empirically useful way of understanding how social problems are defined and emergence of a helping industry around specific social problems in developing countries. This section first explores the social problem industry within which the Chibok girls and their community are ensconced and the various dimensions of exploitation of the victims.

Forms of exploitation of the Chibok girls

The social problem industry generates significant capital. For Bourdieu, capital—'any resource effective in a given social arena that enables one to appropriate the specific profits arising out of participation and contest in it'—is manifested in four major ways (Wacquant 2006: 7). These are economic, cultural, social, and symbolic. The Chibok girls have produced various forms of capital for the claims-makers and newer stakeholders. The forms of exploitation of the Chibok girls are analysed below.

Presidential photo-ops and political mileage
The Buhari administration exploited the Chibok girls' release for symbolic capital and political mileage. For instance, a vigilante group found Amina Darsha Nkeki on 17 May 2016. She was the first Chibok girl found. Amina returned from captivity with a young child and her Boko Haram 'husband'. Amina and

her child were flown to Abuja from Maiduguri for a medical check-up and sent for photo-ops at the presidential villa 48 hours after they were found. Amina Nkeki's visit to the presidency was a huge political affair, despite her frail health after over two years in captivity. President Buhari, the First Lady, Aisha Buhari, the Governor of Borno state, Kashim Shetima, military chiefs, and several other top government officials received Amina and her son. The government was intent on celebrating the moment in the full glare of global television. Amina Nkeki was not in the physical and mental shape for the fanfare as she 'was limping and severely malnourished when she arrived with her baby' (Busari 2016). Besides, the exploitation of Amina's release was ironic, given that security forces were not involved in securing her freedom.

The reception organized to present Amina set the template for subsequent public relations-orientated exploitation of the released Chibok girls. A similar media event at the presidential villa was organized on 19 October 2016 when 21 Chibok girls were released by Boko Haram following negotiations with the government. This was followed by another on 7 May 2017 after 82 Chibok girls were released by Boko Haram. The BBC (2017) caption of one of the pictures taken at the event reads, 'Some (of the girls) were visibly tired after their ordeal.' The haste with which the presidential receptions were organized and the media performances that ensued on each occasion were aimed to reap political capital by showcasing the Buhari administration's success in securing the release of the girls.

However, the events have proven to be impression management strategies to demonstrate that the government was *doing* something. In reality, the security situation in Nigeria had, in fact, worsened since the Buhari administration assumed office (Abubakar 2018). A *New York Times* article captures the condition as a '(d)eadly lack of security' (Akinwotu 2018). Consequently, the occasional negotiated release of the highly prized Chibok girls served the Buhari government's political agenda aimed at masking deteriorating security conditions.

Framing success: The army and the rescue of the Chibok girls
The authorities of the Nigerian army have been engaged in efforts to deploy the release of Chibok girls for positive media attention. The army appears intent on the performative act of being seen to rescue Chibok girls. This has led to a series of other embarrassing episodes. For instance, a *Guardian* (Maclean 2016) report notes the 'desperate bid to claim credit' for the rescue of Amina Nkeki. In May 2016, the army announced that it had rescued a girl, Falmata Mbalala. The army later confirmed that the girl was, in fact, Amina Ali and

argued, 'troops had rescued her in conjunction with Civilian JTF [joint task force], the local vigilante force' (Maclean 2016). Amina's family refuted the army's claim. They insisted that a group of vigilantes found and brought her home.

The army claimed it had another of the kidnapped Chibok girls, Serah Luka. However, Chibok community members and activists contradicted the army's claim. Serah Luka did attend the same school but was not part of the 276 girls kidnapped in April 2014. Female victims who have been rescued from Boko Haram have narrated being vigorously asked by security forces if they were among the Chibok girls.[14] They spoke of being forgotten once they confirmed they were not among the initial Chibok kidnap victims. The Nigerian military was involved in the rescue of 28,150 persons (mainly women and girls) between 19 January 2015 and 27 February 2018. However, none of the victims garnered the media attention given to Amina Nkeki or any of the other Chibok girls.

'From Muslim predators in Africa to Christian predators in America': International media exposure and financial exploitation of the Chibok girls

Nineteen of the Chibok girls who escaped from Boko Haram the night they were captured have also been used to serve the agendas of a web of actors, organizations, and interests outside Nigeria. The interplay of political actors, human rights advocates, school administrators, NGOs, and unsuspecting humanitarians in the United States has led to serious concerns, accusations, and counter-accusations about what entity was exploiting the Chibok girls. Emmanuel Ogebe, a US-based Nigerian lawyer, is at the epicentre of controversies over the manipulation, control, and financial exploitation of the Chibok girls who escaped on the night of their capture. Emmanuel Ogebe facilitated the travel of 10 Chibok girls to the United States during the Jonathan administration.

First, the Chibok girls have been used to raise funds at public events in the United States. Thousands of dollars have been raised in both online and in-person campaigns, with little oversight or accountability. The Nigerian government expressed concerns, in 2016, that NGOs were using the girls as 'tools for making money' in the United States (Haruna 2016). Aishatu Alhassan, Nigeria's minister of women's affairs, informed parents of the girls that the government had ascertained the exploitation of the girls. Yakubu Nkeki Maiva, a representative of the parents, asked the government to take over the girls'

---

[14] Multiple sources among participants.

education. He argued, 'we were told that they were going there to study and not going on tourism. We want them to return home with certificates and not tourists' experiences' (Haruna 2016). A Nigerian government report notes that 'Mr. Ogebe generated a lot of money through these activities and never spent a dime to care for their well-being ... The girls ... accused him of using them as money minting machines' (Hinshaw et al. 2018). Fraud allegations against Ogebe were investigated by the Federal Bureau of Investigation (FBI) in 2016. The FBI 'found Mr. Ogebe had likely been keeping or misappropriating money he raised in the name of the Chibok students, but that he also spent some fraction of that money housing and transporting them ... That made it difficult to prosecute the case' (Hinshaw et al. 2018).

Second, the series of events organized to raise funds ostensibly for the welfare of the Chibok girls necessitated coercing the girls to recount the kidnap ordeal within a few days of arriving in the United States (Interviewee 10)[15] further traumatized the girls. Hinshaw et al. (2018) note that 'Over and over again, they [the girls] say they have been asked by Mr. Ogebe and others to recount an escape most wished to put behind them' and often led audiences to tears. However, the constant retelling of the stories before well-paying audiences became problematic for the integrity of their narrativized experiences. It ensnarled the girls in lies, deceit, and rhetorical embellishments. Hinshaw et al. (2018) note that 'In time, the young Nigerians themselves began to doubt each others' survival stories. The accounts had changed so much in repeat tellings they became dissociated from the actual ordeal.' One of the students claimed that 'We know that they are lies.' She argued that Mr Ogebe and his allies encouraged them 'to embellish their accounts ... to make the story interesting so that people will like it so much' (Hinshaw et al. 2018). One parent, Paul Ali Maiva, said his daughter and a few others were taken to the United States by one Paul Gadzama. He expressed concerns that 'they are being used for show business ... to narrate how they escaped Boko Haram captivity; and then afterwards they will be given money. That was not want we wanted for our children' (Haruna 2016).

In addition, the 106 girls who have remained in Nigeria have also been at the centre of dubious public relations campaigns. For instance, in November 2017, the Nigerian government announced that it had paid the second-semester school fees (₦164.8 million or over $450,000 [US]) to the American University of Nigeria (AUN), Yola for the 106 Chibok girls (Ogunmade 2017). This gave the impression that all the 106 girls were university students at AUN. However,

---

[15] Member of the #BBOG strategic team; personal interview, Abuja 2017.

only six of the girls were university students. A journalist with access to the girls notes that all but six of the girls

> are in university premises but studying a special course. Some of them have been taught at nursery school level. I've been told that some require at least eight years' to proceed to the university level because of the poor education they had prior to the kidnapping incident. Therefore, about 100 of the girls are enrolled in the New Foundation School, 'a school within a school' on the campus of AUN.
>
> (Interviewee 46)[16]

Four other Chibok girls enrolled as undergraduates in September 2018 (Sahara Reporters 2018c). The general reportage of the Chibok matter laid the groundwork for a widespread misperception of the true educational level of the girls. The journalist cited above argues,

> when they escaped, people scrambled. People in the US, thinking they were dealing with girls about to go into the university. You know, they thought that these were girls that were disrupted from being medical doctors and engineers. You know the CNN and BBC thing, which you and I know is a lie. They were not on the way to becoming medical doctors or engineers not with the quality of education they were getting. But these people saw these things on the media and thought it was real and they scrambled to get these girls to school. So you take them to a place like the US and find out that they can't even speak English. So I know it threw a lot of people off balance and for the girls, it was very upsetting.
>
> (Interviewee 46)

Third, some of the girls also appeared to struggle with a diminished sense of self caused by being reduced to one incident on one night of their lives. One of the escaped girls in the United States noted that 'We hate when they call us Chibok girls ... I am Kauna' (Hinshaw et al. 2018). The girls have also experienced chronic instability in their education and residence in the United States (Haruna 2016). Some of the girls have attended five schools within four years (Hinshaw et al. 2018) due to being constantly relocated because of struggles over control by their handlers (Interviewee 10).

Fourth, the Chibok girls' case has enhanced the visibility, relevance, and careers of several stakeholders and claims-makers. Ogebe, for instance, has

---

[16] Nigerian journalist; personal interview, Abuja, July 2018.

appeared before the US Congress and delivered talks at United Nations and human rights-related events organized by transnational NGOs. The Chibok girls are central to his international visibility. Some #BBOG activists in Nigeria also owe their socio-political influence to their involvement in the Chibok issue. Print and electronic media regularly seek them for commentaries on political and human rights affairs. While this is time-consuming, given that many of the #BBOG activists are engaged in other sectors of the economy and do not necessarily earn a living from activism, they have become household names and celebrities in Nigeria. However, the strained relationship between #BBOG in Abuja and the government of Nigeria means that the released girls have had little to no contact with the Abuja #BBOG activists.[17]

The escaped Chibok girls in the United States were also deployed to foster a 'clash of civilization' (Hinshaw et al. 2018) agenda among US politicians. The narratives promoted by Emmanuel Ogebe in particular fed into the predilections of Republican politicians about a war between jihadi zealots and innocent Christians in Nigeria. Ogebe espoused the narrative of 'Christian genocide' in Nigeria and the girls cast as 'symbols of global religious strife' (Hinshaw et al. 2018).[18] Hinshaw et al. (2018) note,

> Mr. Ogebe helped shape U.S. policy toward Africa's most populous country. His calmly narrated accounts of Boko Haram murders of Christians—*he rarely mentioned the sect's more numerous killings of Muslims*—won him friendships with powerful contacts. Republican Congressmen Jason Chaffetz and Chris Smith met him often, as did congresswoman Frederica Wilson, a Miami Democrat [italics added].

Jacob Zenn notes that Ogebe 'knows the trigger words to say that will get attention to his issues in Washington' (cited in Hinshaw et al. 2018). One former White House adviser, Doug Wead, ran one of the schools, the Canyonville Christian Academy in Oregon, which hosted some of the girls. Wead and Ogebe had multiple clashes, 'accusing each other of using the young women for personal and political gain' (Hinshaw et al. 2018). Despite his arguably problematic positionality—denoted by his encouraging the girls that 'people would lose interest if they didn't shop their story to filmmakers', Wead provides a didactic perspective on the use of the Chibok girls in the United States.

---

[17] #BBOG Lagos, however, works closely with the Nigerian government on the released Chibok girls.
[18] The idea of Christian genocide under the Buhari administration has since become widespread among minorities and Southern Nigerians. For more on this theme, see Bishop Hassan Matthew Kukah's presentation to a US Congress committee (The Cable 2021).

He argues that 'This is a tale of girls being passed from Muslim predators in Africa to Christian predators in America' (cited in Hinshaw et al. 2018).

Some actors in the Buhari government also arguably profited from the Chibok girls matter. Ogebe argues that officials in the Buhari administration worked with US media to take the Chibok girls from him. Ogebe claims the five girls being overseen by the Nigerian government are in 'ghetto-like' conditions in Bronx in New York (Sahara Reporters 2018c) and that international donations made to the federal government for the welfare of the girls had not been utilized for that purpose. He claims, 'Some people in the Nigerian government are using the girls to launder funds and over $2 million is said to have been spent on just taking care of five girls.' He criticized the 'adult-education school' in which the girls were enrolled and argued that the government 'lied to the world that they were enrolled in a university'.[19] Ogebe filed a $5 million libel lawsuit against the federal government of Nigeria in 2017. He claimed there was a 'malicious campaign to tarnish his image' (Ogundipe 2017).

The treatment of the Chibok girls constitutes a 'cautionary tale of disgraceful, predatory philanthropy' (Boomer 2018). The interaction of multiple actors noted above feeds into growing concerns over the conflict economy that is developing in Northeast Nigeria. In December 2016, a leading NGO in Nigeria, the Socio-Economic Rights and Accountability Project (SERAP) petitioned the Economic and Financial Crimes Commission (EFCC) to launch an investigation into the whereabouts of ₦500million budgeted for rebuilding the Government Girls Secondary School, Chibok, where the girls were kidnapped (Agency Report 2016). The EFCC launched its investigation into the missing fund in 2017. The exploitation of the Chibok girls is a fraction of a larger economy of graft and miscellaneous criminality in relation to the social impact of the Boko Haram phenomenon. Abdulazeez and Oriola (2018) analyse the activities of institutional and non-institutional actors in embezzling funds for IDPs and use of ghost IDPs, as well as hoarding, theft, and diversion of relief materials intended for IDPs and other victims of Boko Haram. For instance, Babachir Lawal, Secretary to the Federal Government of Nigeria, was indicted by the Senate in 2017 and subsequently removed from office for 'bribery and breach of law in the procurement exercise' related to the Northeast region (Adebayo 2017). Kashim Shetima, who was governor of Borno state when the girls were kidnapped, was highly critical of the role of United Nations agencies and NGOs in the state. Shettima criticized the United Nations Children's Fund

---

[19] No one, at the time of writing, had been sued or convicted for financial malfeasance in relation to the Chibok girls.

(UNICEF) and 126 other organizations in the state for poor performance.[20] He argued that

> The huge chunk of what they are budgeting for Borno goes to service their overheads. I, as a governor don't ride in bullet proof cars; but they spend more than $50, 000 buying bullet proof cars for themselves … They will construct five toilets in Gwoza and fly in helicopters more than seven times to inspect the toilets … *We have become a cash cow; and people are smiling their ways to the banks from the agony of our people*. This is unacceptable. People that are really ready to work are very much welcome here. But people that are here only to use us to make money, may as well leave. We don't need them, since they are only trying to use us to make money.
>
> (cited in Haruna 2017; italics added)

The contextual seven-stage social problem industry model

Tragic social situations or conditions do not automatically become social problems. The kidnapping of the Chibok girls would have likely faded as another in a constellation of security problems in Nigeria. #BBOG helped turn the Chibok kidnapping into a social problem in a sociological sense. The movement made the kidnapping incident gain currency in the global imagination and challenged the Nigerian state and society (Oriola 2021a). In the process, #BBOG engaged in an ideational battlefield with three other entities—the federal government of Nigeria, the army, and the APC. The APC had interest in being seen as an ally of #BBOG until it became the ruling party. This shows the fluidity of claims-making, temporality of alliance, and texture and dynamics of objectives of actors in the social problem industry.

The industry created after a social condition is successfully defined as a social problem is profitable and self-perpetuating. #BBOG's success in turning the Chibok kidnapping into a social problem has had a bifocal consequence. On one hand, it led to global attention on the issue and influenced Nigeria's political context. The advocacy contributed to the first electoral defeat of an incumbent president in Nigeria's history (Adeniyi 2017; JoNathan 2018; Oriola 2021a). On the other hand, #BBOG inadvertently contributed to the creation of a social problem industry, which has generated economic,

---

[20] However, the Governor commended the efforts of the World Food Programme, the International Committee of the Red Cross (ICRC), the Norwegian Refugee Council, the Danish Refugee Council, the International Organization for Migration, and the United Nations High Commissioner for Refugees (UNHCR).

socio-political, and symbolic capital for claims-makers. Rescuing the Chibok girls became a socially desirable activity regardless of actual efforts to find the girls. The Chibok girls became a hot commodity. Being identified with, or perceived as agitating for, their rescue or assisting their community enhanced the legitimacy, street credibility, and visibility of various actors.

In reality, the parents of the girls and the Chibok community have little to show for the activities of the actors in the social problem industry. For example, the Chibok community, under its umbrella organization, the Kibaku Area Development Association (KADA), issued a press statement on 5 February 2020. The statement notes that 20 parents had died from trauma related to the kidnapping; Boko Haram had attacked the community multiple times after the 2014 incident. The statement also notes that an inquiry promised by the government was 'yet to be constituted four years later' and the community had 'no knowledge on their daughters' whereabouts or information from the federal government on when they will be rescued and brought home or if there is any ongoing effort at all' (Omoniyi and Nuhu 2020). The statement challenges the government's persistent claim, since December 2015, that Boko Haram had been 'technically defeated' (BBC News 2015b) and the electoral promise that finding the girls was a priority. While several girls who escaped capture on the night of the abduction have completed university, some of the girls have elected not to return home after years in captivity (Patience 2016). 'Some' of the 112 girls escaped captivity in January 2021.[21]

The global attention generated by #BBOG's success in creating a social problem industry around the Chibok kidnapping has not necessarily translated to concrete action. For example, in March 2016, Andrew Pocock, a former British high commissioner to Nigeria, revealed that Western powers had intelligence about the location of the Chibok girls but chose not to act, and the Nigerian government had never requested that they do so. Therefore, '(d)espite all the BBOG fervour in London and the White House, there was no appetite from Washington or Downing Street to put troops on the ground' (Lamb 2016). Local actors led efforts to secure the release of 107 girls through secret negotiations (Parkinson and Hinshaw 2021).

Besides, the February 2020 KADA statement notes,

> Despite global efforts to renovate, rehabilitate and reopen their school, Government Secondary School, Chibok (with the intention of defeating the terrorists' objective) through the Safe Schools Initiative which was initiated

---

[21] Exact numbers are not available (see Busari 2021).

by the then UN Special Envoy for Global Education, Mr Gordon Brown, in May 2014, following the attack, it has been abandoned and remains closed as an abandoned project, to this day.

Borno state, and Northeast Nigeria in general, have been inundated by local and international NGOs, as previously noted. Many NGOs work with persons displaced by Boko Haram. Others are in Chibok and surrounding areas to provide assistance. However, the results from such activities do not cohere with the huge sums of money expended. The security situation in Northern Nigeria has worsened, with hundreds of students kidnapped by 'bandits' since Chibok. School-focused kidnappings have become the 'norm' (Yusuf 2021).

This study proposes a contextual, seven-stage model in the development of a social problem industry:

1. Overpass stage: a harmful social condition exists. It affects a number of people but the issue and its effects are ignored. This stage is marked by non-attention to the agitations and mobilization by those affected.
2. Elite mobilization stage: this involves intervention by a range of well-situated individuals. They may include political, economic, and religious elite. This stage is significantly influenced by the engagement of such actors and mobilization of social and traditional media.
3. Validation stage: a social condition becomes recognized as a social problem within this stage. This is shaped by establishment of at least one vociferous social group or organization to deal with the 'cause'.
4. Governing authority response stage: this is not always predictable in developing countries. A governing authority may choose to (a) act (e.g. by formulating a policy; passing a law; or directing an agency, committee, or 'czar' to handle the matter) or (b) ignore the social problem. In quasi-democratic or authoritarian contexts, (c) vocal advocates may face persecution through legal or extra-legal means for criticizing the response (or lack thereof) of the governing authority.
5. Bifurcated trajectory stage: the social problem may be (a) resolved or (b) fester. Social actors move on when solutions are provided by the governing authority or resourceful citizens. However, an industry may develop at this stage if the social problem remains unresolved.
6. Internationalization stage: the activities of various actors at the local and national levels may lead to interpellation of international actors. These may include global media giants as well as well-resourced Western-based NGOs and state actors. Émigré groups and citizens of other

states may also begin acts of solidarity on social media and the streets. Their involvement, coverage, and/or demonstrations of solidarity generate significant attention to the social problem but do not guarantee solutions.

7. Dénouement: the social problem may worsen as multi-level actors become self-perpetuating in the social problem industry that has been created. Solving the problem becomes secondary to interested actors. Maintaining appearances becomes a crucial variable as major players seek resources to continue the 'struggle' or 'project'. The social problem remains while industry actors increase in number and intensity.

The Chibok kidnapping provides empirical demonstration of the contextual seven-stage model. First, at the *overpass stage*, the kidnapping of the Chibok girls did not generate any significant attention at the onset. The protest of the mothers of the victims in Chibok was largely ignored, as previously stated. The Nigerian government did not acknowledgment the incident for nearly three weeks. Second, the *elite mobilization stage* ensued when Oby Ezekwesili began to tweet about the Chibok kidnapping and Hadiza Bala Usman started to organize female elite involvement in the matter. The online and offline efforts were the impetus for the mobilization of highly influential female members of the political class and middle-class allies. The mobilization culminated in the Abuja protest on 30 April 2014. The Chibok kidnapping was on the path to validation.

Third, the 30 April 2014 protest, daily gatherings or 'sit-outs' afterwards, and the establishment of the #BBOG movement in Abuja led to the *validation stage* for the Chibok kidnapping. The kidnapping was transformed from a social condition to a social problem. Fourth, the *governing authority response stage* demonstrates the fluidity of how certain states respond to social problems. The Nigerian government did not act quickly to rescue the girls. Rather, the evidence suggests that the belief at the presidential villa was that the incident did not happen. As previously noted, the government then assumed that the girls were kidnapped to embarrass the administration when it became clear that the incident was not a hoax. Therefore, the Nigerian government initially ignored the social problem (i.e. option (b)) and later began to persecute #BBOG (option (c)), as articulated in the section on state repression against #BBOG.

Fifth, the Chibok kidnapping was not resolved and therefore took the less desirable second option—festering of the issue—in the *bifurcated trajectory stage*. Therefore, various social actors became involved and a social problem industry eventually developed. The fifth stage is extremely significant as it follows state action, or lack thereof, and marks the start of the social problem industry. Sixth, the *internationalization stage* set in as the kidnapping issue festered and #BBOG activists began to engage with international media organizations. As previously noted, the framing of the movement also began to emphasize state failure. Global media hegemons, politicians, and celebrities began to get involved. The internationalization dimension of the Chibok kidnapping was in full swing within the first six months of the mobilization of #BBOG. Several #BBOG members became regular political commentators on the issue on television and radio giants around the world.

The seventh and final stage, *dénouement*, demonstrates the current state of efforts to rescue the Chibok girls and the co-mingling of various actors at the local, national, and international level in the social problem industry. About 112 of the girls are back from captivity, but over 100 remain missing. Some are presumed dead. Rescuing the Chibok girls is no longer the primary focus of institutional and non-institutional actors in the social problem industry. Their focus has turned to various projects and assorted concerns in the affected region. For example, some of the NGOs attracted to Borno state, where the girls were kidnapped, have begun to sign office leases of up to 10 years. This is a routine part of the operation of players in the social problem industry as they realize they will have reason to remain for several years.

This model is dynamic rather than unilinear or deterministic. It recognizes that social problems do not have a single or definite pathway and are not always resolved in the short or medium term. Some social problems may terminate at the third or fourth stage. However, an industry may develop around a social problem at the fifth stage. To be clear, the involvement of NGOs in the Chibok area after the 2014 mass kidnapping became defined as a social problem has contributed to the exploitation of the Chibok girls. In 2020, the Borno state government registered 172 local and international NGOs and civil society organizations purportedly providing support to the people. The state governor was concerned that the 'humanitarian system had been fraught with irregularities, duplication of services and alleged corruption' and there was a need to 'sanitise all the operations of the NGOs working in the state' (Haruna 2020).

The contextual seven-stage model supports Blumer's assertion that a 'social problem industry is always a focal point for the operation of divergent and conflicting interests, intentions, and objectives. It is the interplay of these interests and objectives that constitutes the way in which a society deals with any one of its social problems' (Blumer 1971). The contextual seven-stage social problem industry model deviates from Blumer by emphasizing (a) the variegated trajectory of social problems—not all get resolved; (b) the internationalization of social problems; and (c) the particularities of domains outside the West, especially in relation to state response. This model may be useful for investigating or analysing social problems in other contexts.

The decline of #BBOG

In *How Social Movements Die: Repression and Demobilization of the Republic of the New Africa*, Davenport (2015) analyses the life cycle of the Republic of New Africa (RNA). The RNA's objectives included carving out autonomous territories for Black people in Southern United States, obtaining reparations for slavery, instituting a system of government for Black people, and ensuring the participation of African Americans in governance and policy matters. However, the RNA was poorly resourced, had limited capability, and its goals proved too utopian. Davenport interrogates the factors responsible for the 'demobilization' of the RNA (2015: 21). These include its failure to engage in reappraisal. The RNA demobilized because it did not prepare for covert repression from the state and the eclipse of trust within the movement, which insulated leadership from members of the movement.

Davenport's engagement with micro- and meso-sociological approaches to understanding movement demobilization has more analytical utility than a generic universalized approach. One such generic approach argues that social movements pass through four successive stages. These are emergence, coalescence, bureaucratization, and decline (Christiansen 2009). However, the 'employment of invariant models ... assumes a political world in which whole structures and sequences repeat themselves time after time in essentially the same form. That would be a convenient world for theorists, but it does not exist' (Tilly 1995: 1596). Consequently, Davenport's approach, which carefully considers the internal dynamics and political context of a specific social movement (organization) is a more pragmatic way of approaching movement demobilization.

#BBOG protests in the early days involved thousands of people. Over time, the number of participants dwindled. This has coincided with limited involvement of erstwhile partner NGOs, CSOs, and several other interest groups in #BBOG's mass protests. The reduction in numbers of participants in #BBOG protests is a consequence of three major factors. These are

(a) doubts by members and non-members about the efficacy of marches and protests; (b) the degree of discipline and coordination required to participate in #BBOG protests, which alienated partner organizations; and (c) the unanticipated longevity of the movement. Therefore, several committed participants have since moved on—physically out of Abuja and/or emotionally because of burn out.

The question was posed to a member of the strategic team (ST). He noted that

> There is a sense of fatigue, *protest fatigue* across NGOs ... *They couldn't cope with our obsession for coordination, obsession for organization and all that sometimes to the point of being rude and insensitive.* For instance, you can't talk to the media; only appointed #BBOG members can talk to the media. There were instances when some of our leaders had to interrupt live interviews. Those were some of the early days; small issues that affected the larger coalitions we were working with. After a while, we had to deal with having to mobilize ourselves. We couldn't get the numbers out again.
>
> (Interviewee 10; italics added)

The ST member argues that the length of the advocacy has exacerbated 'protest fatigue'. He notes that 'people feel that an obsession for the Chibok girls is now insensitive to the larger problems. People have told us that you guys need to reinvent yourselves.'

There are arguments within #BBOG that the movement could have had far more impact if it had adopted the right approach to engage with the Buhari administration. Several participants cited the 2016 visit of #BBOG to the presidential villa as a turning point.[22] One #BBOG activist argued that the conduct of #BBOG at the presidential villa was 'rude, insolent ... From that day on, anything that has to do with #BBOG Abuja, the presidency was not interested' (Interviewee 32).[23]

The notion that protests and the approach of the movement cannot bring back the girls but merely antagonizes the government has gained traction

---

[22] The President was receiving the head of state of a West African country and sent the Minister of Women Affairs and Social Development, Chief of Defence Staff, and Chief of Staff, among other high-ranking officials, to meet with #BBOG. #BBOG insisted on having the President address them. Several government officials were upset at the insistence of #BBOG. The President eventually entered the meeting room, visibly angry. #BBOG members were divided on the appropriateness of insisting on having the President at the meeting. #BBOG argued that the 'president's countenance and remarks at that meeting 'gave him away as one who regretted being a civilian president as opposed to being a military dictator' (cited in Ajayi 2016).

[23] Female #BBOG member; personal interview, Abuja, July 2017.

among the constituency of #BBOG. For instance, the association of the parents of the missing Chibok girls held a meeting a week up to the 22 August 2016 march of #BBOG and decided not to participate (Vanguard 2016). The chair of the association of Chibok girls' parents, Yakubu Nkeki, argued, 'All we want is our missing daughters and we are ready to work with anybody who will help us find our daughters.' He stated that 'they did not want to antagonize the government, which is in the best position to help them find their missing daughters'. Yana Galang, the women's leader of the Chibok parents' association, also argues that 'We do not want to do anything that the government will not be happy about . . . We are not after any organization that is against any party or religion, and we are supporting the federal government to help us release our girls' (Vanguard 2016). In other words, several parents adopted a strategy of distancing themselves from #BBOG in order not to antagonize the government.

Overall, internal and external sets of factors are gradually catalysing the demobilization of #BBOG. The internal factors are protest fatigue due to the inability to swiftly realize the goal of the movement (the release of all the Chibok girls); internal disagreements over tactics, framing, oligarchization; and the lack of strategy on the direction of the movement. The external factors include changes in the political context and covert repression.[24] The leadership is aware of state efforts to demobilize #BBOG. Ezekwesili notes,[25]

> There is FACTUALLY no problem within BBOG. The so-called 'crisis' was externally induced to destroy some people and ultimately the movement. It has become analytically clear that forces within the FG [federal government] simply adopted a new strategy for dismantling our group which it obviously considers an irritation and found 'some executioners' within the movement as willing collaborators [emphasis original].

The advocacy of #BBOG continues despite the issues highlighted above. Following the rescue of a missing Chibok girl, Salomi Pogu, on 4 January 2018, #BBOG issued a press release appreciating the efforts of the military (Okakwu 2018). #BBOG marched to the presidential villa on 23 January 2018, providing further evidence of #BBOG's relentlessness. However, the strategic direction of the #BBOG movement continues to generate internal debate (see Chapter 4).

---

[24] See Chapter 5 for analysis of the internal and external constraints of #BBOG.
[25] Personal communication, 18 June 2017.

Conclusion

Dwyer and Zeilig (2012: 2) ask, regarding social movements in Africa, 'How have vibrant movements ... failed to develop into broader political forces for radical social and political change?' A nuanced answer must balance the nature of the state and objective analyses of the role of political elites, on one hand, and a 'critical analysis of the politics and composition of social movements themselves' (2012: 3) on the other. This chapter analyses the outcomes of the #BBOG movement. It provides evidence that #BBOG inadvertently prolonged the captivity of the girls through its internationalized framing, protest tactics, and the attention it generated. #BBOG arguably turned the girls into valuable assets in the hands of their abductors. It also shows that several national and international actors are using the girls to pursue their own material and political agenda.

The situation speaks to broader issues on the political economy of conflict and social problems in Africa. Social problems are big businesses. The involvement of NGOs in social problems in Africa remains a contentious issue. The near-wholesale replacement of government by NGOs in many parts of Africa opens up the continent to both scrupulous and unscrupulous actors. The entrenchment of a social problem industry means that a conflict may metastasize because of the activities of unscrupulous actors. The Nigerian government has accused some NGOs of providing relief for Boko Haram fighters, while NGOs maintain they do not discriminate in rendering service (Adeakin et al. 2022). This brings state priority (defeat of terrorists) into confrontation with NGO mission (non-discriminatory services). State abdication of responsibility to citizens therefore comes at a huge price—a lack of control over activities in their jurisdiction. This contributes to the seeming intractability of social problems on the African continent. NGO involvement introduces a dynamic that further complicates conflicts and other social problems.

#BBOG has had several positive outcomes despite legitimate criticisms over its tactics, framing, and confrontations with the government. As one #BBOG member argues, 'the ones [Boko Haram victims] that are nameless and faceless, how well have we recovered them?' (Interviewee 45). The #BBOG experience demonstrates the complications of human rights advocacy in institutionally weak societies, the attitude of the government to the security of human lives, the incapacity of state machinery, the prevalence of patrimonial authority in Africa, and the level of awareness of the average citizen about their rights. In Botswana, considered a major success story in Africa due to stable democratic transitions since independence in 1966 and relatively stellar socio-economic indicators, both the state and society opposed efforts by *Emand Basadi* ('Stand Up Women'), to enact policies favourable to women and expunge laws that discriminated against women (Leslie 2006). Women engaged in contentious politics against the state and members of society who were not accustomed to witnessing public protests by women. The public—men and women—needed to be convinced that there were laws in Botswana that limited women's participation as full citizens. The nature of the state and society therefore plays a major role in the dynamics and outcomes of social movements. The political context also shaped movement outcomes in Egypt, Tunisia, and Libya following the Arab Spring. The differential outcomes were influenced by context—Tunisia and Egypt were effectively 'liberalizing autocracies', while Libya resisted change (Joffé 2011: 507). The outcomes of the Arab Spring have not met expectations in any of the three countries. This supports evidence about the overdetermining influence of the political opportunity structure and the nature of the state in movement outcomes.

#BBOG has helped to promote the education of the girl-child in Northern Nigeria, provided benefits for victims of Boko Haram, and helped the trajectory of non-violent protest movements and a major change in national politics in 2015—the first electoral defeat of an incumbent president.

However, the positive outcomes have not slowed down the decline of #BBOG. As one #BBOG member notes, 'We are struggling for breath now. There's no doubt that the movement has petered out. I have no doubt' (Interviewee 45). Besides, while the national government, which the #BBOG advocacy helped install, has secured over 100 of the girls, the overall picture of protection of human rights and welfare of citizens failed to meet minimum expectations. Ironically, the government engaged in arbitrary arrests and the detention of journalists. It also presided over worsening security conditions in the Northeast, Boko Haram's main enclave, and the entire country. Kidnapping at schools, particularly in Northern Nigeria, intensified (Yusuf 2021).

There are three major lessons for movement activists. First, activists must ask themselves: what is the essence of our advocacy? The answer to that question should shape strategic thinking and cross-articulation of ideas on the link between advocacy and tactics to accomplish the goal of a movement. Some #BBOG members believe that the movement lost focus and some key leaders personalized the struggle. One #BBOG member argues that 'Now the movement is about massaging people's ego. To me it is no longer about the girls' (Interviewee 36). #BBOG had influential, elite co-conveners in government who could have been important intermediaries. This would have necessitated a change of approach and strategy and perhaps a need to redefine the movement. However, the risk of co-optation and possible abandonment of the movement's goal was considered too high by the #BBOG leadership.

Second, social movements must pay particular attention to the changing landscape of political opportunity and the peculiarities of their political process. The protest environment changed once Buhari assumed office as president and some of the movement's elite women accepted positions in government. #BBOG soldiered on as if nothing had changed within the movement and its external environment. The political transition and involvement of some of the co-conveners of the movement in the new government required a degree of re-orientation among those who remained in the advocacy. Third, movement activists need to work hard to prevent factionalization among members. The refusal to change strategies about how to deal with the Buhari government became toxic within the movement. The ensuing social distantiation among elite members worked against #BBOG's objectives.

Overall, political contexts and opportunities will vary from one movement to another but movement activists need to be particularly attentive to the *shifting grounds around them and make effective use of influential allies in government. It appears that #BBOG movement leaders sacrificed pragmatism on the altar of ideological purity.* Nonetheless, #BBOG activists were confronted with a complicated and divided political system. The political system was riddled with ineptitude, potential for graft, and politically motivated statements and actions by key state agents. This complex web of issues influenced the decisions made by #BBOG vis-à-vis framing, tactics, and funding and ultimately shaped the direct and indirect outcomes of the #BBOG movement.

6
Conclusion

This book has investigated the challenges to contemporary women-led movements and human rights advocacy in Africa. The #BringBackOurGirls (#BBOG) movement was founded through an elite middle-class coalition in Nigeria to advocate for the rescue of the Chibok schoolgirls who were kidnapped by Boko Haram. #BBOG transformed the Chibok kidnapping into a social problem in a sociological sense and internationalized the issue. The analysis demonstrates that the Chibok girls were caught in a complex web of multilayered toxic presidential politics and movement dynamics in an environment where some lives do not matter. Besides factors intrinsic to the movement, the outcomes of #BBOG are constituted by, and constitutive of, deeper macro-sociological issues ingrained in the Nigerian state and society. As demonstrated throughout the book, the #BBOG experience has broad implications for peace and security in Africa and the war against terrorism in the Sahel and the Lake Chad Basin.

This is the first scholarly, book-length sociological investigation of the #BBOG movement. The formation, objective, organizational structure, communication process, and protest mobilization of the #BBOG movement are analysed. The analysis demonstrates the inner workings of the #BBOG machinery and the painstaking and strategic efforts that undergird the #BBOG movement. The findings indicate that, contrary to existing presuppositions, the #BBOG movement's cause—the rescue of all the Chibok girls—did not automatically lead to a global media spotlight. Rather, #BBOG activists deployed *media-sense*. Following initial frustrations over lack of media visibility, movement activists adopted a *hybridized communication process*—a combination of the immediacy and time–space compression of social media and the credibility and established audiences of traditional (print and electronic) media. #BBOG engaged traditional and social media in a mutually reinforcing and synergistic manner while anchored on ground mobilization of members and supporters. #BBOG is more than a social media phenomenon. The fixation on #BBOG's use of social media is reductionist in orientation, though well-intentioned. There was far more strategic thinking, rigorous analysis, robust coordination, and offline mobilization than has been credited to the movement to date.

The #BBOG experience embodies the challenges posed by states to contemporary social movements in Africa. States in Africa, which were founded on appeals to universalistic principles and global conventions on human rights, are ironically intolerant of dissent and impede efforts of activists to expand the frontiers of human rights. While earlier social movements formed after decolonization were not autonomous and depended on funding from the state, contemporary social movements in Africa are affected by state repression and partisan politics, despite their relative autonomy. Therefore, the cost of human rights advocacy in sub-Saharan Africa remains high. State-sponsored repression against #BBOG involved intimidation, arrests, surveillance, bomb threats, and ultimately failed plans by the government to change the leadership and install members they considered more agreeable. The impressive pedigree of the elite women of #BBOG ensured a level of protection from some of the most egregious forms of repression within a quasi-democratic environment. Social class attenuated state repression but did not totally protect #BBOG from governmental heavy-handedness against human rights activists.

The #BBOG movement's global ascendance benefited from the social and cultural capital of its elite founders. However, the presence of elite co-conveners of the movement enmeshed #BBOG in Nigeria's toxic political environment. The political activities of the elite women before and during movement activities provided a huge amount of baggage, which influenced perceptions of the movement. #BBOG began to haemorrhage influential elite members shortly after its formation in 2014 and has since experienced multiple existential crises. These were caused by the personal politics of some key leaders or movement superstars, a government-sponsored tour, and the political appointments accepted by some of the elite women leaders of #BBOG after the 2015 presidential elections.

Contemporary social movements in Africa face challenges in relation to inattention to bureaucratization and governance structure. A monolithic #BBOG movement ceased to exist within the first few months of the advocacy. #BBOG faced major internal challenges concerning decision-making and ideological divide over the strategic direction of the movement. These issues fragmented elite and other members who remained. This speaks to the broad challenge of non-governmental organization (NGO) creep into social movements in Africa. The decision of the #BBOG leadership not to change the direction of the movement towards an NGO model and decline funding from multiple international organizations created internal conflicts.

#BBOG members are categorized into five types: the regime-neutral die-hards, regime-change emergency activists, committed pragmatists, non-committal advocates, and totemic elite members. Over time, a small number of persons began to dominate the activities and ideation of #BBOG. Oligarchization—the concentration of power in the hands of a small number of persons—set in as the rescue of the Chibok girls failed to materialize. The four factors responsible for oligarchization within #BBOG are level of commitment to the cause, resources, regime neutrality, and interpersonal relations with top leaders.

The framing of #BBOG was internationalized, but the movement was not transnationalized. #BBOG refused to have formal ties with organizations in Europe and North America that were interested in the cause and willing to provide funding. #BBOG utilized four major master framing techniques. These are the motherist/maternalist, human rights, girl-child's right to education, and state failure framing. #BBOG framing was bifocal in orientation. Motherist or maternalist framing was used for micro-mobilization of women, and the girl-child's right to education also resonated among many supporters in Nigeria. The human rights and state failure framing were largely externally orientated. The state failure framing became the dominant master narrative of #BBOG approximately six months into the advocacy.

#BBOG began to concentrate efforts to secure the rescue of the girls through discursive appeals to the international community. This was a strategic error. Despite its sophistication and painstaking efforts, the error was threefold. First, #BBOG did not think through the step between mobilizing global opinion and actual ground efforts to rescue the girls. Second, #BBOG acted in the belief that the Nigerian government could be shamed or forced to act on an issue in which it had little interest. The government did care about its international image, but factors in the political process and the dynamics of the military served to inhibit efforts. Third, #BBOG relied on the notion of a rescue by concerned Western powers if the Nigerian government was unable or unwilling to act. The movement overestimated the social value of the lives of high-school girls in the Northeast corridor of Nigeria in the global arena of overarching and conflicting national interests and regional rivalry. #BBOG's reliance on interpellating our 'collective humanity' ultimately worked in a lot of ways (e.g. awareness about the problem and the influx of national and international resources into the affected region) but not for its primary cause—the rescue of the Chibok girls.

Social movements in Africa must be cognizant of the contradiction between national political context and international developments. The #BBOG movement's outcomes signpost the tension between national/local context and international opportunity structure. The internationalized framing of #BBOG regarding human rights was effective in generating global attention to the movement but seemed too elitist and utopian to the masses in Nigeria, where approximately 62% of the population was concerned with basic survival. Simply put, #BBOG drew on a globalist language that many of the people did not understand and could not necessarily relate to due to their socio-economic conditions. This was the lesser of two consequential framing narratives. The state failure framing and its emphasis on the corruption and dysfunction of the Nigerian government worked against the movement. The state failure framing refracted across local political conflicts and complicated the dynamics of the socio-political environment by alienating key institutional actors in the Nigerian government and the military architecture. Such crucial national actors or 'ogas' and some elite co-conveners began to distantiate themselves from #BBOG when a confrontational and aggressive tone and language became the centrepiece of #BBOG's framing. The international attention generated by the framing during the Goodluck Jonathan presidency (2010–2015) had historically specific resonance with local contestations for presidential power between the two major political parties, the People's Democratic Party (PDP) and the All Progressives Congress (APC). The APC capitalized on the #BBOG framing for political gain. This was complicated by some co-conveners of the movement, who remained active members of the APC while engaged in the advocacy. The political opportunity structure for the movement dwindled within Nigeria as it lost influential national allies. Parents of some of the kidnapped girls also began to avoid #BBOG.

The refraction of the #BBOG ideation has implications for framing theory. The local political context predominates over opportunities and developments in the international arena (see Bob 2002). In particular, activists and scholars studying social movements in developing countries should carefully consider four major factors vis-à-vis consequences of internationalized framing. The factors are the nearness of mobilization, framing and other movement activities to major events (particularly elections in the political process), the nature of the cause, the primary beneficiaries of the advocacy, and the social position and political antecedents of key movement leaders before and during movement activities.

#BBOG has become a victim of its own success—its cause became internationalized through framing, but elites, celebrities, and miscellaneous actors who symbolically 'joined' the movement to demand the rescue of the Chibok girls were, in fact, not in a position to assist #BBOG to accomplish its objective. Heads of state and governments who expressed 'support' for the movement had other geopolitical priorities and did little to rescue the girls. International organizations that offered support to #BBOG also began to avoid the movement as the issue persisted. Such organizations did not wish to antagonize the Nigerian government, whose cooperation they needed to achieve their goals in sub-Saharan Africa.

The implication is that movement activists in developing regions need to be cognizant that raising awareness or generating global attention to a social problem is not necessarily the same as securing concrete action to solve the problem. Social movements in developing countries with significant transnational appeal, particularly on social media, should be wary about their cause becoming popularized through clicks, 'likes', Tweets, hashtags, and shares. None of these may translate to actual steps to solve the problem unless transnational awareness, in and of itself, is the goal of the movement. The #BBOG experience demonstrates the limits of the social media as a global force for social change and international awareness as a means to an end.

Social movements often produce contradictory outcomes. The outcome of #BBOG regarding the rescue of the Chibok girls is an antinomy. On one hand, the relentlessness of the #BBOG movement contributed to compelling the government to negotiate with Boko Haram for the release of over 100 Chibok girls. This ensured that the case was not abandoned like other victims of Boko Haram. On the other hand, #BBOG inadvertently contributed to the prolonged captivity of the young women. The success of #BBOG in popularizing the cause turned the Chibok girls into prized assets in the hands of Boko Haram. This made the task of rescuing or negotiating their release much more difficult for the military and intelligence agencies. All but two of the #BBOG members who participated in this study believed that the advocacy indirectly delayed the rescue of the girls. The top echelon of the military was unequivocal about how #BBOG complicated their task. Besides, the ransom and key suspects released by the government in exchange for over 100 of the Chibok girls were deployed by Boko Haram to prolong the war.

#BBOG has had numerous impacts despite the outcome of its primary goal. One major impact of the #BBOG movement is its influence in a major political change—the first electoral defeat of an incumbent president in Nigeria's history. The advocacy helped to activate several opportunities and benefits for its constituency. These include welfare provision, scholarships, and medical care. #BBOG has helped to underscore the education and conditions of the girl-child in Northern Nigeria. Multiple citizen-led grassroots advocacy movements have been formed by #BBOG activists to tackle issues relating to education, poverty, and political engagement of citizens.

The #BBOG experience speaks to the ostensible intractability of social problems in the developing world. Local, national, and international actors may exploit a social problem for personal or institutional gain. The utility of the movement in turning the Chibok kidnapping into an international issue has indirectly led to the exploitation of the Chibok girls. The exploitation of the Chibok girls revolves around several institutional and non-institutional actors in Nigeria and the United States. The girls are being exploited to assist the agenda of multifarious government and non-governmental entities. The Chibok girls and their geographic region are being exploited for publicity, financial gain, social visibility, and career advancement of some individuals, while the girls have been compelled to relive the trauma of their abduction through manipulation of their experiences by their handlers. Huge sums of money have been raised to assist Chibok and surrounding areas of the Northeast, with few verifiable results. Social movements in Africa, and the developing world in general, must be wary of providing an avenue for exploitation of the people. This book contributes to social problems theory by proposing a contextual seven-stage model on formation of a social problem industry. This is a dynamic model that is suited to conditions in the developing world and the variegated trajectories of social problems.

The decline of #BBOG offers an important lesson for social movement activists. It raises the question: what is the essence of advocacy? This necessitates strategizing by movement activists on how to deal with political changes in their national contexts. There are two sets of variables responsible for the decline of #BBOG. External factors beyond the control of the movement, such as the change in the political context and opportunity structure (particularly since May 2015, when Muhammadu Buhari was sworn in as president), have played a huge role. The political opportunity structure and overall protest environment shifted when Muhammadu Buhari won the 2015 presidential election. This was further complicated by several #BBOG elite co-conveners who accepted positions in the new government. However, the remaining #BBOG leaders soldiered on as if nothing had happened, but the movement did not remain the same. There was a need to reinvent the movement at that stage despite the risk of co-optation. External factors were complicated by internal variables such as protest fatigue after several years of advocacy, internal fractionalization on issues concerning tactics, framing, oligarchization, and refusal to change strategic direction.

This book demonstrates that conditions in the military speak to broader systemic issues in the society. The military has historically occupied a central space in the body politik of most African states. Therefore, the military is a major site of contestation in the complex web of ethnic, religious, and political identities and loyalties. The military and other security agencies co-constitute, and are influenced by, their political context. The Nigerian military is both a victim and active participant in the politicization of its bureaucracy. The entanglement of the Nigerian military in toxic politics—evident in the labyrinth of political power contestation as well as pre-existing social fractures—has led to its incapacitation in the war against Boko Haram. The embeddedness of the military in toxic politics poses a major problem to national, regional, and global security.

The book argues that 10 major factors within the military interacted with Nigeria's political process and inhibited a swift rescue of the Chibok girls and defeat of Boko Haram. The factors include corruption, intelligence leaks/sabotage, alienation of the public by the military, and shortage of arms and ammunition. Others include inadequate coordination of military/security operations, strategic errors by political leaders, the rise of a series of actors benefiting from the problem, nepotism, toxic politics in the military, and troops' perception of the war against Boko Haram as a 'rubbish mission'.

Reports on the diaries of some of the freed Chibok girls which indicate that the kidnapping was, in fact, 'accidental' as Boko Haram was in their school to steal machinery for construction and its operatives were initially unsure of what to do with the girls (Nwaubani 2017) necessitate further research. Future studies may also consider factors within Boko Haram that led to the desire for negotiation and eventual release of over 100 girls in two tranches. While it may be reasonably inferred that Boko Haram had an interest in securing the release of its members from government custody,[1] and that the organization probably needed the huge amount of cash that was purportedly included in the deals, there is no evidence at the disposal of the researcher to establish the rationale behind the release of the girls. Questions that may be considered in future studies include 'How did Boko Haram perceive the attention attracted by the Chibok girls?', 'Was it becoming logistically difficult to keep the girls?', and 'Why were the girls released to the Buhari government and not Jonathan's?'

Future studies may consider the implications of the 2021 death of Boko Haram leader, Shekau and consolidation of power by Islamic State—West Africa Province (ISWAP). The rise of ISWAP will be consequential in the terrorism landscape in Africa. In addition, future studies may engage Boko Haram members who have been released to their communities to get a sense

---

[1] The five Boko Haram members released in May 2017 appeared in a propaganda video eight days after being exchanged for the girls.

of their motivation, rationalities, and justifications for their actions. This is crucial in order to address simmering grievances, given the shift towards rehabilitation and reintegration of former Boko Haram members. Mayinta Modu, a Boko Haram commander, claimed, in July 2018, that 'many of the girls have accepted the Boko Haram doctrine and don't see any reason to leave their husbands. It's only those that were desperate to come that were released in that swap deal' (Adebayo 2018). This adds a new dimension to the Chibok issue. If confirmed, the claim requires a change of approach. Future studies may engage with Chibok girls who have been reintegrated into their communities to unpack their experiences before, during, and after the kidnapping. Such studies may help engender understanding of why some of their former classmates refused to return to their families and communities.

A longitudinal study of #BBOG movement may be contemplated to understand the transition of the movement after the first decade. Do #BBOG members continue their agitations, expand engagement with issues relating to the girl-child, or find new causes? Following up with the activists on a long-term basis may provide useful material for understanding factors influencing activists and how interests are sustained or lost. The #BBOG movement had yet to decide on its strategic direction beyond the Chibok girls when this book was completed. Leaders have noted that the movement would not simply go away, but at the time of writing, the texture of what #BBOG might transmute into was yet to be decided. Research into #BBOG for the next 5–10 years would be useful to engage with movement transformation in the medium-to-long term.

#BBOG embodies the challenges and outcome of contemporary social movements in Africa. It demonstrates the level of social mobilization that can be engendered through the blend of elite status, maternalist identity, and hybridization of social and traditional media. The movement also signposts the limits of discursive internationalization of issues affecting the Global South, the politics of those offering 'support', and the overall refraction of framing across the labyrinth of the national political context. Activists in Africa are caught within a trifecta of social conditions: an ineffective, politically fractured neocolonial state; a region divided by colonial history, allegiance, language, and conflicting national interests; and an international community that is necessarily driven by rational self-interest. The lesson for grassroots activists, particularly in Africa, is that the national political context and its opportunity structure have an overdetermining influence on the outcomes of their struggles. Consequently, ideological puritanism may have to be substituted for a pragmatic approach which carries the risk of co-optation.

Finally, #BBOG engaged in volunteer, time-consuming, painstaking, on-the-ground as well as online work; framed the cause for multifarious audiences; helped bring global prominence to a problem in the Northeast corridor of Nigeria; and made multiple gains, including the negotiated release of over 100 of the kidnapped girls. The #BBOG movement turned into a global concern the lives of people who were routinely abused or killed without any form of action by the state. #BBOG emphasized that the lives of the Chibok girls mattered and therefore added value to their dignity as right-bearing persons worthy of state intervention. In the process, #BBOG became a barometer for assessing the effectiveness and legitimacy of the government and a global leader in 'lives matter' politics and advocacy.

Bibliography

Abdulazeez, Medinat and Temitope Oriola. 2018. 'Criminogenic patterns in the management of Boko Haram's human displacement situation', *Third World Quarterly*, 39, 1: 85–103.
Abimbola, Michael. 2017. 'Buhari won't bribe critics to keep quiet—Garba Shehu' (3 October), https://newtelegraphonline.com/2017/10/buhari-wont-bribe-critics-keep-quiet-garba-shehu. Accessed 28 December 2017.
Abubakar, Aminu. 2018 (15 August). 'Nigerian soldiers protest as Boko Haram attacks surge', *Yahoo!* (15 August), https://www.yahoo.com/news/nigerian-soldiers-protest-boko-haram-attacks-surge-134153403.html. Accessed 22 August 2018.
Abuja Chronicle. 2018. 'Chibok girls: How Swiss agent, govt officials stole millions of dollars', *Abuja Chronicle* (26 February), http://abujachronicle.com/chibok-girls-how-swiss-agent-govt-officials-stole-millions-of-dollars. Accessed 28 February 2018.
Adeakin, Ibikunle. 2016. 'The military and human rights violations in post-1999 Nigeria: Assessing the problems and prospects of effective internal enforcement in an era of insecurity', *African Security Review*, 25, 2: 129–145.
Adebayo, Bukola. 2018. 'Missing Chibok girls not coming back, Boko Haram commander tells police', CNN, 18 July, https://www.cnn.com/2018/07/18/africa/chibok-kidnapping-suspects-arrested/index.html. Accessed 2 August 2018.
Adebayo, Hassan. 2017. 'SGF Babachir Lawal must be prosecuted for corruption, Senate insists', *Premium Times* (3 May), https://www.premiumtimesng.com/news/headlines/230268-sgf-babachir-lawal-must-prosecuted-corruption-senate-insists.html. Accessed 28 February 2018.
Adeleye, R. A. 1972. 'Mahdist triumph and British revenge in Northern Nigeria: Satiru 1906', *Journal of the Historical Society of Nigeria*, 6, 2: 193–214.
Adeniyi, Olusegun. 2017. *Against the Run of Play: How an Incumbent President Was Defeated in Nigeria*. Lagos: Prestige.
Adepegba, Adelani. 2018. 'Police arrested me in broad daylight—Ezekwesili', *Punch* (24 January), http://punchng.com/police-arrested-me-in-broad-daylight-ezekwesili. Accessed 29 March 2018.
Adesoji, Abimbola O. 2011. 'Between Maitatsine and Boko Haram: Islamic fundamentalism and the response of the Nigerian state', *Africa Today*, 57, 4: 98–119.
Adibe, Jideofor. 2014. 'Explaining the emergence of Boko Haram', *Brookings* (6 May), https://www.brookings.edu/blog/africa-in-focus/2014/05/06/explaining-the-emergence-of-boko-haram. Accessed 28 February 2018.
Adler, C. 1999. 'Violence, gender and social change'. In M. B. Sterger and N. S. Lind (eds), *Violence and Its Alternatives: An Interdisciplinary Reader*. New York, NY: St Martin's Press, pp. 113–128.
Adler, Patricia A. and Peter Adler. 1994. 'Observation techniques'. In Norman K. Denzin and Yvonna S. Lincoln (eds), *Handbook of Qualitative Research*. Thousand Oaks, CA: Sage, pp. 377–392.
Afigbo, A. E. 1972. *The Warrant Chiefs: Indirect Rule in Southeastern Nigeria, 1891–1929*. London: Longman.

Agbiboa, Daniel Egiegba. 2013. 'Living in Fear: Religious Identity, Relative Deprivation and the Boko Haram Terrorism', *African Security*, 6, 2: 153–170.

Agbiboa, Daniel Egiegba. 2014. 'Boko-Haram and the global jihad: 'do not think jihad is over. Rather jihad has just begun'. *Australian Journal of International Affairs*, 68, 4: 400–417.

Agekameh, Dele. 2014. 'Boko Haram insurgency: How Nigeria's intelligence agencies have failed', *Premium Times* (23 April), https://www.premiumtimesng.com/opinion/159197-boko-haram-insurgency-how-nigerias-intelligence-agencies-have-failed-by-dele-agekameh.html. Accessed 26 February 2018.

Agency Report 2016. 'Probe "missing" N500 million Chibok school fund, SERAP tells EFCC', *Premium Times Nigeria*, 28 December, <https://www.premiumtimesng.com/news/more-news/219098-probe-missing-n500-million-chibok-school-fund-serap-tells-efcc.html>. Accessed on 28 July 2021.

Aghedo, Iro. 2014. 'Old Wine in a new bottle: Ideological and operational linkages between Maitatsine and Boko Haram revolts in Nigeria', *African Security*, 7, 4: 229–250.

Aghedo, Iro and Oarhe Osumah. 2012. 'The Boko Haram Uprising: how should Nigeria respond?', *Third World Quarterly*, 33, 5: 853–869.

AFP News Agency. 2014. 'New Nigerian Boko Haram video mocks Bring Back Girls campaign' https://www.youtube.com/watch?v=4ipwr3Myz-Q Accessed 19 November 2023

Ajani, Jide. 2014. 'Funding of terror network; "Boko Haram got over N11bn to kill and maim"', *Vanguard* (2 May) https://www.vanguardngr.com/2014/05/funding-terror-network-boko-haram-got-n11bn-kill-maim. Accessed 26 September 2018.

Ajayi, Omeiza. 2016 (9 September). 'Buhari and BBOG: A love story gone sour', *Vanguard* (9 September), https://www.vanguardngr.com/2016/09/buhari-bbog-love-story-gone-sour. Accessed 19 December 2017.

Akinola, Adeoye O., and Oluwaseun Tella. 2013. 'Boko Haram terrorism and Nigeria's security dilemma: rethinking the state's capacity', *International Journal of Innovative Social Sciences and Humanities Research*, 1, 3: 70–78.

Akinola, Olabanji. 2015. 'Boko Haram insurgency in Nigeria: Between Islamic fundamentalism, politics and poverty', *African Security*, 8, 1: 1–29.

Akinwotu, Emmanuel. 2018 'Deadly lack of security plagues Nigeria as Buhari seeks re-election', *New York Times* (15 August), https://www.nytimes.com/2018/08/15/world/africa/nigeria-zamfara-violence-buhari.html. Accessed 22 August 2018.

Akowe, Tony. 2013. 'Buhari faults clampdown on Boko Haram members', *The Nation* (2 June), http://thenationonlineng.net/buhari-faults-clampdown-on-boko-haram-members. Accessed 20 December 2017.

Amao, Olumuyiwa Babatunde, and Benjamin Maiangwa. 2015. 'Has the Giant gone to sleep? Re-assessing Nigeria's response to the Liberian Civil War (1990–1997) and the Boko Haram insurgency (2009–2015)', *African Studies* 76, 1: 22–43.

Amenta, Edwin. 2006. *When movements matter: The Townsend plan and the rise of social security*. Vol. 176. Princeton University Press.

Alavi, Hamza. 1972. 'The state in post-colonial societies: Pakistan and Bangladesh', *New Left Review*, 74: 59–81.

Albertyn, Catherine. 2003. Towards Substantive Representation: Women and Politics in South Africa. In: Dobrowolsky, A., Hart, V. (eds), *Women Making Constitutions*. London: Palgrave Macmillan. https://doi.org/10.1057/9781403944085_7.

Al-Hussaini, Bassim. 2020a (27 February). '"ISWAP, terror group in Nigeria, rebrands, reversing tradition"', *Premium Times* (27 February), https://www.premiumtimesng.

com/news/headlines/379362-iswap-terror-group-in-nigeria-rebrands-reversing-tradition.html. Accessed 23 March 2020.

Al-Hussaini, Bassim. 2020b. 'New ISWAP boss slays five rebel leaders, silences clerical tones', *Premium Times* (3 March), https://www.premiumtimesng.com/news/headlines/379975-new-iswap-boss-slays-five-rebel-leaders-silences-clerical-tones.html. Accessed 23 March 2020.

Allam, Nermin. 2018. *Women and the Egyptian revolution: Engagement and activism during the 2011 Arab uprisings*. Cambridge: Cambridge University Press.

Allen, Chris. (1999). 'Warfare, endemic violence & state collapse in Africa', *Review of African Political Economy*, 26, 81: 367–384.

Alli, Yusuf. 2017. 'Jonathan: I lost re-election To U.S., UK, France, Local Forces', *Sahara Reporters* (26 April), http://saharareporters.com/2017/04/26/jonathan-i-lost-re-election-us-uk-france-local-forces. Accessed 20 December 2017.

Alli, Yusuf. 2018. '$2.1b deals: Ex-army chief Minimah refunds N1.7b', *The Nation* (26 February), http://thenationonlineng.net/2-1b-deals-ex-army-chief-minimah-refunds-n1-7b. Accessed 28 February 2018.

Amaefule, Everest. 2016. Arms scandal: Buhari orders probe of Ihejirika, Minimah, 52 others', *Premium Times*, (15 July), http://punchng.com/arms-scandal-buhari-orders-probe-ihejirika-minimah-52-others. Accessed 13 January 2017.

Amenta, Edwin, Bruce Carruthers, and Yvonne Zylan. 1992. 'A hero for the aged? The Townsend movement, the Political Medication model, and US old-age policy, 1934–1950', *American Journal of Sociology*, 98: 308–339.

Amnesty International. 2015a. 'Amnesty International 2014/2015 report: The state of the world's human rights', *Amnesty International* (25 February), https://www.amnesty.org/en/documents/pol10/0001/2015/en Accessed 6 March 2018.

Amnesty International. 2015b. '"Stars on their shoulders. Blood on their hands": War crimes committed by the Nigerian Military', *Amnesty International* (2 June), http://www.amnestyusa.org/research/reports/stars-on-their-shoulders-blood-on-their-hands-war-crimes-committed-by-the-nigerian-military. Accessed 15 August 2015.

Amnesty International. 2015c. '"Our job is to shoot, slaughter and kill": Boko Haram's reign of terror in North-East Nigeria', *Amnesty International*, https://www.amnesty.org/en/documents/afr44/1360/2015/en/. Accessed 5 August 2015.

Amnesty International. 2016a. 'Nigeria: Reinstatement of army general implicated in mass murder makes mockery of commitments to end war crimes', *Amnesty International* (1 February), https://www.amnesty.org/en/latest/news/2016/02/nigeria-reinstatement-of-army-general-implicated-in-mass-murder-makes-mockery-of-commitments-to-end-war-crimes. Accessed 2 March 2018.

Amnesty International. 2016b. 'Nigeria: Military must come clean on slaughter of 347 Shi'ites', *Amnesty International* (12 April), https://www.amnesty.org/en/latest/news/2016/04/nigeria-military-must-come-clean-on-slaughter-of-347-shiites. Accessed 29 March 2018.

Amnesty International. 2016c. 'Nigeria: "Bullets were raining everywhere": Deadly repression of pro-Biafra activists', *Amnesty International* AFR 44/5211/2016 (24 November), https://www.amnesty.org/en/documents/afr44/5211/2016/en. Accessed 26 February 2018.

Amnesty International. 2018. 'Nigeria: Reckless police crackdown against unarmed protestors put lives at risk', *Amnesty International* (17 April), https://www.amnesty.org/en/latest/news/2018/04/nigeria-reckless-police-crackdown-against-unarmed-protestors-put-lives-at-risk. Accessed 10 February 2023.

Arendt, Hannah. 1951. *The Origins of Totalitarianism*. New York: Harcourt.
Atoyebi, Olufemi. 2018. 'Ekiti vote buying: Rewarding emerging electoral fraud with victory', *Punch* (22 July), https://punchng.com/ekiti-vote-buying-rewarding-emerging-electoral-fraud-with-victory. Accessed 17 September 2018.
Awojulugbe, Oluwaseyi. 2017. 'Report: Nigeria "lost $32bn" to corruption under Jonathan (updated)', *The Cable* (11 December), https://www.thecable.ng/dfid-nigeria-lost-32bn-corruption-jonathan. Accessed 17 September 2018.
Azzi, Iman. 2011. 'Cairo Leaders: Suzanne Mubarak held Women back', 16 February. Available at: https://womensenews.org/2011/02/cairo-leaders-suzanne-mubarak-held-women-back/ Accessed 22 May 2019.
Bada, Gbenga. 2016. '#BringBackOurGirls: Police IG explains why protest was disrupted', *Pulse* (8 September), http://www.pulse.ng/news/local/bringbackourgirls-police-ig-explains-why-protest-was-disrupted-id5468037.html. Accessed 22 December 2017.
Badejo, Abiodun. 2014. 'Governor Fayose appoints SSG, PA on Stomach Infrastructure, eight others', *Daily Post* (16 October), http://dailypost.ng/2014/10/16/governor-fayose-appoints-ssg-pa-stomach-infrastructure-eight-others. Accessed 13 April 2018.
Baker, Aryn. 2017. 'Boko Haram's other victims', *Time* (27 June), http://time.com/boko-harams-other-victims. Accessed 14 August 2017.
G Bappah, Habibu. 2016. 'Nigeria's military failure against the Boko Haram insurgency', *African Security Review*, 25, 2: 146–158.
Bayart, Jean-François. 2009. *The State in Africa: The Politics of the Belly*, 2nd edn. Cambridge: Polity.
Bayart, Jean-François, Stephen Ellis, and Béatrice Hibou. 1999. 'From kleptocracy to the felonious state?' In Jean-François. Bayart, Stephen Ellis, and Béatrice Hibou (eds) and Stephen Ellis (trans), *The Criminalization of the State in Africa*. Bloomington, IN: Indiana University Press, pp. 1–31.
BBC. 2006. 'Nigeria cartoon protests kill 16' (19 February), http://news.bbc.co.uk/2/hi/4728616.stm. Accessed 24 September 2018.
BBC. 2012a. 'Nigeria's Goodluck Jonathan: Officials back Boko Haram', *BBC News* (8 January), http://www.bbc.com/news/world-africa-16462891. Accessed 30 November 2016.
BBC. 2012b. 'Ngozi Okonjo-Iweala: Nigerian finance minister's mother kidnapped', *BBC News* (9 December), http://www.bbc.com/news/world-africa-20660791. Accessed 18 March 2016.
BBC 2014a. 'Nigeria school raid in Yobe state leaves 29 dead', *BBC News* (25 February), http://www.bbc.com/news/world-africa-26338041. Accessed 23 September 2015.
BBC. 2014b. 'Nigeria: Abuja bomb blast in Wuse district kills 21' (25 June), http://www.bbc.com/news/world-africa-28019433. Accessed 28 December 2017.
BBC. 2014c. Nigeria kidnap: David Cameron joins 'Bring Back Our Girls' campaign, https://www.bbc.com/news/uk-27360712. Accessed 20 November 2023.
BBC. 2015. 'Nigeria Boko Haram: Militants "technically defeated"—Buhari' (24 December), http://www.bbc.com/news/world-africa-35173618. Accessed 20 December 2017.
BBC. 2016. 'Nigerian ex-defence chief Alex Badeh "stole $20m"' (7 March), https://www.bbc.com/news/world-africa-35743795. Accessed 2 March 2018.
BBC. 2017. 'Chibok diaries: Chronicling a Boko Haram kidnapping' (23 October), https://www.bbc.com/news/world-africa-41570252. Accessed 26 September 2018.
BBC. 2018. 'Nigerian snake ate millions of naira, clerk says' (12 February), https://www.bbc.com/news/world-africa-43030827. Accessed 17 September 2018.
BBC. 2021. 'Chad's President Idriss Déby dies after clashes with rebels' (20 April), https://www.bbc.com/news/world-africa-56815708. Accessed 7 October 2021.

Benford, Robert and D. Snow. 2000. 'Framing processes and social movements: An overview and assessment', *Annual Review of Sociology*, 26: 611–639.

Bennett, Lance. 2012. 'The personalization of politics: Political identity, social media, and changing patterns of participation', *Annals of the American Academy of Political and Social Science*, 644, 1: 20–39.

Berriane, Jasmine. 2016. 'Bridging social divides: leadership and the making of an alliance for women's land-use rights in Morocco', *Review of African Political Economy*, 43: 149, 350–364 (29 September), https://doi.org/10.1080/03056244.2016.1214118. Accessed 2 November 2023.

Blumer, Herbert. 1969. 'Social movements'. In Alfred McClung Lee (ed.), *Principles of Sociology*. New York: Barnes & Nobles, pp. 99–120.

Blumer, Herbert. 1971. 'Social problems as collective behavior', *Social problems*, 18, 3: 298–306.

Bob, Clifford. 2002. 'Political process theory and transnational movements: Dialectics of protest among Nigeria's Ogoni minority', *Social Problems*, 49, 3: 395–415.

Bob, Clifford. 2005. *The Marketing of Rebellion: Insurgents, Media and International Activism*. Cambridge: Cambridge University Press.

Bob, Clifford. 2007. '"Dalit rights are human rights": Caste discrimination, international activism, and the construction of new human rights issues', *Human Rights Quarterly*, 29, 11: 167–193.

Bob, Clifford and Sharon E. Nepstad. 2007. 'Kill a leader, murder a movement? Leadership and assassination in social movements', *American Behavioral Scientist*, 50, 10: 1370–1394.

Boomer, Matthew. 2018. 'How Michelle Obama's Crusade To Rescue Schoolgirls From Boko Haram Ended In Their Further Exploitation', *The Federalist*, 5 July, <https://thefederalist.com/2018/07/05/michelle-obamas-crusade-rescue-schoolgirls-boko-haram-ended-exploitation/>. Accessed on 26 July 2021.

Bourdieu, Pierre. 1986. 'The forms of capital'. In J. Richardson (ed.), *Handbook of Theory and Research for the Sociology of Education*. Westport, CT: Greenwood, pp. 241–258.

Bouilly, Emmanuelle, Ophélie Rillon and Hannah Cross. 2016. 'African women's struggles in a gender perspective', *Review of African Political Economy*, 43, 149: 338–349.

Brean, Joseph. 2015. 'The dark side of "rights inflation": Why activists should 'reject the impulse to frame all grievances as human rights', *National Post*, http://news.nationalpost.com/news/canada/why-human-rights-inflation-could-spell-thebeginning-of-the-end-of-social-change. Accessed 30 June 2016.

Breuer, Anita, Todd Landman, and Dorothea Farquhar. 2015. 'Social media and protest mobilization: Evidence from the Tunisian revolution', *Democratization*, 22, 4: 764–792.

Brinkel, Theo and Soumia Ait-Hida. 2012. 'Boko Haram and jihad in Nigeria', *Scientia Militaria, South African Journal of Military Studies*, 40, 2: 1–21.

Britton, Hannah Evelyn. 2005. *Women in the South African Parliament: From Resistance to Governance*. University of Illinois Press. http://www.jstor.org/stable/10.5406/j.ctt1xcp5f.

Brown, Gustav. 2014. 'Does framing matter? Institutional constraints on framing in two cases of intrastate violence', *Mobilization: An International Quarterly*, 19, 2: 143–164.

Brown, M. Helen and Diane M. Hosking. 1986. 'Distributed leadership and skilled performance as successful organization in social movements', *Human Relations*, 39, 1: 65–79.

Bossard, James. 1941. 'Comment', *American Sociological Review*, 6, (June): 320–329.

Busari, Stephanie. 2016. 'Rescued Nigerian schoolgirl not one of the Chibok missing, activist says', *CNN* (20 May), https://www.cnn.com/2016/05/19/africa/nigeria-chibok-girl-escape/index.html. Accessed 22 August 2018.

Busari, Stephanie. 2021. 'Several remaining missing Chibok schoolgirls escape from Boko Haram', *CNN* (29 January), https://www.cnn.com/2021/01/29/africa/nigeria-chibok-girls-escape-intl/index.html. Accessed 26 July 2021.

Cardoso, Fernado Henrique, and Enzo Faletto. 1979. *Dependence and Development in Latin America*. Berkeley, CA: University of California Press.

Carreon, Michelle and Valentine Moghadam. 2015. '"Resistance is fertile": Revisiting maternalist frames across cases of women's mobilization', *Women's Studies International Forum*, 51: 19–30.

Castells, Manuel. 1996. *The Rise of the Network Society*, Volume I. Cambridge, MA: Blackwell.

Castells, Manuel. 2015. *Networks of Outrage and Hope: Social Movements in the Internet Age*. Cambridge: Polity.

Chang, Paul Y. and Alex S. Vitale. 2013. 'Repressive coverage in an authoritarian context: Threat, weakness, and legitimacy in South Korea's democracy movement', *Mobilization: An International Journal* 18, 1: 19–39.

Channels Television. 2014. 'Government sets up fact finding committee on Chibok girls' abduction', *Channels TV* (2 May), http://www.channelstv.com/2014/05/02/govt-sets-up-fact-finding-committee-on-chibok-girls-abduction. Accessed 19 March 2016.

Charmaz, Kathy, and Richard Mitchell. 2001. Grounded theory in ethnography. In *Handbook of Ethnography*. SAGE Publications Ltd, pp. 160–174, https://doi.org/10.4135/9781848608337.

Charrad, Mounira. 2001. *States and Women's Rights: The Making of Postcolonial Tunisia, Algeria, and Morocco*. Berkeley, CA: University of California Press,.

Cheeseman, Nic and Brian Klaas. 2018. *How to Rig an Election*. New Haven, CT and London: Yale University Press.

Chesters, Graeme and Ian Welsh. 2004. 'Rebel colours: "Framing" in global social movements', *Sociological Review*, 52, 3: 314–335.

Chiluwa, I. and P. Ifukor. 2015. 'War against our children: Stance and evaluation in #BringBackOurGirls campaign discourse on Twitter and Facebook', *Discourse and Society*, 26, 3: 267–296 (29 January), https://doi.org/10.1177/0957926514564735. Accessed 2 November 2023.

Christiansen, Jonathan. 2009. 'Four stages of social movements'. In *Sociology Reference Guide: Theories of Social Movements*. Pasadena: Salem Press, pp. 14–25. Available at: https://www.biknotes.com/_files/ugd/b8b6dc_0d2f14d4f5b042e3bb2272da76673f00.pdf#page=18

Clarke, Peter. 1987. 'The maitatsine movement in northern Nigeria in historical and current perspective'. In Rosalind. I. J. Hackett (ed.), *New Religious Movements in Nigeria*. Lewiston, NY: The Edwin Mellen Press, pp. 93–115.

Cole, Teju. 2012. 'The White-savior industrial complex', *The Atlantic* (21 March), https://www.theatlantic.com/international/archive/2012/03/the-white-savior-industrial-complex/254843. Accessed 4 September 2023.

Coleman, Isobel. 2011. 'Is the Arab Spring bad for women?', in Foreign Policy, December 20. Available online at: (accessed 22 May 2019).

Collier, David. 2011. 'Understanding process tracing', *Political Science and Politics*, 44, 4: 823–830.

Comoli, Virginia. 2015. *Boko Haram: Nigeria's Islamist Insurgency*. London: C. Hurst & Co.
Corrigall-Brown, Catherine. 2016. 'Funding for social movements', *Sociology Compass*, 10, 4: 330–339.
Cress, Daniel. and David Snow. 2000. 'The outcomes of homeless mobilization: The influence of organization, disruption, political mediation, and framing', *American Journal of Scoiology*, 105, 4: 1063–1104.
Cummings, Ryan. 2014. 'Why Boko Haram may have kidnapped Chibok's schoolgirls', *Premium Times* (3 May), https://www.premiumtimesng.com/opinion/160044-why-boko-haram-may-have-kidnapped-chiboks-schoolgirls-by-ryan-cummings.html. Accessed 26 September 2018.
Daily Post. 2014. 'Army commander writes to Jonathan, reveals why military cannot defeat Boko Haram', *Daily Post* (16 December), https://dailypost.ng/2014/12/16/army-commander-writes-jonathan-reveals-military-cannot-defeat-boko-haram/. Accessed 17 March 2016.
Daily Trust. 2017. 'You will do better as a comedian', *Daily Trust* (8 September), https://dailytrust.com/you-will-do-better-as-a-comedian-ezekwesili-tackles-garba-shehu/. Accessed 22 December 2017.
Davenport, Christian. 1995. 'Assessing the military's influence on political repression', *Journal of Political and Military Sociology*, 23: 119–144.
Davenport, Christian. 2000. 'Introduction'. In Christian Davenport (ed.), *Paths to State Repression*. Lanham, MD: Rowman & Littlefield Publishers, pp. 1–24.
Davenport, Christian. 2015. *How Social Movements Die: Repression and Demobilization of the Republic of the New Africa*. Cambridge: Cambridge University Press.
DeJesus, Kevin M. 2011. 'Introduction: Political Violence and Armed Conflict in Africa: People, Places, Processes, Effects.' *African Geographical Review*, 30, 1: 5–13.
della Porta, Donatella. 2005. 'Deliberation in movement: Why and how to study deliberative democracy and social movements', *Acta Politica*, 40: 336–350.
Della Porta, Donatella. 2013. 'Democracy inside social movements'. In David A. Snow, Donatella Della Porta, Bert Klandermans, and Doug McAdam (eds), *The Wiley-Blackwell Encyclopedia of Social and Political Movements*, Hoboken, NJ: Blackwell Publishing, pp. 1–4. https://doi.org/10.1002/9780470674871.
della Porta, Donatella and Mario Diani. 1999. *Social Movements: An Introduction*. Oxford: Blackwell Publishing.
Demant, Froukje, and Beatrice de Graaf. 2010. 'How to counter radical narratives: Dutch deradicalization policy in the case of Moluccan and Islamic radicals', *Studies in Conflict & Terrorism*, 33, 5: 408–428.
DeWalt, Kathleen M. and DeWalt, Billie R. 1998. 'Participant observation'. In H. Russell Bernard (ed.), (*Handbook of Methods in Cultural Anthropology*. Walnut Creek, CA: AltaMira Press, pp. 259–300.
Diamond, Larry. 2012. 'Liberation Technology'. In Larry Diamond and Marc F. Plattner (eds), *Liberation Technology: Social Media and the Struggle for Democracy*. Baltimore, MD: The Johns Hopkins University Press, pp. 3–17.
Diani, Mario. 2003. 'Introduction: Social movements, contentious actions, and social networks: "From metaphor to substance?"'. In Mario Diani and Doug McAdam (eds), *Social Movements and Networks: Relational Approaches to Collective Action*, Comparative Politics, online edn. Oxford: Oxford Academic (1 November), https://doi.org/10.1093/0199251789.003.0001. Accessed 18 October 2022.

Dietz, Kelly. 2000. 'Globalized resistance: An event history analysis of indigenous activism', MA thesis, Cornell University.
Di Marco, Graciela. 2009. 'Social justice and gender rights', *International Social Science Journal*, 191: 43–55.
Donnelly, Jack. 2008. 'Human rights and social provision', *Journal of Human Rights*, 7, 2: 123–138.
Douzinas, Costas. 2006. 'Speaking law: On bare theological and cosmopolitan sovereignty'. In Anne Orford (ed.), *International Law and Its Others*. Cambridge: Cambridge University Press.
Downing, John D. H. 2001. *Radical Media: Rebellious Communication and Social Movements*. Thousand Oaks, CA: Sage.
Dunn, Kevin C. 2009 '"Sons of the Soil" and Contemporary State Making: autochthony, uncertainty and political violence in Africa', *Third World Quarterly*, 30, 1: 113–127.
Duthiers, Vladimir, Faith Karimi, and Greg Botelho. 2014. 'Boko Haram: Why terror group kidnaps schoolgirls, and what happens next', *CNN* (2 May), https://www.cnn.com/2014/04/24/world/africa/nigeria-kidnapping-answers/index.html. Accessed 26 September 2018.
Duvall, Raymond D. and Michael Stohl. 1983. 'Governance by terror'. In Michael Stohl (ed.), *The Politics of Terrorism*. New York: Marcel Dekker, pp. 179–219.
Dwyer, Peter and Leo Zeilig. 2012. *African Struggles Today: Social Movements since Independence*. Chicago, IL: Haymarket Books.
Earl, Jennifer. 2003. 'Tanks, tear gas, and taxes', *Sociological Theory*, 21: 44–68.
Earl, Jennifer and Sarah A. Soule. 2006. 'Seeing blue: A police-centered explanation of protest policing', *Mobilization: An International Journal*, 11, 2: 145–164.
Earl, Jennifer, Sarah A. Soule, and John D. McCarthy. 2003. 'Protests under fire? Explaining protest policing', *American Sociological Review*, 69: 581–606.
Economic and Financial Crimes Commission. 2018. 'Finance director reveals how ex-air force chief Dikko, collected N558.2m monthly for 2 Years', *Sahara Reporters* (8 February), http://saharareporters.com/2018/02/08/finance-director-reveals-how-ex-air-force-chief-dikko-collected-n5582m-monthly-2-years. Accessed 28 February 2018.
Edosie, Victor. 2016. 'A new dawn for Ogoni land, as clean up begins', *Daily Trust* (5 June), https://dailytrust.com/a-new-dawn-for-ogoni-land-as-clean-up-begins/. Accessed 30 July 2016.
Elebeke, Emmanuel and Laide Akinboade. 2014. 'BringBackOurGirls: I am not slow—GEJ', http://www.vanguardngr.com/2014/05/bringbackourgirls-slow-gej. Accessed 17 March 2015.
El-Rufai, Nasir Ahmad. 2013. *The Accidental Public Servant*. Ibadan: Safari Books.
Erulka, Annabel and Mairo Bello. 2007. 'The experience of married adolescent girls in Northern Nigeria', http://www.ohchr.org. Accessed 20 November 2015.
Eyerman, Ron. 2002. 'Music in movement: Cultural politics and old and new social movements', *Qualitative Sociology*, 25, 3: 443–458.
Ezekwesili, Obiageli. 2015. 'The #Bringbackourgirls campaign and human rights advocacy in Nigeria', keynote address at the International Week, University of Alberta, https://www.youtube.com/watch?v=LV7ELmEuUAk. Accessed 12 March 2016.
Fallon, Kathleen M. and Julie Moreau. 2016. 'Revisiting repertoire transition: Women's nakedness as potent protests in Nigeria and Kenya', *Mobilization: An International Quarterly*, 21, 3: 323–340 (1 September), https://doi.org/10.17813/1086-671X-20-3-323. Accessed 2 November 2023.

Falola, Toyin. 1998. *Violence in Nigeria: The Crisis of Religious Politics and Secular Ideologies*. Rochester, NY: University of Rochester Press.

Fine, Gary Alan, Beth Montemurro, Bonnie Semora, Marybeth C. Stalp, Dane S. Claussen, and Zayda Sierra. 1998. 'Social order through a prism: Color as collective representation', *Sociological Inquiry*, 68, 4: 443–457.

Forest, James. 2012. 'Confronting the Terrorism of Boko Haram in Nigeria'. JSOU Report 12-5. Joint Special Operations University. Available at: https://apps.dtic.mil/sti/citations/ADA591800 Accessed 15 March 2017.

Francesca Polletta. 2006. 'Mobilization Forum: Awkward movements', *Mobilization*, 11, 4: 475–478.

Francis, Juliana: 2018. 'I worked for Boko Haram because I didn't earn money as JTF member—Boko Haram suspect', *New Telegraph*, 21 July.

Freeman, Jo. 1978. 'Crises and conflicts in social movement organizations', *Chrysalis: A Magazine of Women's Culture*, 5: 43–51.

Fuchs, Christian. 2017. *Social Media: A Critical Introduction*. London: Sage.

Gachihi, Margaret Wangui. 1986. 'The role of Kikuyu women in the Mau Mau', MA thesis, University of Nairobi, http://41.204.161.209/handle/11295/43701. Accessed 6 April 2020.

Gamson, William A. 1975. *The Strategy of Social Protest*. Homewood, IL: Dorsey Press.

Gamson, William A. 1990. *The Strategy of Social Protest*, 2nd edn. Belmont, CA: Wadsworth.

Gans, Herbert. 1972. 'The positive functions of poverty', *American Journal of Sociology*, 78, 2: 275–289.

Geertz, Clifford. 1963. *Old Societies and New State: The Quest for Modernity in Asia and Africa*. New York, NY: Free Press.

George, Alexander and Andrew Bennett. 2005. *Case Studies and Theory Development in the Social Sciences*. Cambridge, MA: MIT Press.

Gerbaudo, Paolo. 2012. *Tweets and the Streets: Social Media and Contemporary Activism*. London: Pluto.

Gheytanchi, Elham and Valentine N. Moghadam. 2014. 'Women, social protests, and the new media activism in the Middle East and North Africa', *International Review of Modern Sociology*, 40, 1: 1–6, http://www.jstor.org/stable/43496487. Accessed 2 November 2023.

Giugni, Marco. 1998. 'Was It Worth the Effort? The Outcomes and Consequences of Social Movements'. Annual Review of Sociology 24 (1): 371–393. https://doi.org/10.1146/annurev.soc.24.1.371.

Glaser, Barney and Anselm Strauss. 1967. *The Discovery of Grounded Theory: Strategies for Qualitative Research*. Mill Valley, CA: Sociology Press.

Godwin, Ameh. 2015. 'Chibok girls were kidnapped to make Jonathan's government look incompetent—Doyin Okupe', *Daily Post* (18 April), http://dailypost.ng/2015/04/18/chibok-girls-were-kidnapped-to-make-jonathans-government-look-incompetent-doyin-okupe. Accessed 17 March 2016.

Goffman, Erving. 1973. *The Presentation of Self in Everyday Life*. Woodstock, NY: The Overlook Press.

Goldstone, Jack. 1980. 'The weakness of organization: A new look at Gamson's *The Strategy of Social Protest*', *American Journal of Sociology*, 85, 5: 1017–1042.

Goodwin, Jeff and James M. Jasper. 1999. 'Caught in a winding, snarling vine: The structural bias of political process theory', *Sociological Forum*, 14: 27–54.

Gould, David J., and Tshiabukole B. Mukendi. 1989. 'Bureaucratic corruption in Africa: Causes, consequences and remedies', *International Journal of Public Administration*, 12, 3: 427–457.

Gramer, Robbie. 2021. 'U.S. lawmakers hold up major proposed arms sale to Nigeria', *Foreign Policy* (27 July), https://foreignpolicy.com/2021/07/27/nigeria-us-arms-sale-lawmakers. Accessed 2 August 2021.

Gray, Simon and Ibikunle Adeakin. 2015. 'The evolution of Boko Haram: From missionary activism to transnational jihad and the failure of the Nigerian Security Intelligence Agencies', *African Security*, 8, 3: 185–211.

Großklaus, Mathias. 2015. 'Appropriation and the dualism of human rights: Understanding the contradictory impact of gender norms in Nigeria', *Third World Quarterly*, 36, 6: 1253–1267.

Guigni, Marco. 1998. 'Was it worth the effort? The outcomes and consequences of social movements', *Annual Review of Sociology*, 246: 371–393.

Gutmann, Amy. 2001. *Michael Ignatieff: Human Rights as Politics and Idolatry*. Princeton: Princeton University Press.

Haenfler, Ross. 2004. 'Rethinking subcultural resistance core values of the straight edge movement', *Journal of Contemporary Ethnography*, 33, 4: 406–436.

Hafez, Sherine. 2012. 'No longer a bargain: Women, masculinity, and the Egyptian uprising', *American Ethnologist*, 39, 1: 37–42.

Hafner-Burton, Emilie M. and Kiyoteru Tsutsui. 2005. 'Human rights in a globalizing world: The paradox of empty promises', *American Journal of Sociology*, 110, 5: 1373–1411.

Hanneman, R. 1985. 'The military's role in political regimes', *Armed Forces and Society*, 2: 29–51.

Harlow, Summer. 2011. 'Social media and social movements: Facebook and an online Guatemalan justice movement that moved offline', *New Media & Society* 14, 2: 225–243.

Haruna, Abdulkareem. 2016. 'Chibok girls in U.S. 'used by NGOs for money' – Minister, Parents', *Premium Times*, 9 September. <https://www.premiumtimesng.com/news/headlines/210138-chibok-girls-u-s-used-ngos-money-minister-parents.html> 26 July 2018.

Haruna, Abdulkareem. 2017. 'Boko Haram: Borno governor lambasts UNICEF, 126 other "nonperforming" NGOs', *Premium Times* (11 January), https://www.premiumtimesng.com/news/headlines/220082-boko-haram-borno-governor-lambasts-unicef-126-nonperforming-ngos.html. Accessed 22 August 2018.

Haruna, Abdulkareem 2020. 'Borno to monitor budgets of 172 registered NGOs, CSOs—Official', *Premium Times* (25 June), https://www.premiumtimesng.com/regional/nnorth-east/399465-borno-to-monitor-budgets-of-172-registered-ngos-csos-official.html. Accessed 26 January 2021.

Hashim, Yahaya, & Walker, Judith-Ann. 2014. 'Marginal Muslims': Ethnic identity & the Umma in Kano. In A. Mustapha (Ed.), *Sects and Social Disorder: Muslim Identities and Conflict in Northern Nigeria* (Western Africa Series). Boydell & Brewer, pp. 126–146. https://doi.org/10.1017/9781782044734.007

Hassim, S. 2003. 'The gender pact and democratic consolidation: Institutionalising gender equality in the South African state', *Feminist Studies*, 29, 3: 505–528.

Helman, Gerald B. and Steven R. Ratner. 1992. 'Saving failed states', *Foreign Policy*, 89: 3–20.

Hemba, Joe. 2014. 'Nigerian Islamists kill 59 pupils in boarding school attack', Reuters (26 February), https://www.reuters.com/article/us-nigeria-violence-idUSBREA1P10M20140226/. Accessed 10 March 2014.

Henkin, Louis. 1990. *The Age of Rights*. New York: Columbia University Press.

Hickey, Raymond. 1984. 'The 1982 Maitatsine uprisings in Nigeria: a note', *African Affairs* 83, 331: 251–256.
Hill, Amelia and Anushka Asthana. 2006. 'Nigeria cartoon riots kill 16', *The Guardian* (19 February), https://www.theguardian.com/world/2006/feb/19/muhammadcartoons.ameliahill. Accessed 24 September 2018.
Hill, Jonathan N. C. 2009. 'Thoughts of home: Civil–military relations and the conduct of Nigeria's peacekeeping forces', *Journal of Military Ethics*, 8, 4: 289–306. https://doi.org/10.1080/15027570903353844. Accessed 18 October 2023.
Hinshaw, Drew, Joe Parkinson, and Gbenga Akingbule. 2018. 'The American ordeal of the Boko Haram schoolgirls', *Wall Street Journal* (13 April), https://www.wsj.com/articles/the-american-ordeal-of-the-boko-haram-schoolgirls-1523661238. Accessed 22 August 2018
Howard, Philip N., Aiden Duffy, Deen Freelon, Muzammil M. Hussain, Will Mari, and Marwa Maziad. 2015. 'Opening closed regimes: What was the role of social media during the Arab Spring?', https://doi.org/10.2139/ssrn.2595096. Accessed 18 October 2023.
Howard, Philip N. and Duffy, Aiden and Freelon, Deen and Hussain, M.M. and Mari, Will and Maziad, Marwa. 2011. Opening Closed Regimes: What Was the Role of Social Media During the Arab Spring? Available at SSRN: https://ssrn.com/abstract=2595096 or https://doi.org/10.2139/ssrn.2595096. Accessed 11 June 2016.
Howe, Sara Eleanor. 2006. 'The Madres de la Plaza de Mayo: Asserting motherhood; rejecting feminism?', *Journal of International Women's Studies*, 7, 3: 43–50.
Human Rights Watch. 2007. '"Chop Fine": The human rights impact of local government corruption and mismanagement in Rivers state, Nigeria', *Human Rights Watch* (31 January), https://www.hrw.org/report/2007/01/31/chop-fine/human-rights-impact-local-government-corruption-and-mismanagement-rivers. Accessed 20 September 2018.
Human Rights Watch. 2014. '"Those terrible weeks in their camp": Boko Haram violence against women and girls in Northeast Nigeria', *Human Rights Watch* (27 October), https://www.hrw.org/report/2014/10/27/those-terrible-weeks-their-camp/boko-haram-violence-against-women-and-girls. Accessed 28 September 2018.
Ibeh, Nnnena. 2014. 'Meet the man who generated #BringBackOurGirls hashtag', *Premium Times* (14 June), http://www.premiumtimesng.com/news/162803-interview-meet-man-generated-bringbackourgirls-hashtag.html. Accessed 25 April 2016.
Ibeh, Nnnena. 2015. 'UN Secretary General, Ban Ki-moon, fails to meet #BringBackOurGirls group', *Premium Times* (24 August), http://www.premiumtimesng.com/news/top-news/188939-un-secretary-general-ban-ki-moon-fails-to-meet-bringbackourgirls-group.html. Accessed 21 March 2016.
Ibekwe, Nicholas. 2014a. 'Ezekwesili blasts Jonathan over "awful" statement to #BringBackOurGirls protesters', *Premium Times* (24 May), http://www.premiumtimesng.com/news/161391-ezekwesili-blasts-jonathan-over-awful-statement-to-bringbackourgirls-protesters.html. Accessed 15 March 2016.
Ibekwe, Nicholas. 2014b. 'Outrage as pro-govt. crowd attacks #BringBackOurGirls campaigners in Abuja', *Premium Times* (29 May), https://www.premiumtimesng.com/news/161650-outrage-as-pro-govt-crowd-attacks-bringbackourgirls-campaigners-in-abuja.html. Accessed 28 December 2017.
Ibhawoh, Bonny. 2018. *Human rights in Africa*. Cambridge: Cambridge University Press.
Ibrahim, Idris and Aisha Yesufu. 2017. 'Onaiyekan joins BringBackOurGirls march', *Premium Times* (11 April), https://www.premiumtimesng.com/news/more-news/228600-onaiyekan-joins-bringbackourgirls-march.html. Accessed 5 January 2018.

Idris, Hamza and Ibrahim Sawab. 2018. 'Factional Boko Haram leader Mamman Nur killed by own fighters', *Daily Trust* (14 September), https://www.dailytrust.com.ng/factional-boko-haram-leader-mamman-nur-killed-by-own-fighters.html. Accessed 17 September 2018.

Igboin, Benson O. 2012. 'Boko Haram sharia reasoning and democratic vision in pluralist Nigeria', *International Studies: Interdisciplinary Political and Cultural Journal (IS)*, 14, 1: 75–93.

Ignatieff, Michael. 2001. 'Human rights as politics'. In Amy Gutmann (ed.), *Human Rights as Politics and Idolatry*. Princeton, NJ: Princeton University Press, pp. 3–52.

Ignatieff, Michael. 2002. 'Human rights, the laws of war, and terrorism', *Social Research*, 69, 4: 1137–1158.

Ikelegbe, Augustine. 2005. 'The economy of conflict in the oil rich Niger Delta region of Nigeria', *Nordic Journal of African Studies*, 14, 2: 208–234.

Institute for Peace and Conflict Resolution Abuja. 2017. '2016 Strategic conflict assessment of Nigeria: Consolidated and zonal reports', *United Nations Development Programme* (18 December), http://www.ng.undp.org/content/nigeria/en/home/library/democratic_governance/strategic-conflict-assessment-of-nigeria-2016.html. Accessed 11 April 2018.

Isa, Daud and Itai Himelboim. 2018. 'A social networks approach to online social movement: Social mediators and mediated content in #FreeAJStaff twitter network', *Social Media + Society* (1 March), https://doi.org/10.1177/2056305118760807. Accessed 18 October 2023.

Isine, Ibanga. 2014a. 'APC's Audu Ogeh apologises over #BringBackOurGirls gaffe', *Premium Times* (21 October), http://www.premiumtimesng.com/news/top-news/169867-apcs-audu-ogbe-apologises-over-bringbackourgirls-gaffe.html. Accessed 11 March 2016.

Isine, Ibanga. 2014b. 'Ogbeh's comment hurts #BringBackOurGirls credibility—Group', *Premium Times* (21 October), http://www.premiumtimesng.com/regional/169874-ogbehs-comment-hurts-bringbackourgirls-credibility-group.html. Accessed 17 March 2016.

Iwuoha, Victor. 2019. 'Clash of counterterrorism-assistance-seeking states and their superpower sponsors: Implications on the war against Boko Haram', *African Security Review*, 28, 1: 38–55.

Iyekekpolo, Wisdom Oghosa. 2020. 'Political elites and the rise of the Boko Haram insurgency in Nigeria', *Terrorism and Political Violence*, 32, 4: 749–767.

Jalali, R. 2013. 'Financing empowerment? How foreign aid to Southern NGOs and social movements undermines grass-roots mobilization', *Sociological Compass*, 7, 1: 55–73.

Joffé, George. 2011. 'The Arab Spring in North Africa: Origins and prospects', *Journal of North African Studies*, 16, 4: 507–532.

Jonathan, Goodluck. 2018. *My Transition Hours*. Ezekiel Press.

Joscelyn, Thomas. 2016. 'Osama Bin Laden's files: Boko Haram's leader wanted to be "under one banner"', *Long War Journal* (4 March), http://www.longwarjournal.org/archives/2016/03/osama-bin-ladens-files-boko-haram-leader-wanted-to-be-under-one-banner.php. Accessed 7 February 2017.

Juris, Jeffrey. 2008. *Networking Futures: The Movements against Corporate Globalization*. Durham, NC: Duke University Press

Kanogo, Tabitha. 1987. 'Kikuyu women and the politics of protest: Mau Mau'. In Macdonald, Sharon, Pat Holden, and Shirley Ardener (eds), *Images of Women in Peace and War*, Women in Society. London: Palgrave, pp. 78–99.

Kassim, Abdulbassit. 2017. 'Blasphemy and freedom of speech in Northern Nigeria: Revisiting Boko Haram's bombing of ThisDay newspaper headquarters in Abuja', Medium (23 April), https://medium.com/@ak61/blasphemy-and-freedom-of-speech-in-northern-nigeria-revisiting-boko-harams-bombing-of-thisday-b9c6c5f38e5c. Accessed 23 September 2018.

Kassim, Abdulbasit and Michael Nwankpa. 2018. *The Boko Haram Reader: From Nigerian Preachers to the Islamic State*. Oxford: Oxford University Press.

Keddie, Nikki. 1994. 'The revolt of Islam, 1700 to 1993: Comparative considerations and relations to imperialism', *Comparative Studies in Society and History*, 36, 3: 463–487.

Kitschelt, Herbert. 1986. 'Political opportunity structures and political protest: Anti-nuclear movements in four democracies', *British Journal of Political Science*, 16: 57–85.

Klandermans, B. 1997. *The Social Psychology of Protest*. Oxford: Blackwell.

Kriesi, Hanspeter. 2004. 'Political context and opportunity'. In David A. Snow, Sarah A. Soule, and Hanspeter Kriesi (eds), *The Blackwell Companion to Social Movements*. Malden, MA: Blackwell Publishing, pp. 67–90.

Lamb, Christina. 2016. 'A fight for the soul of the world', Sunday Times (20 March), http://christinalamb.net/articles/a-fight-for-the-soul-of-the-world/. Accessed 31 March 2016.

Langer, Arnim, Amélie Godefroidt, and Bart Meuleman. 2017). 'Killing people, dividing a nation?', *Analyzing Student Perceptions of the Boko Haram Crisis in Nigeria, Studies in Conflict & Terrorism*, 40, 5: 419–738.

Last, Murray. 2014. 'From dissent to dissidence: The genesis and development of reformist Islamic groups in Northern Nigeria'. In Abdul Raufu Mustapha (ed.), *Sects and Social Disorder: Muslim Identities and Conflict in Northern Nigeria*. Woodbridge: James Currey, pp. 18–53.

Leach, Darcy K. 2005. 'The iron law of *what* again? Conceptualizing oligarchy across organizational forms', *Sociological Theory*, 23, 3: 312–337.

Leadership Editors. 2015. 'Another kind of insurgency', *Leadership*, http://leadership.ng/opinions/431177/another-kind-of-insurgency. Accessed 21 September 2015.

Lederman, Josh. 2017. 'Officials: US approves high-tech attack planes for Nigeria', *AP News* (3 August), https://www.apnews.com/c27a2289b99e49b2b7203fbef36d0580. Accessed 7 August 2017.

Leslie, Agnes Ngoma. 2006. *Social Movements and Democracy in Africa: The Impact of Women's Struggles for Equal Rights in Botswana*. New York: Routledge.

Lim, Merlyna. 2012. 'Clicks, cabs, and coffee houses: Social media and oppositional movements in Egypt, 2004–2011', *Journal of Communication*, 62: 231–248.

Loimeier, Roman. 1997. *Islamic Reform and Political Change in Northern Nigeria*. Evanston, IL: Northwestern University Press.

Loimeier, Roman. 2012. 'Boko Haram: The development of a militant religious movement in Nigeria', *Africa spectrum* 47, 2–3: 137–155.

Loken, Meredith. 2014. '#BringBackOurGirls and the invisibility of imperialism', *Feminist Media Studies*, 14, 6: 1100–1101.

Loseke, Donileen. 1999. *Thinking about social problems: An introduction to constructionist perspectives*. New York: Aldine de Gruyter.

Luckham, Alexander R. 1969. *The Nigerian military: A case study in institutional breakdown*. PhD Dissertation, University of Chicago.

Luckiesh, M. 1938. *Color and Colors*. New York: Van Nostrand.

Mabweazara, Hayes Mawindi. 2015. 'Mainstreaming African digital cultures, practices and emerging forms of citizen engagement', *African Journalism Studies*, 36, 4: 1–11.

Maclean, Ruth. 2016. 'Nigerian president meets schoolgirl who escaped Boko Haram', *The Guardian* (19 May), https://www.theguardian.com/world/2016/may/19/nigerian-president-meet-chibok-schoolgirl-escaped-boko-haram. Accessed 22 August 2018.

Maiangwa, Benjamin, and Olumuyiwa Babatunde Amao. 2015. '"Daughters, brides, and supporters of the Jihad": Revisiting the gender-based atrocities of Boko Haram in Nigeria', *African Renaissance*, 12, 2: 117–144.

Mama, Amina. 1995. 'Feminism or Femocracy? State Feminism and Democratisation in Nigeria', *Africa Development / Afrique et Développement*, 20, 1: 37–58.

Mantzikos, Ioannis. 2014. 'Boko Haram Attacks in Nigeria and Neighbouring Countries: A Chronology of Attacks', *Perspectives on Terrorism*, 8, 6: 63–81.

Mare, Admire. 2014. 'Social media: The new protest drums in Southern Africa?'. In B. Pătrut and M. Pătrut (eds), *Social Media in Politics. Public Administration and Information Technology*, vol 13. Cham: Springer (1 January), https://doi.org/10.1007/978-3-319-04666-2_17. Accessed 2 November 2023.

Marenin, Otwin. 1988. 'The Nigerian state as process and manager: A conceptualization', *Comparative Politics*, 20, 2: 215–232.

Marlow, Christine. 2005. *Research methods for generalist social work*. New York: Thomson Brooks/Cole.

Mason, Paul. 2012. *Why It's Kicking Off Everywhere: The New Global Revolutions*. London: Verso.

Matazu, Hamisi Kabir. 2014. 'Boko Haram gunmen kill 40 students at Federal Govt. college in Yobe', *Sahara Reporters* (25 February), http://saharareporters.com/2014/02/25/boko-haram-gunmen-kill-40-students-federal-govt-college-yobe-dailytrust-newspaper. Accessed 23 September 2015.

Matfess, Hillary. 2017. *Women and the War on Boko Haram: Wives, Weapons and Witnesses*. London: Zed Books.

Matusiak, Matthew C. 2016. 'Dimensionality of local police chiefs' institutional sovereigns', *Policing and Society: An International Journal of Research and Policy*, 26, 7: 753–770. https://doi.org/10.1080/10439463.2014.989156.

Maxfield, Mary. 2015. 'History retweeting itself: Imperial feminist appropriations of "Bring Back Our Girls"', *Feminist Media Studies*. https://doi.org/10.1080/14680777.2015.1116018. Accessed 18 October 2023.

Mazumdar, Tulip. 2015. 'Chibok girls "forced to join Nigeria's Boko Haram"', *BBC Panorama* (29 June), https://www.bbc.com/news/world-africa-33259003. Accessed 28 September 2018.

Mba, N. E. 1982. *Nigerian Women Mobilized: Women's Political Activity in Southern Nigeria, 1900–1965*. Berkeley, CA: University of California.

Mbembé, Achille. 2001. *On the Postcolony*. Berkeley, CA: University of California Press.

Mbembé, Achille. 2003. 'Necropolitics', *Public Culture*, 15, 1: 11–40.

McAdam, D. 1996. 'Conceptual orgins, current problems, future direction'. In D. McAdam, J. McCarthy, and M. Zald (eds), *Comparative Perspectives on Social Movements: Political Opportunities, Mobilizing Structures, and Cultural Framings*, Cambridge Studies in Comparative Politics. Cambridge: Cambridge University Press, pp. 23–40.

McAdam, Doug and David Snow (eds). 1997. *Social Movements: Readings on Their Emergence, Mobilization, and Dynamics*. Los Angeles, CA: Roxbury.

McGowan, Patrick J. 2003. 'African military coups d'etat, 1956–2001: Frequency, trends and distribution', *Journal of Modern African Studies*, 41, 3: 339–370.

Maclean, Ruth and Alice Ross. 2017. '82 Chibok schoolgirls freed in exchange for five Boko Haram leaders', *The Guardian* (7 May), https://www.theguardian.com/world/2017/

may/07/chibok-schoolgirls-familes-await-as-82-are-freed-by-boko-haram-exchange-prison. Accessed 17 December 2017.

McQue, Katie. 2017. 'Nigeria rejected British offer to rescue seized Chibok schoolgirls', *The Guardian* (4 May), https://www.theguardian.com/world/2017/mar/04/nigeria-declined-uk-offer-to-rescue-chibok-girls. Accessed 1 March 2018.

McVeigh, Tracy. 2014. 'Michelle Obama raises pressure over kidnapped schoolgirls', *The Guardian* (11 May), http://www.theguardian.com/world/2014/may/10/michelle-obama-nigeria-presidential-address. Accessed 18 March 2014.

Meagher, Kate and Abdul Raufu Mustapha. 2020. 'Introduction: Faith, society and Boko Haram'. In Kate Meagher and Abdul Raufu Mustapha (eds), *Overcoming Boko Haram: Faith, Society, and Islamic Radicalization in Northern Nigeria*. Woodbridge: James Currey, pp. 1–29.

Mensah, Joseph. 2005. 'On the ethno-cultural heterogeneity of blacks in our "ethnicities"', *Immigration and the Intersections of Diversity*, Spring: 72–77.

Merry, Sally Engle. 2006. 'Transnational human rights and local activism: Mapping the middle', *American Anthropologist*, 108, 1: 38–51.

Meyer, David S. 2004. 'Protest and political opportunities', *Annual Review of Sociology*, 30: 125–145 (10 February), http://www.jstor.org/stable/29737688. Accessed 2 November 2023.

Michel, Sonya. 2012. 'Maternalism and beyond'. In Rebecca Plant (ed.), *Beyond Maternalism: Motherhood and Method*. New York: Bergahn Books, pp. 22–37.

Michels, Robert. [1911] 1962. *Political Parties: A Sociological Study of the Oligarchical Tendencies of Modern Democracy*. New York: Free Press.

Miller, Walter Richard Samuel. 1936. *Reflections of a Pioneer*. London: Church Missionary Society.

Miners, Norman. J. 1971. *The Nigerian Army, 1956–1966*. London: Mathuen.

Milman, Noa. 2014. 'Mothers, Mizrahi, and poor: Contentious media framings of mothers' movements', *Intersectionality and Social Change: Research in Social Movements, Conflicts and Change*, 37: 53–82. https://doi.org/10.1108/S0163-786X20140000037002. Accessed 18 October 2023.

Minkoff, Debra, and Walter W. Powell. 2006. 'Nonprofit mission: Constancy, responsiveness, or deflection?'. In Walter W. Powell and Richard Steinberg (eds), *Nonprofit Sector: A Research Handbook*. Second Edition. New Haven, CT: Yale University Press, pp. 591–611.

Misri, Deepti. 2011. '"Are you a man?": Performing naked protest in India', *Signs: Journal of Women in Culture and Society*, 36, 3: 603–625.

Mkhize, Gabi and Nwabisa Mgcotyelwa-Ntoni. 2019. 'The impact of women's movements' activism experiences on gender transformation policies in democratic South Africa', *Agenda*, 33, 2: 9–21.

Mohammed, Kyari. 2015. 'The message and methods of Boko Haram'. In Marc-Antonine Perouse de Montclous (ed.), *Boko Haram: Islamism, Politics, Security and the State in Nigeria*. Los Angeles, CA: Tsehai Publishers, pp. 3–69.

Mojeed, Musikilu. 2015. 'Nigeria-based journalist arrested in Cameroon, accused of spying for Boko Haram', *Premium Times* (29 August), http://www.premiumtimesng.com/news/top-news/189201-nigeria-based-journalist-arrested-in-cameroon-accused-of-spying-for-boko-haram.html. Accessed 14 September 2015.

Mojeed, Abdulkareem. 2021. 'EXCLUSIVE: NPA saga: At last, Hadiza Bala Usman receives suspension letter', *Premium Times* (8 May), https://www.premiumtimesng.com/news/

top-news/460323-exclusive-npa-saga-at-last-hadiza-bala-usman-receives-suspension-letter.html. Accessed 2 August 2021.

Munshi, Neil. 2019. 'Graft and mismanagement claims taint Nigeria oil clean-up', *Financial Times* (28 December), https://www.ft.com/content/33485e22-104e-11ea-a225-db2f231cfeae. Accessed 2 August 2021.

Musa, Njadvara. 2017. 'AfDB votes $1million to rebuild Chibok school', *The Guardian* (28 April), https://guardian.ng/news/afdb-votes-1m-to-rebuild-chibok-school. Accessed 19 December 2017.

Muslim Students' Society of Nigeria (MSSN), University of Ibadan. 2018. 'About', https://www.mssnui.org/about. Accessed 22 September 2018.

Mustapha, Abdul Raufu. 2014. 'Understanding Boko Haram'. In Abdul Raufu Mustapha (ed.), *Sects and Social Disorder: Muslim Identities and Conflict in Northern Nigeria*. Woodbridge: James Currey, pp. 147–198.

Mustapha, Abdul Raufu, and Bunza, Mukhtar. 2014. Contemporary Islamic sects & groups in northern Nigeria. In A. Mustapha (Ed.), *Sects and Social Disorder: Muslim Identities and Conflict in Northern Nigeria* (Western Africa Series). Boydell & Brewer, pp. 54–97. https://doi.org/10.1017/9781782044734.005

Mustapha, Abdul Raufu, and Kate Meagher. 2020. Overcoming Boko Haram: faith, society & Islamic radicalization in northern Nigeria. Oxford: James Currey.

Mutum, Ronald. 2015. 'Tribal, religious sentiments fuel B/Haram crisis—Minimah', *Daily Trust*, 6 August, https://dailytrust.com/tribal-religious-sentiments-fuel-b-haram-crisis-minimah/. Accessed 15 October 2016.

National Bureau of Statistics. 2010. *Annual Abstract of Statistics*. Abuja, FCT: Hossrael Prints & Publishers.

Nepstad, Sharon and Clifford Bob. 2006. 'When do leaders matter? Hypotheses on leadership dynamics in social movements', *Mobilization: An International Quarterly*, 11, 1: 1–22. https://doi.org/10.17813/maiq.11.1.013313600164m727. Accessed 2 November 2023.

Ngwodo, Chris. 2015 (8 August). 'How the North Was Lost', *Premium Times*, Available at: https://opinion.premiumtimesng.com/2015/08/08/how-the-north-was-lost-by-chris-ngwodo/?tztc=1. Accessed 2 April 2016.

Nilsson, Marco. 2015. 'Foreign fighters and the radicalization of local jihad: Interview evidence from Swedish jihadists', *Studies in Conflict & Terrorism*, 38, 5: 345.

Noonan, Rita. 1995. 'Women against the state: Political opportunities and collective action frames in Chile's transition to democracy', *Sociological Forum*, 10, 1: 81–111.

Nwaubani, Adaobi Tricia. 2017. 'Nigeria's Chibok girls say kidnap by Boko Haram was accidental', *Reuters* (16 August), https://www.reuters.com/article/us-nigeria-boko-haram-chibok-iduskcn1ax0ay. Accessed 21 August 2017.

Nwabughiogu, Levinus. 2015. 'Hate campaign: Buhari fights back, bars AIT from covering his activities', *Vanguard* (27 April), http://www.vanguardngr.com/2015/04/hate-campaign-buhari-fights-back-bars-ait-from-covering-his-activities. Accessed 13 January 2017.

Nyabola, Nanjala. 2018. *Digital Democracy, Analogue Politics: How the Internet Era Is Transforming Politics in Kenya*. London: Zed.

Nyiayaana, Kialee. 2018. 'MOSOP since 1995: Somewhere between hope and despair?' In Cyril Obi and Temitope Oriola (eds). *The Unfinished Revolution in the Niger Delta: Prospects for Environmental Justice and Peace*. New York and London: Routledge, pp. 12–27.

Obike, Grace. 2017. 'Chibok girls: #BBOG marches to Aso Rock on Tuesday', The Nation (31 July), http://thenationonlineng.net/chibok-girls-bbog-marches-aso-rock-tuesday. Accessed 22 December 2017.

Odunsi, Wale. 2017. 'Stop acting like opposition—Nigerian government carpets BBOG', *Daily Post* (23 January), http://dailypost.ng/2017/01/23/stop-acting-like-opposition-nigerian-government-carpets-bbog. Accessed 20 December 2017.

Office of Gordon and Sarah Brown. 2014. 'Safe Schools Initiative launched' (7 May), http://gordonandsarahbrown.com/2014/05/safe-schools-initiative-launched. Accessed 19 December 2017.

Office of the Senior Special Assistant to the President on SDGs. 2017. 'NIGERIA: Sustainable development goals (SDGs) indicators baseline report, 2016', *United Nations Development Programme* (30 October), http://www.ng.undp.org/content/nigeria/en/home/library/mdg/nigeria-sdgs-indicators-baseline-report-2016. Accessed 11 April 2018.

Ogbeche, Daniel. 2016. 'Chibok girls: Oby Ezekwesili warns Buhari's daughter, Hadiza, against associating BBOG with fund-raiser group', Daily Post (22 October), http://dailypost.ng/2016/10/22/chibok-girls-oby-ezekwesili-warns-buharis-daughter-hadiza-associating-bbog-fund-raiser-group. Accessed 25 December 2017.

Ogene, Ashionye. 2014. 'Abandonment of "Bring Back Our Girls"', *Al Jazeera* (14 October), http://www.aljazeera.com/indepth/features/2014/10/abandonment-bring-back-our-girls-2014101494119446698.html. Accessed 16 March 2016.

Ogundipe, Samuel. 2017. 'Sacked guardian of Chibok girls in U.S. slams $5 million suit on Nigerian govt', *Premium Times*, 9 February. <https://www.premiumtimesng.com/news/top-news/223020-sacked-guardian-chibok-girls-u-s-slams-5-million-suit-nigerian-govt.html> (26 July 2021). Accessed 9 April 2020.

Ogundiya, Ilufoye. 2009. 'Political corruption in Nigeria: Theoretical perspectives and some explanations', *The Anthropologist*, 11, 4: 281–292.

Ogunmade, Omololu. 2017. 'FG pays N164.7m tuition fees for Chibok girls', *This Day* (27 November), https://www.thisdaylive.com/index.php/2017/11/27/fg-pays-n164-7m-tuition-fees-for-chibok-girls. Accessed 17 December 2017.

Ogunyemi, Bukola. 2018. 'NPA under Hadiza Bala-Usman', *Leadership* (4 July), https://leadership.ng/2018/07/04/npa-under-hadiza-bala-usman. Accessed 30 September 2018.

Ojedokun, Usman, Yetunde Ogunleye, and Adeyinka Aderinto. 2021. 'Mass mobilization for police accountability: The case of Nigeria's #EndSARS protest', *Policing: A Journal of Policy and Practice*, 15, 3: 1894–1903.

Ojukwu, Odumegwu. 1989. *Because I am involved*. Ibadan: Spectrum Books Limited.

Okakwu, Evelyn. 2016a. 'After public condemnation, Nigeria police backtrack, pledge to allow peaceful protests in Abuja', *Premium Times* (10 September), http://www.premiumtimesng.com/news/headlines/210179-public-condemnation-nigeria-police-backtrack-pledge-allow-peaceful-protests-abuja.html. Accessed 21 August 2017.

Okakwu, Evelyn. 2016b. 'Dasukigate Court Drama: EFCC witness says AIT boss Dokpesi got N2.1 billion through due process', *Premium Times* (19 October), http://www.premiumtimesng.com/news/headlines/213080-dasukigate-court-drama-efcc-witness-says-ait-boss-dokpesi-got-n2-1-billion-due-process.html. Accessed 13 January 2017.

Okakwu, Evelyn. 2016c. '#Dasukigate: Court sends ex-Defence Chief, Alex Badeh, to prison', *Premium Times*, https://www.premiumtimesng.com/news/headlines/199686-breaking-dasukigate-court-sends-ex-defence-chief-alex-badeh-to-prison.html?tztc=1 Accessed 20 November 2023.

Okakwu, Evelyn. 2018. 'BBOG group reacts to release of Chibok girl, insists on protest marches', *Premium Times* (4 January), https://www.premiumtimesng.com/news/top-news/254489-bbog-group-reacts-release-chibok-girl-insists-protest-marches.html. Accessed 5 January 2018.

Okolie, Ifeanyi. 2018. 'How we abducted Chibok girls in 2014—Boko Haram commanders', *Vanguard* (21 July), https://www.vanguardngr.com/2018/07/how-we-abducted-chibok-girls-in-2014-boko-haram-commanders. Accessed 28 September 2018.

Okonta, Ike. 2006. 'Behind the mask: Explaining the emergence of the MEND militia in Nigeria's oil-bearing Niger Delta', Niger Delta: Economies of Violence Working Papers. Working Paper No. 11. Berkeley, CA: University of California, Institute of International Studies.

Olukoya, Sam. 2002. 'Eyewitness: Nigeria's Sharia amputees', *BBC* (19 December), http://news.bbc.co.uk/2/hi/africa/2587039.stm. Accessed 23 September 2018.

Omoniyi, Tosin and Salome Nuhu. 2020. '"We're being targeted for "annihiliation"', Chibok residents say', *Premium Times* (5 February), https://www.premiumtimesng.com/news/headlines/375788-were-being-targetted-for-annihilation-chibok-residents-say.html. Accessed 25 February 2020.

Onapajo, Hakeem. 2017. 'State repression and religious conflict: The perils of the state clampdown on the Shi'a minority in Nigeria', *Journal of Muslim Minority Affairs*, 37, 1: 80–93.

Onapajo, Hakeem and Ufo Okeke Uzodike. 2012. 'Boko Haram terrorism in Nigeria: Man, the state and the international system', *African Security Review*, 21, 3: 24–39.

Onapajo, Hakeem, Ufo Okeke Uzodike, and Ayo Whetho. 2012. 'Boko Haram terrorism in Nigeria: The international dimension', *South African Journal of International Affairs*, 19, 3: 337–357.

Onuoha, Felix. 2014. 'Nigeria Islamists better armed, motivated than army: Governor', *Reuters* (17 February), https://www.reuters.com/article/us-nigeria-violence/nigeria-islamists-better-armed-motivated-than-army-governor-idUSBREA1G1AO20140217. Accessed 2 March 2018.

Onuoha, Freedom C. 2010. 'The Islamist challenge: Nigeria's Boko Haram crisis explained', *African Security Review*, 19, 2: 54–7.

Onuoha, Freedom C. 2012. 'Boko Haram: Nigeria's Extremist Islamic Sect', *Al Jazeera Centre for Studies*, 29, 2: 1–6.

Opoola, Lateefat. 2018. 'BBOG to sue FG over abduction of Dapchi schoolgirls', *Daily Trust* (13 March), https://www.dailytrust.com.ng/bbog-to-sue-fg-over-abduction-of-dapchi-schoolgirls.html. Accessed 14 March 2018.

Oriola, Temitope. [2013] 2016. *Criminal Resistance? The Politics of Kidnapping Oil Workers*. London and New York: Routledge.

Oriola, Temitope B. 2017. '"Unwilling cocoons": Boko Haram's war against women', *Studies in Conflict and Terrorism*, 40, 2: 99–121.

Oriola, Temitope B. 2020. 'Reflections on women's resistance and social change in Africa'. In Sandra Walklate, Kate Fitz-Gibbon, Janemaree Maher, and Jude McCulloch (eds), *The Emerald Handbook of Feminism, Criminology and Social Change*. Bingley: Emerald, pp. 235–252.

Oriola, Temitope. 2021a. 'Framing and movement outcomes: The #BringBackOurGirls Movement', *Third World Quarterly*, 42, 4: 641–660.

Oriola, Temitope. 2021b. 'Nigerian soldiers and the war against Boko Haram', *African Affairs*, 120, 479: 147–175.

Oriola, Temitope. 2023. 'The exploitation of Nigeria's Chibok girls and the creation of a social problem industry', *African Affairs*, 122, 486, adac042, https://doi.org/10.1093/afraf/adac042. Accessed 18 October 2023.

Oriola, Temitope and Olabanji Akinola. 2017. 'Ideational dimensions of the Boko Haram phenomenon', *Studies in Conflict & Terrorism*. https://doi.org/10.1080/1057610X.2017.1338053. Accessed 18 October 2023.

Osumah, Oarhe. 2013. 'Boko Haram insurgency in Northern Nigeria and the vicious cycle of internal insecurity', *Small Wars & Insurgencies*, 24, 3: 536–560.

Owete, Festus. 2016a. 'Dasukigate: Leadership newspaper returns its share of N9 million', *Premium Times* (29 January), http://www.premiumtimesng.com/news/headlines/197655-dasukigate-leadership-newspaper-returns-share-n9m.html. Accessed 13 January 2017.

Owete, Festus. 2016b. '#Dasukigate: Another newspaper, Blueprint, returns N9m', *Premium Times* (2 February), http://www.premiumtimesng.com/news/top-news/197832-dasukigate-another-newspaper-blueprint-returns-n9m.html. Accessed 13 January 2017.

Oxford Dictionary of Islam. 2018. 'Northern People's Congress', Available at: https://www.oxfordreference.com/display/10.1093/oi/authority.20110803100239410?d=%2F10.1093%2Foi%2Fauthority.20110803100239410&p=emailAAoOPgFzMIoQA Accessed 12 March 2018.

Oyeniyi, Bukola A. 2014. 'One voice, multiple tongues: Dialoguing with Boko Haram', *Democracy and Security*, 10, 1: 73–97.

Oyefusi, Aderoju. 2008. 'Oil and the Probability of Rebel Participation among Youths in the Niger Delta of Nigeria', *Journal of Peace Research*, 45, 4: 539–555.

Oyèrónké Oyěwùmí. 2003. 'Introduction: Feminism, sisterhood and other foreign relations'. In Oyèrónké Oyěwùmí (ed), *African Women and Feminism: Reflecting on the Politics of Sisterhood*, Trenton: Africa World Press, pp. 1–24.

Oyewole, Samuel. 2013. 'Boko Haram and the challenges of Nigeria's war on terror', *Defense & Security Analysis*, 29, 3: 253–262.

Oyeyipo, Shola, Segun James, and Jameelah Sanda. 2016. 'The politics that shaped the Chibok story', This Day (18 April), https://www.thisdaylive.com/index.php/2016/04/18/the-politics-that-shaped-the-chibok-story. Accessed 28 September 2018.

Parkinson, Joe and Drew Hinshaw. 2017. 'Two bags of cash for Boko Haram: Freedom for the world's most famous hostages came at a heavy price', *Wall Street Journal* (24 December), https://www.wsj.com/articles/two-bags-of-cash-for-boko-haram-the-untold-story-of-how-nigeria-freed-its-kidnapped-girls-1513957354. Accessed 28 February 2018.

Parkinson, Joe and Drew Hinshaw. 2021. *Bring Back Our Girls: The Untold Story of the Global Search for Nigeria's Missing Schoolgirls*. New York: Harper.

Patience, Martin. 2016. 'How did Nigeria secure the 21 Chibok girls' release from Boko Haram?', BBC (15 October), https://www.bbc.com/news/world-africa-37667915. Accessed 26 September 2018.

Pileggi, Tamar. 2018. 'Whistleblower: Cambridge Analytica used Israeli firm to hack Nigerian president', Time of Israel (27 March), https://www.timesofisrael.com/whistleblower-cambridge-analytica-used-israeli-firm-to-hack-nigerian-president. Accessed 28 September 2018.

Pilkington, Ed. 2009. 'Shell pays out $15.5m over Saro-Wiwa killing', *The Guardian* (9 June), https://www.theguardian.com/world/2009/jun/08/nigeria-usa. Accessed 23 June 2016.

Premium Times. 2014a. 'DSS, sack Marilyn Ogar now', *Premium Times*, Editorial (20 August), https://www.premiumtimesng.com/investigationspecial-reports/167031-editorial-dss-sack-marilyn-ogar-now.html. Accessed 28 December 2017.

Premium Times. 2014b. 'How ex-Gov Modu Sheriff sponsored Boko Haram-Falana', *Premium Times* (4 September), https://www.premiumtimesng.com/news/top-news/167724-how-ex-gov-modu-sheriff-sponsored-boko-haram-falana.html#sthash.vyfjiYYc.dpuf. Accessed 14 April 2018.

Premium Times. 2014c. 'EXCLUSIVE: Secret Intelligence report links ex-Governor Sheriff, Chad president to Boko Haram sponsorship', *Premium Times* (12 September), https://www.premiumtimesng.com/news/headlines/168053-exclusive-secret-intelligence-report-links-ex-governor-sheriff-chad-president-to-boko-haram-sponsorship.html. Accessed 13 April 2018.

Premium Times. 2015a. 'Chibok girls' abduction: Jonathan campaign insists Gov. Shettima is culpable', *Premium Times* (11 March), http://www.premiumtimesng.com/news/top-news/178276-chibok-girls-abduction-jonathan-campaign-insists-gov-shettima-is-culpable.html. Accessed 17 March 2016.

Premium Times. 2015b. 'Nigerial internet users increase to 97 million—NCC', *Premium Times* (21 November), http://www.premiumtimesng.com/news/headlines/192485-nigeria-internet-users-increase-to-97-million-ncc.html. Accessed 15 March 2015.

Premium Times. 2015c. 'Tribune, Telegraph, two other newspapers disown Obaigbena, over ex-NSA Dasuki payment claim', *Premium Times* (12 December), http://www.premiumtimesng.com/news/top-news/195015-tribune-telegraph-two-other-newspapers-disown-obaigbena-over-ex-nsa-dasuki-payment-claim.html. Accessed 13 January 2017.

Premium Times. 2016a. 'Kaduna govt says 347 Shiites killed by Nigerian troops given secret mass burial', *Premium Times* (11 April), https://www.premiumtimesng.com/news/headlines/201615-kaduna-govt-says-347-shiites-killed-by-nigerian-troops-given-secret-mass-burial.html. Accessed 26 February 2018.

Premium Times. 2016b. 'Why I won't end "stomach infrastructure" programme—Fayose', *Premium Times* (2 August), https://www.premiumtimesng.com/regional/ssouth-west/207981-why-i-wont-end-stomach-infrastructure-programme-fayose.html. Accessed 13 April 2018.

Premium Times. 2018. 'Police arrest ex-minister, Oby Ezekwesili', *Premium Times* (23 January), https://www.premiumtimesng.com/news/headlines/256437-police-arrest-ex-minister-oby-ezekwesili.html. Accessed 29 March 2018.

Presley, Cora Ann. 1988. 'The Mau Mau rebellion, Kikuyu women, and social change', *Canadian Journal of African Studies/Revue Canadienne des Études Africaines*, 22, 3: 502–527.

Punch. 2015. US Sending Arms To Nigeria', *Punch*, 17 August. https://www.alltimepost.com/2015/08/us-sending-arms-to-nigeria-report/#google_vignette Accessed 12 September 2016.

Punch. 2016a. 'Boko Haram: Journalist, Ahmed Sarkida, arrested in Abuja', *Punch* (5 September), http://punchng.com/journalist-ahmed-salkida-arrested-abuja. Accessed 12 March 2018.

Punch. 2016b. 'Chibok girls: Police stop BBOG protest again', *Punch* (6 September), http://punchng.com/chibok-girls-police-stop-bbog-protest. Accessed 28 December 2017.

Ramdani, Nabila. 2012. 'Egyptian women: "They were doing better under Mubarak"'. Available at https://www.theguardian.com/world/2012/jun/04/egyptian-women-better-under-mubarak. Accessed 22 May 2019.

Reuters. 1992. '163 Nigerians dead as a military plane crashes near Lagos', *Reuters* (28 September), http://www.nytimes.com/1992/09/28/world/163-nigerians-dead-as-a-military-plane-crashes-near-lagos.html. Accessed 26 December 2017.

Reuters. 2014. 'U.S. deploys surveillance aircraft over Nigeria to find girls', *Reuters* (12 May), http://www.reuters.com/article/us-nigeria-girls-usa-idUSBREA4B0ZO20140513. Accessed 21 March 2016.

Reuters. 2021a. Northeast Nigeria insurgency has killed almost 350,000 – UN', Available at: https://www.reuters.com/world/africa/northeast-nigeria-insurgency-has-killed-almost-350000-un-2021-06-24/#:~:text=ABUJA%2C%20June%2024%20(Reuters),(UNDP)%20said%20on%20Thursday. Accessed 30 June 2021.

Reuters. 2021b. 'Boko Haram fighters pledge to Islamic State in video, worrying observers', Available at: https://www.reuters.com/world/africa/boko-haram-fighters-pledge-islamic-state-video-worrying-observers-2021-06-27/. Accessed 1 July 2021.

Rodrigues, Maria. 2011. 'Rethinking the impact of transnational advocacy networks', *New Global Studies*, 5, 2, https://doi.org/10.2202/1940-0004.1124. Accessed 18 October 2023.

Roeflofs, Portia. 2014. 'Framing and blaming: Discourse analysis of the Boko Haram uprising, July 2009'. In Marc-Antoine Perouse de Montclos (ed.), *Boko Haram: Islamism, Politics and the State in Nigeria*, West African Politics and Society Series, vol. 2. Ipskamp Drukkers, Enschede, Netherlands: African Studies Centre and IFRA, pp. 110–131.

Ross, Will. 2015. 'Nigeria: What next for the rescued Boko Haram captives?', *BBC* (8 May), http://www.bbc.com/news/world-africa-32625811. Accessed 22 September 2015

Rowell, Andy and Eveline Lubbers. 2010. 'Ken Saro-Wiwa was framed, secret evidence shows', Independent (5 December), https://www.independent.co.uk/news/world/africa/ken-saro-wiwa-was-framed-secret-evidence-shows-2151577.html. Accessed 26 March 2020.

Sanusi, Lamido Sanusi. 2017. 'Chibok and the mirror in our faces', *Osun Defender*, https://www.osundefender.com/chibok-mirror-faces-emir-sanusi/. Accessed 19 November 2023.

Sahara Reporters. 2016. 'Nigerian army releases 566 Boko Haram family members to Borno State government', *Sahara Reporters* (16 September), http://saharareporters.com/2016/09/16/nigerian-army-releases-566-boko-haram-family-members-borno-state-government. Accessed 19 September 2020.

Sahara Reporters. 2017a. 'Focus of your struggle too narrow, Emir of Kano tells BBOG', *Sahara Reporters* (14 April), http://saharareporters.com/2017/04/14/focus-your-struggle-too-narrow-emir-kano-tells-bbog. Accessed 21 August 2017.

Sahara Reporters. 2017b. 'Exclusive: Freed Chibok schoolgirl attempts suicide to protest going to Atiku-owned school', *Sahara Reporters* (7 September), http://saharareporters.com/2017/09/07/exclusive-freed-chibok-schoolgirl-%E2%80%8Eattempts-suicide-protest-going-atiku-owned-school. Accessed 26 September 2018.

Sahara Reporters. 2018a. 'Dapchi girls: Yobe Police Command faults military claim on withdrawal of troops', *Sahara Reporters* (26 February), http://saharareporters.com/2018/02/26/dapchi-girls-yobe-police-command-faults-military-claim-withdrawal-troops. Accessed 28 February 2018.

Sahara Reporters. 2018b. 'Boko Haram gives reason for release of Dapchi girls, denies ceasefire talks with FG', *Sahara Reporters* (9 April), http://saharareporters.com/2018/04/09/boko-haram-gives-reason-release-dapchi-girls-denies-ceasefire-talks-fg. Accessed 9 April 2018.

Sahara Reporters. 2018c. 'Chibok girls' sponsor says some people in Buhari's govt using the girls to launder funds', *Sahara Reporters* (6 June), http://saharareporters.com/2018/

06/06/chibok-girls-sponsor-says-some-people-buharis-govt-using-girls-launder-funds. Accessed 22 August 2018.

Sahara Reporters. 2019a. 'My grandson asked me why they call me "Liar Mohammed", Lai Mohammed tells senate', *Sahara Reporters* (30 July), http://saharareporters.com/2019/07/30/my-grandson-asked-me-why-they-call-me-%E2%80%98liar-mohammed%E2%80%99-lai-mohammed-tells-senate. Accessed 25 March 2020.

Sahara Reporters. 2019b. 'Dispute over money causes deadly terrorists infighting in Nigeria—Report', *Sahara Reporters* (3 August), http://saharareporters.com/2019/08/03/dispute-over-money-causes-deadly-terrorists-infighting-nigeria-report. Accessed 23 March 2020.

Samuel, Malik. 2021. 'Boko Haram teams up with bandits in Nigeria'. Institute for Security Studies (ISS) Today. Available at: https://issafrica.org/iss-today/boko-haram-teams-up-with-bandits-in-nigeria Accessed 10 March 2021.

Sändig, Jan. 2015. 'Framing protest and insurgency: Boko Haram and MASSOB in Nigeria', *Civil Wars*, 17, 2: 141–160.

Saro-Wiwa, K. 1992. *Genocide in Nigeria: The Ogoni Tragedy*. Port Harcourt: Saros International.

Sawer, Marian. 2007. 'Wearing your politics on your sleeve: The role of political colours in social movements', *Social Movement Studies*, 6, 1: 39–56.

Schmid, Alex P. 2015. 'Challenging the narratives of the "Islamic State", International Centre for Counter-Terrorism', The Hague Research Paper. Available at: https://www.jstor.org/stable/pdf/resrep29429.pdf Accessed 20 June 2017.

Schmitz, Hans Peter. 2001. 'When networks blind: Human rights and politics in Kenya'. In Thomas Callaghy, Ronald Kassimir, and Robert Latham (eds), *Intervention and Transnationalism in Africa: Global–Local Networks of Power*. New York: Cambridge University Press, pp. 149–172.

Scott, Ben. 2014. 'In defense of #BringBackOurGirls and hashtag activism', *Slate* (16 May), http://www.slate.com/blogs/future_tense/2014/05/16/bringbackourgirls_a_defense_of_hashtag_activism.html. Accessed 2 March 2015.

Seidman, Gay W. 2005. 'Monitoring multinationals: Corporate codes of conduct'. In Joe Bandy and Jackie Smith (eds), *Coalitions across Borders: Transnational Protest and the Neoliberal Order*. Lanham, MD: Rowman & Littlefield, pp. 163–183.

Sen, Amartya. 1999. *Development and Freedom*. New York: Alfred A. Knopf.

Sengupta, Somini. 2019. 'The story of the Boko Haram schoolgirls, by a reporter who takes it personally', New York Times (9 July), https://www.nytimes.com/2019/07/09/books/review/beneath-the-tamarind-tree-isha-sesay.html. Accessed 3 August 2021.

Sesay, Aisha. 2019. *Beneath the Tamarind Tree: A Story of Courage, Family, and the Lost Schoolgirls of Boko Haram*. New York: HarperCollins.

Shadjareh, Massoud and Abed Choudhury. 2014. 'Nigeria report: The Zaria massacres and the role of the military', Islamic Human Rights Commission, https://www.ihrc.org.uk/nigeria-report-the-zaria-massacres-and-the-role-of-the-military/.

Shehu, Garba. 2016. '#Dasukigate: Buhari orders probe of Badeh, other ex-generals', *Premium Times*, press release (15 January), http://www.premiumtimesng.com/news/headlines/196809-dasukigate-buhari-orders-probe-of-badeh-other-ex-generals.html. Accessed 13 January 2017.

Shekau, Abubakar. 2014. 'Boko Haram leader: "We will sell the girls on the market"—video', *The Guardian* (6 May), http://www.theguardian.com/world/video/2014/may/06/boko-haram-sell-girls-market-video. Accessed 14 September 2015.

Siollun, Max. 2015. 'How Goodluck Jonathan lost the Nigerian election', *The Guardian* (1 April), https://www.theguardian.com/world/2015/apr/01/nigeria-election-goodluck-jonathan-lost. Accessed 20 December 2017.

Sjoberg, Gideon; Elizabeth A. Gill, and Norma Williams. 2001. 'A sociology of human rights', *Social Problems*, 48, 1: 11–47.

Sloss, David. 1999. 'The domestication of international human rights: Non-self-executing declarations and human rights treaties', *Yale Journal of International Law*, 24: 129–221.

Smith, Alexander. 2016. 'Ansaru: Boko Haram splinter group sows terror in Nigeria', *NBC News* (10 April), https://www.nbcnews.com/storyline/missing-nigeria-schoolgirls/ansaru-boko-haram-splinter-group-sows-terror-nigeria-n551661. Accessed 24 September 2018.

Smith, Helena. 2016. 'Shocking images of drowned Syrian boy show tragic plight of refugees', *The Guardian* (2 September), http://www.theguardian.com/world/2015/sep/02/shocking-image-of-drowned-syrian-boy-shows-tragic-plight-of-refugees. Accessed 25 April 2016.

Smith, Mike 2015. *Boko Haram: Inside Nigeria's Unholy War*. London: I. B. Tauris & Co. Ltd.

Snow, D. and Benford, R. D. 1988. 'Ideology, frame resonance, and participant mobilization', *International Social Movement Research* 1: 197–217.

Snow, David and Benford, Robert 1992. 'Master frames and cycles of protest'. In Aldon Morris and Carol McClurg Mueller (eds), *Frontiers in Social Movement Theory*. New Haven, CT: Yale University Press, 133–155.

Snow, David, and Scott Byrd. 2007. 'Ideology, framing processes, and Islamic terrorist movements'. *Mobilization: An International Quarterly*, 12, 2: 119–136.

Sneyd, L. Q., A. Legwegoh, and E. D. G. Fraser. 2013. 'Food riots: Media perspectives on the causes of food protests in Africa', *Food Security*, 5: 485–497 (18 June), https://doi.org/10.1007/s12571-013-0272-x. Accessed 2 November 2023.

Soeters, Joseph and Audrey Van Ouytsel. 2014. 'The challenge of diffusing military professionalism in Africa', *Armed Forces & Society*, 40, 2: 252–268.

Solomon, Hussein. 2012. 'Counter-terrorism in Nigeria', *RUSI Journal*, 157, 4: 6–11, https://doi.org/10.1080/03071847.2012.714183. Accessed 18 October 2023.

Sputnik International. 2018. 'Analyst reveals real reason behind Boko Haram kidnappings', Sputnik News (23 February), https://sputnikglobe.com/20180223/boko-haram-girls-hostage-1061919258.html.

Stebbins, Robert A. 2001. 'What is exploration', *Exploratory research in the social sciences*, 48: 2–17.

Stern, Jessica. 2003. 'The protean enemy', *Foreign Aff.*, 82, 27.

Stern, Paul C., Thomas Dietz, Troy D. Abel, Gregory A. Guagnano, and Linda Kalof. 1999. 'A value-belief-norm theory of support for social movements: The case of environmentalism', *Human Ecology Review*, 6, 2: 81–97.

Stoddard, Edward. 2019. 'Revolutionary warfare? Assessing the character of competing factions within the Boko Haram insurgency', *African Security*, 12, 3–4: 300–329.

Szeftel, Morris. 2000. 'Clientelism, corruption and catastrophe', *Review of African Political Economy*, 85: 427–441.

Tandy, Sara. 2014. '#Slacktivism: Social media and the pitfalls of inefficacy', https://www.tandfonline.com/doi/pdf/10.1080/14680777.2015.1116018.

Tarrow, Sidney. 1996. 'Social movements in contentious politics: A review article', *American Political Science Review*, 90, 4: 874–883. https://doi.org/10.2307/2945851. Accessed 30 October 2023.

Tarrow, Sidney. 2005. 'The dualities of transnational contention: "Two activist solitudes" or a new world altogether?' *Mobilization: An International Journal*, 10, 1: 53–72.

Taylor, Verta and Nella Van Dyke. 2007. '"Get up, stand up": Tactical repertoires of social movements'. In David A. Snow, Sarah A. Soule, and Hanspeter Kriesi (eds), *The Blackwell Companion to Social Movements*. Malden: Blackwell, pp. 262–293.

Temple, Uwalaka and Jerry Watkins. 2018. 'Social media as the fifth estate in Nigeria: An analysis of the 2012 Occupy Nigeria protest', *African Journalism Studies*, 39, 4: 22–41.

The Cable. 2017. 'Garba Shehu: Buhari has abolished settlement—no critic will be paid to keep quiet', https://www.thecable.ng/buhari-deserves-credit-rebuilding-destroyed-says-garba-shehu Accessed 19 November 2023.

The Cable. 2021. 'Full text: What Kukah told US congress committee on foreign affairs', *The Cable* (19 July), https://www.thecable.ng/full-text-what-kukah-told-us-congress-committee. Accessed 26 July 2021.

The Telegraph. 2015. 'Boko Haram killed woman in labour', *The Telegraph* (16 January), https://www.telegraph.co.uk/news/worldnews/africaandindianocean/nigeria/11351805/Boko-Haram-killed-woman-in-labour.html. Accessed 28 September 2018.

Thornton, A. 2019. 'These countries have the most women in parliament', *World Economic Forum* (12 February), https://www.weforum.org/agenda/2019/02/chart-of-the-day-these-countries-have-the-most-women-in-parliament. Accessed 30 May 2019.

Thurston, Alexander. 2018. Boko Haram: *The History of an African Jihadist Movement*. Princeton: Princeton University Press.

Tilly, Charles. 1979. 'Social movements and national politics', CRSO Working Paper No. 197. Ann Arbor, MI: University of Michigan, Center for Research on Social Organization, https://deepblue-lib-umich-edu.login.ezproxy.library.ualberta.ca/bitstream/handle/2027.42/50971/197.pdf?sequence=1. Accessed 28 March 2018.

Tilly, Charles. 1995. 'To explain political process', *American Journal of Sociology*, 100: 1594–1610.

Tilly, Charles. 1999. 'From interactions to outcomes in social movements'. In Marco Giugni, Doug McAdam, and Charles Tilly (eds), *How Social Movements Matter*. Minneapolis, MN: University of Minnesota Press, pp. 253–270.

Tonwe, Daniel A. and Surulola J. Eke. 2013. 'State fragility and violent uprisings in Nigeria', *African Security Review*, 22, 4: 232–243, https://doi.org/10.1080/10246029.2013.838794. Accessed 18 October 2023.

Tripp, A., Casimiro, I., Kwesiga, J., and Mungwa, A. 2008. *African Women's Movements: Transforming Political Landscapes*. Cambridge: Cambridge University Press. https://doi.org/10.1017/CBO9780511800351.

Tukur, Sani. 2015a. 'South Africa returns seized $15 million to Nigerian government', *Premium Times* (18 January), http://www.premiumtimesng.com/news/top-news/186871-south-africa-returns-seized-15-million-to-nigerian-government.html. Accessed 21 March 2016.

Tukur, Sani. 2015b. 'Election postponement: March 28 must be sacrosanct, Buhari warns', *Premium Times* (9 February), https://www.premiumtimesng.com/news/top-news/176486-election-postponement-march-28-must-sacrosanct-buhari-warns.html. Accessed 5 March 2018.

Tukur, Sani. 2015c. 'Court papers show how ex-NSA Dasuki allegedly shared N13.6bn arms money to cronies, politicians', *Premium Times* (14 December), http://www.premiumtimesng.com/news/headlines/195173-court-papers-show-how-ex-nsa-dasuki-allegedly-shared-n13-6bn-arms-money-to-cronies-politicians.html. Accessed 17 March 2016.

Tukur, Sani. 2017a. 'SHOCKING REVELATION: 100,000 killed, two million displaced by Boko Haram insurgency, Borno Governor says', Premium Times, Available at: https://www.premiumtimesng.com/news/headlines/223399-shocking-revelation-100000-killed-two-million-displaced-boko-haram-insurgency-borno-governor-says.html?tztc=1 Accessed 15 February 2017.

Tukur, Sani. 2017b. 'Nigeria buys new aircraft from Russia', *Premium Times* (6 January), http://www.premiumtimesng.com/news/headlines/219772-nigeria-buys-new-aircraft-russia.html. Accessed 2 August 2017.

Tukur, Sani and Agency Report. 2017. 'Red Cross explains role in securing release of 82 Chibok girls', *Premium Times* (8 May), http://www.premiumtimesng.com/news/headlines/230681-red-cross-explains-role-securing-release-82-chibok-girls.html. Accessed 7 August 2017.

Turner, Terisa and Leigh S. Brownhill, 2004. 'Why women are at war with Chevron. Nigerian subsistence struggles against the International Oil Industry', *Journal of Asian and African Studies*, 39, 1–2: 63–93.

Udounwa, Solomon Effiong. 2013. *Boko Haram: Developing new strategies to combat terrorism in Nigeria*. US Army War College.

Ukeje, Charles. 2004. 'From Aba to Ugborodo: Gender identity and alternative discourse of social protest among women in the oil delta of Nigeria', *Oxford Development Studies*, 32, 4: 605–617, https://doi.org/10.1080/1360081042000293362. Accessed 2 November 2023.

Ukpong, Cletus. 2017. '82 Chibok girls: Why we helped Nigeria negotiate with Boko Haram—Switzerland govt', *Premium Times* (9 May), http://www.premiumtimesng.com/news/top-news/230786-82-chibok-girls-helped-nigeria-negotiate-boko-haram-switzerland-govt.html. Accessed 7 August 2017.

UNDP (United Nations Development Programme). 2016a. 'About Nigeria', http://www.ng.undp.org/content/nigeria/en/home/countryinfo. Accessed 4 July 2016.

UNDP. 2016b. 'Nigeria SDGs Indicators Baseline Report 2016', http://www.ng.undp.org/content/nigeria/en/home/library/mdg/nigeria-sdgs-indicators-baseline-report-2016. Accessed 11 April 2018.

UNICEF. 2016. 'Annual results report 2016: Gender equality', https://www.unicef.org/media/49166/file/2016arr_gender.pdf Accessed 20 November 2023.

Urkidi, Leire and Mariana Walter. 2011. 'Dimensions of environmental justice in anti-gold mining movements in Latin America', *Geoforum*, 42, 6: 683–695.

Valiente, Celia. 2003. 'Mobilizing for recognition and distribution on behalf of others? The case of mothers against drugs in Spain', In Hobson, Barbara (ed), *Recognition Struggles and Social Movements: Contested Identities, Agency and Power*. Cambridge: Cambridge University Press, pp. 239–259.

Van Allen, Judith. 1975. 'Aba Riots or the Igbo women's war?—Ideology, stratification and the invisibility of women', *Ufahamu: A Journal of African Studies*, 6, 1: 11–39.

Van Maanen, John, Peter K. 2001. Manning, Marc Miller: Series editors' introduction. In: Stebbins, Robert (ed), *Exploratory research in the social sciences*. Thousands Oak, CA: SAGE, pp. v–vi.

Vanguard. 2009. 'Boko Haram resurrects, declares total jihad', *Vanguard* (14 August), https://www.vanguardngr.com/2009/08/boko-haram-ressurects-declares-total-jihad. Accessed 12 September 2018.

Vanguard. 2014. 'Jonathan's administration playing dirty politics with Chibok girls' plight—APC', *Vanguard* (28 September), https://www.vanguardngr.com/2014/09/jonathans-administration-playing-dirty-politics-chibok-girls-plight-apc. Accessed 28 September 2018.

Vanguard. 2016. 'Chibok parents: Why we boycotted BBOG march', *Vanguard* (23 August), https://www.vanguardngr.com/2016/08/chibok-parents-boycotted-bbog-march. Accessed 5 January 2018.

Vanguard. 2017. 'Nigeria's Jonathan blames Obama for 2015 election defeat', *Vanguard* (27 April), http://www.vanguardngr.com/2017/04/nigerias-jonathan-blames-obama-2015-election-defeat. Accessed 21 August 2017.

Wacquant, Loïc. 2006. 'Pierre Bourdieu', in Rob Stones (ed), *Key contemporary thinkers*. London and New York: Macmillan, pp. 261–276.

Waldek, Lise, and Shankara Jayasekara. 2011. 'Boko Haram: the evolution of Islamist extremism in Nigeria', *Journal of Policing, Intelligence and Counter Terrorism*, 6, 2: 168–178.

Waylen, Georgina. 2007. 'Women's mobilization and gender outcomes in transitions to democracy: the case of South Africa', *Comparative Political Studies* 40, 5: 521–546.

Weeraratne, Suranjan. 2017. 'Theorizing the Expansion of the Boko Haram Insurgency in Nigeria', *Terrorism and Political Violence*, 29, 4: 610–634, https://doi.org/10.1080/09546553.2015.1005742

Widener, Patricia. 2007. 'Benefits and burdens of transnational campaigns: A comparison of four oil struggles in Ecuador', *Mobilization: An International Quarterly*, 12, 1: 21–36.

Wienner-Bronner, Danielle. 2014. 'Nigerian military officers court-martialed for giving Boko Haram weapons', *The Atlantic* (3 June), https://www.theatlantic.com/international/archive/2014/06/nigerian-generals-arrested-for-giving-boko-haram-weapons/372052. Accessed 26 February 2018.

Williams-Elegbe, Sope. 2015. 'Citizens' response to irresponsible (or constrained) leadership as a catalyst for change: A critical assessment of leadership and followership in Nigeria', *Journal of Corporate Citizenship*, 60: 27–40.

Wilson, James Q. 1973. *Political Organizations*. New York: Basic Books.

Young, Iris Marion. 2003. 'The logic of masculinist protection: Reflections on the current security state', *Signs: Journal of Women in Culture and Society*, 29, 1: 1–25.

Yesufu, Aisha. 2017. oral statement at BBOG sit-out.

Yusuf, Kabir. 2021. 'Seven years after Chibok, mass kidnapping of students becoming norm in Nigeria', *Premium Times* (22 June), https://www.premiumtimesng.com/news/top-news/469110-timeline-seven-years-after-chibok-mass-kidnapping-of-students-becoming-norm-in-nigeria.html. Accessed 26 July 2021.

Zaidi, Manzar. 2009. 'A Taxonomy of Jihad', *Arab Studies Quarterly*, 31, 3: 21–34.

Zald, Mayer N. and Roberta Ash. 1966. 'Social movement organizations: Growth, decay and change'. *Social Forces*, 44, 3: 327–341.

Zartman, I. William. 1995. *Collapsed States: The Disintegration and Restoration of Legitimate Authority*. Boulder, CO: Lynne Rienner.

Zenn, Jacob. 2012. 'Northern Nigeria's Boko Haram: The prize in Al-Qaeda's Africa strategy', Jamestown Foundation Report, Washington, DC.

Zenn, Jacob. 2013. 'The Islamic movement and Iranian intelligence activities in Nigeria', *CTC Sentinel*, 6(10), 13–18, https://ctc.usma.edu/the-islamic-movement-and-iranian-intelligence-activities-in-nigeria. Accessed 22 September 2018.

Zenn, Jacob. 2014. 'Boko Haram and the kidnapping of the Chibok schoolgirls', *CTC Sentinel*, 7, 5: 1–8.

Zenn, Jacob. 2020. 'Chronicling the Boko Haram Decade in Nigeria (2010-2020): distinguishing factions through videographic analysis', *Small Wars & Insurgencies*, 31, 6: 1242–1294.

Zucker, Lynne G. 1987. 'Institutional theories of organization', *Annual Review of Sociology*, 13, 1: 443–464.
Zweigenhaft, Richard L. and G. William Domhoff. 1997. 'Sophisticated Conservatives and the integration of prep schools: The creation, funding, and evolution of the "A Better Chance" program'. In J. H., Stanfield II (ed.), *Research in Social Policy: Social Justice Philanthropy*. Greenwich, CT: Yale University Press, pp. 169–90

Index

For the benefit of digital users, indexed terms that span two pages (e.g., 52–53) may, on occasion, appear on only one of those pages.
'n.' after a paragraph number indicates the footnote number.

A
Abacha, Sani (General), 17, 74, 148
AbbaKaka, Fati, 86–87
Abdulazeez, Medinat, 222–223
Abdullahi, Abubakar, 86–87
Abdullahi, Ibrahim: '#BringBackOur-Daughters'/'#BringBackOurGirls', 63
Abiola, MKO (Chief), 17
Abubakar, Abdulsalam (General), 17
Abuja #BBOG, 60–61, 61 n.15, 65, 166, 202–203, 220–221
ACN (Action Congress of Nigeria), 212
Adamawa state, 37, 52, 212
Adamu, Naomi, 53–54
Adeakin, Ibikunle, 41–42
Adeleye, R. A., 24
Adeniyi, Olusegun, 209, 211–212
Africa
　#BBOG experience and African states, 2
　Chibok kidnapping as prism for understanding terrorism and human rights advocacy in, 56
　framing and human rights movements in, 118
　human rights, 235
　military forces in African states, 175–176, 239–240
　'politics of the belly', 13–14
　social problem industry, 231
　see also developing countries/Global South; social movements (Africa/Global South)
African Union, 77
AFRISEI (Africa Support and Empowerment Initiative), 113
Agbiboa, Daniel Egiegba, 32, 47
Aghedo, Iro, 47

Ahmad, Attahiru (Caliph), 23
AIT (Africa Independent Television), 101 n.40, 177–178
Akinjide, Olajumoke, 74–75
Akinola, Olabanji, 39–46
Akume, Sesugh, 86–87, 99–100, 104, 157–158, 195–196, 208
Alhassan, Aishatu, 218–219
Ali, Amina, 217–218
Allen, Manasseh, 86–87, 107
　Sambisa tour, 161–163
Amnesty International, 44, 60, 77, 80, 180–181
ANC (African National Congress), 200
ANCWL (African National Congress Women's League), 164–165
ANRP (Abundant Nigeria Renewal Party), 157–158
Ansaru (Vanguard for the protection of Muslims in Black Africa), 47–48
APC (All Progressives Congress), 212
　2015 elections, 9, 17–18, 143–144, 155, 212
　#BBOG and, 223, 233
　#BBOG framing and, 150, 236–237
　#BBOG leaders, appointment into key positions of APC-led government, 144–145, 156–157, 210, 233, 235, 239
　#BBOG leaders as members of, 132, 143–144, 236–237
　Boko Haram and, 9
　Buhari, Muhammadu and, 9, 17–18
　Chibok kidnapping and toxic politics, 54–55
　military forces and, 9
　state failure framing and, 12, 144

Usman, Hadiza Bala as APC
    member, 143
  see also Buhari, Muhammadu
    (General)/Buhari government
Arab Spring, 68, 98, 231–232
  see also Egypt; Tunisia
Arendt, Hannah, 147
arms and military equipment
  challenges in defeat of Boko Haram and
    shortage of, 9, 122, 139–140,
    176–177, 240
  'Dasukigate', 177–178
  limited foreign military support for the
    Nigerian government to fight Boko
    Haram, 139–140
  Nigeria's elections and, 13
Ash, Roberta, 65
Associated Press, 103
Ateba, Simon, 61–62 n.16
authoritarian/quasi-democratic contexts
  human rights advocacy, 3–4
  Nigeria: between authoritarian and
    democratic state, 74, 188, 197–198
  social movements (Africa/Global South)
    in, 1, 3–4, 20–21, 111, 117–118, 139,
    142–143, 149–150, 198, 201, 225
Awolowo, Obafemi (Chief), 15
Aylan Kurdi, 147
Azikiwe, Nnamdi, 16

B
Babangida, Ibrahim (General), 17
Babangida, Maryam, 57–58
Badeh, Alex (Chief of Defence Staff), 143,
    183–184, 183–184 n.33
Baker, Aryn, 207
Bako (Reverend), 28, 32
Balewa, Sir Abubakar Tafawa, 15–16
Ban Ki Moon (UN Secretary
    General), 144–145
al-Barnawi, Abu Musab, 48–49
al-Barnawi, Khalid, 47–48
Baruwa, Tunji, 86–87
Bashir, Abu, 48
Bayart, Jean Francois, 13–14, 135
BBC (British Broadcasting
    Corporation), 28, 53–54, 80, 102,
    133, 178, 217

#BBOG (#BringBackOurGirls movement)
  '#BringBackOurGirls', 75
  core values, 81, 110, 126–127
  credibility, 104–105, 113, 114, 164,
    173–174, 197–198
  criticism of, 64, 112–113, 112–113 n.50,
    130–131, 145, 163, 185, 209–210,
    231–232
  decline of, 202–203, 228, 232, 239
  demobilization of, 230
  grievances, 65, 135–136
  'HUMANITEEDS', 81, 84, 125–127
  as 'networked social movement', 68
  as NGO, 158–159, 173–174, 208,
    235–236
  non-violent nature of, 1, 12, 96,
    193–194, 208–209, 232
  objective, 1, 78, 118–120, 124, 173–174,
    232–234
  'ReleaseOurGirls' hashtag, 75–76
  scholarly work on, 64
  as self-funded grassroots movement, 80
    n.21, 112–115, 137–138, 173,
    209–210, 235–236
  as 'single-issue' movement, 78, 138
  as sociological phenomenon, 1–2
  visual symbols and symbolism, 82
  website, 78
  as women-led social movement, 1–2,
    65, 115
#BBOG: advocacy, 1, 242
  #BBOG's innovativeness, 12
  double bind of involvement of elite
    women/mothers in grassroots
    advocacy, 3
  human rights advocacy, 76–77, 96, 124,
    193–194, 197–198
  see also #BBOG: lessons for improved
    advocacy; Chibok kidnapping and
    social problem industry
#BBOG: chants/slogans/messages, 83,
    125, 125 n.12, 127
  #BBOG banners, 63–64, 70, 95, 111, 129
  '#BringBackOurGirls' tweet, 63, 72
  chant, 83–85, 94, 125
  message: 'It could have been me', 96
  message: 'Would you be silent if your
    daughter was missing?', 95, 129

#BBOG: chants/slogans/messages (*Continued*)
  Nigeria's national anthem, 93–94
  slogan: 'The fight for the Chibok girls is the fight for the soul of Nigeria and the world', 77
#BBOG: communication process, 98, 103*f*
  Al Jazeera, 102
  BBC, 102
  #BBOG, ignored by some media channels, 101 n.40
  #BBOG, social media-led movement, 101, 234–235
  #BBOG leadership as only ones permitted to speak with the media, 110
  #BBOG's credibility, 104–105, 115–116
  #BBOG's innovativeness, 12
  #BBOG's *media sense*, 12, 234–235
  '#BringBackOurGirls' tweet, 63, 72
  Channels Television, 101, 101 n.40
  CNN, 102
  Facebook, 12, 19, 99–100, 104, 107
  global media spotlight, 19, 100, 234–235
  individual handles, 103–104
  individual social media platforms, 103
  journalists, 12, 100–101, 103, 104–105, 108
  media engagement, 87, 97, 100, 104–105, 126, 194–195
  social media, 99–100, 102, 107–108, 115–116, 194, 196
  social media and #BBOG's origins, 63–64, 99–102
  social media/traditional media hybridized communication, 1–2, 12, 19, 87, 97, 99–100, 102, 103, 115–116, 234–235
  SCT (strategic communication team), 87, 97, 99–104
  ST (strategic team), 103–104
  tactics of protest and social media, 102–103, 103*f*
  traditional media, 99–102, 104–105, 108, 115–116
  traditional media and internationalization of #BBOG movement, 102
  Twitter, 19, 99–101, 103–104, 152, 194, 196
  weekly compendium, 100–101
  WhatsApp, 59 n.14, 100, 103, 107–108, 154 n.5, 155
#BBOG: core framing tasks, 119–125
  diagnostic framing, 120–122
  motivational framing and mobilization of #BBOG members, 125
  prognostic framing, 122
  see also #BBOG: framing
#BBOG: documents, 88
  'ABC of our demands', 122–123
  'Citizens' solution to end terrorism: The voice of Nigerians' manual, 124–125
  'Strategic Angle to #BringBackOurGirls', 21, 78, 202
#BBOG: framing, 3, 20, 64–65, 119, 149
  #BBOG outcomes and, 4–5, 211
  as bifocal in orientation, 4, 20, 127–128, 138–139, 236
  closeness of mobilization to major events (elections), 4–5, 150
  framing theory and, 4–5, 150–151, 237
  lessons for grassroots movements, 20, 119, 139, 144–145, 149–150
  master frames, 4, 127–135
  nature of the cause, 4–5, 150–151
  partisan politics, 3–4, 143, 236–237
  primary beneficiaries of movement activities, 4–5, 150
  refraction of, 3, 145, 150, 236–237, 241
  social positionality of key movement leaders, 4–5, 150
  see also #BBOG: core framing tasks; #BBOG framing internationalization; framing; girl-child's right to education framing; human rights framing; motherist/maternalist framing; state failure framing
#BBOG: framing internationalization, 4–5, 92, 128, 138, 149–150, 236
  alienation of key national actors, 3–4, 118–119, 142–144
  assumption: Nigerian government could be compelled/shamed into taking action, 5, 145, 236

assumption: Western powers would help, 5, 140, 145, 236
#BBOG as victim of its own success, 118–119, 144, 237–238
consequences of, 128, 136, 149–150, 231, 236–237, 241
difficulty for the military to find the girls, 142
failure to think through the step between mobilizing opinion and practical efforts to rescue the girls, 5, 145, 236
global elites, 5, 127–128
international arena *vs* local political process, 145
'international embarrassment', 5, 79–80, 135, 144, 144–145 n.33, 186
international media, 79–80
limited foreign military support for the Nigerian government to fight Boko Haram, 139–140, 147, 224
little international support in the Chibok girls's rescue, 8–9, 237–238
political opportunity structure, 5, 236–237
shutting avenues for collaboration, 118–119, 142–145
as strategic error, 5, 118–119, 142–143, 236
see also #BBOG: internationalization
#BBOG: internal divisions, 6, 230, 233
back-channel approach, 158–159, 210
#BBOG/military forces relationship, 185–186
#BBOG as NGO, 158–159, 173–174, 235–236
Buhari's supporters, 155, 158
conciliatory approach, 6, 155, 158, 160–161, 173–174, 190, 210
decision-making disagreements, 6–7, 125 n.14, 168–172, 235–236
elite women, appointment into key positions of APC-led government as source of division, 157
engagement with the government, 6, 109, 143, 173–174, 210, 211, 229, 233
framing internationalization, 143, 230, 239
ideological blocs within #BBOG, 158
ideological puritanism *vs* pragmatism, 5–6, 158–159, 173–174, 241
membership categories, 6–7, 158–161, 197
non-diplomatic no-nonsense approach, 6
oligarchization, 168–172, 230, 239
organizational structure, debates on, 88, 168–169
personal political stances within the movement, 155–158, 197, 235
protest tactics, 6, 109, 210, 230, 239
Sambisa tour controversy, 10–11, 160–161, 163
self-funding, disagreements on, 113–114, 209–210, 235–236
strategic direction of #BBOG, debates over, 173, 230, 233, 235–236, 239
'super-star' activists, 6–7, 197, 235
Yesufu's criticism of the person and administration of President Buhari, 155
Yesufu video controversy, 152–154
see also #BBOG: membership; #BBOG: oligarchization
#BBOG: internationalization, 93, 226–227, 234, 242
#BBOG and international NGOs, 2, 80 n.21, 127–128, 136–137
internationally orientated discursive strategy, 79–80
refusal of foreign financial support, 80 n.21, 112–113, 137–138
refusal to formal transnationalization, 5, 119, 138, 149–150, 236
spreading all around the world, 63–64, 95, 96, 137–138
traditional media and, 102
transnationalization, 80 n.21, 136–138
wide international support, 77, 144, 187–188
see also #BBOG framing internationalization; transnationalization
#BBOG: lessons for improved advocacy
advocacy, essence of, 232–233, 239
back-channel approach, 5–6, 158–159

#BBOG: lessons for improved advocacy (*Continued*)
 framing, 20, 119, 139, 144–145, 149–150, 237
 funding, 114–115
 governance, 173, 197
 government, engagement with, 233
 ideological puritanism *vs* pragmatism, 5–6, 158–159, 233, 241
 internal divisions, 233
 local *vs* international support, 8–9, 149–151, 238
 in local struggles: *think local and act local*, 3–4, 151
 membership criteria, 167, 197
 oligarchization, 6–7, 173, 197
 outcomes, 201–202, 241
 partisan politics, 157, 197
 political opportunity, 159, 163, 164, 198, 233, 241
 Sambisa tour, lessons for movement advocates, 163–164, 198
 social media, 115–116, 150–151, 238
 social problem industry, 7
 state-friendly narratives and framing, 5–6, 142–143, 149–150
 state repression, 193–195, 197
 strategizing on direction in the face of contexts, 197, 239
 toxic politics, 149–150, 163–164
#BBOG: membership, 19, 88
 #BBOG's internal divisions and, 6–7, 158–161, 197
 committed pragmatists, 6–7, 158–161, 235–236
 ethno-religious diversity, 71, 73–74, 76–77, 94
 freerider problem, 166–167
 general assembly of members at the 'sit-out', 88, 169–170
 non-committal advocates, 6–7, 159, 235–236
 offline membership, 1–2
 regime-change emergency activists/'Buharists' 6–7, 155, 158, 160–161, 235–236
 regime-neutral die-hards, 6–7, 158, 235–236

 snapshot of members' profiles, 88, 89*f*, 90*f*, 91*f*
 'strategic cabal' members, 170–171
 totemic elite members, 6–7, 159
 universalized approach to membership, 166, 169–170
 who is a #BBOG member?, 166, 171
 see also #BBOG: oligarchization
#BBOG: mobilization, 105–109, 241
 ad hoc committees, 107
 #BBOG banners, 63–64, 70, 95, 111, 112, 129
 #BBOG internal discipline vis-à-vis mass protests, 109
 #BBOG protest mobilization matrix, 106–107, 106*f*
 'Don't do list', 110
 effectiveness of, 120–121
 evolution of mobilization for mass protests, 107
 interest groups (NGOs/CSOs), 108
 journalists, 108
 law enforcement agencies, 106–109
 mixed crowds, 111
 motivational framing and mobilization of #BBOG members, 125
 protest themes, 107
 rigorous planning, 109–111, 115
 social media, 107–108
 social media/offline work combination, 12
 speech acts at sit-outs, 125, 127, 134
 stakeholders invited to mass protests, 107
 see also #BBOG: tactics of protest
#BBOG: oligarchization, 167, 235–236
 2017: 10 June decisions of the ST, 170–172
 bureaucratization, 169–170
 decision-making, 168–172, 235–236
 governance, 169–170, 172
 internal democracy, 168–169, 171–172
 internal divisions over, 168–172, 230, 239
 interpersonal relations with #BBOG top leaders, 6–7, 173, 235–236
 lessons for improved advocacy, 6–7, 173, 197

level of commitment, 6–7, 169, 173, 235–236
organizational structure, debates on, 168–169
regime neutrality, 6–7, 173, 235–236
resources, 6–7, 173, 235–236
sources of oligarchization, 6–7, 173
see also #BBOG: internal divisions; #BBOG membership; oligarchization
#BBOG: organizational structure, 85–88, 86f, 169
ad hoc committees, 87–88
#BBOG leader, 85
debates on, 88, 168–169
deputy ST chair, 154, 170, 195
general assembly of members at the 'sit-out', 88
SCT (strategic communication team), 87, 99–100
security task force, 189–190, 193
ST (strategic team), 86, 88, 172–173
#BBOG: origins and rise, 1, 56, 60–61
2014: 30 April inaugural mass protest (Abuja), 63–64, 92, 101, 120–121, 129, 226
'#BringBackOurGirls' tweet, 63
Ezekwesili, Obiageli, 63–64, 72
gender and Nigeria's patriarchal ideational infrastructure, 69
nature of the Nigerian state and political opportunity, 69, 74
positive transformation of the movement, 69, 76
social and cultural capital of co-conveners, 69, 72, 234
social media, 63–64, 99–102
Usman, Hadiza Bala, 63–64
#BBOG: outcomes and impact, 3, 21, 205, 231–234, 238, 242
106 girls back/113 still missing, 21, 202, 205–206, 232, 238
assessing the #BBOG movement's outcomes, 209
#BBOG, social class dimension and impact on outcomes, 3, 10
#BBOG framing and, 4–5, 211
Chibok girls's wellbeing: psychotherapy/activities for rehabilitation, 11–12, 202–203, 206–207, 211, 238
contradictory outcomes, 11, 207, 232, 238
education of the girl-child in Northern Nigeria, 11–12, 207–210, 232, 238
envisaging outcomes: #BBOG movement's three scenarios, 202
human rights advocacy, 208–210, 231–232
IDPs, support for, 11–12, 208
impacts on its cause and the broader political process, 11
non-violent protest in Nigeria, 12, 208–209, 232
nurturing the humanitarian drive and leadership skills of several members, 208, 238
political change, 12, 209, 232, 238
political context/organizational variables approaches, 201–202, 211–213
prolonging inadvertently the Chibok girls' captivity, 203, 231, 238
schools in Northeast Nigeria, 11–12, 208
tension between national/local context, 236–237
see also social movement outcomes
#BBOG: social class dimension, 19–20
double bind of involvement of elite women/mothers in grassroots advocacy, 3
elite middle-class coalition, 1–3, 71, 187, 234
ethno-religious diversity of the core group, 71, 73–74
kinship networks, 73–74
Nigerian government and, 5–6, 187, 192–193, 196
outcomes, impact on, 3, 10
social and cultural capital of co-conveners, 69, 72, 105, 127, 150, 187, 196–198, 226, 234–235
'social motherhood' identity and social class status of #BBOG conveners, 130, 150

#BBOG: social class dimension (*Continued*)
   state repression: kinship and social networks of co-conveners as protection to #BBOG, 187, 197–198, 235
   support from international players and male elites, 73
#BBOG: strategies on Chibok girls' rescue, 78
   internationally orientated discursive strategy, 79–80
   kinetic approach/military operations, 79–81
   reorientation of how to 'rescue' the Chibok girls, 79–81
   strategizing on how to 'rescue' the Chibok girls, 78
#BBOG: tactics of protest, 65, 91–97, 115, 211, 231
   30 April 2014 inaugural mass protest (Abuja), 63–64, 92, 101, 120–121, 129, 226
   2014 unplanned protest, 109–110, 115
   annual Chibok girls' lecture, 97, 207–208
   celebrity marches, 105–106
   Chibok girls' ambassador tactic, 96
   daily protests, 74–75, 83–84, 93
   days of action, 95, 102, 133
   debates and internal division over, 6, 109, 210, 230, 239
   'Global Week of Action', 95, 105
   media engagement, 87, 97, 100, 105, 126
   protest fatigue, 229–230, 239
   reduction in numbers of participants in protests, 228–229
   'silent marches', 95–96
   sit-outs, 76–77, 88, 93, 102–103, 105, 109–110, 125–127, 152, 159, 166–167, 189–190, 202–203
   social media and, 102–103, 103*f*
   street marches/mass protests, 95, 99–100, 105, 106–107, 106*f*, 166–167, 191
   see also #BBOG mobilization
#BBOG and state repression, 10, 93, 110, 189–195, 226, 235
   attacks by state-sponsored thugs, 10, 188, 189, 193–194
   attempts to sponsor chaos and leadership change in the movement, 10, 188, 192, 195, 235
   #BBOG's strategies in countering state repression, 10, 193–195, 197
   bomb threats, 10, 188, 189, 235
   covert repression, 188, 230
   gender-related issues, 187
   intimidation through false arrests, 10, 188, 195, 235
   journalists, attacks on and arrest of, 189, 232
   kinship and social networks of co-conveners as protection to #BBOG, 187, 197–198, 235
   law enforcement agencies and infiltration of #BBOG ranks, 109
   lessons for improved advocacy, 193–195, 197
   marches, prevention of, 190, 208–209
   smear campaigns, 10, 114, 188, 190, 194–195
   strength-from-within/strength-from-without, 187–188, 196, 197–198
   see also state repression
#BBOG and toxic politics, 20, 71, 74–76, 145
   #BBOG: lessons for improved advocacy, 149–150, 163–164
   #BBOG leaders, appointment into key positions of APC-led government, 144–145, 156–157, 210, 235
   #BBOG members: embedding the movement in toxic politics, 156–158, 235
   Jonathan government: casting of #BBOG as opposition tool, 114–115, 120–122, 132, 135, 137–138, 143, 144, 150, 185, 190–191, 203
   partisan politics, 20, 135, 157–158
   see also toxic politics
Bello, Abdullahi, 23
Bello, Ahmadu, 16
Bello, Muhammed, 23
Benford, R.D., 119, 127–128

Biafra Republic, 16 n.7, 17
  killing of pro-Biafra protesters by the military, 180, 188, 197–198
Bin Laden, Osama, 41
Blumer, Herbert, 65, 215–216, 227–228
Bob, Clifford, 118, 195 n.42
Boko Haram, 29, 61–62
  APC and, 9
  #BBOG and, 120
  Buhari, Muhammadu and, 43, 80–81, 212–213
  Chibok kidnapping, 1, 49
  divisions within Boko Haram and Islamic State, 47
  evolution of, 33, 45–46, 56
  as existential threat to Nigeria, 29–30, 44
  extremism, 32, 41–42, 44
  FTO designation, 42–43, 58–59
  government's negotiations with, 11–12, 186, 205–206, 238
  grievances, 32, 42–44, 47
  imprisonment of Boko Haram family members, 51–53
  ISIS and, 33, 41, 44, 47–48, 56
  meaning of the term 'Boko Haram', 29–30
  Modu Sheriff, Ali and, 14–15, 29, 46, 122
  NGOs and, 231
  as 'Nigerian Taliban'/'Black Taliban', 29–30, 41
  Nigeria's politics and the rise and spread of, 13–15, 46
  objectives, 33, 44
  origins, 29–30, 29–30 n.1
  poverty and, 45–47, 181
  al-Qaeda/AQIM and, 33, 41, 47, 53, 56
  recruitment, 45, 181
  scholarship on, 56–57
  secularism, repudiation of, 30–31, 44
  Sharia law, 32, 44, 45, 47, 122
  state repression and Boko Haram's violence, 31, 42–43, 47, 51, 121
  as 'technically defeated', 80–81, 212–213, 224
  terrorism, 37, 41–44, 47, 56
  as transnational organization, 41, 47
  use of Boko Haram as tool to win elections, 14–15
  'We speak as Boko Haram' (2009 official statement), 29–31, 44–45
  see also Chibok kidnapping; ISWAP; Shekau, Abubakar; Yusuf, Muhammad
Boko Haram: challenges in defeat of, 9, 122, 176–184, 240
  alienation of the public by the military, 9, 176–177, 180–181, 240
  corruption, 9, 122, 176–178, 185, 240
  fratricidal struggles within Boko Haram and ISWAP, 49
  inadequate coordination of security operations, 9, 176–177, 240
  ineffective national leadership during the Jonathan presidency, 176
  intelligence leaks/sabotage/disloyalty, 9, 176–180, 185, 240
  limited foreign military support for the Nigerian government to fight Boko Haram, 139–140, 147, 224
  military professionalism, decline in, 176, 183–184
  nepotism, 9, 176–177, 183–184, 240
  politicization of the war against Boko Haram, 181–182
  rise of actors benefiting from the problem, 9, 176–178, 184, 240
  role of politics in national security architecture, 176
  shortage of arms and ammunition, 9, 122, 139–140, 176–177, 240
  'strategic blunders' of political leaders, 9, 176–177, 240
  toxic politics in the military, 9, 176–177, 179, 181–184, 240
  troops' perception of the war against Boko Haram as 'rubbish mission', 9, 176–177, 184, 240
Boko Haram: ideology, 47
  Chibok kidnapping and ideology, 51–52
  ideological divides, 47
  injustice master frame, 42–43, 47
  Islamism: missionary, activist, and jihadist Islamism, 41–42
  master frames, 42–44

Boko Haram: ideology (*Continued*)
  return to true Islam master frame, 42
  Salafism, jihadism and
    Salafi-jihadism, 29–30, 39, 56
  war against the infidel master
    frame, 42–44
Boko Haram: trends, targets, and
  tactics, 19, 33, 41–42, 49
  armed assault, 37
  attacks, injured, fatalities, 34, 34*f*
  attacks, injured, fatalities by attack
    type, 37, 38*f*
  bombing/explosion, 37, 44, 45
  civilians, 35–37
  distribution of attacks, persons injured,
    and fatalities by country, 35, 35*f*
  educational institutions, 35–37, 51–52
  hostage-taking/kidnapping, 37, 47,
    52–53, 61–62
  killings, 80
  Muslims, attacks on, 47–48
  Nigeria's political process and, 37–38
  political violence in Nigeria and Boko
    Haram, 33
  suicide bombing, 37, 39*f*, 40*f*, 44, 46
  targets, 35–37, 36*f*
  territorial scope of action, 37–38, 44, 47
  see also Buni Yadi; Chibok kidnapping;
    Dapchi kidnapping
Boomer, Matthew, 222–223
Borno state, 225
  Boko Haram and, 47
  Boko Haram's suicide bombing
    attacks, 37, 44
  Borno government as responsible for
    abduction and failure to rescue the
    Chibok girls, 122
  Modu Sheriff, Ali and Boko
    Haram, 14–15, 29, 46, 122
  NGOs at, 225, 227
  Sharia law, 29
  see also Chibok kidnapping
Bossard, James, 215 n.13
Botswana, 231–232
Bourdieu, Pierre, 72, 216
Britain and Nigeria
  1914 establishment of Nigeria, 15–16,
    23
  1906 Satiru rebellion, 24–25, 31

British colonialists, 15–16, 23–26, 31,
    66–67
  'indirect rule', 23
  Sokoto Caliphate, 25
Brown, Gordon, 208, 224
BudgIT, 74
Buhari, Aisha, 216–217
Buhari, Muhammadu/Buhari government
  1983 military coup, 17
  2011 elections, 17
  2015 elections, 9, 17–18
  APC and, 9, 17–18
  #BBOG and, 6, 144–145 n.33, 173, 185,
    191–192, 196, 203, 211, 212–213, 229,
    239
  #BBOG members as Buhari's
    supporters, 155, 158
  Boko Haram and, 43, 80–81, 212–213
  Chibok kidnapping and, 80–81,
    212–213
  Christian genocide under, 221 n.18
  clean-up of the Ogoni
    environment, 148–149
  exploitation of Chibok girls, 216
  humanitarian services in Nigerian
    Northeast, 114
  see also APC
Buhari-Bello, Hadiza, 113
Buni Yadi (Federal Government College):
    2014 Boko Haram's attack, 35–37,
    51–52, 69–70, 69–70 n.7, 133

C
Cameron, David, 102, 187–188
Cameroon, 35
capital, 72
  Chibok girls and, 216
  social and cultural capital of #BBOG
    co-conveners, 69, 72, 105, 127, 150,
    187, 196–198, 226, 234–235
Castells, Manuel, 68
celebrities and personalities, 8–9, 76, 77,
    102, 132–133, 187–188, 202–203,
    226–227, 237–238
  #BBOG activists as, 220–221
  celebrity marches, 105–106
  personalities at the sit-out, 102
Charrad, Mounira, 73–74
Chibok girls

106 girls rescued, 21, 202, 205–206, 219–220, 227, 232
112 girls still missing/failure to rescue all the girls, 21, 56, 64, 202, 227
as "brain-washed" by Boko Haram, 80
girls who escaped on the night of kidnapping, 1 n.1, 50, 52, 224
girls who escaped on the night of kidnapping: US travel, 218–219, 221
killed by Boko Haram, 80
parents of, 206, 218–219, 224, 229–230, 236–237
psychotherapy and activities for rehabilitation, 11–12, 202–203
as slaves, 54
trauma suffered by, 52
as 'wives' to the fighters, 53–54, 71, 77, 80–81, 240–241
Chibok Government Secondary School, 1, 224
Chibok kidnapping (2014, Borno state), 1, 61–62
2016 release of Chibok girls, 52–53, 81, 217
2017 release of Chibok girls, 52–53, 81, 95–96, 141, 205–206, 217, 240 n.1
as accidental, 51, 54, 240
Alhaji, Maita (Abu), 50
Boko Haram and, 1, 49
Buhari, Muhammadu and, 80–81, 212–213
education of young girls/their right to education and, 52, 70
ideology and, 51–52
impact of, 52
Jonathan administration and, 54–55, 63–64, 74–75
Jonathan administration's reluctance/delay in acknowledging the kidnapping, 54–55, 63, 74–75, 120–121, 135, 211–212, 226
lack of security at the school, 50
military forces: false information on rescue of the girls, 54–55, 74–75, 121–122
Nigerian lethargic state/failure to act, 55, 63–65
politicization of the Chibok issue, 181–182
as prism for understanding terrorism and human rights advocacy in Africa, 56
prisoner exchange and, 52–53, 186, 205–206, 238, 240
prolonged captivity, 11, 58–59, 79, 84–85, 142, 203, 231, 238
ransom, 11, 50, 53, 205, 238
reasons for Boko Haram's kidnapping, 51–53
released girls during the kidnapping, 50
as revenge for imprisonment of Boko Haram family members, 51–53
revenue as reason for, 53
Sambisa Forest, 10–11, 50, 54, 203–204
Shekau, Abubakar and, 50–52, 54
taking captives as legitimate warfare, 53–54
toxic politics and, 54–55, 234
Chibok kidnapping and social problem industry, 2, 7, 223
#BBOG and, 223–224, 234
exploitation of Chibok girls and their community, 7, 216–218, 227, 231, 239
framing success: the army and the rescue of the Chibok girls, 217
international media exposure and financial exploitation of the Chibok girls, 218
NGOs, 218–221, 227, 239
predatory philanthropy, 222–223
presidential photo-ops and political mileage, 216
see also social problem industry
Chile, 93–94, 200–201, 211–212
Chiluwa, I., 99
CLEEN Foundation, 45–46
co-optation (by the government), 57–58, 74, 111–112, 241
#BBOG and, 6, 57, 194–195, 211, 232–233, 239
political opportunity and, 198
Corrigall-Brown, Catherine, 111
corruption
Boko Haram's recruitment and, 45–46
Buhari's war against, 183–184 n.33
bureaucratic corruption, 13

corruption (*Continued*)
  challenges in defeat of Boko Haram and corruption, 9, 122, 176–178, 185, 240
  citizens, 13
  'Dasukigate', 177–178
  Democratic Republic of Congo, 13
  embezzling funds for victims of Boko Haram, 222–223
  military forces, 13, 122, 177–178, 181–182 n.31, 183–184 n.33, 185
  Nigeria, 13, 23, 222–223
  see also EFCC
Cote d'Ivoire, 13
Cress, Daniel, 199

D
Dan Fodio, Usman, 16 n.7, 22–23, 27, 32
Dapchi kidnapping (2018, GGSTC/Government Girls Science and Technical College, Yobe), 48, 61–62, 61–62 n.17, 209–210 n.7
Dasuki, Sambo (retired Colonel), 177
Davenport, Christian, 228
Democratic Republic of Congo, 13
developing countries/Global South, 1
  human rights advocacy, 3–4, 151
  intractability of social problems in, 7, 231, 239
  nebulous nature of international 'support' for grassroots movements in, 8
  social problem industry, 7–8, 231
  see also social movements (Africa/Global South)
Diani, Mario, 65
Dietz, Kelly, 144
Dikko, Mohammed Umar (Air Marshall), 178
Douzinas, Costas, 147
Duvall, Raymond D., 186–187
Dwyer, Peter, 231

E
Earl, Jennifer, 187
Ecuador, 137, 149
education
  #BBOG's impact on education of the girl-child in Northern Nigeria, 11–12, 207–210, 232, 238
  #BBOG's impact on schools in Northeast Nigeria, 11–12, 208
  Boko Haram's approach to female education, 35–37, 51–52, 133, 134
  Chibok kidnapping, impact on education of young girls/right to education, 52, 70
  educational institutions as Boko Haram's targets, 35–37, 51–52
  NEPU and mass education, 25–26
  Northern Nigeria, girl-child's education in, 134
  Western education as motive of conflict, 26, 29–32, 51–52
  see also girl-child's right to education framing
EFCC (Economic and Financial Crimes Commission), 177–178, 181–182 n.31, 222–223
Egypt, 68, 99
  Egyptian revolution/Tahrir Square, 98–99, 165, 231–232
  Islamism, 165
  Mubarak, Hosni, 98, 165, 201, 205
  Mubarak, Suzanne, 57–58, 201
  women and political revolution, 98, 165, 205
  women's movement in, 165
EiE (Enough is Enough), 74
elections (Nigeria)
  1959 elections, 16
  1979 elections, 17
  1993 elections, 17
  1999 elections, 17
  2011 elections, 17
  2015 elections, 9, 17–18, 150, 177–178, 182, 183–184, 209, 232
  2018 elections, 14 n.4
  APC, 2015 elections, 9, 17–18, 143–144, 155, 212
  arms and ammunitions, 13
  ballot box stuffing, 14
  #BBOG framing and, 4–5, 143, 150, 209, 223–224, 232
  bribery, 14, 177–178
  contestation, 13
  ethnic/religious polarization, 17–18
  Jonathan, Goodluck/PDP, 17–18, 55, 209

money-for-vote scheme, 14 n.4
rigging, 13, 182
use of Boko Haram as tool to win elections, 14–15
violence, 14
El-Rufai, Nasir, 85–86, 156, 157
El Saadawi, Nawal, 201
Emand Basadi ('Stand Up Women'), 231–232
Emir of Kano, 72–73, 97, 138–139, 207–208
#ENDSARS protests, 1–3, 188
Ezekwesili, Obiageli (Oby), 6, 20, 58–59, 71, 125 n.12, 204, 230
   2014 UNESCO forum speech, 63, 72
   2017: 10 June ST decisions, 170–171
   2018 arrest, 195–196
   APC convention speech, 156
   #BBOG: human rights framing, 131–133
   #BBOG: origins, 63–64, 72
   '#BringBackOurGirls' tweet, 63, 72, 226
   on Buni Yadi attack, 69–70
   critique of the government, 120, 156, 205–206
   as founding member of Transparency International, 85
   funding, stance on, 113–114
   as leader of the #BBOG movement, 85, 192–193
   'Madam Due Process', 72
   media and, 101 n.40, 102
   as member of #BBOG ST, 86–87
   as Obasanjo/PDP government's minister, 6, 63, 72, 156, 187
   Sambisa tour, 160–162
   social and cultural capital of, 72, 85, 125 n.15, 127, 187
   Twitter, 63, 72, 103–104, 196

F
Facebook, 68, 98, 99
   #BBOG, 12, 19, 99–100, 104, 107
Falana, Femi, 196
Fayemi, Kayode, 14 n.4
Fayose, Ayo, 14
Federation of South African Women, 164–165
feminism, 164

Egypt, 57–58, 165, 201
FEMEN (Special Force of Feminism), 91–92
Iran, 98
'secular'/'Islamic' feminism, 165
state-sponsored feminism, 57–58, 201
framing
   authoritarian/quasi-democratic contexts, 4–5, 117–118, 139, 142–143, 149–150
   #BBOG framing and framing theory, 4–5, 150–151, 237
   Boko Haram: ideological master frames, 42–44
   core framing tasks: diagnostic, prognostic, and motivational framing, 119
   cultural resonance in the social context, 117
   frame, definition, 127–128
   framing local struggles using global-speak, 138, 236–237
   framing/political context link, 213
   motherist framing, 128–129
   as process, 117
   social movements, 117, 237
   social movements (Africa/Global South), 117–118
   see also #BBOG framing; #BBOG: framing internationalization; human rights framing
future research, suggestions on, 240–241

G
Galang, Yana, 229–230
Galtimari panel, 15
Gamson, William A., 186–187, 202
Gans, Herbert, 214–215
gender-related issues, 58
   #BBOG and state repression, 187
   Boko Haram's approach to gender, 35–37, 69–70, 133
   conflict dynamics of Islamic fundamentalist movements, 31–32
   gender and Nigeria's patriarchal ideational infrastructure, 69
   gender-related activism, 200–201
   motherist framing and, 128–131

gender-related issues (*Continued*)
  SGBV (sexual and gender-based violence), 44, 77
  see also women
Gheytanchi, Elham, 98
girl-child's right to education framing (#BBOG framing), 4, 133, 138, 236
  cultural bias against the education of the girl-child, 134
  founded on ongoing global narrative, 134
  location of the kidnapping as symbolic, 134
  Nigerian audience/context, 20, 137, 138–139, 141–142, 236
  see also #BBOG: framing; education
Global South, *see* developing countries/Global South; social movements (Africa/Global South)
Goodwin, R. H. (Major), 25
Gowon, Yakubu (General), 17
Gray, Simon, 41–42
Großklaus, Mathias, 118, 138
GTD (Global Terrorism Database), 19, 33, 37–38
Guardian (newspaper), 177–178, 204, 207, 217–218

H
Hafner-Burton, Emilie M., 147
Hinshaw, Drew, 205, 218–222
human rights, 131, 145–146
  Africa, 235
  global regime of human rights as 'double-edged sword', 147
  Nigeria's human rights record, 139–140, 188
human rights advocacy
  authoritarian/quasi-democratic contexts, 3–4
  #BBOG's human rights advocacy, 76–77, 96, 124, 193–194, 197–198
  #BBOG's impact on human rights advocacy, 208–210, 231–232
  Chibok kidnapping as prism for understanding terrorism and human rights advocacy in Africa, 56

involvement of elites in grassroots advocacy, 3
local struggles: *think local and act local*, 3–4, 151
social movements (Africa/Global South), 2–4, 118, 146–147, 151, 165, 235
transnationalization of human rights discourses, 146–147
vernacularizing human rights, 146–147
women's rights movements, 2–3, 67, 200–201, 231–232
see also #BBOG: lessons for improved advocacy; human rights framing
human rights framing, 145–147
  framing and human rights movements in Africa, 118
  limited impact, 148
  successful transnational rights campaigns in the Global South, 148
human rights framing (#BBOG framing), 4, 131, 236
  disappointment at lack of impact, 146–148
  international/Western audience, 20, 133, 138–139, 146, 236
  justification and legitimization of #BBOG's existence, 132
  limited cultural resonance in Nigeria, 146–147, 236–237
  as politically motivated and as embarrassment, 146–147
  social class dimension, 132–133
  see also #BBOG: framing
Human Rights Watch, 49, 54, 60

I
Ibrahim, Bashiru, 86–87
Ibrahim, Jibril, 86–87, 110
Ibrahim, Jimoh, 73
ICRC (International Committee of the Red Cross), 141
IDPs (internally displaced persons), 95, 108, 113, 225
  #BBOG, impact on support for, 11–12, 208
  embezzling funds for IDPs and use of ghost IDPs, 222–223

IDP camp bombing by the military, 163–164, 185, 205–206
Ifukor, P., 99
Ignatieff, Michael, 145–146
Iliya, Dauda, 86–87
IMN (Islamic Movement in Nigeria), 26–27
al-Quds Day massacre, 27, 197–198
ING (interim national government), 17
international support
　#BBOG, lessons for improved advocacy: local *vs* international support, 8–9, 149–151, 238
　political change in Nigeria and, 12
　social movements and, 8, 111–112, 115, 149, 151, 238
　US and UK, largely symbolic support given by, 141
　see also #BBOG: framing internationalization; #BBOG: internationalization
Internet, 12, 68, 101
internet activism, 1, 57, 69, 115–116
　women's cyberactivism, 98
Iran, 26–27, 98
ISIS (Islamic State of Iraq and Syria)
　2018: school girls kidnapped in Dapchi, 48
　Boko Haram and, 33, 41, 44, 47–48, 56
Islam (Nigeria)
　Shia Islam, 26–27
　Sufism, 45–46
　Sunni Islam, 26–27, 39–41
Islamic movements (Nigeria), 22–23
　1804 Fulani jihad, 22–23, 27
　1906 Satiru rebellion, 24–25, 31
　conflict dynamics of Islamic fundamentalist movements, 31–32
　extremism, 32, 41–42, 44, 45–46
　fundamentalism, 28, 45–46, 56
　Iran and Northern Nigeria, 26–27
　Islamic violence as political violence, 29
　Islamism: missionary, activist, and jihadist Islamism, 41–42
　Mahdist movements, 24–25
　in Northern Nigeria, 22, 31–32
　radicalization, 26–27, 32, 45–46
　religious dissidence, 22–24
　sectarian/religious violence, 27–29, 31–32
　see also Boko Haram; Dan Fodio, Usman; ISWAP; jihadism; Sharia law
ISWAP (Islamic State West Africa Province), 240–241
　2018: school girls kidnapped in Dapchi, 48
　2021 June: consolidation of power, 49, 56
　Ba Idrisa (Abdullahi Umar Al Barnawi), 48–49
　Ba Lawan, 48–49
　al-Barnawi, Abu Musab, 48–49
　Boko Haram, 41, 49
　Shekau, Abubakar and, 48–49
　violence within, 48–49

J
Jackson, Paul, 53
Jalali, R., 111–112
jihadism, 45–46, 139
　Boko Haram, 29–30, 33, 39, 47, 56
　Fulani jihadists, 23
　global jihadi terrorism, 47, 56, 139
　see also terrorism
Jonathan, Goodluck/Jonathan administration
　2011 elections, 17
　2015 elections, 17–18, 55, 209
　#BBOG, ignored by, 203
　Chibok kidnapping, 54–55, 63–64, 74–75
　Chibok kidnapping, reluctance/delay in acknowledge of, 54–55, 63, 74–75, 120–121, 135, 211–212, 226
　'Dasukigate', 177
　failures/ineptitude, 55–56, 76, 121, 135–136, 209
　PDP and, 17–18
　state failure framing, 4, 12, 135–136, 142–143
　toxic politics: casting of #BBOG as opposition tool, 114–115, 120–122, 132, 135, 137–138, 143, 144, 150, 185, 190–191, 203
　see also PDP; state failure framing
Juris, Jeffrey, 69

K

Kabrik, Maureen, 86–87, 195–196
KADA (Kibaku Area Development Association), 107, 161–162, 224
Kaduna, 2015 killing of Shi'ites by the military, 180, 188, 197–198
Kano, 37
Kano, Aminu, 25–26
Kenya, 13, 69
  nude protests, 92
  transnationalizing local struggles, 137
Khalid, Mouhammed (Chief Imam), 105–106
kidnapping
  Boko Haram and, 37, 47, 52–53, 61–62
  Nigeria, normality of kidnapping, 2–3, 50, 61–62, 132–133, 225
  ransom, 132–133
  of students at schools, 61–62, 225, 232
  see also Chibok kidnapping; Dapchi kidnapping
Kingibe, Babagana, 73–74
Kingibe, Ireti, 72–74, 86–87, 187
Kitschelt, Herbert, 202
Klein, Naomi, 136–137
Kpotum, Ibrahim Idris (Inspector General), 190

L

Lagos #BBOG, 202–203
Last, Murray, 22–23
Lawal, Babachir, 222–223
Lawan, Kaka Shehu, 14–15
Leadership (newspaper), 70, 101, 140, 177–178
Liberia, 13
Libya, 231–232
'lives matter' politics, 1–2, 242
Loimeier, Roman, 32
Loseke, Donileen, 214
Luckham, Alexander R., 175–176
Luka, Serah, 218

M

Madhi, Saudatu, 72, 86–87, 210
Madres de la Plaza de Mayo (Mothers of the Plaza de Mayo, Argentina), 83, 128
Maitatsine, 27–28, 56
Maiva, Paul Ali, 219
Maiva, Yakubu Nkeki, 218–219
Malala (Yousafzai), 102, 187–188
Malala Fund, 128
Mare, Admire, 98–99
Marenin, Otwin, 135
Marks, James 'Spider' (US Major General), 147
Marwa, Muhammed, 27–28
Mason, Paul, 99
Mazumdar, Tulip, 80
Mbalala, Falmata, 217–218
Mbembé, Achille, 14
Meagher, Kate, 22, 29
media
  Sambisa tour, 10–11, 160, 161
  see also #BBOG: communication process; social media
Melaye, Dino, 73
Merry, Sally Engle, 146–147
Michels, Robert, 167–168
military forces (Nigeria)
  #BBOG/military forces relationship, 175, 185–186, 191, 203, 223
  #BBOG as responsible for the Chibok girls' long captivity, 11, 203–204, 238
  #BBOG state failure framing: alienation of key political and military actors, 20, 138–139, 141–143, 185, 186
  Chibok kidnapping: false information on rescue of the girls, 54–55, 74–75, 121–122
  corruption, 13, 122, 177–178, 181–182 n.31, 183–184 n.33, 185
  fragmentation in the army, 175–176, 239–240
  framing success: the army and the rescue of the Chibok girls, 217
  IDP camp bombing by, 163–164, 185, 205–206
  inability to rescue the Chibok girls, 175–185
  as ineffective against Boko Haram, 9, 239–240
  infiltration of armed forces by persons sympathetic to Boko Haram, 178–179

inhibited efforts to rescue the Chibok girls, 9
internal decay of, 4
killing of pro-Biafra protesters by the military, 180, 188, 197–198
military coups/counter-coups, 16–17
military professionalism, decline in, 176, 183–184
Nigerian ethno-religious divisions and, 9, 16, 181–184
partisan politics, 9, 182, 239–240
people rescued from Boko Haram by, 203–204, 218
repressive relationship with civilians, 9, 180–181, 186, 188
scholarship on military performance in the war against Boko Haram, 176
toxic politics in, 9, 17–18, 176–177, 179, 181–184, 239–240
US military support and clash with Nigerian government/military forces, 139–140
war crimes by, 180–181, 180–181 n.28
see also Boko Haram: challenges in defeat of; Sambisa tour
Miners, Norman, 16
Minimah, Kenneth (Lieutenant General), 181–182, 181–182 n.31
Miss World controversy (2002), 29, 32
Modu, Mayinta, 240–241
Modu Sheriff, Ali, 14–15, 29, 46, 122
Moghadam, Valentine N., 98
Mohammed, Ajoke, 73–74
Mohammed, Isa, 28
Mohammed, Lai, 160, 160 n.9, 161, 190, 205–206, 210
Mohammed, Murtala (General), 73–74
Morocco, 73–74, 92, 98
Mosley, Ramaa, 63 n.1
motherist/maternalist framing (#BBOG framing), 4, 71, 128, 236
    as de-emphasized/abandoned, 136, 141–142
    missing girls as 'daughters' and 'sisters', 70, 129
    motherhood, mothering, and maternal identity elements, 128
    Nigerian audience/context, 20, 137, 138–139, 141–142, 236
    patriarchy and, 130–131
    practical gender interests, 128–129, 131
    problematics of, 130–131
    'social motherhood' identity and social class status of #BBOG conveners, 130, 150
    success of, 129–130, 141–142
    see also #BBOG: framing
Movimiento Cívico Nacional (Guatemala), 99
Mozambique, 67
MSSN (Muslim Students' Society of Nigeria), 26–27
Mubarak, Hosni, 98, 165, 201, 205
Mubarak, Suzanne, 57–58, 201
Muhammed, Murtala (General), 17, 114, 187
Muhammed Oyebode, Aisha, 114
Muslim Brotherhood, 39–41
    Freedom and Justice Party, 201
Mustapha, Abdul Raufu, 22, 29, 31, 45–46
Mustapha, Zannah, 141

N
Namibia, 67
NCNC (National Council of Nigeria and the Cameroons), 16
nepotism, 9, 13–14, 176–177, 183–184, 240
Nepstad, Sharon E., 195 n.42
NEPU (Northern Elements Progressive Union), 25–26
NESG (Nigerian Economic Summit Group), 74
New York Times, 217
NGOs (non-governmental organizations), 225
    #BBOG and international NGOs, 2, 80 n.21, 127–128, 136–137
    #BBOG mass protests and, 106–108, 111
    #BBOG as NGO, 158–159, 173–174, 208, 235–236
    Boko Haram and, 231
    in Borno state, 225, 227
    Chibok kidnapping, social problem industry and, 218–221, 227, 239
    foreign aid and, 111–112
    IDPs, support for, 208

NGOs (non-governmental organizations) (*Continued*)
  social problem industry and, 7, 213–214, 225, 227, 231
  state priority (defeat of terrorists) *vs* NGO mission (non-discriminatory services), 231
  transnationalization and, 136–137
Niger Delta
  1990s insurgency, 13, 31 n.3
  2000s insurgency, 74
  2002 nude protest against Chevron, 91–92
  kidnapping, normality of, 50
  military violence in, 180
  Niger Delta movement, 74, 148–149
  see also Ogoni movement
Nigeria
  1960 independence, 16
  1967–1970 Civil War, 17, 29–30
  Boko Haram's attacks, 33, 35, 40*f*
  British colonialists and, 15–16, 23–26, 31, 66–67
  complexity and politics, 13
  ethnic and religious diversity/polarization, 15–18, 189
  human rights record, 139–140, 188
  kidnapping, normality of, 2–3, 50, 61–62, 132–133, 225
  military coups/counter-coups, 16–17
  Nigerian Constitution, 16, 29, 124
  Northeast zone, 18
  North/South divide, 16, 182, 183, 189, 211–212
  population, 15
  states and geopolitical zones, 18
  see also Adamawa state; Borno state; Northern Nigeria; Yobe state
Nigerian government/state
  #BBOG and, 120–121, 124, 138, 203, 210, 223
  between authoritarian and democratic state, 74, 188, 197–198
  corruption, 13, 23, 222–223
  deflecting responsibility, 74–75
  lethargic state, 5–6, 71
  negotiations with Boko Haram, 11–12, 186, 205–206, 238
  Nigerian presidency as responsible for the abduction and failure to rescue the Chibok girls, 120
  Nigerian security architecture as responsible for the abduction and failure to rescue the Chibok girls, 121
  'politics of the belly', 14
  as 'private indirect government', 74–75
  'stomach infrastructure', 14
  Twitter, ban on, 188
  see also #BBOG and state repression; co-optation; state failure framing
Nkeki, Amina, 80–81, 216–218
Nkeki, Yakubu, 229–230
Northern Nigeria
  #BBOG's impact on education of the girl-child in Northern Nigeria, 11–12, 207–210, 232, 238
  #BBOG's impact on schools in Northeast Nigeria, 11–12, 208
  #BBOG members as Buhari's supporters, 155, 157
  Boko Haram and, 32, 46
  conflict dynamics of Islamic fundamentalist movements, 31–32
  education of the girl-child, 11–12
  girl-child's education in, 134
  Iran and, 26–27
  Islamic movements, 22, 31–32
  kidnapping of students after Chibok case, 225, 232
  poverty, 46, 134
  Sharia law, 28–29, 44
NPAN (Newspaper Proprietors Association of Nigeria), 177–178
NPC (Northern People's Congress), 15–16, 25–26
NSA (National Security Adviser): 'Dasukigate', 177–178
NTA (Nigerian Television Authority), 101 n.40
Nuhu, Salome, 224
Nur, Mamman, 48–49
Nwaubani, Adaobi Tricia, 54
Nyabola, Nanjala, 69
Nzeogwu, Kaduna (Major), 16

O
Obaigbena, Nduka, 177–178

Obama, Barack, 102, 140
Obama, Michelle, 102, 130, 187–188
Obasanjo, Olusegun (General), 17, 76, 86, 156
Occupy Grahamstown, 98–99
'Occupy' movement, 98–99
Occupy Nigeria, 74, 98–99
Ogar, Marilyn, 190–191
Ogbeh, Audu, 143–144
Ogebe, Emmanuel, 218–222
Ogoni movement, 74, 148–149
  MOSOP (Movement for the Survival of Ogoni People), 148–149, 195
  Ogoni Nine, extrajudicial execution of, 31 n.3, 148–149, 188, 195
Ojukwu, Odumegwu (Colonel), 16 n.7, 17
Okoroafor, Jeff, 86–87, 195–196
Okunaye, Mariam, 107
Okupe, Doyin, 137–138, 144
oligarchization, 167–168
  bureaucratization as 'form' of, 167–168
  see also #BBOG: oligarchization
Olukolade, Chris (Major General), 74–75, 112–113, 142
Oluwale, Rotimi, 86–87
Omoniyi, Tosin, 224
Onaiyekan, John (Catholic Archbishop of Abuja diocese), 105–106
Oriola, Temitope, 39–44, 65, 214–215, 222–223
Osumah, Oarhe, 47
Oyebode, Aisha, 72, 187
Oyěwùmí, Oyèrónkẹ́, 57
Ozor, Florence, 109–110
  as #BBOG ST chair, 86–87, 154, 166–167, 169–170, 172–174, 195

P
Parkinson, Joe, 205
PDP (People's Democratic Party)
  2015 elections, 9, 17–18
  military forces and, 9
  see also Jonathan, Goodluck/Jonathan administration
Peace Corps of Nigeria, 113
Pinochet, Augusto, 93–94, 142–143, 211
Pocock, Andrew, 224
Pogu, Salomi, 230
political opportunity

#BBOG: framing internationalization, 5, 236–237
#BBOG: lessons for improved advocacy, 159, 163, 164, 198, 233, 241
#BBOG: origins and rise, 69, 74
co-optation and, 198
political process approach, 68
social movements (Africa/Global South), 20–21, 198, 200–201
state failure framing, 211, 236–237
poverty, 18, 214–215
Boko Haram's recruitment and, 45–47, 181
Northern Nigeria, 46, 134
Premium Times (newspaper), 103, 122, 152–153, 189, 191
protest
  29 April 2014: Chibok women's march (protest of victims' mothers), 3, 120–121, 129, 226
  #BBOG's impact on non-violent protest in Nigeria, 12, 208–209, 232
  food protests, 92
  nude protests in Africa, 91–92
  social media and, 98
  social movement and, 91–92, 109
  social movements (Africa/Global South), 91–92
  see also #BBOG: tactics of protest

Q
al-Qaeda
  Ansaru and, 47–48
  AQAP (al-Qaeda in the Arabian Peninsula), 53
  AQIM (al-Qaeda in the Islamic Maghreb), 33, 41, 53, 56
  Boko Haram and, 33, 41, 47, 53, 56

R
#ReleaseOurGirls, 76 n.13, 189
Republic of Benin, 148–149
research, 56–58
  data analysis, 60
  data collection, 58–60
  methodological approach, 58
  political process approach, 67–68
  scope and limitations, 60
Rimi, Abubakar, 28

RNA (Republic of New Africa), 228
Rosenberg, Rodrigo, 99
Russia, 140
Rwanda, 13, 67

S
Sambisa Forest
  Chibok kidnapping, 10–11, 50, 54, 203–204
  women and children kept at, 203–204
Sambisa tour, 10–11, 159, 185, 203, 210, 235
  Allen, Manasseh, 161–163
  #BBOG, existential crisis for, 10–11, 160–161
  #BBOG fragmentation over, 10–11, 160–161, 163
  #BBOG's conditions for accepting the invitation, 161
  #BBOG's report on the tour, 162–164
  Ezekwesili, Obiageli, 160–162
  fears for #BBOG members's lives, 161–162
  journalists, 160–162
  lessons for movement advocates, 163–164, 198
  media and, 10–11, 160, 161
  Mohammed, Lai, 160, 160 n.9, 161
  political manoeuvring, 10–11, 160, 161
  Sambisa tour invitation, 160–161
  social media and, 161
  Usman, Ibrahim, 162
  Yesufu, Aisha, 161–162
Samuel, Sarah, 53
Sanda, Lugwa, 52
Sanusi, Muhammad II (Emir of Kano), 97, 97 n.36, 207–208
Saraki, Bukola, 194
Sarkida, Ahmed, 61–62 n.16
Saro-Wiwa, Ken, 148–149, 195
Sawer, Marian, 82
Schmitz, Hans Peter, 137
secularism, 30–32, 44
Seidman, Gay W., 149
Senegal, 67
Sengupta, Somini, 147–148
SERAP (Socio-Economic Rights and Accountability Project), 196, 222–223
Sesay, Isha, 147–148

al-Shabaab, 41, 79–80
Shagari, Alhaji Shehu, 17
Sharia law, 23, 25, 32
  Boko Haram, 32, 44, 45, 47, 122
  Borno state, 29
  IMN, 27
  Northern Nigeria and, 28–29, 44
  punishments, 28
  see also Islamic movements
Shehu, Emman, 86–87
Shekau, Abubakar, 41, 51, 203–204
  Chibok kidnapping, 50–52, 54
  death/suicide, 49, 240–241
  ISWAP and, 48–49
Shettima, Kashim, 44, 122 n.5, 216–217, 222–223
Shonekan, Ernest (Chief), 17
Sierra Leone, 13
Snow, David, 119, 127–128, 199
social media, 68
  #BBOG: lessons for improved advocacy, 115–116, 150–151, 238
  as 'Fifth Estate', 98–99
  'hashtag activism'/'slacktivism', 64, 69, 99
  interpenetrative capacity, 99
  Kenya, 69
  as 'liberation technology', 99
  malleability of social networks, 68 n.5
  offline actions and effective activism, 99
  protest and, 98
  Sambisa tour, 161
  social movements and, 98–99, 115–116, 150–151
  social movements in Africa/Global South, 98–99, 238
  see also #BBOG: communication process; Facebook; Twitter; WhatsApp; Youtube
social movement
  anthems, slogans, chants, and songs, 83
  bureaucratization, 167–168
  capital and, 72
  challenges faced by, 164
  core values, 81
  definition, 65
  as embedded in national politics, 156
  framing and, 117, 237
  funding, 111, 115

internal democracy, 168–169
membership, tiered approach, 166–167
movement demobilization, 228
movement's acceptance as legitimate actor, 159
'networked social movement', 68
oligarchization, 167–168
political process approach, 67–68
protests, 91–92, 109
SMO (social movement organization), 65
social media and, 99, 115–116, 150–151
stages: emergence, coalescence, bureaucratization, and decline, 228
state repression and, 186–187
symbolic support, 141
symbolism and, 82, 93–96
see also #BBOG: lessons for improved advocacy; transnationalization
social movement outcomes, 199, 238
internal organizational variables, 199–200, 213
need for a broad-based approach to, 200–202, 213
political contexts, 199–200, 202, 213, 231–232, 241
procedural impacts, substantive impacts, structural impacts of movements, 202
social movements in Africa, 200–202, 231, 241
'success' 'as a set of outcomes', 202
social movements (Africa/Global South)
anti-colonialist movements, 146–147
in authoritarian/quasi-democratic contexts, 1, 3–4, 20–21, 111, 117–118, 139, 142–143, 149–150, 198, 201, 225
#BBOG and, 6–7, 57
Botswana, 231–232
challenges of contemporary social movements, 164, 197, 234–236, 241
Chilean women's movement, 200–201, 211–212
collaborating with the government, 10–11, 164, 198
Egyptian women's movement, 165
elite women's involvement in, 20–21, 57–58
foreign aid/international support and, 8, 111–112, 115, 149, 151, 238

framing and, 117–118
human rights advocacy, 2–4, 118, 146–147, 151, 165, 235
internal challenges, 6, 197
legitimacy, 10–11
movement actors as tolerated, 74
in Nigeria, 74
nude protests in Africa, 91–92
outcomes, 200–202, 231, 241
political opportunity, 20–21, 198, 200–201
protests, 91–92
risks to a movement's acceptance as legitimate actor in a cause, 10, 159
social media and, 98–99, 238
South African women's movements, 164–165, 200
state abdication of responsibility to citizens, 231
state funding, 111–112, 115, 201, 235
state repression, 235
state-sponsored women's rights movements, 201
successful transnational rights campaigns in the Global South, 148
trifecta of social conditions, 241
women-led movements in Africa, 57, 66–68, 92, 115, 164, 201, 231–232
women's rights movements, 2–3, 67, 200–201, 231–232
see also #BBOG: lessons for improved advocacy
social problem, 213
'central deficiencies' in the sociology of social problems, 215
five-stage model regarding life course of a social problem, 215
intractability of social problems in developing countries, 7, 231, 239
social problem industry, 213–214, 227–228
in developing countries/Africa, 7–8, 231
as international business, 7, 231
motives for getting involved in, 214, 239
NGOs and, 7, 213–214, 225, 227, 231
profits generated by, 214, 216, 223–224
self-perpetuation of, 7–8, 214–215, 223–224, 227, 231

social problem industry (*Continued*)
  see also Chibok kidnapping and social problem industry
social problem industry: contextual seven-stage model, 7, 216, 225–228, 239
  1: overpass stage, 7–8, 225, 226
  2: elite mobilization stage, 7–8, 225, 226
  3: validation stage, 7–8, 225, 226
  4: governing authority response stage, 7–8, 225, 226
  5: bifurcated trajectory stage, 7–8, 225, 226–227
  6: internationalization stage, 7–8, 225, 226–227
  7: dénouement stage, 7–8, 225, 227
  Chibok kidnapping and, 226–227
  as dynamic and context-dependent, 7–8, 227, 239
Sokoto Caliphate, 23–25, 32
Sonibare, Bukky, 86–87, 102, 154, 160–161
Soulaliyate movement (Morocco), 92
South Africa, 67, 98–99, 149, 180
  anti-apartheid movement, 93, 118, 164–165
  women in politics, 164–165, 200, 205
  women's movements, 164–165, 200
Soyinka, Wole, 76
state
  abdication of responsibility to citizens, 231
  state funding and social movements in Africa/Global South, 111–112, 115, 201, 235
  state-sponsored feminism, 57–58, 201
  state-sponsored women's rights movements, 201
  see also co-optation; Nigerian government/state; state failure framing; state repression
state failure framing (#BBOG framing), 4, 79–80, 135, 137, 211, 226–227, 236
  alienation of key political and military actors, 20, 138–139, 141–143, 185, 186, 236–237
  APC and, 12, 144
  critique of the Nigerian government, 136, 236–237
  international audience, 20, 136, 138–139, 142–143, 236
  Jonathan government, 4, 12, 135–136, 142–143
  'language of international embarrassment', 135–136
  Nigeria as failed state, 135, 142–143, 236–237
  overpoliticization, 135
  political opportunity structure, 211, 236–237
  toxic politics, 20, 135, 138–139, 236–237
  see also #BBOG: framing
state repression
  Boko Haram's violence and, 31, 42–43, 47, 51, 121
  covert repression, 188, 228, 230
  extrajudicial killings, 27, 31 n.3, 31, 148–149, 188, 195
  leaders' assassination, 195, 195 n.42
  military forces and, 188
  movement framing and, 117–118
  Nigeria, 188
  regime type and, 188
  social movements in Africa, 235
  'threat' perspective, 186–187
  'weakness' approach, 186–187, 197–198
  'weakness-from-within/weakness-from-without' approach, 187
  see also #BBOG and state repression; Ogoni movement
Stebbins, Robert A., 58
Stohl, Michael, 186–187
#stopkony, 1
Sun, 177–178
Switzerland, 141

T
Tarrow, Sidney, 65, 68, 136–137
Temple, Uwalaka, 98–99
terrorism, 138–139, 147–148
  #BBOG: 'Citizens' solution to end terrorism: The voice of Nigerians' manual, 124–125
  Chibok kidnapping as prism for understanding terrorism and human rights advocacy in Africa, 56

counterterrorism foreign support as uneven and fragmented, 176
global jihadi terrorism, 47, 56, 139
see also Boko Haram; ISIS; jihadism; al-Qaeda
This Day, 55, 177–178
thugs
  political thugs, 13
  state-sponsored thugs, 10, 188, 189, 193–194
Thurston, Alexander, 13, 29–30
Tilly, Charles, 228
Time Magazine, 207
toxic politics
  APC, Chibok kidnapping and toxic politics, 54–55
  Chibok kidnapping, 54–55, 234
  military forces, 9, 17–18, 176–177, 179, 181–184, 239–240
  state failure framing, 20, 135, 138–139, 236–237
  see also #BBOG and toxic politics
transnationalization
  #BBOG, 80 n.21, 136–138
  #BBOG, refusal to formal transnationalization, 5, 119, 138, 149–150, 236
  framing local struggles using global-speak, 138, 236–237
  of human rights discourses, 146–147
  of local struggles, 136–137, 149, 238
  NGOs and, 136–137
  successful transnational rights campaigns in the Global South, 148
  TNAs (transnational advocacy networks), 137–138
Trump administration, 140
Tsambido, Hosea, 86–87
Tsutsui, Kiyoteru, 147
Tunisia, 68, 73–74, 98, 231–232
Twitter ('X'), 68, 99, 194
  2018 arrest of #BBOG members, 196
  #BBOG, 19, 99–101, 103–104, 152, 194, 196
  '#BringBackOurGirls' tweet, 63, 72
  Ezekwesili, Obiageli, 63, 72, 103–104, 196
  Nigerian government ban on, 188
Twitterati, 68–69

Yesufu, Aisha, 152, 154

U
Umaru, Sanni, 45
UN (United Nations), 128, 138, 144–145, 187–188
UNDP (UN Development Programme), 44
UNEP (UN Environment Programme), 148–149
UNESCO (UN Educational, Scientific and Cultural Organization), 63
UNICEF (UN Children's Fund), 77, 222–223
Unity Fountain (Abuja), 76 n.13, 76–77, 94–95, 208–209, 208–209 n.6
  #BBOG marches, 95, 108, 110, 195–196
  #BBOG sit-outs, 94–95, 137–138, 169–170, 187–188, 208–209
Unity and Jihad in West Africa, 41
US (United States)
  Chibok girls: not a priority, 147–148
  Chibok girls who escaped on the night of kidnapping: US travel, 218–219, 221
  counterterrorism support as uneven and fragmented, 176
  limited foreign military support for the Nigerian government to fight Boko Haram, 139–140, 147, 224
Usman, Hadiza Bala, 20, 140, 226
  as APC member, 143
  appointment into key positions of APC-led government, 144, 156, 210
  #BBOG: origins, 63–64
  identity as mother, 71, 129
  media and, 102
  as member of #BBOG ST, 86–87
  social and cultural capital of, 72–73, 187
Usman, Ibrahim, 162
Usman, Yusufu Bala, 63–64 n.2, 72–73
Uwais, Maryam, 72, 157
  appointment into key positions of APC-led government, 157, 210
  as member of #BBOG ST, 86–87
  social and cultural capital of, 73, 187
Uwais, Mohammadu, 73

V

Vanguard, 29–31, 55, 229–230
violence
  Danish cartoon-related violence, 29
  elections and, 14
  IMN, 27, 197–198
  Islamic violence as political violence, 29
  Maitatsine confrontation with state security forces, 28
  military forces (Nigeria), 9, 180–181, 186, 188
  sectarian/religious violence, 27–29, 31–32
  SGBV (sexual and gender-based violence), 44, 77
  see also state repression

W

Wakil, Asiha, 141
Wall Street Journal, 205
Watkins, Jerry, 98–99
Wead, Doug, 221–222
WhatsApp, 59 n.14, 100, 103, 107–108, 154 n.5, 155
Widener, Patricia, 137, 149
Wilson, Frederica, 102
WNC (Women's National Coalition), 200
women
  Aba women's war, 66
  anti-colonial struggle and, 66–67
  #BBOG as women-led social movement, 1–2, 65, 115
  Boko Haram's approach to 'place' of women in society, 51–52, 133
  challenges of contemporary women-led social movements in Africa, 164
  conflict dynamics of Islamic fundamentalist movements, 31–32
  cyberactivism, 98
  Egypt, women and political revolution, 98, 165, 205
  gender-based violence against women, 44
  Kikuyu women in Mau Mau revolution, 66–67
  NEPU and rights of women, 25–26
  politics, participation of African women in, 67, 164–165
  Sokoto Caliphate and women's role in society, 23
  South African women in politics, 164–165, 200, 205
  women-led movements in Africa, 57, 66–68, 115, 164, 201, 231–232
  women-led movements in Africa, tactical divide among, 92
  women's rights movements, 2–3, 67, 200–201, 231–232

Y

Yar'Adua, Alhaji Umaru, 17, 209
Yerima, Ahmed Sani, 28
Yesufu, Aisha, 20, 58–59, 125 n.12
  2018 arrest, 195–196
  as #BBOG ST chair, 86–87, 152, 153–154, 170, 195
  criticisms of the person and administration of President Buhari, 152, 154–155
  as 'mascot' of #BBOG, 152, 155, 156
  Sambisa tour, 161–162
  Twitter, 152, 154
  video criticizing President Buhari, 152–154
Yobe–Borno Forum, 107
Yobe state
  Boko Haram and, 35–37, 41–42, 47
  see also Buni Yadi; Dapchi kidnapping
YouthHub Africa, 108
Youtube, 68, 99
Yunfa, 22–23
Yusuf, Muhammad, 33
  extrajudicial killing of, 31, 42–43, 121–122
  founder/leader of Boko Haram, 32, 41, 42–43

Z

al-Zakzaky, Ibrahim, 26–27
Zald, Mayer N., 65
Zeilig, Leo, 231
Zenn, Jacob, 26–27, 47, 221–222